Anti-Semitism and Anti-Zionism in Historical Perspective

This book presents the reflections of historians from Israel, Europe, Canada and the United States concerning the similarities and differences between anti-Zionism and anti-Semitism primarily in Europe and the Middle East.

Spanning the past century, the essays explore the continuum of critique from early challenges to Zionism and they offer criteria to ascertain when criticism with particular policies has and has not coalesced into an "ism" of anti-Zionism and anti-Semitism.

Including studies of England, France, Germany, Poland, the United States, Iran and Israel, the volume also examines the elements of continuity and break in European traditions of anti-Semitism and anti-Zionism when they diffused to the Arab and Islamic.

This book was previously published as a special issue of *The Journal of Israeli History*.

Jeffrey Herf is Professor of Modern European History at the University of Maryland in College Park.

Anti-Semitism and Anti-Zionism in Historical Perspective

Convergence and Divergence

Edited by
Jeffrey Herf

 Routledge
Taylor & Francis Group

LONDON AND NEW YORK

First published 2007 by Routledge
2 Park Square, Milton Park, Abingdon, Oxon, OX14 4RN

Simultaneously published in the USA and Canada
by Routledge
270 Madison Ave, New York, NY 10016

Routledge is an imprint of the Taylor & Francis Group, an informa business

© 2007 Taylor & Francis Ltd

Typeset in Minion 10.5/13pt by the Alden Group, Oxford

British Library Cataloguing in Publication Data
A catalogue record for this book is available from the British Library

Library of Congress Cataloging in Publication Data
A catalog record for this book has been requested

ISBN10 0-415-40069-4
ISBN13 978-0-415-40069-5

CONTENTS

Acknowledgments

I would like to thank the following people and institutions who contributed to the conference entitled "Convergence and Divergence: Anti-Semitism and Anti-Zionism in Historical Perspective", held from 24 to 25 March 2004 at Brandeis University. It has been a pleasure to work with Anita Shapira and Derek Penslar in shaping the themes and inviting contributors to the conference. The conference was made possible with financial and institutional support from the Chaim Weizmann Institute for the Study of Zionism and Israel at Tel Aviv University, the Sarnat Center for the Study of Anti-Jewishness at Brandeis University, and the American Jewish Committee (AJC). Professors Susannah Heschel, Jerry Muller and Anson Rabinbach served as moderators on several panels and made valuable contributions to conference discussions. Thanks are also due to Steven Bayme of the AJC for his comments at the conference, as well as for facilitating support from the AJC. Sylvia Fuks Fried, executive director of the Tauber Institute at Brandeis, superbly handled the details of the conference. Philippa Shimrat, the assistant editor of this journal, has expertly guided this volume on its way to completion. Thanks most of all to the contributors to this conference, who wrote fine papers and responded quickly and thoughtfully to this editor's suggestions and comments.

Jeffrey Herf

Introduction

Jeffrey Herf

After the Holocaust, anti-Semitism began a gradual decline and loss of respectability in Western Europe and the United States. Though the communist governments in Europe claimed to be undergoing a similar shift, the "anti-cosmopolitan campaigns" and then anti-Zionist campaigns of the period from the 1950s to the end of the Cold War gave new life to anti-Semitic stereotypes. The hostility of the Western New Left to Israel and then the emergence of Islamic fundamentalism in recent decades have led to renewed concern that the secular anti-Zionism of the radical left is making common cause with the religiously inspired anti-Semitism of the radical Islamists. The articles in this special issue address issues raised by such concerns. They were first presented at a conference entitled "Convergence and Divergence: Anti-Semitism and Anti-Zionism in Historical Perspective" held in March 2004 at Brandeis University. The conference was organized by the editors of this journal with the support of the Chaim Weizmann Institute for the Study of Zionism and Israel at Tel Aviv University, the Sarnat Center for the Study of Anti-Jewishness at Brandeis University, and the American Jewish Committee. Contemporary events—especially the second *Intifada* and its global consequences—overshadowed the gathering and were an impetus for its organization. The sobriety of these essays reflects the realities of the moment in which they were written.

In our invitation to the conference, we asked participants to reflect on the following three broad areas. First, what have been the similarities and differences between anti-Zionism and anti-Semitism? How did European anti-Semitic ideology of the late nineteenth through mid-twentieth centuries view Zionism, and how did those views change over time? In the West since 1948, when and why have criticisms of Israeli policies or aspects of Israeli society crystallized into "anti-Zionism"—that is, a rejection of the legitimacy of the Jewish state itself—and under what conditions and circumstances has anti-Zionism echoed the themes, symbols and discourse of anti-Semitism? How have the codes of anti-Zionism and anti-Semitism served as conceptual frameworks for interpreting major events such as the founding of the State of Israel, the Arab-Israeli conflict and Israel's links to the United States? What criteria should one offer to ascertain when criticism of and disagreement with particular policies of the State of Israel have coalesced into an "ism" of anti-Zionism and/or anti-Semitism?

Second, how and why has anti-Semitism, historically rooted and concentrated in European Christian culture, diffused into the Arab and Islamic world? What elements of continuity and discontinuity coexist there with traditions rooted in the Islamic heritage? Have Muslim and Arab anti-Zionists and anti-Semites merely borrowed European ideas and adapted them to new circumstances, or are they also innovators who have introduced new elements to anti-Semitic themes? How have Arab governments and opinion-shaping elites interpreted Israeli modernity, and do these interpretations echo previous associations between hostility to the Jews and their identification with aspects of modernity? What practical, political impact and importance have these ideas had on the policies of Arab governments? What has been the balance over time between antagonisms rooted in the political conflict between Israel, the Palestinians and the Arab states and hatreds due instead to religiously inspired anti-Semitism?

Third, how have the contours of the debate within Israel since its founding evolved regarding the motivations of its critics and enemies and the mixtures of anti-Semitism and anti-Zionism among its critics?

In his 1986 work, *Semites and Anti-Semites: An Inquiry into Conflict and Prejudice*, Bernard Lewis addressed the first two of these issues, the differences and overlaps between anti-Semitism and anti-Zionism, and the impact of European anti-Semitism on the Arab and Islamic world.[1] In a work that remains essential for thinking about these issues, Lewis clearly distinguished between the political conflict surrounding Zionism and then Israel but also pointed to instances in which hatred of the Jews as Jews had entered into the Arab and Islamic political culture. He also demonstrated that the ideological virulence and degrees of violence of Jew hatred in the Arab and Islamic world were *not* traditional elements of the culture and politics of Islam but rather have been the results of a relatively recent, twentieth century process of transmission and diffusion of anti-Semitism from Europe yet have emerged as a distinctive and now indigenous elaboration of classic anti-Semitic themes. In this volume contributors explore these issues again seeking to understand the relationship the political-military conflict between Israel and the Arabs, on the one hand, and the existence of anti-Semitism which is as much or more its cause as its effect.

*

The essays regarding the European dimension begin with Derek Penslar's comparative cultural historical analysis. He notes that anti-Zionism was peripheral to the major anti-Semitic texts and movements of nineteenth- to mid-twentieth-century Europe yet was central for Arab thinking about Jews and Judaism. If modern European anti-Semitism can be described as "a psychosomatic illness" that expressed "systemic intolerance" aggravated by socio-economic crisis due to rapid modernization, anti-Zionism in the Arab world was an "allergic reaction" that was a response to discrete political events and policies—that is, Jewish migration and then the formation of the

State of Israel. While European anti-Semitism "originated in fantasy... the latter was a debilitating, even fatal, response to a genuine substance." Indeed, "Zionism did not exist as a discrete phenomenon" in the writings of prominent European anti-Semites but was subsumed to be a chapter in the larger history of an international Jewish conspiracy. In the Arab and Muslim world, despite disparaging remarks about Jews in the Koran, anti-Zionism for much of the twentieth century was the product of a "specific political conflict" in Palestine and Israel more than of the anti-Jewish elements within the Muslim tradition.

David Myers's discussion of "principled Jewish anti-Zionism" recalls the criticism of German-Jewish philosophers such as Hermann Cohen and Franz Rosenzweig. These neo-Kantian, Jewish anti-historicists saw Zionism as, in their view, a regrettable "return to history." In the period of apparently successful Jewish assimilation in Germany before Nazism, they affirmed the creative potential of Jewish life in exile and alienation in the diaspora. Myers argues that such a principled anti-Zionism can "contribute to discussions about the future contours of the State of Israel," specifically the debate over "whether Israel can and should remain a Jewish state (or a state of the Jews), as opposed to becoming a state of all its citizens." Aware that anti-Zionism in the current context can become linked to anti-Semitism, Myers reminds us that this "has not always been the case .... And perhaps it need not be the case in the future."

Shulamit Volkov, who has so fruitfully examined the ideological package of anti-Semitism as a cultural code for anti-modernism in late-nineteenth- to mid-twentieth-century Europe, poses similar issues regarding the function of anti-Zionism for the Western and international left since the 1960s. She argues that as Jews came to symbolize modernity and its reputed ills in Europe, so in the Middle East and in the Western left since 1967 Israel became a symbol for the West and the policies of imperialism and colonialism. The result has been an anti-Zionism as a cultural code which has presented the persecuted as guilty, thus making them "legitimate targets for hatred." Opposition to Israel and elements of anti-Semitism borrowed from the past became "part of the overall anti-imperialist syndrome." Yet Volkov also notes that the anti-Semitism of the Nazi regime was no longer a search for a scapegoat or a diversion but became a goal in itself. In response to her own question of whether or not this has happened with anti-Zionism, she responds "perhaps." More important in her view is the "identity assumed between the policies of the United States ... and those of the State of Israel" concerning the Palestinians, Arabs and Islam, and the need to take responsibility for diminishing the force of anti-Semitism and anti-Zionism through demonstrating a commitment to peace.

My own contribution concerns Nazi Germany, the classic case of convergence between anti-Zionism and anti-Semitism. In light of Soviet and Arab campaigns during the Cold War to posit a link between Zionism and Nazism, this convergence is not as taken for granted in parts of the world as the historical facts demand that it should be. The realities were that while the Nazi regime in the 1930s permitted limited Jewish emigration to Palestine, at no time in the entire history of the Nazi Party or Nazi regime did Hitler or any other key decision maker favor the establishment of a Jewish state in Palestine. On the contrary, the consistent view from the top down was that a Jewish state would serve as another center, indeed perhaps as "the Vatican" of the international Jewish conspiracy. As such it would pose a dire threat to Nazi Germany, at war, as its leaders believed it to be, with this international Jewish enemy. My article examines efforts during World War II to diffuse the messages of Nazi anti-Semitism into the Arab and Islamic world through the Berlin-based broadcasts of Amin al-Husseini, the Grand Mufti of Jerusalem. Neither in ideology nor in policy was the Nazi regime ever in favor of the establishment of a Jewish state in Palestine.

In his synthetic essay, Andrei Markovits argues that European antipathy to Israel should be understood as part of an anti-American mood. He also points to changes in the connection between anti-Americanism and anti-Semitism in Europe in general. While anti-Semitism and anti-Americanism were not always part of the same current, they "have become inseparable both conceptually and empirically." Though anti-Americanism since the eighteenth century has been primarily a prejudice of elites, the recent period stands out because, "for the very first time a solid majority of European publics ... bear negative attitudes towards the United States ...." In the imaginations of the prejudiced, the combination of Judaism and Americanism offered a negative symbiosis of capitalism and profit seeking, universalism, individualism and erosion of established traditions against which Europeans defined themselves. Like other contributors to this volume, Markovits notes that familiar right-wing anti-Semitism remains beyond the pale of respectable speech. It is left and left-liberal opinion that sets the tone in many prestige papers and on television, and which led Europeans in the first decade of this century to respond to surveys by labeling Israel as the greatest threat to peace, ahead of Iran, the United States, Iraq, Afghanistan and Pakistan. Markovits has a particularly sharp eye for double standards and hypocrisy evident in European responses to a variety of international conflicts. He raises the question of whether a European identity may emerge as part of a negation of stereotypes of the United States and Israel.

Joseph Bendersky's contribution draws on his deeply researched and important history of anti-Semitism in the American military. His is a story of traditional anti-Semitism rooted in an overwhelmingly Christian officer corps which gradually diminished following World War II and then gave way to support for and cooperation with Israel from the late 1960s and 1970s. Though the crude anti-Semitism of the first half of the century gradually eroded, it was Israel's victory in the Six Day War that convinced American military leaders that Israel was also a strategic asset in the Cold War and served, more than it undermined, American interests in the region.

Four contributions deal with Britain, France, Germany and Poland in recent decades.

David Cesarani examines anti-Zionism in Britain since World War I. He writes of a pattern of attitudes of "extraordinary longevity and resilience" in which the Jews are accused of exorbitant power, wealth and influence used for destructive purposes. In the interwar period, such views appeared primarily in major mass-circulation papers of the political right. While there was more sympathy for Zionism on the British left, some of its leading representatives also distinguished between "good" Jewish workers and "bad" Jewish capitalists, so that at times "the pro-Zionist discourse of the left coexisted with anti-Semitism." In the postwar decades, hostility to Jews and to Israel lingered on in British society, especially in its upper strata, but ceased to be an issue for political mobilization. Indeed, in the 1960s, Labour politicians such as Harold Wilson, Richard Crossman and Michael Foot were emphatically pro-Zionist.

Cesarani—and other contributors—mark the emergence of the New Left and the Six Day War in 1967 as a historic turning point in the history of anti-Zionism and anti-Semitism in Britain, as a result of which its dominant expression moved from right to left. The New Left viewed Israel as a hegemonic regional power allied to the USA while the Palestinian cause took its place among national liberation movements antagonistic to American interests. As the Jewish community in Britain made Israel an important component of Jewish identity, Marxist, Maoist and Trotskyist groups seeking to root themselves in Black and Asian immigrant populations deployed anti-Zionism as a matter of both conviction and political expediency. By the 1980s, leaders of the New Left, such as London's current Mayor Ken Livingstone, were in positions of power in municipal governments where "anti-Zionism went from doctrine to policy." By the time the Palestinians launched the terrorist campaign in 2000, a convergence of anti-Zionism and anti-Jewish discourse occurred "not at the fringes, but at the center of British political and cultural life," in the "niche publications of the left," the *New Statesman*, the *Guardian* and the *Independent*. The notion that "rich Jews comprise a worldwide network of power and influence that is covertly behind world affairs has transferred comprehensively from the right to the left" and was being voiced as well in Britain's Muslim mosques and neighborhoods.

France, with Europe's largest Jewish community, has been in the center of debates about these issues. Pierre Birnbaum's historical overview recalls that representatives of the anti-Semitic French right in the twentieth century, such as Edouard Drumont, Louis-Ferdinand Céline and Drieu la Rochelle, dreamed that Zionism would be a "solution" to the Jewish question in Europe. With slogans such as "France for the French! The Jews in Palestine!" they supported Zionism in the hopes that it would get rid of the Jews in France, and restore an ethnic and religious definition of the nation in contrast to that of universalist republicanism. Yet Drumont and others also juxtaposed conventional anti-Semitic features of the Jews to the noble, sober and honest Arabs. The Jews in Palestine would establish yet another capitalist plutocracy of an Anglo-Saxon sort long detested by Catholic counter-revolutionaries. Hence anti-Zionism also became an undercurrent of French right-wing ideology in an effort to combat imperialist domination of the world led by the Americans and British.

In recent years, Birnbaum notes, members of the French far right praised Saddam Hussein, called the first Gulf War "a Jewish war" and joined the anti-Israel chorus. By 2002 Jean-Marie Le Pen and the National Front were calling for "one bullet for the Zionists, one bullet for the cosmopolitans, one bullet for the Yanks." In recent years, the radical right has entered into an unlikely alliance with radical Muslims, bound together by anti-Semitism and hostility to the United States, to the war in Iraq and to Jews in France. Birnbaum asks if an alliance of far right and far left is reasserting itself at a moment in which French Jews are "less able than in the past to count on the protection of the state" and have been assimilated in much public discourse to a conquering Israel and the Anglo-Saxon world that is being rejected by French official strategy.

As comprehensive as this volume seeks to be, it lacks a contribution about the anti-Zionist campaigns launched by the Soviet Union. While the literature on that topic is extensive, scholarly work in English dealing with events in Poland is scarce. Thus we are pleased to be able to include Dariusz Stola's excellent and detailed account of the anti-Zionist campaign in Poland in 1967–68, which draws on his research in the only recently available archives of the Polish government and security services. The campaign took shape in the aftermath of Israel's victory in the Six Day War and evolved into a domestic anti-Jewish purge that led to firings, dismissals and then large-scale emigration of thousands of Jews from Poland. Władysław Gomułka, the head of the Communist Party and government, suggested that a "fifth column" of Jewish Polish citizens who applauded the victory of Zionism and Western imperialism should emigrate from Poland. The Polish Security Services, the Politburo and the Polish military all expressed fears about a "Zionist threat" within Poland and blamed Zionists for student rebellion in 1968.

Like Volkov, Stola views the anti-Zionism of 1968 as a "complex and subtle code" whose use was "a sign of obedience and loyalty to the party" but also, "like other conspiracy theories," served to "alleviate the painful inability to understand the complex modern world." Yet, despite its irrational foundation and illusory visions of Zionist plots, the anti-Zionist campaign served as a useful tool in fighting youth rebellion, strikes and popular unrest. On the other hand, the anti-Zionist campaign fostered a "profound disillusionment" among segments of the Polish intelligentsia. It dealt "a final blow" to their hopes for "socialism with a human face" and led some of them on a path to dissidence and then opposition in the 1980s.

In recent years the intertwining of anti-Semitism and anti-Zionism in the early decades of the German Democratic Republic (East Germany) has been extensively examined in work by Sigrid Meuschel, Mario Kessler and Thomas Haury, as well as in my own work.[2] As this work is now well known, we are not including a separate essay on the topic. Suffice it to say that the history of communism in the Soviet Union and East and Central Europe in the post-1945 era is central to understanding the history of anti-Zionism as a distinct ideological perspective. For the East German Communists in the postwar decade, purges of Jewish-identified Jews in the Communist Party, as well as of non-Jewish Communists who expressed solidarity with the then new State of Israel, were accompanied by clearly anti-Semitic arguments about conspiracies linking Jews with international, American and Israeli conspiracies. In so doing, they evoked elements of the Marxist tradition which had associated the Jews with despised capitalism as well as currents of German nationalism which linked the "cosmopolitan"

Jews to the despised West and the United States. In light of this scholarship, as well as the considerable work on the Soviet Union and the Jews, it is now well established that the international resonance of anti-Zionism and the diffusion of anti-Semitic stereotypes in the decades following the Holocaust should, as François Furet demonstrated a decade ago, be placed prominently in the central historical narratives of communism in Europe.[3]

Angelika Timm examines the foreign-policy implications of the "anti-cosmo-politan" purges in the German Democratic Republic (East Germany). East Germany became a leading foe of Israel and a loyal friend and supporter both of the Arab states and of the Palestine Liberation Organization (PLO) in their wars with Israel. She situates this historical peculiarity in the context of the Cold War, East German membership in the Warsaw Pact and political competition with West Germany inside Europe and in the Middle East for recognition, as well as in communist ideology. Timm's distinctive contribution lies in the examination of the interaction between communist ideology and the definition of national interest in the sphere of foreign policy. "The pro-Arab and anti-Israeli foreign policy of the GDR should be viewed, above all, in the context of the Middle East policy of the Warsaw Pact countries." That policy included establishment of diplomatic ties with key Arab states in 1969 in a successful effort to gain international recognition, and provision of military support and training bases for the PLO beginning in the 1970s. East Germany never established diplomatic relations with Israel. Timm confirms that classic anti-Semitic themes of a worldwide Jewish conspiracy accompanied East German participation in the Soviet bloc's anti-Zionist campaigns, and she notes the particularly close and long-standing bonds between the GDR and Arafat.

As the volume lacks a contribution dealing specifically with these issues in the West German or unified German context, I would make the following points. First, like the New Left elsewhere, the West German New Left since 1967 became increasingly hostile to Israel and placed it in the camp of the imperialist enemy. Second, because this was a German New Left, such an ideological shift had the consequence of seemingly liberating its advocates from the burdens of German history—in much the same way that anti-fascist East German ideology and policy presumed to do—and leading instead to hyper-identification with the Palestinian cause, including its armed struggle. Third, by the mid-1970s, when such views had led to active cooperation between West German and Palestinian terrorists in violent attacks against Jews, important liberal and left-liberal voices, most notably future foreign minister Joschka Fischer and future interior minister Otto Schilly, recoiled from the West German left's flirtation with anti-Zionism and anti-Semitism. In the crisis of the recent years, the German government clearly expressed solidarity with Israel and denounced terrorism and anti-Semitism.[4] Although, as Markovits notes, a convergence of anti-Americanism with hostility to Israel has found some respectability in German politics and the press in recent years, the German government over the past several decades remains the most supportive of Israel among the large states in the European Union.

Essays by Arieh Kochavi and Anita Shapira consider the Israeli debates about these issues. Kochavi examines campaigns against Israel in the United Nations and the International Criminal Court as well as Israel's diplomatic and legal response. He discusses the UN's response to the battle in Jenin, Belgium's failed effort to put Prime Minister Ariel Sharon on trial for war crimes, and the ICC's attempts to bring legal arguments against the security fence Israel is building. He notes that in the Israeli government, "the long-held suspicion of the UN and its organs has now expanded to the international legal arena." Kochavi concludes that Israel "has apparently lost the contest for public opinion" that accompanied these efforts, yet his essay also underscores the importance of the existence of a Jewish state with the diplomatic and legal expertise to counter such campaigns.

Anita Shapira examines how Zionists and then Israelis have interpreted both anti-Semitism and anti-Zionism. She reminds us that the founding Zionist generations believed that establishment of a Jewish state would produce a change in the relationship between Jews and non-Jews that would bring an end to anti-Semitism. After the full revelations of the Holocaust in 1945 and with the establishment of the Jewish state in 1948, Israelis regarded anti-Semitism as a residue of European fascism and Nazism, while anti-Zionism was seen as a straightforward result of the political and military struggle with the Arabs. The Soviet Union's role in defeating Nazi Germany and in supporting Israel in 1948 deepened the association of the left with support for the Jews. Yet by the 1960s, the Soviet Union, the Western left and Third World governments had placed Israel in the camp of Western imperialism. By 1975 this "pernicious anti-Zionism" culminated in the UN's definition of Zionism as a form of racism. Shapira notes that debates over anti-Zionism and anti-Semitism were shaped by Israeli domestic politics. While the political right saw anti-Semitism as the cause of hostility to Israel, the left argued that anti-Zionism rooted in political arguments about the conflict in the Middle East fanned the flames of anti-Semitism. Islamic fundamentalism, however, has introduced a new and even more menacing element into the picture, and today most Israelis do not differentiate between anti-Zionism and anti-Semitism.

The Palestinian, Arab and Islamic context is profoundly influenced by the emergence of Islamic fundamentalism and the renewal of religiously inspired anti-Semitism. Meir Litvak examines this dimension in his analysis of Holocaust denial in Iran, a phenomenon he calls "a manifestation of anti-Semitism disguised as anti-Zionism." Ayatollah Khomeini made anti-Zionism and anti-Semitism core elements of Iran's revolutionary ideology by blending interpretation of passages from the Koran with conventional, secular anti-imperialist rhetoric. To his successors he bequeathed a fusion of anti-Semitism and anti-Zionism that seamlessly fused political and religious hatreds. For the Islamists, the founding of the State of Israel served as another chapter in the Jewish-Christian conspiracy against Islam. The Jewish state was simultaneously the representative in the Middle East of a despised Western secular modernity. The official Iranian view is that the State of Israel should disappear, to be replaced by an Islamic state. Litvak notes that Holocaust denial in Iran brings the Iranians into sympathetic contact with Holocaust deniers from Europe's radical right. He also points to the prevalence of the equation of Zionism with Nazism in Iranian political discourse.

*

Despite their differences in context and origins, Nazism and Islamic fundamentalism are the two limit cases of convergence of anti-Semitism and anti-Zionism. In both, the existence of such an ideology, and of activists who espoused it, radicalized international politics and the domestic politics of many nations. The issue of the possible future of convergence is inseparable from the future of radical Islam. However, as a number of the contributors make clear, the expression of anti-Semitic stereotypes in anti-Zionist agitation, especially conspiracy theories of vast Jewish power, has accompanied secular anti-Zionism in the Soviet bloc campaigns of the Cold War, the propaganda of Arab states and parts of the Western left as well. While the open expression of anti-Semitic views fell out of fashion, certainly in Europe after the Second World War and the Holocaust, such views have lived on in the cultural codes and interpretive frameworks of anti-Zionism. Indeed, one of the implications of this volume is that "anti-Zionism" can take its place alongside anti-Semitism as a related but distinct chapter of the modern history of ideologies. That chapter does not include the European Jewish critics of Zionism before 1933 or, for example, those within Israel who have opposed the presence of settlements in the occupied territories. Yet, as a number of contributors point out, the obsession with Israel and its alleged misdeeds and the lack of empathy toward the Israeli victims of terrorist attacks call for an explanation that points more to the mentality of observers than to the facts in the Middle East. Historians examine ideologies in a context. In the context of contemporary history, it is apparent that "anti-Zionism" as a cultural code is inseparable from anti-Semitic views which could not be so easily expressed as such after the Holocaust. As any observer of Israeli politics quickly perceives, criticism of particular policies of the Israeli government is commonplace and is distinct from "anti-Zionism." I conclude that in the historical context of recent decades, certainly since the 1960s and into coming decades, there is no politically and historically significant divergence between what anti-Semitism and anti-Zionism have come to mean as distinct ideologies in world politics. One has become the handmaiden of the other.

The conclusions implied and stated by the contributors to this volume are sobering. The evidence in this volume will not reveal how large a role anti-Semitism and anti-Zionism will play in years to come in world politics. Yet it is reasonable to assume that both will continue to play a role. In any case, for victims of terror, it makes no difference if its practitioners call themselves anti-Semites or anti-Zionists. Following Israel's withdrawal from the Gaza strip in 2005 there were hopes that Palestinians would turn to more moderate leadership. In January 2006, they did the opposite when they delivered a solid electoral majority to Hamas, a political party, social movement and ideological passion which was and remains unequivocal in making no distinction between antisemitism and antizionism and which engages in terrorism in order to destroy the Jewish state. In historical perspective, the election of Hamas represents a clear example of convergence between antisemitism and antizionism. Only time will tell if this revival of antisemitic hatred will gave way to a willingness to coexist with the Israel. In this collection, a fine group of historians have drawn on past work and pointed to future avenues for research. They have done so in a sobering moment without illusions but also without abandoning hope that a historical perspective may shine some light into contemporary affairs.

Notes

[1] Bernard Lewis, *Semites and Anti-Semites: An Inquiry into Conflict and Prejudice* (New York: W.W. Norton, 1986; reissued with new Afterword, 1999).

[2] See Herf, *Divided Memory*; Haury, *Antisemitismus von Links*; Kessler, *Die SED und die Juden*; Meuschel, *Legitimation und Parteiherrschaft in der DDR*.

[3] Furet, *Le passé d'une illusion* (English translation, *The Passing of an Illusion*), is a synthetic work that brings anti-Semitic and anti-Zionist campaigns into the main narrative of modern communism.

[4] The literature on anti-Semitism and anti-Zionism in the West German and German context is extensive. See Herf, *Divided Memory*; Kloke, *Israel und die deutsche Linke*; Koenen, *Das rote Jahrzehnt*. For the German government's response to the crisis of recent years in the Middle East, see speeches by Foreign Minister Joschka Fischer available at the website of the German Foreign Ministry. See, for example, *Rede von Bundesaußenminister Fischer zur Nahostpolitik vor dem Deutschen Bundestag, Berlin, 13.02.2004*, at www.auswaertiges-amt.de/www/de/infoservice/ presse/presse_archiv? archiv_id = 5366.

References

Furet, François. *Le passé d'une illusion: Essai sur l'idée communiste au XXE siècle*. Paris: Editions Robert Laffont, 1995.

———. *The Passing of an Illusion: The Communist Idea in the Twentieth Century*. Translated by Deborah Furet. Chicago: University of Chicago Press, 1999.

Haury, Thomas. *Antisemitismus von Links: Kommunistische Ideologie, Nationalismus und Antizionismus in der frühen DDR*. Hamburg: Hamburger Edition, 2002.

Herf, Jeffrey. *Divided Memory: The Nazi Past in the Two Germanys*. Cambridge, MA: Harvard University Press, 1997.

Kessler, Mario. *Die SED und die Juden—zwischen Repression und Toleranz*. Berlin: Akademie Verlag, 1995.

Kloke, Martin W. *Israel und die deutsche Linke: Die Geschichte eines schwierigen Verhältnisses*. 2nd ed. Frankfurt/Main: Haag and Herchen, 1994.

Koenen, Gerd. *Das rote Jahrzehnt: Unsere klein deutsche Kulturrevolution, 1967–1977*. Frankfurt/Main: Fischer Verlag, 2002.

Lewis, Bernard. *Semittes and Anti-Semites: An Inquiry into Conflict and Prejudice*, New York: W.W. Norton, 1999.

Meuschel, Sigrid. *Legitimation und Parteiherrschaft in der DDR*. Frankfurt/Main: Suhrkamp, 1992.

Anti-Semites on Zionism: From Indifference to Obsession

Derek J. Penslar

In his classic Zionist manifesto *The Jewish State* (1896), Theodor Herzl claimed that the "Jewish Question" was "neither a social nor religious one, even if it at times takes on these or other colorings. It is a national question, and in order to solve it, we must make it into an international political question, which will be managed through counsel with the civilized nations of the globe."[1] Herzl believed that the anti-Semitism of his day contained certain elements of what he called "legitimate self-defense," for emancipated Jews were particularly well-suited for commerce and the professions, thus creating "fierce competition" with bourgeois Gentiles. Economic issues, however, were, in Herzl's view, epiphenomenal, for no matter how Jews earned their livelihood, no matter how greatly they contributed to the wealth and welfare of the lands in which they lived, they were decried as strangers and parasites. Thus for Herzl, as for millions of Jews from his time to our own, Zionism has appeared to be a rational response to an irrational and ineradicable form of prejudice.

Herzl believed that anti-Semites themselves would appreciate the desirability and feasibility of the Zionist project and would gladly help ensure a smooth transfer of unwanted Jews from Europe to Palestine. In fact, however, most anti-Semitic ideologues in *fin-de-siècle* Europe were indifferent to or dismissive of Zionism. Believing that Jews were incorrigibly dishonorable and work-shy, anti-Semites considered Zionism to be at best an impracticable fantasy, as Jews would not willingly leave the fleshpots of the West to take on the arduous task of rebuilding their ancient Oriental homeland. At worst, Zionism was thought to represent yet another tentacle in the vast Jewish conspiracy to extend financial and political control over the entire globe. Over the period 1880–1940, as anti-Semitism became a mobilizing, all-embracing ideology in much of Europe, the latter view gained prominence, although the process was gradual, uneven, and specific to certain countries.

Over the same period, the Arab world witnessed an eruption of anti-colonial and nationalist sentiment, often directed against the Zionist project. Whereas Zionism was peripheral to European anti-Semitism, it was central to Arab sensibilities about Judaism and Jews. In both environments anti-Semitism was a response to apparently inexplicable upheavals and an expression of virulent *ressentiment,* yet the function of Zionism in anti-Semitic discourse in Europe, compared to that in the Middle East, suggests the need to draw a distinction between systemic intolerance, aggravated by socio-economic crisis, and political strife, driven by discrete events and policies. To employ a medical metaphor—quite appropriate, since all forms of anti-Semitism are pathological—European anti-Semitism may be compared to a psychosomatic illness, whereas its Arab counterpart more closely resembles a toxic allergic reaction. The former originated in fantasy yet crippled the entire body politic; the latter has been a debilitating, even fatal, response to a genuine substance.

Whereas most of the literature on the relationship between anti-Semitism and anti-Zionism focuses on contemporary developments, there is much to be gained through a historical approach, through grasping underlying assumptions and visceral feelings about Zionism when they were first expressed, before they were affected by contingencies and rapidly changing events on the ground. Historical developments could either mitigate or intensify anti-Jewish feeling. An example of the former would be the temporary alliance between Zionism and Nazism in the guise of the Transfer (*Ha'avarah*) Agreement of the 1930s, which facilitated German-Jewish emigration to Palestine. The power of events to deepen anti-Semitic grooves is demonstrated in the Arab world, where Israel's military victories in 1948, 1956 and 1967 generated a tidal wave of anger and compelled a search for explanations for the Arabs' ignominious defeat in the arcane realms of anti-Semitic fantasy. In the early 1900s, however, and particularly after the proclamation of the Balfour Declaration in 1917 and the rapid growth of the Jewish National Home thereafter, Zionism was a sufficiently powerful presence on the international scene and within Palestine itself to command attention without being so influential that it had to be accorded de facto acceptance or utterly demonized.

This article focuses primarily on Europe, and it does so for two reasons: I have some expertise in the area; and despite the vast literature on the history of European anti-Semitism, its conceptual stance vis-à-vis Zionism has, surprisingly, not been properly elucidated. The discussion of Arab anti-Semitism and anti-Zionism is briefer and more synthetic, but it is placed within a comparative analytical framework whose novel features will, I hope, stimulate experts in the modern Middle East to further, fuller reflection on the subject.

Zionism in European Anti-Semitic Discourse

Classic, nineteenth-century anti-Semitism identified the Jew with modern capitalism and the rapid transformation of society and culture that came in its wake. Ancient and medieval tropes of Jewish avarice, murderous hatred of Gentiles, and black-magical practices mutated into the modern stereotype of an international Jewish conspiracy. Tellingly, the myth of a global Jewish financial cabal flourished among early socialist thinkers in France and Germany during the 1840s, a decade of economic turmoil due in part to the impact of industrialization on the peasants and artisans who constituted the bulk of the population. The metonymic association between Jew and capitalism, and by extension with modernity as such, was a driving force behind late-nineteenth-century political anti-Semitism, described appositely by the German socialist leader August Bebel as "the socialism of the stupid man."

Intriguingly, the discourse on Jewish restoration to Palestine, a discourse that intensified with the writings of the former socialist Moses Hess in the 1860s and, of course, with the establishment of the Zionist movement in the 1880s, attracted little sustained attention from anti-Semitic ideologues. To be sure, one can find scattered statements in writings on the "Jewish Question," dating back to the Enlightenment, about shipping Jews out of Europe and back to Palestine. Scholars have painstakingly accumulated such statements by the likes of Johann Gottfried von Herder, Johann Gottlieb Fichte, Pierre-Joseph Proudhon, Heinrich von Treitschke and Adolph Stöcker, among others, but they have failed to note that these utterances were merely barbed quips or enraged outbursts, and rarely led to a sustained engagement with Zionism even after Theodor Herzl brought it onto the stage of public opinion.

One apparent exception was the Hungarian anti-Semitic activist Győző Istóczy, who is the subject of a recent biography by Andrew Handler, provocatively titled *An Early Blueprint for Zionism*. Handler draws the title from a speech of 1878 on "The Restoration of the Jewish State in Palestine," delivered by Istóczy from the floor of the Hungarian Diet, of which he was an elected member. Reflecting an anti-Russian and pro-Turkish sentiment as much as an anti-Semitic worldview, Istóczy claimed that such a state would revive "the enfeebled and backward East" by introducing Jewish wealth and energy, "a vigorous, powerful and new element and an influential ingredient of civilization."[2] Istóczy offered few specifics as to how this plan would be implemented, and subsequent to the speech Istóczy soon let the matter drop, as it encountered strong disapproval from his fellow parliamentarians. Thus this "early blueprint" for Zionism was, in fact, quite sketchy and faded quickly. For the next twenty years, Istóczy pursued the usual anti-Semitic agenda of attacking alleged Jewish domination in finance, commerce and journalism within Europe. It is true that in 1906 he began to speak in support of the now-established political Zionist movement, but by 1911 he had lost interest, largely due to the Young Turk government's opposition to massive Jewish immigration to Palestine.[3]

By and large, anti-Semitic ideologues of the *fin de siècle* paid Zionism little heed, and when they did think about it, dismissed it as a trick, perpetrated by the agents of the international Jewish conspiracy. In the French journalist Edouard Drumont, perhaps the most successful anti-Semitic scribbler of the period, we have the interesting case of an anti-Semite whose interest in Zionism waxed and waned, fading away altogether when Drumont decided that Zionism did not stand a chance against its rivals, assimilationist and plutocratic Jews, who also happened to be, in Drumont's view, the greatest threats to the world as a whole.

Drumont's daily newspaper, *La Libre Parole*, greeted the First Zionist Congress of 1897 with great fanfare. Apparently confirming Herzl's views that anti-Semites and Zionists would find a meeting of minds and form a productive collaboration, the newspaper wrote, in its customary sneering tone, "Not only does [*La Libre Parole*] offer, freely and enthusiastically, publicity for the [Zionist] colonists, but if it were ever—an inconceivable thing—a question of money that caused the Jews to hesitate, it takes upon itself the commitment to take up a subscription whose immense success is not in doubt."[4] Yet right from the start Drumont saw a snake in the Zionist garden, Jewish "haute-banque," that cabal of powerful Jewish financiers whose economic interests depended on the maintenance of a vast global Jewish network and would thus be harmed by the mass movement of Jews to Palestine.[5]

A decade later, as the Zionist movement appeared to shake off the lethargy that had gripped the movement since Herzl's death in 1904, Drumont devoted considerable energy to drumming up anti-Semitic support for Zionism. At the time of the Eighth Congress in 1907, Drumont wrote that Zionism represented the "future of the Jewish Question and, consequently, the future of humanity as a whole." Were the Jews removed from Europe to Palestine, "this Jewish Question, which ... dominates all human affairs, including the Social Question, would be resolved, at least for the time being, and the world would finally know a period of calm and relative security." Drumont even expressed admiration for Zionists, whom he contrasted unfavorably with their opponents:

> The Jew who aspires to reconstitute a homeland is worthy of esteem. The Jew who destroys the homeland of others is worthy of every kind of scorn. The Jew who wants to have a flag and a religion is a virtuous Jew, and we will never proffer against him any hurtful word .... We have therefore all sorts of reasons to prefer the Zionist Jews over those arrogant Hebrews who aspire not only to involve themselves in our affairs but also to impose their ideas and their will upon us, who treat us in our own homeland as representatives of an inferior race, as vanquished and pariahs.[6]

Drumont and his contributing journalists consistently praised Herzl, and especially Max Nordau, for his fiery and unapologetic Jewish nationalism, while they pilloried the principled assimilationism of French-Jewish notables such as Joseph Reinach and Emile Cahen, editor of *Les Archives Israélites*.

By 1913, however, Drumont had changed his tune. On the eve of the Eleventh Zionist Congress, Drumont warned darkly that "this conference will probably be the last, and this racket will have sounded Zionism's death-knell."[7] Reproducing verbatim large sections from his 1907 articles on the subject, Drumont added a new twist: The "great Jews" Herzl and Nordau have been vanquished by the combined forces of assimilationists and Jewish high finance. Drumont accused the former of shifting the Zionist Organization's focus away from international diplomacy, aimed at obtaining a Jewish homeland secured by public law, and enmeshing the movement in *Gegenwartsarbeit*, political and cultural activity in the diaspora. Even worse, according to Drumont, was the work of "the great Jews, the aristocrats of banking," who, like Maurice de Hirsch, had always been hostile to Zionism, and who had now created Territorialism:

> It is no longer a matter of reconstituting in Palestine or elsewhere a Jewish nation having its land, its flag and its religion, but only of creating Jewish colonies for the use of poor and miserable Jews who would go establish themselves in distant territories. During this time, the ambitious Jews, having pushed from view their shabby brethren, would enjoy, more than ever, the unquestioned authority and enormous power that they wield in the country where, as in France, they have become the masters and the rulers.

It matters little that Drumont was wrong on both points—both *Gegenwartsarbeit* and Territorialism developed from within the heart of the Zionist movement—rather, the key here is that Drumont placed the contest between Zionism and its enemies within sturdy and venerable anti-Semitic frameworks of conspiracy led by Jewish plutocrats and cultural domination by assimilated Jewish intellectuals. Drumont's views on Zionism were not influenced by, nor did they influence, his general anti-Semitic worldview. Drumont was willing to endorse Zionism if it appeared to confirm his preexisting views that Jewish nationhood was ineradicable, but in the blink of an eye he was quite willing to disown it, especially since, on the eve of and during World War I, Zionist goals increasingly appeared to conflict with French imperial interests and the sensibilities of Roman Catholics in the Middle East.[8]

As we expand our chronological horizon into the twentieth century, it appears that in France, Zionism, although occasionally applauded or derided, was peripheral to the anti-Semitic imagination. Adulatory literature written in France about Drumont in the decades following his death—literature that includes generous extracts from his work—does not make so much as a mention of Zionism. Such writing does, however, faithfully reproduce Drumont's own *idées fixes* about Jewish responsibility for the corruption, social upheaval and financial scandals that were making life hell for the little man.[9] More important, during France's darkest and most shameful hours in the Second World War, the Vichy regime devoted little time and effort to the issue of

Zionism, and when the matter did come up, attitudes were instrumental, based on the needs of the moment. In 1943, when a German victory no longer seemed assured and the mass deportations of Jews were provoking considerable discontent in France, the Vichy regime toyed with pro-Zionist proposals to facilitate mass Jewish emigration to Palestine and endorse the creation of a Jewish state. Unlike the Nazis, who had come out clearly against Jewish statehood at the time of the Partition Controversy of 1937 and put an end to Jewish emigration to Palestine in 1940 as part of the transition from a policy of mass expulsion to one of genocide, Vichy leaders, admittedly steeped in anti-Semitic yearnings to rid France of the Jews, were willing to ponder what the chief of Marshal Pétain's civilian staff called "the only truly effectual solution [to the Jewish Question] that is both completely humane and Christian."[10]

Similarly, Italian fascism adopted an instrumental approach to Zionism, opposing it when it clashed with Catholic interests or appeared to be a tool of British expansionism in the eastern Mediterranean, and embracing it when it was thought that Zionists might sever their alliance with Britain and turn to Italy as their protector. This flexibility reflected the ambiguous legacy of Italian anti-Semitism in the post-unification era. On the one hand, Italian Catholicism could espouse no less fierce an anti-Semitism than its French counterpart, as seen in the stridently Judeophobic Vatican periodical *La Civiltà Cattolica*, which argued that the Jewish religion was corrupt, materialistic and long superseded by Christianity, and that the Jews comprised:

> an ambiguous nation, because, at the same time, it [the Jewish community] is the same and the Other, as the other nations of the world where they have settled: [they are] Jewish Italians, French, Germans, English, Americans, Rumanians, and Poles, that is to say, the Jews enjoy dual nationality. It seems that they carry 'a harvest of' advantages to the country where they sit, and that the country will reap these advantages, their financial skills and intelligence. But these advantages are, directly or indirectly, consciously or unconsciously, used methodically to get the upper hand and secure power for the Jewish nation, controlling high finance so that more or less veiled, they will control everybody.[11]

Nonetheless, due to the relative strength of the secular Italian state vis-à-vis the vanquished Church, anti-Semitism did not become a political force in the early twentieth century. The Italian kingdom, with its Jewish cabinet ministers, mayors and prime minister, was a country with many Dreyfuses, yet no Dreyfus Affair.

Ironically, the relative weakness of political anti-Semitism in early-twentieth-century Italy made possible a more serious and pragmatic engagement with Zionism than was the case in France, where Zionism's political program was engulfed by the anti-Semitic fog generated by the Dreyfus Affair. Accordingly, during the early years of Mussolini's rule, there were numerous meetings between Mussolini and the leaders of Italian and international Zionism, and although in the late 1920s Mussolini unhesitatingly turned against Zionism in order to satisfy the interests of the Vatican, with which he negotiated a Concordat in 1929, in the early 1930s Mussolini once again announced a favorable stance towards Zionism, inviting the World Zionist Organization to convene in Italy and hoping (rather improbably) that pro-Italian

Jewish immigrants to Palestine could gain sufficient influence to overturn the British Mandate.[12]

In Germany, by contrast, from the 1870s onward anti-Semites were wont to judge Zionism more harshly, as a manifestation of ongoing global Jewish chicanery. Wilhelm Marr, who is credited with coining the term "anti-semitism" in the late 1870s, wrote here and there throughout the 1880s about shipping all of Europe's Jews to Palestine, where they could put their boundless energy and resources to work in creating a model polity, a *Musterstaat*. Yet this relatively sanguine attitude did not survive the passage of time, as Marr's anti-Semitic worldview grew ever darker and more bitter. Marr wrote at the time of the First Zionist Congress of 1897 that "the entire matter is a foul Jewish swindle, in order to divert the attention of the European peoples from the Jewish problem."[13] Marr did not elaborate on his opposition to Zionism, for, as with Drumont and the other anti-Semites we have analyzed thus far, Zionism was far from central to Marr's concerns.

The logical connection between conspiratorial anti-Semitism and an adamant rejection of Zionism may be found in the work of Marr's contemporary, Eugen Dühring, author of what was perhaps the most relentlessly brutal anti-Semitic tract of the late nineteenth century, *The Jewish Question as a Question of Racial Noxiousness for the Existence, Morals and Culture of Nations* (1881). This book, which went through six editions up to 1930, offers an opportunity to observe how an acutely intelligent but deranged individual responded to Zionism as the movement gained prominence from the 1880s through the end of the First World War. We see that it was precisely the depth of Dühring's anti-Semitism that prevented him from taking Zionism seriously and considering it outside of the prepackaged framework of a Jewish financial and cultural stranglehold over all of Europe. In the 1892 edition, Dühring devotes over seventy pages to elaborately detailed "solutions" to the Jewish Problem—solutions including reducing the numbers of Jews in, or barring them altogether from, the civil service, professions, journalism and teaching, and laying punitive taxes on Jewish-owned banks and other enterprises. In short, Dühring advocates the de-emancipation of European Jewry. Claiming that the Jews are racially incorrigible, Dühring dismisses Zionism in a couple of paragraphs, beginning with the following observation:

> Moreover I do not believe that the Jews, if they were to really unite in a territory, be it a Jewish colony in Palestine or some other settlement, would be prevented from renewing their obtrusive nomadism. Nomadism is their world-historical natural condition. Without it and alone among themselves they would eat one another alive, for other peoples would not be among them. Such a thing as a Jewish state would mean the destruction of the Jews by the Jews.[14]

Thus, Dühring goes on to argue, Jews would always prefer living under the most oppressive conditions among Gentiles rather than among their own kind.

As Dühring aged, his language grew ever more bilious and threatening. In the posthumously published 1930 edition of the work, incorporating changes and additions made by the author ten years before, Dühring claimed that throughout history no political force had been able to contain the Jewish menace. The Roman conquest of Palestine merely spread the Jewish disease into the diaspora, expulsion decrees in medieval Europe were ineffective, and ghettoization served only to strengthen Jewish solidarity. In turn, today's Zionists sought to dupe honest Europeans, who would like to see the Jews leave for Palestine, by selling them shares in various Zionist enterprises, all designed to enrich their Jewish directors. Moreover, a Jewish state, even if one were to be established, would only accentuate Jewish power; the Jewish snake that encircled the globe would now have a head:

> This would entail pushing history back, thereby making necessary something like a second Roman clearing action. It would mean going back to the beginning, where the matter would be brought to an end in an entirely different and far more comprehensive sense. (*Es hiesse zum Anfang zurückzukehren, wo in einem ganz andern und weit durchgreifenderen Sinne ein Ende zu machen ist.*)[15]

A chilling, and prescient, threat indeed, yet one made in passing, via a few sentences, after which Dühring returns to his favorite themes of Jewish control over most aspects of politics, economics and culture in the Western world.

The significance of Dühring's text lies not only in what he says but also in the popularity and durability of his book, and the apparently paradoxical combination of a lack of serious interest in Zionism and a blanket condemnation of it. One encounters a similar case in the writings of Theodor Fritsch, whose *Antisemitism Catechism*, also published under the title *Handbook of the Jewish Problem*, went through thirty-six editions and a total print-run of 155,000 copies between 1886, when it first appeared, and 1934, a year after Fritsch's death.

Although the book was expanded considerably over time, its basic structure remained intact. First came an overview of the allegedly noxious role played by Jews throughout history from antiquity to the present, then a chapter of citations from contemporary Jewish writers attesting to the Jews' status as a separate nationality, followed by a chapter on the Jewish presence in malevolent secret societies. First and foremost among them were the Alliance Israélite Universelle (in fact, a philanthropic, educational and lobbying organization established in Paris in 1860) and the Russian *kahal*, an imaginary network of Russian-Jewish communities, as dreamed up by the Russian convert Iakov Brafman in a notorious book of 1868. The 1907 edition of Fritsch's book does not even mention Zionism in its chapter on Jewish secret societies, although the Anglo-Jewish Association (whose purview was similar to that of the Alliance) is singled out for condemnation, along with that venerable object of anti-Semitic fantasy, Freemasonry. In the chapter of statements by Jews claiming a unique national identity, most of the statements are from anti-Zionists, such as the Viennese Orthodox rabbi, Leopold Kohn, or individuals who were or may have been Zionists but are not identified as such (for example, the American rabbi, Berhardt Felsenthal). There is abundant, albeit wildly inaccurate, analysis of the socio-economic situation and political life of the Jews in Germany's neighboring lands, but no treatment of the Zionist movement, its diplomatic activities, or events on the ground in Palestine.[16]

In the 1934 edition, the chapter on "Jewish Organizations and Parties" expanded to include material on a vast array of Jewish political bodies, and Zionism finally received its own subsection, but it only amounted to two pages out of more than five hundred in the book, and "Zionism" does not appear in the otherwise exhaustive index. Fritsch induces a frisson of fear as he details the evil deeds of the shadowy Russian-Jewish *kahal* or the omnipotent Alliance, "the central node for the realization of all Jewish special interests, implementing on any occasion the power of the whole of Jewry," and which has been responsible for everything from agitation on behalf of Captain Alfred Dreyfus to rallies for the condemned Italian-American anarchists Sacco and Vanzetti. Zionism, on the other hand, is dismissed out of hand: Herzl and Nordau were frauds, lacking in imagination or ability; and the Zionist project would have been stillborn had it not been for wartime collusion between the British government and the Rothschilds, by which a promise of a Jewish national home in Palestine was made in return for international Jewish assistance to defeat Germany. Intriguingly, Fritsch does not credit the Zionists with the power and influence that one might expect from a virulent anti-Semite. Fritsch focuses instead on the British, who, he claims, have no intention of allowing a Jewish state to be set up in Palestine, as it would conflict with their imperial interests. Besides, Palestine is too small and its economy too undeveloped to accommodate large numbers of Jews, and the current Jewish community in Palestine is mostly urban, and hence no less corrupt and parasitical than its diaspora counterpart. The only good thing about Zionism, concludes Fritsch, is that it has "transformed previously in large measure inactive and apolitical Arabs into convinced opponents of the Jews."[17]

Like any anti-Semitic ideologue, Dühring and Fritsch had to simultaneously fabricate falsehood and deny reality. Not only did they demonize Zionist international diplomatic and fundraising activity, they also ignored the growth of the Jewish National Home, which was rooted in notions of Jewish bodily and cultural renewal. Like utraviolet light, invisible to the naked eye, many aspects of the Zionist project simply could not be perceived within the optical field of anti-Semitism. One encounters precisely this sort of conceptual blindness in the somewhat more genteel, but no more palatable, tome by Houston Stewart Chamberlain, *The Foundations of the Nineteenth Century* (1899). In the midst of a massive (and highly negative) historical analysis of Judaism and Jews comes a remarkable observation that the Hebrew language died out four hundred years before Christ. (Apparently Chamberlain knew nothing about rabbinic literature.) Moreover:

> Its adoption many centuries later was artificial and with the object of separating the Jews from their hosts in Europe . . .. The absolute lack of feeling for language among the Jews today is explained by the fact that they are at home in no language—for a dead language cannot receive new life by command—and the Hebrew idiom is as much abused by them as any other.[18]

Thus when a Jew speaks Hebrew he does not speak Hebrew, just as a laboring Jew in a Palestinian vineyard does not truly labor. For these anti-Semites, Zionism is nothing but smoke and mirrors, and the only appropriate response is to conjure it away.

An association between Zionism and Jewish criminality became central to Nazi ideology, pioneered by Alfred Rosenberg, who claimed in 1922 that Zionism was an anti-German movement that drew support from reactionary capitalists (the Rothschilds) and Communists ("Jewish" Bolsheviks) alike. Drawing on Rosenberg and Dühring, Adolf Hitler, writing in *Mein Kampf*, would claim that Jews had no intention of constructing a legitimate state in Palestine, or ability to do so, but rather wished to make it into a clearing house for their international economic swindling operations. "[E]ndowed with sovereign rights and removed from the intervention of other states," a Jewish state would become "a haven for convicted scoundrels and a university for budding crooks."[19] (Thus the intellectual pedigree of the notorious contemporary Holocaust denier Ernst Zundel's characterization of Israel as "a gangster enclave in the Middle East.")[20]

Even in Nazi ideology, however, Zionism was little more than an addendum to a well-worn diatribe against international Jewish political machinations and inveterate malevolence. The presence of the Zionist movement did not substantively add to or detract from preexisting modes of anti-Semitic sensibility. The conceptual irrelevance of Zionism behind modern European anti-Semitism is demonstrated all the more clearly by the most significant text in the history of twentieth-century anti-Semitism, *The Protocols of the Elders of Zion.*

The precise authorship of the *Protocols* remains obscure, but scholars concur that the work was composed by agents of the Russian secret police in Paris during the 1890s. The *Protocols* were the most notorious expression of Jewish conspiracy theory, which originated among opponents of the Enlightenment and French Revolution. Specifically, the *Protocols* were inspired by Hermann Goedsche's novel *Biarritz* (1868), a section of which depicts the assembly of a Jewish cabal at a Prague cemetery. Much of the *Protocols'* text, however, was plagiarized from a second, wholly innocuous work, Maurice Joly's *A Dialogue in Hell* (1864), which employed a fictional dialogue between the philosophers Machiavelli and Montesquieu in order to satirize the authoritarian rule of French Emperor Napoleon III. The authors of the *Protocols* lifted many of Machiavelli's speeches verbatim and put them into the mouths of Jewish conspirators. Yet the authors of the *Protocols* transmuted Joly's text while plagiarizing it, in that Joly presented Machiavelli as a cynical realist, whereas the *Protocols* depict the Jews as the embodiment of preternatural, all-consuming evil.[21]

Anti-Semitism in *fin-de-siècle* western and central Europe could be a form of lower-middle-class protest; in Germany and Austria, it took the form of "Christian Socialism" and nourished the populist demagoguery of Vienna's mayor Karl Lueger. In Russia, on the other hand, anti-Semitism was often reactionary, a rejection of modernity in any form and a paean to rigid hierarchical rule by a hereditary nobility. These sentiments pervade the *Protocols*, which were written primarily in order to sabotage Russia's halting moves towards economic modernization by associating liberalization with Jewish conspiracy. The link between Russia, reaction and the *Protocols* was strengthened by their publication in St. Petersburg in 1903. The *Protocols* were disseminated throughout Russia by members of the ultra-rightist Black

Hundreds, and Tsar Nicholas and Tsarina Alexandra commanded that Orthodox priests declaim the *Protocols* in the churches of Moscow.[22]

In its early editions, a variety of origins were attributed to the *Protocols*, and only after the First World War do we see a popularization and routinization of the claim that they transcribe deliberations from the First Zionist Congress. The references to Herzl and the Congress come at the very beginning of the texts, and nothing in the text of the *Protocols* itself touches upon Zionism, although the *Protocols* were forged at the time of the beginnings of political Zionism in the late 1890s. Significantly, in editions of the *Protocols* issued before 1917, the international Jewish body referred to most often as generating the text is the Alliance. (A spectacular but anomalous exception was the work of the Russian reactionary Paquita de Shishmareff who, writing under the pseudonym L. Fry, claimed that the Zionist intellectual Ahad ha-Am had penned the *Protocols*.)[23] Just as the internationalist dimension of the Alliance's name and activities stoked the anti-Semitic imagination of the *fin de siècle*, so could the increased visibility of the Zionist movement in the wake of the Balfour Declaration and establishment of the British Mandate over Palestine encourage anti-Semites to interpret the Basel Congress as, citing Norman Cohn, "a giant stride towards Jewish world-domination."[24] But the actual Zionist program, enunciated at Basel in 1897 and legitimized in part by the British in 1917 and 1920, of creating a Jewish National Home in Palestine is overlooked in the interwar editions of the *Protocols*. Even the notorious paraphrase of the *Protocols* serialized in Henry Ford's *Dearborn Independent* in 1920, which claims that the Sixth Zionist Congress predicted the outbreak of world war and that the Zionist movement represents the tip of an iceberg of international Jewish power, only engages issues relating to Jewish political activity in interwar Europe, specifically the minority-rights treaties, which allegedly singled Jews out for favorable treatment.[25]

To sum up, Zionism did not exist as a discrete phenomenon in the minds of European anti-Semites during the half-century prior to the Holocaust. It was merely a placeholder for a host of conspiratorial fantasies that were rooted deep in the nineteenth century and in a search for an identifiable agent responsible for the bewildering social and political transformations sweeping Europe like a storm. Jews were of course only occasional representatives, rather than creators or agents, of these processes, as the anti-Semite's Jew was little more than a reflection and reification of European society itself. Granted, although European anti-Semitism was riddled with contradictions and highly irrational, it was not wholly illogical. It attributed to the Jew only selected attributes of the human psyche, such as arrogance, cupidity and a thirst for power. The anti-Semite's Jew was not stupid, brutish or enslaved to passion. Bridging the clashing stereotypes of the Jewish capitalist and Communist was an underlying and unifying reality: the Jews' historic prominence in the economy's distributive sector and as agents of economic change. Even so, the visibility of Jews in commerce and the medical and legal professions was a symptom, not a cause, of a capitalist economic order with a meritocratic impetus and a permeable elite. The "Jewish Question" in modern Europe did not amount to anything more than a deceptively tangible avatar of the "social question." Zionism as an ideology and political movement did not impinge upon the lives of Europeans as did other forces associated with Jews, such as capitalism, Bolshevism or cultural modernism.

Anti-Semitism and Anti-Zionism in the Arab World

The function of Zionism in modern Arab anti-Semitism is radically different from that of its European counterpart. Simply put, whereas European anti-Semites regarded Zionism as a manifestation of Judaism, in the Middle East Jews and Judaism have, for the past century or more, been defined in terms of Zionism. We may take as a starting point the argument made in 1978 by Yehoshafat Harkabi, an Israeli scholar of the modern Arab world and Israeli security policy, that Arab anti-Semitism was the product of a specific political conflict—the century-long struggle with the Zionist movement, the *Yishuv* (pre-state Jewish community in Palestine) and the State of Israel—as opposed to the Islamic religious tradition as such or a fundamental inability of Islamic lands to tolerate Jews in their midst.[26] In an earlier work, Harkabi had documented at considerable length the extent of Judeophobic fantasy in the Arab world, and he made no effort now to deny or belittle the findings from his previous research.[27] But Harkabi came to question the value of cataloguing hostile statements about Israel or Jews without taking into account the historical circumstances in which they emerged or noting, as one could see during the era of the Camp David peace accords, that the same government directives that stoked anti-Semitic rhetoric could also staunch it, and that Arab attitudes towards Israel were shaped as much by specific Israeli policies and actions as they were by inherited, pervasive anti-Semitic stereotypes.

Harkabi's argument, and my own here, are not to be confused with that of post-1948 Arab propagandists who have presented the history of the Jews in the lands of Islam as uniformly stable and prosperous, blessed by Islam's enlightened and tolerant attitude towards its protected minorities, an attitude overturned solely by the injustices and cruelties against Arabs perpetrated by the State of Israel.[28] Obviously, the fate of Jews in *dar al-Islam* has been often an unhappy one, molded in part by the Judeopohobic motifs that are imbedded in Islam's foundational texts. In addition to the Koran's many polemical comments about Jews and its accounts of Jewish treachery against Muhammad, a traditional biography of Muhammad attributes his death to poisoning by a Jewish woman, and an equally venerable historical text claims that Shi"ism, which sundered Islamic unity, was instigated by a Yemenite Jew.[29] Such texts, however, mean little when not considered in the context of medieval Jewish life in the lands of Islam, where despite constant discrimination the Jews lived in greater security, and were far less often the subject of chimeric fantasy, than in Europe, where persecutions and expulsions of Jews often followed accusations of ritual murder, desecration of the sacred host and consorting with the Devil. As Mark Cohen has argued convincingly in his comparative history of Jewish life in medieval Christendom and *dar al-Islam*, in the latter acts of expulsion and forced conversion were highly exceptional.[30] Today, many critics of Muslim anti-Semitism place great stock in Moses Maimonides" celebrated *Letter to the Jews of Yemen* (1172), in which the renowned scholar claimed that the lot of Jews had been far worse under Muslim than under Christian rule. Yet this was a *cri de coeur* issued in a time of extreme, and atypical, persecution.

In the nineteenth century, notions of a Jewish international political and financial conspiracy were exported to the Middle East, largely via French and Francophone Christian clerics. Intriguingly, however, during the late Ottoman era Arab opposition to Zionism was not necessarily anti-Semitic. Palestinian Arabs expressed rational fears of displacement from a land in which they had long been resident, and Ottoman officials worried about the creation in the empire of a new minority problem akin to that presented by the Armenians.[31] Intellectuals in Egypt and Syria conceived of Jews in complex ways, combining a realistic assessment of the Zionist movement's accomplishments with an exaggerated belief in Jewish power. For example, the *fin-de-siècle* Muslim reformer Rashid Ridha, who followed the Dreyfus Affair carefully and denounced anti-Semitism in print, wrote in 1899 that Muslims and Arabs would be wise to emulate Jewish solidarity, which had allowed them to preserve their language and culture despite many centuries of dispersion. Moreover, the Jews deserved praise for having adopted scientific knowledge and accumulated great wealth. The Jews, wrote Ridha, "lack nothing but sovereign power in order to become the greatest nation on the face of the earth, an objective they pursue in a normal manner. One Jew [Herzl] is now more respected than an Oriental monarch [Ottoman sultan Abdul Hamid.]"[32] There are obvious shades of hostility and exaggeration in Ridha's image of Jews as comprising a unified, wealthy and powerful collective, but his concern was the reality presented by the immigration of tens of thousands of Jews into Palestine, not, as in the case of European anti-Semitism, broad social transformations in which Jews played no significant causal role.

The secular Arab nationalist Najib Azuri, writing in 1905 in his classic work *Le Reveil de la nation arabe*, described Jews as a people engaged in a concerted drive to establish a state in what they perceived to be their homeland. "On the final outcome of this struggle," Azuri noted darkly (and, one hopes, not presciently), "between these two peoples, representing two opposing principles, will depend the destiny of the entire world."[33] Azuri's casual reference to Jews as a people points out an interesting distinction between early-twentieth-century Arab anti-Zionism, on the one hand, and both European anti-Semitism and later forms of Arab anti-Zionism, on the other. It was a staple of European anti-Semitism that Judaism comprised both a nation and a religion. Unlike European anti-Semitism, which imagined Jews to constitute an unassimilable and noxious nation, defying the quid pro quo of assimilation for emancipation, in the decades after Azuri, Arab propaganda had to develop an opposite argument that the Jews did not constitute even a retrograde nation, for to admit as much might open the way to accepting the legitimacy of the principles of Zionism.

In the twentieth-century Arab world, the interlacing of anti-Semitic motifs with opposition to Zionism occurred in a direct response to increased Jewish immigration to Palestine. It is no coincidence that the *Protocols of the Elders of Zion* first appeared in Arabic in 1925, during the fourth, and largest yet, wave of Zionist immigration to Palestine. (The translation, from the French, was the work of a Catholic priest, Antoine Yamin, in Egypt.) The following year, an article in a periodical of the Jerusalem Latin Patriarchate announced the presence of the Arabic translation of the *Protocols* and urged the faithful to read them in order to understand what the Zionists had in store for Palestine. During the disturbances of the years 1928–29, Haj Amin al-Husseini, the mufti of Jerusalem, publicized portions of the *Protocols* in connection with alleged Jewish plots to conquer the Temple Mount. Thus although the translation was done by a Christian cleric, infused with European anti-Semitic sensibilities, the text was immediately introduced into the context of the new and unique political conflict between Arabs and Jews for control over Palestine.[34]

To be sure, during the interwar period Arab anti-Semitism was nourished by sources outside of Palestine. The rapid social mobility and prominence of Jews in Middle Eastern lands under colonial rule, and the economic and administrative links between Jews and colonial regimes, instilled a powerful anti-Semitic element into Arab nationalism, for which Jews served as metonymic representations of the West. In some instances, as in Iraq during the Second World War, German political and intellectual influences catalyzed pro-Nazi nationalist movements that imbided racial anti-Semitism from its most potent source. A ruthless dedication to creating a culturally homogenous Arab nation led in Iraq to the massacre of thousands of Assyrian Christians in 1933 and of some 400 Jews during the *Farhoud* of 1941.[35] During the 1930s and 1940s, Middle Eastern anti-Semitism was strengthened further by the increasing popularity of socialism and communism among Arab intellectuals. Jews were defined by the Arab left as in league with their fascist persecutors, while royalists and fascist sympathizers leapt to wild conclusions from the disproportionate involvement of Jews in the communist parties in Egypt and Iraq. The important common element behind these contradictory expressions of Arab anti-Semitism during the interwar period was the adoption of common European views of the Jew as universal solvent, the destroyer of social order and bringer of chaos, housed in both the left and right ends of the political and economic spectrum. Arab anti-Semitism even adopted European notions of preternatural Jewish sexual powers. The secular and socialist-inspired youth so visible among the Zionist immigrants prompted Arab accusations that Jews were sexually promiscuous as well as carriers of Bolshevism—indeed, the Arab word for "communist" was *ibahi*, "permissive."[36]

Nonetheless, up to 1948 Arab anti-Semitism did not routinely function, as it did in Europe, as a totally unbounded discourse, attributing every ill of modern humanity to Jewish influence. And within Palestine itself, anti-Semitism grew directly out of conflict with the Zionist movement and its gradual, yet purposeful settlement of the country. The dominant tone was set as early as 1920, when in a play entitled *The Ruin of Palestine*, performed in Nablus, the comely daughter of a Jewish tavern keeper seduces two wealthy Arabs and coaxes out of them their money and even the deeds to their properties, leaving the Arabs with no resource other than suicide, before which they wail "the country is ruined, the Jews have robbed us of our land and honor!"[37]

Our focus thus far on the period before 1948 sharpens our perception of the novel qualities of Arab anti-Semitic discourse generated since the creation of the State of Israel. As opposed to traditional Muslim Judeophobia, post-1948 Arab anti-Semitism featured a transition from a view of the Jew as weak and degraded to a belief in Jewish global power. Traditional Islam scorned the Jew; post-1948 Arab anti-Semitism has blended contempt with fear. The fear stems from the apparent inability of Arabs to stop what has seemed to them to be a gradual, yet carefully planned and executed, Jewish takeover of Palestine, a land whose sanctity and significance have grown in the face of what appears to be a repetition of the Crusades, a European assault against the heartland of the Islamic world. The growth of a secular Arab nationalism, uniting Christians and Muslims in a common battle against Western colonialism, has expanded the purview of this alleged new crusade from a Muslim holy land to the Middle East as a whole. Older forms of contempt for Jews have, in recent decades, taken the form of the widespread view that, humiliating though it was to be subjugated by Christian Europe, it has been all the more galling to witness Palestine falling under the rule of Jews.

Indeed, the trope of assaulted Arab dignity is perhaps the most common theme in contemporary Arab anti-Semitism. Western pundits are wont to attribute this discourse to an atavistic shame-culture, in which codes of personal honor, particularly male honor, bind a rigid socio-religious hierarchy that privileges status over achievement and resists the formation of a liberal, inclusive, egalitarian and democratic Western-style civil society. It is not my brief to determine whether such views are accurate or whether they are the product of facile Orientalist fantasies. What is clear, however, is that the discourse on dignity in the Middle East stems primarily from a sense of overwhelming helplessness rather than from merely wounded pride. However much the Arab powers may have bickered over the fate of Palestine during the 1940s, the loss of Palestine to a Jewish state was seen as the defining catastrophic event of the era, or, as Constantine Zurayq described it in 1956, *al-naqba* (the disaster), a term that gained universal currency in decades to come:

> The defeat of the Arabs in Palestine is no simple setback or light, passing evil. It is a disaster in every sense of the word and one of the harshest trials and tribulations with which the Arabs have been afflicted throughout their long history—a history marked by numerous trials and tribulations.[38]

Regardless of how one apportions responsibility for *al-naqba*, the conquest of the West Bank and Gaza in 1967, the ensuing occupation of those territories and the steady settlement of Jews therein, all of these phenomena are historical realities, as is Israel's close relationship—particularly since 1967—with the United States, which is widely seen in the Middle East as the last remaining great colonial power. There is an immeasurable gap between this scenario and that of modern Europe, where Jews as a collective wielded no power, conquered no land, expelled no family from its home.

There are strains of post-1948 Arab anti-Semitism that absorbed the Manichean qualities of Nazism, elevating the Jew into a global, even cosmic, evil, which must be annihilated, not only within Palestine but wherever he may be found. Such viewpoints are espoused vigorously by Muslim fundamentalists in many lands. They trace their intellectual pedigree to Sayyid Qutb, the intellectual father of the Muslim Brotherhood, who, while in Egyptian prisons during the 1950s, embroidered a European-style anti-Semitism into his massive commentary on the Koran. Qutb's anti-Semitism was ontological, perceiving Jews as incorrigibly evil and associated with all the world's ills, including capitalism, communism, atheism, materialism and modernism.[39] During the 1960s, Qutb, like fundamentalist leaders elsewhere in the Middle East, devoted most of his effort to toppling secular Arab leaders. Developments over a period of fifteen years— the 1967 war, the Sadat peace initiative, the Iranian Revolution, and Israel's invasion of Lebanon—transformed Muslim fundamentalism, causing anti-Zionism, according to Emmanuel Sivan, to "take pride of place, presented as the modern-day incarnation of the authentically Islamic hostility to the Jews."[40]

Nonetheless, the older, Palestinocentric streak in Arab anti-Semitism lives on in our own day, as in the 2002 Egyptian television series *Horseman without a Horse*, which was based in part on the *Protocols of the Elders of Zion*, but in which the Jewish conspiracy to control the world was replaced by a specific plot to take control of Palestine. Moreover, it is significant that the *Protocols* come in and out of fashion in Egypt; they were popular under Nasser, but fell out of circulation in the wake of Camp David, only to return after the failure of the Oslo Peace Accords. Arab anti-Semitism in any form is repugnant, but those forms that wax and wane in response to developments in Arab-Israeli relations are qualitatively different from the Manicheanism of extremist Muslim fundamentalists who, no less than the Nazis, imagine Jews as literally the handmaids of Satan and call for their eradication from the face of the globe. It is essential to draw a clear distinction between these two different forms of anti-Semitism, one of which may be malleable, subject to change in a dynamic and constructive political environment, while the other kind is incurable and must be confronted with unequivocal condemnation, isolation and, when necessary, forceful suppression.

Conclusion

This article's comparative framework will not please those who see European and Arab anti-Semitism as of a piece and who associate anti-Zionism with anti-Semitism *tout court*. Some of my critics have responded with a comparison of their own, claiming that Jews in modern times have featured an exaggerated, perhaps unique capacity for self-criticism, and that this practice has led Jews, particularly Jewish intellectuals, whether in nineteenth-century Germany or in early-twenty-first-century North America and Israel, to internalize anti-Semitic assaults against them and to labor in vain to ingratiate themselves with their persecutors. The frequently cited example of nineteenth-century German Jews relates a pathetic tale of individuals who responded to anti-Semitic accusations of Jewish vulgarity and parasitism by encouraging circumspect public behavior, the utmost probity in business affairs and the promotion of reputable, honorable occupations in crafts among poor Jewish youth. Of course, nothing German Jews did could possibly mitigate anti-Semitism, let alone assuage the genocidal fury of the Nazis. Similarly, argue many staunch supporters of Israel today, leftist Israelis and their counterparts in the Jewish diaspora are urging that Israel make massive, and ultimately self-destructive, territorial and political sacrifices in an illusory pursuit of peace. According to this pessimistic worldview, for most Arabs peace can only come in the wake of Israel's destruction, either spectacularly, by force, or gradually, through its transformation into a binational state, whose Jewish component would over time be overwhelmed by a rapidly growing Arab population, and whose Jewish character would accordingly fade away.

I respond to this objection by noting that Israel, unlike the Jewish global conspiracy of the European anti-Semitic imagination, does exist. Precisely because Arab anti-Semitism's fantasies are far more thoroughly grounded in reality than are those of their European predecessors, a necessary, although admittedly insufficient, precondition for deconstructing those fantasies will be a radical transformation of Israel's borders and policies towards Arabs both within and outside of the state. As Yehoshafat Harkabi wrote in the wake of the Camp David summit, "It is not the change of images . . . which will lead to peace, but peace which will lead to the change of images."[41] Unlike the decline of anti-Semitism in post-1945 Europe, which was not the work of Jews but rather the result of the crimes and guilt of European society as a whole, in the Middle East Jews are obliged to make fateful political decisions in the hopes that such decisions will stimulate equally constructive action on the part of Israel's neighbors and the Palestinians under her control, that these multilateral actions will in fact lead to peace, and that peace will lead to a change of Arab images of Jews. This time around, anti-Semitism grows out of a political conflict in which Jews are empowered actors, not figments of the imagination. For this reason, although the chances for accommodation between Israel and the Arab world may appear slim, conditions are vastly more favorable than they were in pre–World War II Europe, not simply because the Jewish state possesses military power, but also because it has the capacity to take actions that may weaken the *raison d'être* of Arab anti-Semitism.

Notes

[1] Herzl, *Der Judenstaat*, 9–10.
[2] Handler, *An Early Blueprint for Zionism*, 42–51.
[3] Ibid., 152.
[4] "Un Congrès israélite," *La Libre Parole*, 17 August 1897.
[5] "Le Sionisme et la haute banque," *La Libre Parole*, 4 September 1897.
[6] "Le Congrès sioniste," *La Libre Parole*, 20 August 1907.
[7] "L'Agonie du sionisme," *La Libre Parole*, 11 September 1913.
[8] "Le Congrès sioniste: Nouvelle orientation," *La Libre Parole*, 31 August 1913; Busi, "Anti-Semites on Zionism," 18–27.

[9] Bernanos, *La Grande Peur des bien-pensants.*

[10] André Lavagne, cited in Marrus and Paxton, *Vichy France and the Jews,* 315. Compare the treatment of Vichy's flirtation with Zionism on 310–15 with Francis Nicosia's discussion of changes in Nazi policy towards Zionism over the years 1937–40 in his *The Third Reich and the Palestine Question,* chaps. 7–9.

[11] "Intorno alla Questione del Sionismo," *La Civiltà Cattolica,* 2 April 1938, a. 89, v. II, quad. 2107, 76.

[12] Biagini, *Mussolini e il sionismo,* 14, 23–24, 49–52, 63, 72, 78, 122, 128, 137.

[13] Zimmermann, *Wilhelm Marr,* 88.

[14] Dühring, *Die Judenfrage als Frage der Rassenschädlichkeit,* 122–23.

[15] Ibid., 127–78.

[16] I have compared the 1886, 1892, 1907 and 1910 editions of the work, which was published at first by the author in Leipzig, but which as of 1907, if not earlier, was published by the Hanseatischer Druck- und Verlags-Anstalt in Hamburg.

[17] Fritsch, *Handbuch der Judenfrage,* 170. Similarly, Fritsch's book *The Riddle of the Jew's Success,* published in many editions during the 1920s, does not even raise the issue of Zionism in its final chapter about World War I and Jewish control over wartime finance.

[18] Chamberlain, *Foundations of the Nineteenth Century,* 1:477n.

[19] For Rosenberg's and Hitler's views on Zionism, see Nicosia, *The Third Reich and the Palestine Question,* 20–8; and Wistrich, *Hitler's Apocalypse,* 154–63 (citation from *Mein Kampf* on 155).

[20] Cited by Marvin Kurz, "Ernst Zundel Is More Dangerous Than You Realize," *The Globe and Mail,* 26 February 2003, A15.

[21] On the history of the *Protocols,* see Cohn, *Warrant for Genocide;* Segel, *A Lie and a Libel;* and Bronner, *A Rumor about the Jews.*

[22] Bronner, *A Rumor about the Jews,* 92.

[23] Thanks to Steven Zipperstein for this observation.

[24] Cohn, *Warrant for Genocide,* 108. See also Segel, *A Lie and a Libel,* 71–79.

[25] See the excerpts in Levy, ed., *Antisemitism in the Modern World,* 169–77.

[26] Harkabi, "On Arab Antisemitism Once More," 227–40. The Hebrew edition of the book in which this article appeared, based on a 1978 conference, was published in 1980.

[27] The book *Arab Attitudes To Israel,* published in English in 1971, first appeared in Hebrew in 1967.

[28] Cohen, *Under Crescent and Cross,* 3–14.

[29] Nettler, "Islamic Archetypes of the Jews," 63–73.

[30] Cohen, *Under Crescent and Cross,* 167.

[31] Porath, "Anti-Zionist and Anti-Jewish Ideology," 217–26.

[32] Be'eri, "The Jewish-Arab Conflict during the Herzl Years," 13.

[33] Muhmamad Muslih, *The Origins of Palestinian Nationalism,* 75, 77–78 (quote on 78).

[34] Rubinstein, ""Ha-protokolim shel ziknei tziyon" ba-sikhsukh ha-aravi-yehudi," 37–42.

[35] Simon, *Iraq between the Two World Wars.*

[36] Porath, "Anti-Zionist and Anti-Jewish Ideology," 223.

[37] Muslih, *Origins of Palestinian Nationalism,* 169.

[38] Zurayk, *The Meaning of the Disaster,* 2.

[39] Berman, *Terror and Liberalism,* 85–6.

[40] Sivan, "Islamic Fundamentalism, Antisemitism, and Anti-Zionism," 82.

[41] Harkabi, "On Arab Antisemitism Once More," 238.

[42] For a clear discussion of convergence and divergence between antisemitism and anti-Zionism, see Lewis, *Semites and Anti-Semites:* An Inquiry into Conflict and Prejudice (New York: W.W. Norton, 1999), pp. 11–23.

References

Be'eri, Eliezer. "The Jewish-Arab Conflict during the Herzl Years." *The Jerusalem Quarterly*, no. 41 (1987): 3–18.

Berman, Paul. *Terror and Liberalism*. New York: Norton, 2003.

Bernanos, Georges. *La Grande Peur des bien-pensants, Edouard Drumont*. Paris: B. Grasset, 1931.

Biagini, Furio. *Mussolini e il sionismo*. Milan: M & B, 1998.

Bronner, Stephen Erich. *A Rumor about the Jews: Reflections on Antisemitism and the* Protocols of the Learned Elders of Zion. New York: St. Martin's Press, 2000.

Busi, Frederick. "Anti-Semites on Zionism." *Midstream* (February 1979): 18–27.

Chamberlain, Houston Stewart. *Foundations of the Nineteenth Century*. New York: Howard Fertig, 1968.

Cohen, Mark. *Under Crescent and Cross: The Jews in the Middle Ages*. Princeton: Princeton University Press, 1994.

Cohn, Norman. *Warrant for Genocide: The Myth of the Jewish World Conspiracy and the Protocols of the Elders of Zion*. New York: Harper & Row, 1967.

Dühring, Eugen. *Die Judenfrage als Frage der Rassenschädlichkeit für Existenz, Sitte und Cultur der Völker*. 4th ed. Berlin: H. Reuther, 1892.

———. *Die Judenfrage als Frage des Rassencharakters und seiner Schädlichkiten für Eistenz und Kultur der Völker*. 6th ed. Leipzig: O.R. Reisland, 1930.

Fritsch, Theodor. *Handbuch der Judenfrage*. 36th ed., 146–155M. Leipzig: Hammer-Verlag, 1934.

Handler, Andrew. *An Early Blueprint for Zionism: Győző Istóczy's Political Antisemitism*. East European Monographs. Boulder: Columbia University Press, 1989.

Harkabi, Yehoshafat. "On Arab Antisemitism Once More." In *Antisemitism through the Ages*, edited by Shmuel Almog. Oxford: Pergamon, 1988.

Herzl, Theodor. *Der Judenstaat*. 8th ed. Berlin: Jüdisches Verlag, 1920.

Levy, Richard S., ed. *Antisemitism in the Modern World: An Anthology of Texts*. Lexington, MA: T.C. Heath, 1991.

Marrus, Michael, and Robert O. Paxton. *Vichy France and the Jews*. New York: Schocken, 1981.

Muslih, Muhammad Y. *The Origins of Palestinian Nationalism*. New York: Columbia University Press, 1988.

Nettler, Ron. "Islamic Archetypes of the Jews: Then and Now." In *Anti-Zionism and Antisemitism in the Modern World*, edited by Robert Wistrich. London: Macmillan, 1990.

Nicosia, Francis. *The Third Reich and the Palestine Question*. Austin: University of Texas Press, 1985.

Porath, Yehoshua. "Anti-Zionist and Anti-Jewish Ideology in the Arab Nationalist Movement in Palestine." In *Antisemitism through the Ages*, edited by Shmuel Almog. Oxford: Pergamon, 1988.

Rubinstein, Elyakim. ""Ha-protokolim shel ziknei tziyon" ba-sikhsukh ha-aravi-yehudi be-eretz yisra'el bi-shnot ha-esrim." (The Protocols of the Elders of Zion in the Arab–Jewish Conflict in the Land of Israel in the 1920s). *Ha-Mizrah he-Hadash* 26 (1977): 37–42.

Segel, Binjamin. *A Lie and a Libel: The History of the* Protocols of the Elders of Zion. Lincoln, NE: University of Nebraska Press, 1995.

Simon, Reeva Spector. *Iraq between the Two World Wars: The Militarist Origins of Tyranny*. 2d ed. New York: Columbia University Press, 2004.

Sivan, Emmanuel. "Islamic Fundamentalism, Antisemitism, and Anti-Zionism." In *Anti-Zionism and Antisemitism in the Modern World*, edited by Robert Wistrich. London: Macmillan, 1990.

Wistrich, Robert. *Hitler's Apocalypse: Jews and the Nazi Legacy*. London: Weidenfeld and Nicolson, 1985.

Zimmermann, Moshe. *Wilhelm Marr: The Patriarch of Antisemitism*. New York: Oxford University Press, 1986.

Zurayk, Constantine. *The Meaning of the Disaster*. Beirut: Khayat's College Book Co-operative, 1956.

Can There Be a Principled Anti-Zionism? On the Nexus between Anti-Historicism and Anti-Zionism in Modern Jewish Thought

David N. Myers

On the face of it, the equation between anti-Semitism and anti-Zionism that stands at the heart of this issue of *The Journal of Israeli History*—and of much recent public debate—is not self-evident.[1] Or perhaps it is better to say that without careful contextualization and delineation, the equation should not be bandied about freely. That I feel compelled to belabor this rather obvious point results from a complex series of developments in the Middle East, Europe and North America since the outbreak of the Al-Aksa *Intifada* in late September 2000. Among them, a resurgent anti-Semitism, particularly in Europe, has had a noticeable effect in widening an already vast gulf between unquestioning critics of Israel and unquestioning supporters. This growing gap leads us to wonder whether opposition to the State of Israel, or the Zionist ideology underlying it, must invariably succumb to anti-Semitism. Can there be, in short, a principled anti-Zionism?

That there can be an unprincipled anti-Zionism, informed by and consonant with anti-Semitism, is widely recognized. Recent affirmation of this comes from a rather unlikely source: high-ranking Catholic leaders meeting with Jewish counterparts in Buenos Aires in July 2004.[2] At this meeting, the Catholic leaders accepted the logic frequently articulated by Jews that attacks on Israeli government policy at times bear within them an animus that crosses the bounds of legitimate criticism into the terrain of anti-Semitism.

But given how charged today's political climate is, is it possible to hold to a principled anti-Zionism? Merely to raise this question is to invite hostility. Within the organized Jewish world, its mention risks severe castigation, partly due to the fear of granting solace to haters of Jews and partly due to the fact that Zionism has become an important pillar of faith for many modern Jews. In fact, it is not simply (or even primarily) Zionism that has attained this status. Israel and its representative institutions have become central foci of identity for many Jews.[3] This is particularly so in the diaspora where cynicism about those institutions and their efficacy is far less pronounced than it is in Israel. Hence, the actions of the Israeli government are often considered above reproach, and all the more so in times of crisis.[4] One consequence in the current environment is that even *pro*-Zionist critics of Israeli government policy are subjected to sharp accusations by fellow Jews, including claims of self-hatred and betrayal. The kind of exaggerated language invoked reflects a state of heightened anxiety that at times borders on delusion. For example, we read the verdict of Abraham Foxman, national director of the Anti-Defamation League, who opens his 2003 book *Never Again?* with the following assessment: "I am convinced that we currently face as great a threat to the safety and security of the Jewish people as the one we faced in the 1930s—if not a greater one."[5] What seems to be startling hyperbole is made all the more so by the locus of Foxman's concern. At least five of eight chapters in *Never Again?* deal with anti-Semitism not in the Muslim or Arab world, but in the United States. And the axis around which much of this potent new anti-Semitism swivels, according to Foxman, is anti-Israel agitation.

This kind of alarmism grossly distorts, to my mind, the reality on the ground *in the United States*.[6] But what complicates the picture—indeed, what compels us to recalibrate our political bearings—is that the reality on the ground in other venues, principally Europe, is quite different. The first unreleased report of the European Monitoring Centre on Racism and Xenophobia in March 2003—and the second published report in April 2004—chronicle the demonstrable rise in anti-Semitic word and deed in various European countries, especially since 2002. The reports go on to discuss the ways in which the Middle East conflict, agitation against Israel, and the facile equation of Israelis and Jews are contributing factors to this phenomenon.[7]

Against this background, itself haunted by the long shadow of anti-Semitism in Europe, the questions invariably arise: When is criticism of Israel legitimate? And when does it stray into that lamentably familiar terrain of anti-Semitism? Two concise criteria may help clarify the link between criticism of Israel and anti-Semitism: exclusion and group stigmatization. In the first instance, when criticism of Israel exists in a near-total vacuum, as if Israel is the sole state worthy of condemnation in the international order, one must wonder about the motivations behind this selective attention.[8] This is not to deny the debilitating and corrupting nature of Israel's occupation of the West Bank and Gaza. It is to suggest that an exclusive focus on Israel's misdeeds often ignores other state-sponsored violence of a similar or greater scale elsewhere. Second, when criticism of Israel shifts its target from the actions of Israel's political leaders to the character of Jews, Israeli or diaspora, a red line has been crossed. Charles de Gaulle's famous words in November 1967 that the Jews had become "un peuple d'élite, sûr de lui-meme et dominateur" (an elite people, sure of itself and dominating) may have crossed that line.[9] Despite his later qualifications of this judgment, de Gaulle's words tapped into an old discursive strand in anti-Semitic language that has gained new momentum in recent times. It is the claim, readily associated with the *Protocols of the Elders of Zion*, that Jews are clannish, exclusive and capable of political fealty only to themselves.

These two criteria may help in ferreting out the anti-Semites from among Israel's critics. And this is an important task. But they do not necessarily provide traction in addressing the core question with which we opened our deliberations: the putative equation of anti-Semitism and anti-Zionism. If the hallmark of anti-Zionism today is opposition to the idea of a Jewish state, is it possible to imagine an anti-Zionist who is possessed of good will towards Jews—that is, who rejects the claim that Israel is uniquely inhumane among the world's nations or that it reflects and draws from an ignominious Jewish character?[10] Can there be an anti-Zionist whose opposition to Zionism is in fact motivated by good will towards Jews and Judaism? In fact, there are a good number of such critics, some of the most prominent of whom were or are themselves Jews. If the latter fail by any reasonable standard to be counted as *sonei Yisrael* (haters of Israel)—and not simply because of their origins, but also because of their views—then the equation between anti-Zionism and anti-Semitism quickly becomes subject to challenge, modification and refinement. It is with this proposition in mind that we now begin to excavate a historical tradition—or set of traditions—of Jewish anti-Zionism that seems to escape the stain of anti-Semitism.

Beyond Time, against Zion

In the crowded marketplace of ideas in *fin-de-siècle* (and early-twentieth-century) Europe, Zionism was but one of the ideologies competing for the hearts of the Jewish masses. The Bund, the Autonomists, Reform Judaism, the Agude (i.e. Agudat Yisrael)—all saw Zionism as a competitor whose underlying rationale and territorial ambition were fundamentally flawed. It is a measure of Zionism's impressive success and good fortune—as well as the tragic murder of millions of Europe's Jews—that these voices of opposition disappeared by the end of the first half of the twentieth century. While we do not dwell in the world of the counter-factual, it is hard to avoid asking what might have been the fate of opposition to Zionism—such as the Bund or the Agude—had the large concentration of eastern European Jews avoided the Nazi terror.

Without the tools to answer this question, we must retreat to what is more tangible. For the purposes of this article, I will first examine a current of anti-Zionism uncovered in the course of research for a book on anti-historicism in modern (and, more particularly, German) Jewish thought.[11] In the second section of the article, I will trace a second and intersecting current of Jewish criticism of Zionism. The third section extends the discussion to our times and observes a curious inversion whereby one of the most visible strands of Zionism today has itself appropriated the language and logic of anti-historicism. The net effect is *not* an exhaustive account of anti-Zionism, but rather a historically informed meditation on the central question announced at the outset.

1. Anti-Historicism and Anti-Zionism in Prewar Europe

One of Zionism's boldest wagers was that it would not merely restore the Jewish people to the land of Israel, but that it would restore the Jewish people to history as well. In classical Zionist thought, diaspora Jews were prisoners of historical contingency (and prey to the caprice of often hostile hosts). But at another, perhaps more important level, diaspora Jews existed beyond the laws of normal historical contingency in an extraterritorial and ahistorical domain: *Galut*. The task of Zionism was to pull Jews back into the flowing current of history, not as petrified detritus but as active and purposeful swimmers.[12]

In the course of being restored to history, Jews would be able to observe and write their own history with new perspicacity. The most notable of the first-generation Jewish scholars at the Hebrew University, Gershom Scholem, wrote in 1937 that the road from Exile to Zion afforded Jews "an historic point of view from within"—within, that is, the vibrant current of history itself.[13] Scholem's statement suggests that the Zionist "return" was a bridge to both ontological and epistemological transformation. Restoration to history would create a new lens *onto* history.

It was while studying Scholem and other founding fathers of Jewish studies in Jerusalem that I often wondered whether their double act of historicization met resistance from other Jews, perhaps from a set of European Jewish alter egos. After all, it was the relentless historicization of life that prompted Ernst Troeltsch, the Protestant theologian and historian, to declare in 1922 a "crisis of historicism."[14] Troeltsch's call culminated a half-century of intense criticism of history as ontological plane and scholarly method extending back to Friedrich Nietzsche's 1874 essay, "Vom Nutzen und Nachteil der Historie" (On the use and abuse of history for life).

Were there Jewish critics of historicism who, like their Christian contemporaries, expressed concern about the debilitating effects of history on their religious tradition? Indeed, there were Jewish thinkers who saw in history a grave threat to the integrity of

Judaism. We might logically expect such fear issuing from the ranks of "traditionalists"—for whom immersion in subjects or methods beyond the canon of classical Jewish texts was discouraged or proscribed. We will return to the traditionalist camp below. But there was also an intriguing critique of historicism that issued not from the avowedly insular, but from those Jews who proudly embraced the surrounding secular culture. What is even more intriguing is that these thinkers' concern about history often overlapped with their critique of Zionism.

The progenitor of this lineage was a contemporary of Friedrich Nietzsche's who would gain renown as one of the leading Jewish and German philosophers in the last decades of the nineteenth century and the first decades of the twentieth: Hermann Cohen (1842–1918). Already in his first article as a budding neo-Kantian philosopher in 1871, Cohen voiced reservations about the hegemonic impulses of the historical method within the *Geisteswissenschaften*.[15] His fear was twofold: first, that the contextual logic of historicism led to fragmentation and atomization—in stark contrast to philosophy's quest for holism and coherence; and second, that history was on the verge of supplanting philosophy as the pride of the "human sciences."

Over the course of his subsequent career, Cohen periodically returned to a critique of historicism. Often enough, he did so by attacking his erstwhile teacher at the Jewish Theological Seminary in Breslau, Heinrich Graetz. Graetz represented for Cohen the antithesis of a stable philosophical demeanor. His "emotional perversity" resulted in equal parts from his personality, the historical vocation and his ideological stance—the last a form of which Cohen labeled in 1874 "Palestinian."[16] This curious pre-Zionist label referred less to a territorial proclivity on Graetz's part than to a preference for the material and mundane features—what Cohen called the "saftige Frucht"—of history.[17]

In Cohen's reading, the methods of the historian were exclusively (and regrettably) attuned to this kind of materialist, "Palestinian" perspective; as such, they failed to grasp the grandeur of Judaism as a soaring and timeless ethical system. On similar grounds, Cohen later extended his critique of Graetz's "Palestinian" perspective to Zionism per se, which he bitterly opposed. Indeed, Cohen's anti-Zionism was as pronounced and public as his fealty to neo-Kantianism—and that was hardly coincidental, since the two derived from a shared resistance to a sensory-driven materialism. As Cohen made clear in his famous polemic with Martin Buber from 1916, Judaism did not require territorial autonomy in order to survive. On the contrary, "political integration into the modern nation-state"—the bane of Zionism—was the best guarantee of Judaism's survival.[18]

A number of provisional conclusions can be offered at this point that serve as signposts for our future discussion. First, Hermann Cohen was hardly a marginal figure in German-Jewish culture of the late nineteenth and early twentieth centuries. On the contrary, he was the most famous Jewish philosopher of his day, a German patriot and a passionate opponent of anti-Semitism. Second, his deep-seated belief in the union of *Deutschtum und Judentum* anchored his conviction in the viability of a vibrant Jewish life in the diaspora and, conversely, his steadfast opposition to Zionism.[19]

The example of Cohen reminds us that appreciation—even glorification—of the diaspora was a respectable position in his day and shortly after. The early decades of the twentieth century in Europe, we recall, witnessed a robust debate between Zionists and their opponents over the ideal locus of Jewish existence. In Germany, it suffices to say that not all Jews—in fact, only a small minority—shared the Zionists' belief that exiting the diaspora and returning to the homeland was imperative.[20] But neither did all German Jews believe that their task was, as the nineteenth-century Eduard Gans once prophesied, to disappear like a river into the ocean of European society. There was a middle ground inhabited by the likes of Cohen, strongly committed to their Jewish and German identities and convinced that the true Zion did not lie in Palestine. Redemption was possible even—perhaps only—in *Golus*.

We see clear traces of this stance in Hermann Cohen's student and friend from Berlin, Franz Rosenzweig (1886–1929). The two differed by generation, background and philosophical proclivity. Whereas Cohen was the flag-bearer of nineteenth-century neo-Kantianism, Rosenzweig belonged to a younger generation of intellectuals hungry for a new and more urgent philosophical language—what Peter Gordon has called a "counter-lexicon of religion, vitalism, and *Existenz*."[21] And yet, for all of their differences, Cohen met Rosenzweig at an important crossroads. The year was 1913, and the young Rosenzweig had decided to leave behind the professional study of history (at Freiburg with Friedrich Meinecke) and commit himself anew to Jewish learning, most particularly with Cohen in Berlin. In Cohen, he was encountering not only one of the great German philosophers of the day, but the man in whom "twentieth-century Jewish theology in Germany emancipated itself from a sterile Historicism."[22] And so it seems fair to assume that Cohen's periodic, if determined, chiseling away at the edifice of historicism reinforced Rosenzweig's own skepticism about history.

In any event, Rosenzweig's famous return to Judaism clearly marked an escape from history—as professional vocation and method. But it also signaled release from the gravitational pull of historical contingency. To illustrate this point, we must recall another shared trait of Cohen the teacher and Rosenzweig the student: their skepticism over Zionism. It would be mistaken to maintain that Rosenzweig was as unequivocal in his condemnation of Zionism as Cohen. He was more a Zionist agnostic than a confirmed opponent.[23] But similarly to Cohen, Rosenzweig insisted on neither a return to history nor a return to Zion.

In 1919–20, Rosenzweig delivered a series of lectures in his hometown of Kassel that revealed his views about the distinctiveness of the Jewish people. In one of these lectures, Rosenzweig spoke of Jews as a people born and tested not in its own territory, but in exile, a condition that steeled them for "battle on behalf of the exalted life and *against descent into the contingency of land and time*."[24] There was no ambition here to restore the Jews to the normal flow of history. For, as Rosenzweig, declared: "The Jewish spirit breaks through the shackles of time. Because it is eternal and aims for the Eternal, it disregards the omnipotence of time. Indeed, it walks unperturbed through history."[25]

This image of a Jewish spirit "unperturbed" by history stands in stark contrast to the Zionist ideal of a return to history. At the same time, Rosenzweig did not surrender an inch of the Jewish claim to national uniqueness. He was as staunch in opposition to assimilation as the Zionists, and thus charted a third way between those Jews who sought salvation in Germany and those who sought salvation in Palestine. We might say that Rosenzweig sought salvation neither in terrain nor, for that matter, in any *space*.[26] Like a number of other Weimar Jewish intellectuals, he sought refuge in a particular kind of time, not the dynamic and fast-moving chronological time that measures historical change, but *Jetztzeit*, an eternal and unchanging present in whose midst the possibility of messianic transformation—even of a measure of eternity—was always alive.[27] By pointing to this present (and the transformative potential inhering in it), Rosenzweig was holding at bay the Zionist desire for return—to history, to Zion, to a normal national existence. Simultaneously, he was pushing towards a new evaluation, even valorization, of *Galut*.

Some years after Rosenzweig's Kassel lectures, another young German-Jewish thinker, Leo Strauss (1899–1973), offered up one of the most enigmatic descriptions of the Exilic condition uttered in his day. Drawn to Zionism as a youth in Kirchhain, Strauss was increasingly attracted, as an aspiring young academic in Weimar times, to the logic of political Zionism. And yet, in an essay in 1923 devoted to the early Zionist Max Nordau, he called attention to the common thread that linked Zionism and its apparent opposite, assimilationism. Zionism, through its quest for normalization, had the ironic effect of accentuating "the dejudaizing tendency" so characteristic of assimilation.[28] This critical observation of Zionism sets in relief a comment made earlier in the essay when Strauss was summarizing, it would appear, Nordau's view of Exile. He noted the simultaneously preservative and destructive forces that framed Exile, the net effect of which was to afford Jews "the maximum possibility of existence by means of a minimum normality."[29]

Eugene Sheppard has written more extensively on Strauss's notion of *Galut* than I can here.[30] But it is interesting to note that while Strauss was hardly an avowed anti-Zionist (or a self-professed Diasporist), his remark about *Galut* appears, as a matter of literary style and context, to be as attributable to his own stance as to Max Nordau's. This is interesting to us, because the formulation is far from the classic Zionist "negation of the diaspora." On the contrary, it reflects a posture of ambivalence and even (if we read "between the lines," as Strauss would later counsel) a veiled appreciation of the creative capacity of Jews under difficult conditions. Of course, this is all the more interesting to us in light of Strauss's later claim in *Persecution and the Art of Writing* (1952) that conditions of political persecution are conducive to the communication of profound esoteric truths.

This later assertion does not allow us to conclude that Leo Strauss was unequivocal about the glories of Exile in 1923. He was simply too complex, ambiguous and tortuous a thinker, even at age twenty-four, for that. That said, we can use his 1923 formulation as more than a summary of Max Nordau's (or his own) views of *Galut*. For our purposes, it can serve as an epigram for those early-twentieth-century German

Jews who struggled between the poles of Zionism and assimilationism and, in the process, contemplated the prospects of a robust Jewish existence in the diaspora.[31] We have seen here that Hermann Cohen and Franz Rosenzweig struggled, each in his own way, to delineate a Judaism that defied the gravitational pull of base historical contingency. Concomitantly, each was prepared to countenance, at least for a time, the prospect of Jewish political alienation in Exile rather than Zionist normalization. And perhaps most germane, neither of them (nor Leo Strauss for that matter) can be judged in the least as anti-Jewish.

2. Between Tradition and Revision: Postwar Legacies

The intellectual heirs of this tradition of thought are not many. The erasure of German-Jewish culture in the Nazi terror, followed by the creation and growing prominence of the State of Israel, diluted the logic of Jewish anti-Zionism and Zionist agnosticism.[32] One can point to a small number of postwar legatees of the German-Jewish intellectual tradition like Jakob J. Petuchowski and Steven Schwarzschild, both German-born Reform rabbis who served as academics in the United States. Schwarzschild, for example, feared that a Zionist return to history would jeopardize a cherished ethical quality of the Jew—the sense of alienation, of being "always and everywhere a stranger except in Judaism and with God."[33] In a similar vein (but different field), the literary critic George Steiner has long celebrated the Jew's Exilic cosmopolitanism: "Instead of protesting his visitor-status in gentile lands, or, more precisely, in the military camps of the diaspora, the Jew should welcome it."[34]

In addition to Steiner, Schwarzschild and Petuchowski, we can note a diverse array of Jewish critics in the diaspora ranging from Simon Rawidowicz[35] to Michael Selzer[36] to groups such as the American Council for Judaism and Breira.[37] Meanwhile, the State of Israel has produced its own diverse lineage of Jewish critics of Zionism (such as Uri Avnery, Boas Evron, the group Matzpen) whose ranks grew after the Six Day War and then swelled even more after the Israeli invasion of Lebanon in 1982.

However, there is a second and more concerted source of Jewish critique of Zionism to which we must now turn our attention: that emerging out of Orthodox and, often, *haredi* (ultra-Orthodox) circles. Contemporary observers are well aware of the staunchly anti-Zionist and anti-Israeli line of the small *haredi* group, Neturei Karta.[38] This group gained renown for its highly visible expressions of support of the Palestinian national cause in the 1970s. But in fact the movement's roots extend much deeper into the fierce anti-Zionism of traditionalist Orthodox Jews in Europe that surfaced at the turn of the twentieth century. It was this sentiment that gave rise to the creation in 1912 of Agudat Yisrael (or Agude), a coalition of various Orthodox bodies (for example, German, Hungarian and Polish) assembled to combat the growing secularization and assimilation of European Jews, one of whose principal manifestations was Zionism.

Among the leading German proponents of the Agude was Isaac Breuer (1883–1946), a contemporary of the Weimar-era intellectuals mentioned earlier and a figure who returns our attention to the link between anti-historicism and anti-Zionism.[39] Grandson of the renowned neo-Orthodox rabbi, Samson Raphael Hirsch, Breuer lived out his own version of the Hirschian ideal of *Torah im derekh eretz* (stringent Torah observance complemented by openness to secular culture). He was a university-trained lawyer with a deep and abiding reverence for Kant. Moreover, he was a frequent critic of the bourgeois materialism of the separatist community that his grandfather created in Frankfurt and in which he was born and raised. In this regard, he shared an important concern with leading Jewish intellectuals in Frankfurt, including Franz Rosenzweig and members of the city's Institut für Sozialforschung.

At the same time, Breuer not only remained scrupulously observant throughout his life; he also inherited his grandfather's belief that the essential ideals of the Torah did not change over time and thus were immune from the ravages of history. Breuer refined this notion by suggesting that the chief bearer of Torah Judaism, the Jewish people, actually inhabited a different realm of existence than the gentile nations—the realm of *Metageschichte* (Metahistory). As a *Gottesnation*, a divinely elected people, the Jews soared above the fast-moving current of prosaic history.[40] Consistent with this view, Breuer regarded Zionism as "the most dreadful enemy that has ever arisen against the Jewish nation."[41] For Zionism sought nothing more than to re-immerse Jews into the current of history through a return to political power. The mission of the Jewish nation was to resist this profanation. Life in Exile was a good defense against this danger. It taught Jews, Breuer declared in 1918, "to abjure the path of sovereignty, the striving for political power." Over the course of the Jews' long dispersion, "*Golus* became the school of the messianic nation."[42]

Breuer's view of Exile resonates with that of other Weimar-era Jewish intellectuals, who contemplated the creative potential of a diaspora existence. What separated Breuer from these intellectuals, though, was his decision in 1936 to leave Germany and move to Palestine—the very site of Zionist dreams! To be sure, Hitler's rise to power was sufficient incentive to leave Germany. But in fact, Breuer's decision was more complicated. Zionism was a source of revulsion to him, but evidently also of vertiginous allure. His ambivalent posture, according to a recent biographer, amounted to a kind of counter- or "alternative Zionism."[43] A man who knew Breuer well from Frankfurt, Baruch Kurzweil, could only explain his attitude in this way: "Huge contradictions swim around in the depths of his soul."[44]

Space does not permit a full unpacking of these contradictions. It is enough to say that Isaac Breuer symbolized a line of thought—an Orthodox critique of the Zionist descent into history—that paralleled and at times overlapped with the German-Jewish lineage discussed earlier. Curiously, Breuer's own paradoxical passage from Frankfurt to Jerusalem presaged the continuation of that line of thought in Israel. The aforementioned Baruch Kurzweil (1907–72), the irascible and iconoclastic literary critic, gained notoriety in Israeli intellectual circles for his barbed attacks against Gershom Scholem and the "Jerusalem School," whom he accused of genuflecting before the "god of ... the normalization and historicization of Judaism."[45]

As with previous critics, Kurzweil traced in Zionism and historicism a coarse materialism that threatened the exalted spiritual status of Judaism. This position could also be said to characterize the thought of an equally irascible and iconoclastic Israeli Orthodox thinker, Yeshayahu Leibowitz (1903–94). With his decidedly unsentimental demeanor, Leibowitz insisted that each individual Jew was required to accept the burden of Halakhic observance as a reflection of his/her submission to "Divine supervision." It was this "supervision," not the return to Zion or history, that lent the Jewish people its distinctiveness.[46] In fact, the attempt of some Zionists to apotheosize the return to the land was, for Leibowitz, an act of idol worship.[47]

As is well known, this perspective is shared by a good number of ultra-Orthodox Jews—those who, unlike Breuer, Kurzweil or Leibowitz—eschew engagement with modern secular culture. Most prominently, Rabbi Joel Teitelbaum (1887–1979), the Satmar Rebbe and a towering figure in twentieth-century ultra-Orthodoxy, was as unrelenting a Jewish critic of Zionism as ever was. According to Rabbi Teitelbaum,

> if we place all the immodesty and promiscuity of the generation and the many sins of the world on one side of the scale, and the Zionist state on the other side of the scale by itself, it would outweigh them all. Zionism is the greatest form of spiritual impurity in the entire world.[48]

Zionism's cardinal sin was to violate a number of oaths to which God had sworn the Jewish people, principally the proscription against Israel's "breaching the wall" (*she-lo ya'alu ba-homah*) by entering the land of Israel (Babylonian Talmud Ketubot 111A). Indeed, it was the Zionist attempt to throw off the heavy yoke of Exile and undertake an active return to history that marked a heretical usurpation of divine prerogative. God's punishment for this transgression, Teitelbaum argued in one of his most well-known and controversial assertions, was the Holocaust.[49]

As marginal and repugnant as such a view is, it is undeniable that Teitelbaum's views about Zionism are perfectly acceptable to thousands, if not hundreds of thousands, of Jews the world over—such as the *Edah Haredit* (ultra-Orthodox community) in Jerusalem, as well as Hasidic communities in Brooklyn, Monsey, Kiryas Joel and New Square, and *haredim* in Europe and Australia. The question that these *haredi* critics—and their more centrist Orthodox coreligionists—raise is the very one that we broached at the outset: can anti-Zionists—in this case, people who are single-mindedly devoted to the perpetuation of the Jewish people and Judaism—be anti-Semitic? There has in fact been a consistent anti-Zionist refrain from traditionalist Jews for as long as there has been a Zionist movement. Were they motivated by hate or bias?

If intent were the sole measure, then none of those discussed above—from *haredim* to liberal German Jews—would qualify as an anti-Semite. None wished ill either of the Jewish people or of the Jewish religious tradition. On the contrary, all were deeply concerned for the well-being of Jews and Judaism. Nor is it clear that the effect of their words was deleterious in any meaningful way. Expressions of anti-Zionism or Zionist agnosticism coming from those examined above neither hastened the Nazi reign of terror nor impeded the Zionist march to political realization. If we find little trace of anti-Semitic intent or effect, we are hard-pressed to designate the Jewish critics of Zionism mentioned here as anti-Semites.

3.   Jewish Anti-Zionism: The Contemporary Question

The historical survey I have offered, incomplete as it is, has followed a variety of twentieth-century Jewish thinkers who departed from the increasingly normative path of Zionism, not out of animus for Jews, but rather out of deep concern. This deep concern, we repeat, did not have a noticeably deleterious effect on Zionism. On the contrary, it could be argued that these Jewish critics—from the time of the Bund—have pushed Zionism to sharpen and refine its own ideological distinctiveness.

Can the same be said about today, with the Israel-Palestine conflict and a rise in anti-Semitic activity looming ominously in the backdrop? One important difference from earlier times is that Zionism has lost much of its steam, owing both to its successes (such as the realization of the Herzlian vision of a bourgeois political state) and its failures (chiefly, the unresolved conflict with the Palestinians, exacerbated by the occupation). It is the latter perception that has prompted a loosely organized group of Israeli intellectuals (such as Yitzhak Laor, Uri Ram, Amnon Raz-Krakotzkin, Ilan Pappé), often brought together under the rubric of post-Zionism, to criticize the underlying principles of Zionism. This body of criticism has generated a torrent of responses, including many insisting that the so-called post-Zionists are themselves responsible for the death of Zionism.[50]

I sense that the opposite is the case. That is, the very challenge posed by the newer critics of Zionism has had the effect of reviving Zionism, or at least of providing much-needed energy to the debate over Zionism's purpose. In this sense, I would echo Jonathan Freedland's observation, in one of the most insightful essays on the link between anti-Zionism and anti-Semitism, that Zionists ignore at their own peril the arguments of their critics, particularly those who cannot be deemed anti-Semitic; Freedland mentions as an example Israeli Member of Knesset Azmi Bishara, and we might add the Jewish critics who have been discussed here.[51] It is important to recall that we have focused exclusively on Jewish critics of Zionism so as to consider the most plausible conditions for an anti-Zionism untainted by the stain of anti-Semitism.[52] But we must also state what will appear more or less obvious, depending on the eye: namely, not all non-Jewish critics of Zionism can be deemed anti-Semites, especially if they avoid those criteria (selectivity of focus and group stigmatization) that distinguish legitimate from illegitimate criticism.

One of the key questions for present-day critics of Zionism who are not anti-Semites is the deep structural issue of whether Israel can and should remain a Jewish state (or a state of the Jews), as opposed to becoming a state of all its citizens. This question has been much discussed in Israel throughout the 1990s, but assumes increasing urgency as the demography of Israel and Palestine continues to shift in favor of the Arab side.[53] Is it better to avoid the claims of those critics who argue that the basic character of Israel can no longer be maintained? Or can principled critics of Zionism, even anti-Zionists—for example, those who oppose the idea of a Jewish state but are committed to a state of all its citizens, *as well as to the well-being of Jews*— contribute to discussions about the future contours of the State of Israel? Might it be that they offer a vision of the future that is as likely to be realized as is preserving the status quo?

In recalling the provocative and thought-provoking role of Jewish critics of Zionism in the past, I am inclined to answer these questions affirmatively. I am further inclined to believe that the debate engendered by the current Israeli critics is important, as a matter of public discourse and moral conscience, to the future of the State. Clearly not all will agree. At a minimum, it is advisable to move beyond the equation of critique of Zionism and group betrayal, for it has a chilling effect on debate over issues of key import to the Jewish future.

Should one be unmoved by this call, I propose in conclusion another benefit to retracing the path of Jewish critics of Zionism. This path serves as a revealing backdrop to a significant development in the recent history of Zionism—namely, the emergence of a form of expression that subverts the earlier impulse to return to history. One of the tasks of this essay was to excavate a group of diaspora Jewish thinkers who came to appreciate the status of Exile beyond time and space, set against the Zionist desire for historical normalcy. Ironically, it may be that the staunchest—perhaps even the last— Zionists left in Israel today share an important characteristic with these diaspora thinkers. I refer to the messianically imbued settlers of the West Bank and Gaza, inspired by the teaching of Rabbis Kook *père et fils*. Whereas the elder A. I. Kook bestowed a powerful kabbalistic language upon the notions of Exile and Zion, his son (Z. Y. Kook) thoroughly conflated the ideals of "historical necessity" and "cosmic redemption."[54] At this juncture of history and cosmos, the messianic settlers who follow in the path of the Kooks take flight from the older, largely secular Zionist vision that sought a return to mundane history. At the same time, their quest for a new plane of messianic history paradoxically recalls that of anti-Zionist Orthodox Jews like Isaac Breuer and the Satmar Rebbe.[55] But it adds an explosive and dangerous tonic: political and military power.

And so contemporary Zionists, like the anti-Zionists studied here, seek to escape history—in large measure, by sacralizing it. But of course, neither group fully succeeds. Both are condemned to live in history's fast-moving current. Within that current, both are often motivated by the desire to advance the Jewish commonweal. This is particularly important to bear in mind with regard to the Jewish critics of Zionism. To be sure, there is no guarantee that all critics of Zionism will be similarly disposed. As we have seen in recent years, criticism of Zionism can slip from legitimate and morally compelling grounds to the murky terrain of group stigmatization. But the gist of this article has been to suggest that this has not always been the case in the past. And perhaps it need not be the case in the future.

Notes

[1] On the subject of the new anti-Semitism, see, inter alia, Chesler, *The New Anti-Semitism*; Dershowitz, *The Case for Israel*; Foxman *Never Again?*; and Iganski and Kosmin, eds., *A New Anti-Semitism?*. There have also been some rather searching journalistic pieces by Ian Buruma: "How to Talk about Israel," *New York Times Sunday Magazine*, 31 August 2003 and "The Myth of the New Anti-Semitism," *The Nation*, 15 January 2004; and by Omer Bartov: "He Meant What He Said," *The New Republic*, 29 January 2004.

[2] See "Vatican Leaders Condemn Anti-Zionism," *Jewish Telegraphic Agency*, 8 July 2004.

[3] The most recent National Jewish Population Survey (2000–2001) indicates that a strong majority of American Jews remain "emotionally attached to Israel" and feel a "common destiny" with Israeli Jews. See the NJPS findings on Israel at http://www.ujc.org/content_display.html?ArticleID = 83868. Meanwhile, Jacob Neusner gave voice to these sentiments when he noted of American Jews: "The sole commitment shared by nearly all, uniquely capable of producing common action, is that the State of Israel must live." See his introduction to Neusner, ed., *Israel and Zion in American Judaism*, xi. See also the comprehensive article on the American Jewish project of "Israel advocacy" by Raffel, "History of Israel Advocacy," 103–80. On the other hand, it is essential to note that some observers have traced a decline in American Jewish support for Israel since the high-water mark of 1967. See, for example, Rosenthal, *Irreconcilable Differences?*

[4] According to New York labor leader Victor Gotbaum, the Holocaust was an important turning point in his uncritical embrace of Zionism and Israel: "Since I helped to liberate Buchenwald, I feel Zionism as a *faith*. I can never be critical of Israel." Quoted in Moore, *To the Golden Cities*, 18.

[5] Foxman, *Never Again?* 4.

[6] Leon Wieseltier has brilliantly refuted this claim in "Hitler is Dead: Against Ethnic Panic," *The New Republic*, 27 May 2002.

[7] In the earlier report, the authors argue that "one cannot deny that there exists a close link between the increase of anti-Semitism and the escalation of the Middle East conflict." See Bergmann and Wetzel, "Manifestations," 16. Meanwhile, the second and more fragmented report states that "it seems clear that the Middle East conflict has a negative impact on the lives of the Jewish communities." See "Perceptions."

[8] Akin to this form of selectivity is the October 2003 poll sponsored by the European Union in which Israel was deemed the leading threat to world peace. See "European Polls Call Israel a Big Threat to World Peace," *International Herald Tribune*, 31 October 2003.

[9] De Gaulle's comment was made in response to a question at a press conference on 27 November 1967. For a transcript, see www.obsarm.org/dossiers/damo/palestine/de-gaulle.htm.

[10] For the purposes of this article, I use the terms "anti-Zionist," "Zionist agnostic" and "critic of Zionism" relatively interchangeably. While there are obvious gradations among them, the common denominator is the shared challenge to the wisdom of territorial concentration and political sovereignty for Jews in the Land of Israel.

[11] Indeed, much of the following discussion of Hermann Cohen, Franz Rosenzweig, Leo Strauss and Isaac Breuer draws from Myers, *Resisting History*.

[12] The Zionist impulse to "return to history" has received some new and interesting attention. Most significantly, Raz-Krakotzkin argues that this impulse was animated by a powerful, if not always articulate, "theological" ambition that marked an unwitting absorption of a Christian eschatological scheme: that is, Zionism marked the move from Exilic disfavor to salvation ("Ha-shivah el ha-historiyah," 249–76); see also the earlier essay by Schweid, "Ha-shivah el ha-historiyah," 673–83.

[13] Scholem, "Kabbala at the Hebrew University," 8.

[14] Troeltsch, "Die Krisis," 573.

[15] See Cohen, "Zur Kontroverse."

[16] See Cohen's letter to F. A. Lange from 5 September 1874, discussed in Liebeschütz, "Hermann Cohen," 3–4.

[17] Cohen, "Grätzens Philosophie," 203.

[18] The exchange between Cohen and Buber between July and September 1916 is translated in Mendes-Flohr and Reinharz, *The Jew in the Modern World*, 571–77.

[19] Cohen, *Jüdische Schriften*, 237–318.

[20] See the figures on German Zionists in Poppel, *Zionism in Germany*, 176.

[21] Gordon, "Under One Tradewind," 66.

[22] Altmann, "Theology," 194.

[23] As Stéphane Mosès shows, Rosenzweig at various points in his life, particularly in the 1920s, appeared quite understanding of the Zionist impulse, and even sympathetic to Jewish settlement in Palestine. For instance, Mosès recalls that Rosenzweig once wrote in his diary in 1922 that "the Jew who lays down roots in the diaspora loses his creative Jewish and religious powers." See Mosès, "Franz Rosenzweig," 324. For a broader review of Rosenzweig's ambivalence toward Zionism, see also Meir, *Kokhav mi-Ya'akov*, 105–19.

[24] Rosenzweig, "Geist und Epochen," 537 (my emphasis).

[25] Ibid., 537 (my emphasis), 538. It is important to note that Karl Barth, Rosenzweig's theological contemporary, described Christianity in somewhat parallel terms, as a religious faith that refused to succumb to the temporal. See Ogletree, *Christian Faith*, 92–6.

[26] This is certainly true relative to Hermann Cohen's embrace of Germany. At the same time, Rosenzweig's notion of *Zweistromland*—the "land of two streams" as his collected Jewish writings were called—hints at a fertile coexistence between Jewish and non-Jewish (e.g. German) culture.

[27] Rosenzweig understood *Weltgeschichte* not as a story of the past and surely not of the gentile past. Rather, "it is *now*"—a living present whose bearers long ago buried their one-time contemporaries (i.e the Greeks). Rosenzweig, "Jüdische Geschichte," 539, 542–43.

[28] Strauss, "Der Zionismus bei Nordau," 317, 319; Myers, *Resisting History*, 127.

[29] Strauss, "Der Zionismus bei Nordau," 318.

[30] Sheppard, "Leo Strauss."

[31] In fact, these meditations were not restricted to an esoteric circle of philosophers. As Michael Brenner has shown, Weimar Berlin, with figures like Simon Dubnow in residence, boasted a minor revival of earlier Diasporist ideas in communal discourse, one of whose by-products was a moderately successful, if short-lived, political party, the Jüdische Volkspartei. Brenner, "The Jüdische Volkspartei," 219–43.

[32] A proper mapping of these interrelated phenomena would take note of the earlier critique of political Zionism offered by Central European Jews in Palestine (many of them self-identified Zionists) through the organizational mouthpieces of Brit Shalom and the Ihud faction from the 1920s up to 1948. See, for example, Ratsabi, *Between Zionism and Judaism*, and the more dated study by Hattis, *The Bi-National Idea*. A number of these figures—e.g. S. H. Bergmann, Martin Buber and the American-born Judah L. Magnes—strongly preferred a binational political arrangement in Palestine to Jewish sovereignty. Another member of this group, the scholar of nationalism Hans Kohn, left Palestine in frustration over what he saw as the errant course of the Zionist ideal. See, for example, Kohn's essay, "Zion and the Jewish National Idea," originally published in *The Menorah Journal*, no. 1–2 (autumn–winter 1958) and reprinted in Selzer, ed., *Zionism Reconsidered*, 175–212. Mention must also be made of the forceful critique of another German Jewish intellectual and lapsed Zionist who did not settle in Palestine, Hannah Arendt. In 1945 Arendt published "Zionism Reconsidered," in which she asserted that the growing push toward a Jewish state in Palestine would create an "insoluble 'tragic conflict'"—or worse, "as many insoluble conflicts as there are Mediterranean nations" (214–15). A more extended

mapping of Jewish criticism of Zionism would also register the appearance of the American Council for Judaism, which mounted an energetic campaign against Zionism in the 1940s under the leadership of Rabbi Elmer Berger. See Kolsky, *Jews against Zionism*.

[33] See Schwarzschild, *Franz Rosenzweig*, 14, as well as Menachem Kellner's discussion of Schwarzschild's opposition to Zionism in *The Pursuit of the Ideal*, 12. See also Petuchowski, *Zion Reconsidered*.

[34] Steiner, "The Wandering Jew," *Petahim* 1, no. 6 (1968): 21, quoted in the informative discussion in Sagiv, "George Steiner's Jewish Problem". Sagiv's analysis of Steiner comports with the gist of the present article when he notes that "Steiner's opposition to Zionism and his challenge to Jewish collective existence contain no hint of what is often called Jewish self-hatred." See "George Steiner's Jewish Problem," 2. I thank Ruth Gavison for calling my attention to Sagiv's article.

[35] Rawidowicz repeatedly expressed concern that a growing Zionist triumphalism would lead to neglect or even "negation" of the diaspora. This is a leitmotif of his 900-page study, *Bavel vi-Yerushalayim*, especially the second part, "1948 and the Jewish Question."

[36] One of Selzer's key angles of critique of Zionism is its dominance by Ashkenazic Jews and concomitant discrimination of Sephardic Jews, which he outlines in the provocatively entitled *The Aryanization of the Jewish State*. Selzer concludes this book with a call for a renewed diaspora nationalism: "The foundations of a Dubnovian, autonomous Jewish life are already well established outside Israel, particularly in the United States" (118).

[37] See the account of Gorny, *The State of Israel*, as well as the voices assembled in Kushner and Solomon, eds, *Wrestling with Zion*.

[38] For an insider's account of the group, see Domb, *The Transformation*.

[39] See Myers, *Resisting History*, 130–56.

[40] Breuer, *Messiasspuren*, 18.

[41] Ibid. *Judenproblem*, 89; Myers, *Resisting History*, 154.

[42] Breuer, *Messiasspuren*, 44, 79.

[43] Morgenstern, *Vom Frankfurt nach Jerusalem*, 231.

[44] Kurzweil, "Yitzhak Breuer," in idem, *Le-nokhah ha-mevukhah*, 117.

[45] Ibid. See also "Al ha-to'elet ve-al ha-nezek shel mada'ei ha-yahadut," in idem, *Be-ma'avak al erkhei ha-yahadut*, 209.

[46] See Leibowitz, *He'arot le-farshiyot ha-shavu'a*, 112. Leibowitz insisted that "the abiding and constant element in Jewish history, the *Halakhah*, is essentially ahistoric." Leibowitz, "Ahistorical Thinkers," 97.

[47] According to Leibowitz, "exalting the land itself to the rank of holiness is idolatry *par excellence*." Leibowitz, "The Uniqueness," 86–87.

[48] See http://www.jewsagainstzionism.com/quotes/teitelbaum.html#SomeWords.

[49] Teitelbaum, *Sefer va-yo'el Moshe*, 5, 8.

[50] For a sampling of the debate between "post-Zionists" and their critics, see, inter alia, Ginossar and Bareli, eds, *Tziyonut*; Weitz, *Bein hazon le-reviziyah*; and Silberstein, *The Postzionism Debates*.

[51] Freedland has offered one of the best and most credible accounts of the relationship between anti-Semitism and anti-Zionism (or varieties of anti-Zionism). Freedland's discussion of MK Bishara introduces an important category of anti-Zionist expression to the tradition under discussion—Israeli, particularly Israeli Arab, anti-Zionism. Freedland, "Is Anti-Zionism Antisemitism?" 127.

[52] In this regard, one is reminded of an apocryphal story told about the arch Jewish anti-Zionist, the Satmar Rebbe. It is a story whose moral is at once compelling and repellent, intuitive and immoral. Once a politician in New York came to visit Rabbi Teitelbaum to ask for his endorsement. Apparently, the politician knew with whom he was dealing and avoided any

mention of Israel. However, at the end of their meeting, the Satmar Rebbe asked the politician what his stance on Israel was. With some hesitation, the politician admitted that he was a strong supporter of Israel. Surprisingly, the Rebbe responded with approval. Later, he explained to his "perplexed followers ... that non-Jewish opposition to the state of Israel is rooted in hatred of the Jews." In other words, it was dangerous and threatening—in fact, anti-Semitic—for a non-Jew to oppose Zionism. The accompanying logic—that which guided the Satmar Rebbe throughout his life—was that it was not only possible but obligatory for a Jew to oppose Zionism. See Nissan Ratzlav-Katz, "The Wisdom of the Satmar Rebbe," *Arutz Sheva*, 28 March 2003 (www.israelnationalnews. com/article.php3?id = 2129). The Satmar Rebbe's logic is similar to that of one who believes ethnic jokes are legitimate only when told by a member of the in-group. On the one hand, such logic violates our sense of basic fairness regarding human nature (by imputing ill will to the outside critic). On the other, it hardly seems unreasonable to maintain that Jews would feel a deeper sense of commitment to Jewish survival than non-Jews, and thus might oppose Zionism out of altruism rather than malice.

[53] See the section dealing with this question, particularly the contribution by Israel Supreme Court Justice Aharon Barak, in Walzer, Lorberbaum and Zohar, eds, *The Jewish Political Tradition*, 545–61. See also the recent attempt by Yakobson and Rubinstein to compare Israel's version of democracy to that of other nations in *Yisra'el u-mishpahat ha-amim*, as well as Gavison, *Yisra'el ki-medinah yehudit ve-demokratit*.

[54] See Ravitzky, *Messianism*, 125–56, and more generally chapter 3.

[55] Ravitzky calls attention to the affinity between religious Zionist and religious anti-Zionist messianism in ibid., 138.

References

Altmann, Alexander. "Theology in Twentieth-Century German Jewry." *Leo Baeck Institute Year Book* 1 (1956): 194.

Arendt, Hannah. "Zionism Reconsidered." In *Zionism Reconsidered: The Rejection of Jewish Normalcy*, edited by Michael Selzer. London: Macmillan, 1970.

Bareli, Avi, and Pinhas Ginossar, eds. *Tziyonut: Pulmus ben zmanenu* (Zionism: A contemporary controversy). Beer Sheva: Ben-Gurion University, 1996.

Bergmann, Werner, and Julianne Wetzel. "Manifestations of Anti-Semitism in the European Union." Vienna: The European Monitoring Centre on Racism and Xenophobia, 2003 (http://eumc.eu. int/eumc/as/PDF04/AS-Main-report-PDF04.pdf).

Brenner, Michael. "The Jüdische Volkspartei—National-Jewish Communal Politics during the Weimar Republic." *Leo Baeck Institute Year Book* 35 (1990): 219–43.

Breuer, Isaac. *Messiasspuren*. Frankfurt: R. L. Hammon, 1918.

———. *Judenproblem*. Halle: O. Hendel, 1918.

Chesler, Phyllis. *The New Anti-Semitism: The Current Crisis and What We Must Do about It*. San Francisco: Jossey-Bass, 2003.

Cohen, Hermann. "Deutschtum und Judentum." *Jüdische Schriften*. Vol. 2. Berlin: C.A. Schwetschke, 1924.

———. "Grätzens Philosophie der jüdischen Geschichte." In *Jüdische Schriften*. Vol. 2. Berlin: C.A. Schwetschke, 1924.

———. "Zur Kontroverse zwischen Trendelenburg und Kuno Fischer." In *Schriften zur Philosophie und Zeitgeschichte*. Vol. 1. Berlin: Akademie Verlag, 1928.

Dershowitz, Alan. *The Case for Israel*. Hoboken, NJ: John Wiley & Sons, 2003.

Domb, Jerahmeel Israel Isaac. *The Transformation: The Case of the Neturei Karta*. Brooklyn: Hachomo, 1989.

Foxman, Abraham. *Never Again? The Threat of the New Anti-Semitism*. San Francisco: Harper, 2003.

Freedland, Jonathan. "Is Anti-Zionism Antisemitism?" In *A New Antisemitism? Debating Judeophobia in 21st-Century Britain*, edited by Paul Iganski and Barry Kosmin. London: Profile Books, 2003.

Gavison, Ruth. *Yisra'el ki-medinah yehudit ve-demokratit: Metahim ve-sikuyim* (Israel as a Jewish and democratic state: Tensions and prospects). Jerusalem: Van Leer Institute, 1999.

Gordon, Peter Eli. "Under One Tradewind: Philosophical Expressionism from Rosenzweig to Heidegger." Ph.D. diss., University of California, Berkeley, 1997.

Gorny, Yosef. *The State of Israel in Jewish Public Thought: The Quest for Collective Identity*. New York: New York University Press, 1994.

Hattis, Susan Lee. *The Bi-National Idea in Palestine during Mandatory Times*. Haifa: Shikmona, 1970.

Iganski, Paul, and Barry Kosmin, eds. *A New Anti-Semitism? Debating Judeophobia in 21st-Century Britain*. London: Profile Books, 2003.

Kellner, Menachem, ed. *The Pursuit of the Ideal: Jewish Writings of Steven Schwarzschild*. Albany: State University of New York Press, 1990.

Kohn, Hans. "Zion and the Jewish National Idea." In *Zionism Reconsidered: The Rejection of Jewish Normalcy*, edited by Michael Selzer. London: 1970.

Kolsky, Thomas A. *Jews against Zionism: The American Council for Judaism, 1942–1948*. Philadelphia: Temple University Press, 1990.

Kurzweil, Baruch. *Be-ma'avak al erkhei ha-yahadut* (In the struggle for the values of Judaism). Jerusalem: Schocken, 1969.

———. *Le-nokhah ha-mevukhah ha-ruhanit shel dorenu* (Facing the spiritual confusion of our times). Ramat Gan: Bar-Ilan University, 1976.

Kushner, Tony, and Alisa, Solomon, eds. *Wrestling with Zion: Progressive Jewish-American Responses to the Israeli-Palestinian Conflict*. New York: Grove Press, 2003.

Leibowitz, Yeshayahu. "Ahistorical Thinkers in Judaism." In *Judaism, Human Values, and the Jewish State*, edited by Eliezer Goldman. Cambridge, MA: Harvard University Press, 1972.

———. "The Uniqueness of the Jewish People." In *Judaism, Human Values, and the Jewish State*, edited by Eliezer Goldman. Cambridge, MA: Harvard University Press, 1972.

———. *He'arot le-farshiyot ha-shavu'a* (Comments on the weekly Portions). Jerusalem: Akademon, 1988.

Liebeschütz, Hans. "Hermann Cohen and His Historical Background." *Leo Baeck Institute Year Book* 13, no. 2 (1968): 3–4.

Meir, Ephraim. *Kokhav mi-Ya'akov: Hayav ve-yetzirato shel Franz Rosenzweig* (A star from Jacob: The life and works of Franz Rosenzweig). Jerusalem: Hebrew University, 1994.

Mendes-Flohr, Paul, and Jehuda Reinharz. *The Jew in the Modern World*. New York: Oxford, 1995.

Moore, Deborah Dash. *To the Golden Cities: Pursuing the American Jewish Dream in Miami and L.A.* New York: Maxwell Macmillan International, 1994.

Morgenstern, Matthias. *Vom Frankfurt nach Jerusalem: Isaac Breuer und die Geschichte des "Austrittsstreits" in der deutsch-jüdischen Orthodoxie*. Tübingen: J.C.B. Mohr, 1995.

Mosès, Stéphane. "Franz Rosenzweig mul ha-tziyonut" (Franz Rosenzweig confronting Zionism). In *Ha-Tsiyonut u-mitnagdeha ba-am ha-yehudi* (Zionism and its Jewish opponents), edited by Haim Avni and Gideon Shimoni. Jerusalem: Ha-sifriyah ha-tziyonit, 1990.

Myers, David, N. *Resisting History: Historicism and Its Discontents in German-Jewish Thought*. Princeton: Princeton University Press, 2003.

Neusner, Jacob, ed. *Israel and Zion in American Judaism: The Zionist Fulfillment*. New York and London: Garland, 1993.

Ogletree, Thomas W. *Christian Faith and History: A Critical Comparison of Ernst Troeltsch and Karl Barth*. New York: Abingdon Press, 92–96.

"Perceptions of the Antisemitism in the European Union: Voices from Members of the European Jewish Communities." European Monitoring Centre on Racism and Xenophobia, April 2004 (http://eumc.eu.int/eumc/as/PDF05/AS-interviews.pdf).

Petuchowski, Jakob J. *Zion Reconsidered*. New York: Twayne Publishers, 1966.

Poppel, Stephen M. *Zionism in Germany, 1897–1933*. Philadelphia: Jewish Publication Society of America, 1977.

Raffel, Martin, J. "History of Israel Advocacy." In *Jewish Polity and American Civil Society: Communal Agencies and Religious Movements in the American Public Square*, edited by Alan Mittleman, Jonathan D. Sarna, and Robert Licht. Lanham, MD: Rowman & Littlefield, 2002.

Ratsabi, Shalom. *Between Zionism and Judaism: The Radical Circle in Brith Shalom, 1925–1933*. Boston: Brill, 2002.

Ravitzky, Aviezer. *Messianism, Zionism, and Jewish Religious Radicalism*. Chicago: University of Chicago Press, 1993.

Rawidowicz, Simon. *Bavel vi-Yerushalayim* (Babylon and Jerusalem). London and Waltham, MA: Ararat, 1957.

Raz-Krakotzkin, Amnon. "Ha-shivah el ha-historiyah shel ha-ge'ulah" (The return to the history of redemption). In *Ha-tziyonut veha-hazarah le-historiyah: Ha'arakhah me-hadash* (Zionism and the return to history: A reassessment), edited by S.N. Eisenstadt and M. Lissak. Jerusalem: Yad Yitzhak, 1999.

Rosenthal, Steven, T. *Irreconcilable Differences? The Waning of the American Jewish Love Affair with Israel*. Hanover, NH: University of New England Press, 2001.

Rosenzweig, Franz. *Der Mensch und sein Werk: Zweistromland*. The Hague: Martinus Nijhoff, 1984.

Rubinstein, Amnon, and Alexander Yakobson. *Yisra'el u-mishpahat ha-amim* (Israel and the family of nations). Tel Aviv: Shocken, 2003.

Sagiv, Assaf. "George Steiner's Jewish Problem." *Azure*, no. 15 (Summer 2003) (www.azure. org.il/15-sagiv.htm).

Scholem, Gershom. "Kabbala at the Hebrew University." *The Reconstructionist* 3, no. 10 (1937): 8–12.

Schwarzschild, Steven. *Franz Rosenzweig (1886–1929): A Guide for Reversioners*. London: The Education Committee of the Hillel Foundation, 1960.

Schweid, Eliezer. "Ha-shivah el ha-historiyah ba-hagut ha-yehudit shel ha-me'ah ha-esrim" (The return to history in twentieth-century Jewish thought). In *Hevrah ve-historiyah* (Society and history), edited by Y. Cohen. Jerusalem: 1980.

Selzer, Michael. *The Aryanization of the Jewish State*. New York: Black Star Publishing Co., 1967.

———, ed. *Zionism Reconsidered: The Rejection of Jewish Normalcy*. London: Macmillan, 1970.

Sheppard, Eugene R. "Leo Strauss and the Politics of Exile." Ph.D diss., UCLA, 2001.

Silberstein, Laurence J. *The Postzionism Debates: Knowledge and Power in Israeli Culture*. New York and London: Routledge, 1999.

Strauss, Leo. "Der Zionismus bei Nordau." In *Gesammelte Schriften*, edited by Heinrich Meier. Stuttgart: J.B. Metzler, 1997.

Teitelbaum, Yoel. *Sefer va-yo'el Moshe*. Brooklyn: Deutsch, 1959.

Troeltsch, Ernst. "Die Krisis des Historismus." *Die Neue Rundschau* 33 (1922): 572–90.

Walzer, Michael, Lorberbaum, M., and N. Zohar, eds. *The Jewish Political Tradition*. Vol. 2. New Haven: Yale University Press, 2003.

Weitz, Yehiam. *Bein hazon le-reviziyah: me'ah shnot historiyografiyah tziyonit* (Between vision and revision: A hundred years of Zionist historiography). Jerusalem: Hebrew University, 1997.

Readjusting Cultural Codes: Reflections on Anti-Semitism and Anti-Zionism

Shulamit Volkov

Twenty-five year ago the Leo Baeck Institute *Yearbook* published an essay of mine under the title "Anti-Semitism as a Cultural Code."[1] I was astonished at the attention it received, since I had hardly had a chance to try it on a live audience before publication and expected only a limited reaction, if at all. My single presentation of the text at a conference at St. Antony's College, Oxford, had drawn a rather hostile response from some of the participants and there seemed to be no reason to expect others to react differently. In the end it was probably the ringing title, based on a variation upon a well-known essay of Clifford Geertz, that contributed to the modest fame of this piece.[2] Concepts based on anthropological and ethnographic research were becoming fashionable at the time in other historiographical contexts, too, and the introduction of the term "cultural code" in relation to the problematics of anti-Semitism seemed timely.[3] I myself had some grave doubts. I took seriously the critique of historians, dealing both with German and with German-Jewish history, and have tried on several occasions during the following years to re-examine the validity of this term and work out its implications.[4]

In view of the antiquity of this entire episode and for the purposes of this article, let me recapitulate what still seems relevant to me in the arguments laid out in that paper and in some of the additional, related work, I did thereafter.[5] At the time, I was working on the so-called modern anti-Semitic movement in Germany of the last third of the nineteenth century. This has been a major focus of research since the end of World War II and many historians then—as now—believed that here lay the roots of Nazi anti-Semitism and the ultimate explanation for the Holocaust. The novelty of that modern anti-Semitism, it was generally agreed, was twofold. It substituted a racial theory, or rather pseudo-theory, for the old religious hatred, and it brought to fruition for the first time the political potential of Jew-hating. Both these characteristics, ran the argument, were later exploited to the full by Hitler and his followers.

I, however, tended to minimize the importance of these factors. I thought that racialism was grafted upon old motivations for Jew-hating rather than substituted for them, and that if anything, the meager success of the mushrooming anti-Semitic political parties at the time could have served to show *the limits* of its recruiting power. Instead, I suggested, anti-Semitism had another function in Imperial Germany. It served as a code, a signal for a much larger and more important political and cultural phenomenon at that time: that of antimodernism. An entire section of German society was by then deeply unsettled by the implications of an advanced industrialism and its concomitant value-system and life-style, I argued. Apparently, all of the typically antimodern social elements, and not only in Germany, were also infected by anti-Semitism. In their eyes, Jews stood for modernity, for success under its auspices, for the chance of manipulating its advantages, while destroying all remnants of the old world. Anti-Jewish attitudes were not particularly *important* for most of these people, it seemed to me. But precisely because these were marginal to their overall worldview, their expression could serve them as a mark of a radical position on other, more important matters. It became a political symbol in the context of the late nineteenth century; or even more generally, it was becoming a cultural code, indicating the overall acceptance of a certain cultural choice.

Beyond its descriptive value, this thesis had a number of advantages from my point of view. It allowed me to explain, for instance, the overtly anti-Jewish position of some Jews, who belonged to what I saw as the antimodern camp, and to do that without using the concept of self-hatred, which I have treated then, and still do today, with a great deal of skepticism.[6] It also—more importantly no doubt—allowed me to suggest that Nazi anti-Semitism, never merely a code or a sign but a source of a full-fledged program of annihilation, was itself a novelty considering this background. The change in the meaning of anti-Jewish rhetoric introduced by the Nazis was far-reaching, but was, surprisingly perhaps, not immediately apparent. Many Jews—and Germans—tended to misread Hitler's intentions. *They* were still using the cultural tools of a previous era, I argued, not realizing that the language, their very own language, was meanwhile being transformed and its meaning changed. The meaning of anti-Semitism had thus shifted, but it was not easy to perceive the shift.

Furthermore, and crucial in many respects, the cultural-code thesis helped explain the open *anti*-anti-Semitic line taken by the left in pre–World War I Europe, especially no doubt in Germany and in France. Now, any long-term view of anti-Semitism could not fail to show an anti-Jewish streak in the various movements of the left. Some historians, such as Edmund Silberner in an earlier generation and Robert Wistrich later on, claimed, indeed, that anti-Semitism had always been constitutive to the left, especially to the revolutionary left.[7] And examples could be brought not only from thinkers and ideologues such as Proudhon, Marx or Eugen Dühring but also from the French socialists' procrastination in defending Dreyfus in *fin-de-siècle* France, from the position of most Austrian socialists on a variety of Jewish issues and from the many common asides against Jews in the social democratic press throughout the German *Kulturraum*.[8] Moreover, even the most decent European socialists, entirely uncontaminated by explicit anti-Semitism, were hostile to the idea and the ideals of Jewish nationalism and to any and all manifestations of Zionism.[9]

Still, from the first decade of the twentieth century, European socialists clearly saw the inner bond between anti-Semitism and antimodernism, and were able to diagnose its meaning for socialism. In France, anti-Semitism called forth the various aspect of anti-Republicanism. In Germany, it indicated opposition to everything related to the new world of industrialism and democratization. Because anti-Semitism served as a cultural code for an outspoken posture more or less clearly associated with the right, the socialists repeatedly felt they had to distance themselves from it, at least publicly. They were careful not to appear as Philosemites—to use a contemporary term—but as a rule, stayed clear from any anti-Semitism in the *Öffentlichkeit*.[10]

All of these points provided supporting evidence for my cultural-code thesis and helped manifest some of its implications for the historical period I then tried to illuminate. Before I attempt to apply this idea in other contexts and examine its validity today, let me say something about the route that led me to adopt this original thesis. The application of the concept of cultural-code to my work had two sources, as is so common in historiography: professional and autobiographical, or personal. It grew, first of all, out of my previous work on the master-artisans in Germany during what we then used to call "die Grosse Depression" (the Great Depression). Indeed, it was rather easy to demonstrate the instrumental role—that is, the *function*—of Jew-hating within the organizational and political efforts of these small handicraft masters at the time. Their deep uneasiness with modernity was all too often translated into an anti-Semitic verbiage, though rarely into anything more threatening than that. They were not revolutionaries. They were usually even ready to *defend* the "system"—but they truly believed it had been corrupted. Their enemy was not capitalism, they often argued, but the Jews who had led it to inhuman excesses; not liberalism as such, but the Jews who misinterpreted and misrepresented it; it was not the modern state that was responsible for neglecting their interests, but the Jews who thought of theirs only, and so forth. The link between anti-Semitism and the fear of modernity was clearly apparent among the men I then investigated.[11]

But it was not only my academic work that led me to seek the possibly symbolic function of anti-Semitism in modern society. More important perhaps was my first-hand experience with anti-Zionism on the Berkeley campus during the 1960s and in some of the German towns visited immediately afterwards. By then, anti-Zionism was clearly a constant theme among members of the so-called New Left—men and women who considered themselves the revolutionaries of those heroic years. Strangely enough, at least from my perspective, anti-Zionism was often particularly strong among Jews. No doubt, the realization that perhaps not only anti-Zionism but also anti-Semitism may be seen as a part of a larger, more comprehensive ideological "package deal" first occurred to me as I observed my American Jewish friends operating as they did within the various left-wing groupings during these years.

In some ways, of course, their anti-Zionism could merely be considered a continuation of the anti-Zionist position of so many liberal Jews *before* the Holocaust. In the prosperous Jewish communities of the West during the early decades of the twentieth century, Jews opposing Zionism were surely more common than Jews supporting it. But after the Holocaust, this "balance of power" clearly shifted. Following the realization of the dimensions of mass extermination under the Nazis and the tragic effects of the closed-door policies of so many countries during the war, it seemed no longer *bon ton* to oppose Zionism—neither principally nor in practice. Both Jews and non-Jews, on the left and the right, proceeded much more carefully now along the lines of the old pro- and contra-Zionism debate. In fact, it was only after the Israeli victory in 1967, when the existence of Israel seemed finally secure and its policies of occupation began to draw criticism, that anti-Zionism began to play the role of a cultural code within the ideological set-up of the New Left, in America as well as in Europe. Once again, we were dealing with an ideational package deal. Its main components were anticolonialism, a somewhat vague but often violent anticapitalism and a deep suspicion vis-à-vis the policies of the United States, not only in Vietnam but also, often especially, in Latin America. In some countries this package now also included the emerging ecological argument. On the whole, this was clearly no longer the old antimodern package, though it still had some similarities with it. Moreover, it was now no longer located on the right but on the left. But despite all-important differences, here too a particular form of anti-Jewish posture was made to serve as a symbol, an indication of belonging, a cultural code. The package deal had been transformed; its social and political focus relocated; but the general mechanism of its operation was in many ways the same.

An additional perspective then helped convince me of the validity of my interpretation. By the late 1960s and the early 1970s, expressions of anti-Israel, if not clearly anti-Zionist, sentiments were also voiced ever more frequently by representatives of the so-called developing countries, members of the now extinct "Third World." Occasionally, such attitudes were based on solidarity with the Arab cause, no doubt. But the general anti-Jewish, indeed anti-Semitic, twist given to such basically political attitudes required further explanation. It was at this stage that the anticolonial struggle no longer focused on straightforward demands for independence on the part of the colonized and began to display its cultural contours. The overall set of values and norms typical of the imperialist West and its inherent list of priorities were turned into targets for attack at this point. It was an attack on cultural conceit, on disregard for the suffering of non-white peoples, on the traditional paternalism and cultural arrogance of the colonizers. Finally, and through a vague adoption of old anti-Semitic claims and suppositions, the Jews became a symbol of that West. They stood for its essence and its vices. By attacking them one was finally up in arms against all and every manifestation of Western culture. The persecuted were as guilty as the persecutors among the colonialists. Even the most downtrodden among them were no longer privileged. Even they were legitimate targets for hatred. Jewish claim for special consideration because of the Holocaust and its horrendous consequences seemed especially outrageous to spokesmen from the Third World. In view of their own devastation, the Holocaust elicited little sympathy. A combination of opposition to Israel, often while linking its policies to the evils of South African apartheid and a reliance on a borrowed, European anti-Semitic tradition, became a part of the overall anti-imperialist syndrome. It may not have been particularly important to those applying it, but it served them well to signify their position.

Personally, then, it was above all the case of anti-Zionism among left-wing activists during the late 1960s and spokesmen of the Third World somewhat later on that I first diagnosed as a cultural code for a larger political-intellectual package and that has since served me for interpreting both contemporary and historical situations. A look at France in the late nineteenth century, during the Dreyfus affair, offered an excellent historical case study. It appeared that as the affair became a major public issue, it consolidated on the one side the anti-Dreyfusards, who were part of the general anti-Republican camp in the Third Republic of the late 1890s, and on the other, the Dreyfusards—namely, the Republican forces, despite the inner controversies that raged among them.[12] A decade earlier, one could still locate anti-Semitic attitudes across much of the social and political spectrum of France. In the years between 1887 and 1889, the *Socialist Review*, the official newspaper for the socialist movement, published a series of anti-Semitic articles, though it occasionally gave voice to milder positions, too. The Blanquist and Proudhonist traditions within the socialist left in France were laden with anti-Semitic materials. But when an anti-Dreyfusard and a generally anti-Jewish position became a mark of the anti-Republican camp, French socialists, much like their German comrades under different circumstances, found it necessary to distance themselves from it. This became particularly evident in the aftermath of Emil Zola's public *J'accuse* in 1898 and when the violent message of the Anti-Semitic League was made apparent in the streets of Paris. Like the social democrats in the *Kaiserreich*, the French socialists too never managed to rid their membership entirely of anti-Semitic prejudices, but in public and in their open political pronouncements, they left no doubt as to the side they chose to take.[13]

Here too, then, a position on the so-called Jewish question, not in itself of paramount importance, came to indicate a belonging to a larger camp, signifying loyalty to a larger ideological package deal, a political stand and an overall cultural choice. In both Germany and France of the turn of the twentieth century, however, it was often unclear whether anti-Semitism served as a code for a general antimodern and anti-Republican stand, or whether an outspoken *anti*-anti-Semitism fulfilled this role for the modern, emancipatory—and in France, Republican—camp. A decision along these lines, I believe, depends on the prominence of the anti-Semitic issue within each context. A position on a certain issue could be considered a code, it seems to me, only if and when it plays a rather marginal role for the men and women concerned. Thus, I have elsewhere argued, antifeminism, another creed of the conservative, antimodern bloc in pre–World War I Europe, could not serve as a code, because already by the last decade of the nineteenth century and the first of the twentieth it was a major issue; neither a sign for something else nor a code for more important matters.[14]

To sum up, we have so far relied upon two assumptions in trying to interpret anti-Semitism—or anti-Zionism too—as cultural codes. The first is that cultural as well as social and political views come in packages, in the form of ideational syndromes; the second, that only relatively minor issues, though of the kind that are common enough in public discourse, can serve as codes, signifying larger, more important syndromes. Much of the criticism that has been voiced against my thesis came from those who objected to one or the other of these assumptions. The first kind of objection, however, was not usually sounded on theoretical grounds. The fact that people's belief-system has the form of more or less well-integrated compounds or "syndromes" was rarely contested. Opposition usually came from historians, familiar with the complexity and diversity of Germany during the period under consideration, who claimed that a division of its society into two camps, recognizable by their attitudes to Jews, was an unwarranted simplification.

This, usually oral, controversy was from the start intertwined with a more comprehensive and, no doubt, more important one—that dealing with the validity of the *Sonderweg* thesis in German historiography. My paradigm, the paradigm of a split society, in which two major political camps and two subcultures were set against each other, seemed to fit that thesis well enough. It seemed to support the *Sonderweg* view, according to which social, political and cultural developments, most particularly since the late nineteenth century, prepared the ground for the later victory of National Socialism.[15] Moreover, this thesis included the claim that it was some shortcoming in the process of modernization and in the way modernity had been received and internalized in Germany that was the source of its uniqueness vis-à-vis its European neighbors. The alternative view, originally proposed by Geoff Eley and David Blackbourn precisely at the time I published my "cultural code" paper, disputed this uniqueness altogether and stressed the bourgeois nature of German society at the time of the *Kaiserreich*, its modernity and its similarity to other societies in *fin-de-siècle* Europe.[16] Accordingly, Germany was pluralistic and diversified, so that a breaking line along issues of emancipation and anti-Semitism could not gain the importance of a general cultural code. A number of studies by English historians on some of the early-twentieth-century political associations, such as the Navy League and the Pan-German League, argued that anti-Semitism had in fact been negligible even among members of the popular right.[17] Later, some German historians too, above all the late Thomas Nipperdey, took up the same argument and likewise claimed that other, reform-oriented associations, too, though sometimes antimodern in orientation, were not anti-Semitic.[18] Recently, a young scholar from Jerusalem, Gideon Reuveni, has argued that if consumers' organizations rather than producers' interest-groups were to be investigated, anti-Semitism would be found even less frequently among their members.[19] In other words: a variety of other lines of division were more significant for the social world of the *Kaiserreich*, overshadowing the general left-right division, or indeed the anti-Semitic versus the anti-anti-Semitic camp, too.

There were, no doubt, other divisions within German society at the turn of the century and there were likewise quite a few cases in which familiar ideological package deals proved unreliable. Some of the better-known examples were to be found among artists, such as the poet Stefan George, whose artistic modernity clearly did not match his reactionary social and political views. Artists, after all, are expected to excel in breaking up conventional wisdom. Ideational package deals are such conventions *par excellence*. Similarly, to be sure, there were also men on the left who continued to parade their anti-Semitism. Vienna at the turn of the century knew quite a few of them.[20] Ideational package deals are rough tools and clearly not everyone succumbs to their spell. Still, on the whole they are very pervasive and extremely powerful. While the Pan-German League had been careful on the Jewish issue for sometime, it eventually adopted anti-Semitism—always central in its Berlin chapter—with a vengeance. The Navy League may have been less than outspoken on that matter, since it was an association representing above all the interests of the upper bourgeoisie—by no means obvious candidates for upholding the cultural views of the antimodern right.

A variety of reformers, too, fighting for the abolition of alcohol or tobacco, for instance, were unlikely to get involved publicly on the Jewish issue, as theirs was not a typically right-wing agenda, old or new. Furthermore, there were clearly numerous variations within each camp, not just with regard to the Jews. Elements of the right held different attitudes towards Christianity, to take one example. Despite the prominence of the Junkers within this milieu, to take another, others within it were vocal opponents of the old aristocracy. Material interests, too, tended to divide members of the same cultural bloc. Still, on some major issues these people saw eye to eye. Mosse's "German Ideology" was crucial to them. They relied heavily upon an antimodern mentality, including a systematic rejection of the tenets of liberalism, democracy and socialism. They all too often reveled in nostalgic visions of a long-lost golden past and had various utopian plans for the future. An antagonistic attitude towards Jews could easily be found among them. It sometimes sprang from a deep-seated Christian education; occasionally from some kind of xenophobia or from a situation of professional competition. The function of their publicly paraded anti-Semitism was frequently the same: to indicate their basic cultural choices, to qualify them in the eyes of their peers, to define them vis-à-vis their adversaries.

The second type of criticism directed at the cultural-code thesis was in a way merely the other side of the same coin. If some historians of Wilhelmine Germany thought this thesis gave too much weight to the issue of anti-Semitism, others felt it underestimated its significance. Such underestimation could pertain to a particular case—in a particular place and time—or it could be claimed for the overall development of anti-Semitism, from its inception and up to National Socialism. Surely, both these reproaches deserve some consideration. In fact, there is a tradition of sorts, according to which historians of anti-Semitism insist on considering all its manifestations as outgrowths of a permanent antipathy towards Jews, based on ancient controversies and conflicting social relationships. Every attempt to disengage a particular case from that linear, age-old story is therefore strictly rejected. Let me mention here as an example Jacob Katz's elaborate attempt to dismiss Eleonora Sterling's interpretation of the 1819 Hep-Hep riots in Germany as "displacement" of hostility and violence from issues of modernization to anti-Jewish rioting. Katz, an open-minded historian and a pleasant colleague, refused to acknowledge such an interpretation. His famous essay on the Hep-Hep riots is an extended effort to reject it, dismissing the significance of contemporary issues and stressing the role played by a continuous European tradition of Jew-hating in this case.[21] He was also ill at ease with the cultural-code idea. Now, there is no question that the choice of the Jews as targets for violence—actual in the early nineteenth century and in most cases only verbal in its later years—was not arbitrary. It clearly relied on the anti-Jewish sentiment embedded in Christian culture. But a historical view of the manifestations of this sentiment must also consider the particular context in which such sentiments were activated and their particular function at a certain point in time. The fact is, after all, that though Jews were not much appreciated at *all* times, they were actively resented and persecuted only in *particular* places and at *particular* times. Beyond acknowledging the persistence of anti-Jewish feelings, it is the historian's role to explain how and why a certain form of anti-Semitism characterizes certain societies at certain times.

Still, concentrating upon the function of anti-Semitism within a particular historical context and beyond the effect of its permanent existence, while not necessarily detracting from its significance—so I believe—is surely a way of avoiding its overestimation. We have all gone through what might be called "the Goldhagen stage" about a decade ago. It was a reminder of how history could be read backward, by choosing only the supporting evidence. However anti-Semitic Germany was during the late nineteenth century, indeed, it was clearly likewise a land of what at that time seemed a uniquely successful emancipation. Contemporary Jews from across Europe who sent their sons—and sometimes even their daughters—to study and live in Imperial Germany were not simply blind or ignorant. Its society embodied for them the potential of existing freely and creatively as Jewish citizens of a modern state. It was not an existence free of anti-Semitism, to be sure, but this issue was largely under control, according to most observers. Let us not forget that the anti-Semitism that provoked the emergence of Zionism then and there was mainly manifested in Russia of the pogroms and in France of the Dreyfus affair. Indeed, the cultural-code thesis suggests the *relative* unimportance of anti-Semitism at the time. While it does not deny its existence, it does try to avoid inflating its influence merely in view of what was to come later. It provides a perspective of the period under consideration, which is dependent upon its own parameters, seeking to preserve its own "directness to God," to use Ranke's terminology, or uphold its special uniqueness, in more modern terms.

Before I move forward in time, examining the validity of the idea of cultural code for more contemporary situations, let me first take a small detour in order to further undermine the claim to exclusivity of explanations that rely on the heritage of anti-Semitism only. In fact, the historiography of anti-Semitism has for many years applied another term that carried with it a symbolic connotation and related Jew-hating to particular events, chronologically and geographically—namely, the "scapegoat." The word itself, as is well known, indicates an ancient Jewish ritual, in which guilt is symbolically laden upon a he-goat that is then sent to a no-man's land among the mountains of Jerusalem. By analogy it was often argued that Jews were made to carry blame for various catastrophes, such as a variety of social ills or the plague, primarily during the Middle Ages. Turning against Jews in some of the early-modern episodes seems to have followed a similar pattern, too, and even later attacks on Jews, instead of on landlords for instance or on exploiting capitalists, were often interpreted along the same lines. Like the cultural-code paradigm, scapegoating too does not stand outside the tradition of Jew-hating, since it is that tradition that qualifies the Jews in particular crisis situations to take the blame. But the cultural-code model seems to depend on this tradition even more heavily, since it also relies on the symbolic applications of this tradition, including scapegoating. In other words, being a later phenomenon, it relies not only on the tradition of despising the Jews but also on that of making symbolic use of this hatred in a variety of social and cultural situations. In comparison with scapegoating, the cultural-code mechanism is more general, applicable to times of stability, or even growth and prosperity, not only to days of wrath.

Furthermore, scapegoating is basically a psychological tool, the workings of which are presumably always the same, while coding is a cultural process taking different shapes in different times and places. It may have been born out of the same mechanism in Germany and France of the late nineteenth century, but in each case it served a somewhat different purpose. It surely serves different purposes when it is found to be a practice on the right as opposed to the left. It is a better instrument for historians, because it takes into account both change and repetition. It clearly stresses the shifting functions of anti-Semitism and provides a way of thinking about *difference*, not only about continuity.

Thus, while antipathy towards Jews is to some degree a cultural constant, my model rejects the approach of observing the history of anti-Semitism as cyclical or spiral. This antipathy, I argue, is neither always the same, nor does it follow a pattern of rising intensity. The nineteenth century, accordingly, ought not to be considered a "rehearsal for destruction," nor Nazism the peak of an ongoing, gradual development. It did build upon "the longest hatred," of course, but finally introduced—as had happened in the past—a radical new variation upon the old theme. Nazi anti-Semitism was not simply yet another step in the long march towards extermination, but in many important ways was a new departure. It was, in any case, a diversion from the path of anti-Semitism during the Second Reich. It was only under Nazism that anti-Semitism lost its symbolic role and became most emphatically an end in itself. For Hitler, indeed, though anti-Semitism may not have always been the highest priority, it was in any case a separate, central issue, one that probably became ever more crucial as his other goals seemed less and less realizable. Under the rule of National Socialism, anti-Semitism no longer stood for other issues. It was not a way of avoiding social criticism, nor a sign of belonging to a particular cultural or political camp. The attack upon the Jews became a major policy matter under Nazism, a goal to be pursued relentlessly, under all circumstances. Perhaps here lay the danger of anti-Semitism as a cultural code: at a certain point it might lose its symbolic nature and turn almost imperceptibly into a full-scale attack.

Is that what we are experiencing today? If indeed the joint anti-Zionist and anti-Israel language of the left in the 1960s and 1970s served as a cultural code to indicate belonging to the camp of anti-imperialism, anticolonialism and a new sort of anticapitalism, has it now lost its symbolic meaning? Is it now a matter of direct and full-scale attack upon the Jews? I do not know. Perhaps. Surely, the context has been transformed. A number of additional elements have meanwhile been added to the ideational package deal that characterized the left during the 1960s: the specter of globalization, for instance, the growing importance of the ecological agenda, and so forth. Even more important now is the identity assumed between the policies of the United States, always a target for attack, especially from the European left, and those of the State of Israel. Today, however, following over five years of unprecedented conflict in the Middle East, opposition to Israel can hardly be regarded as a code for some other evil. In addition to a more open anti-Semitism among xenophobic groups on the right, the subculture of the left, even of the center-left, can no longer consider its position towards Israel a side-issue, ripe to serve as a cultural code. This has become a major concern now. The last public opinion poll in Europe documented, in fact, not so much a rising level of anti-Semitism as a rising anxiety vis-à-vis the worldwide implications of the Israeli-Palestinian conflict. Our traditional enemies may not need to adjust their position to the new situation, but we may have already passed the moment in which our friends too could use their attack against us as a sign of other beliefs and commitments. We may be approaching the stage in which we really are the target of their resentment, fear and hatred.

Unlike previous occasions, however, this time we are no longer pawns in someone else's chess game. It is up to us now to act. We could take action that would prove our commitment to peace and our concern for the well-being of others. We could set out to convince those who either were against us or at the very best were using their opposition to us as a code for their opposition to more important forces, that we understand the severity of the hour. Unfortunately, there seems to be no step taken in this direction. It is apparently easier to blame all others, to complain of anti-Semitism or anti-Zionism, to measure incessantly their intensity, but never to take any responsibility for trying to diminish their force.

Notes

[1] Volkov, "Anti-Semitism as a Cultural Code."

[2] See Geertz, "Ideology as a Cultural System," in his *The Interpretation of Cultures*, 193–233. Geertz, who uses terms such as 'cultural patterns' or 'symbolic systems,' finds the term 'code' rather less appropriate. On that see his "Thick Description: Toward an Interpretive Theory of Culture," also in ibid., 3–30, especially 9, where he critically discusses Gilbert Ryle's ethnographic approach and a term he used, "established codes."

[3] A more favorable reaction to the term and its potential use was forthcoming after a lecture and publication of a subsequent paper, Volkov, "Le Texte et la Parole."

[4] See Volkov, "Anti-Semitismus und Antifeminismus," 62–81.

[5] For the relevant bibliography, see Volkov, "Anti-Semitism as a Cultural Code," and "Le Texte et la Parole."

[6] See Volkov, "Selbstgefäligkeit und selbshaß," inidem, *Anti-Semitismus als kultureller Code*, 181–96.

[7] Silberner, *Sozialisten zur Judenfrage*; Wistrich, *Socialism and the Jews*.

[8] See Leuschen-Seppel, *Sozialdemokratie und Anti-Semitismus*, especially chap. 5.

[9] See, above all, the unfortunately rather neglected book of Na'aman, *Marxismus und Zionismus*.

[10] See Volkov, "The Immunization of Social Democracy against Anti-Semitism."

[11] See Volkov, *The Rise of Popular Antimodernism in Germany*.

[12] See Volkov, "Le Texte et la Parole," and the bibliography there. An English version can be found in Furet, ed., *Unanswered Questions*.

[13] For this issue see, among the many new books on this subject, Birnbaum, *The Anti-Semitic Moment*.

[14] See Volkov, "Antisemitismus und Antifeminismus."

[15] For a critique of my work from this perspective, though without reference to the cultural-code thesis, see Eley, *From Unification to Nazism*.

[16] By now the literature on the *Sonderweg* debate is enormous, indeed, but still critical for understanding its origins is Eley and Blackbourn, *The Peculiarities of German History*. The earlier German version was published in Frankfurt a. M., 1980.

[17] See Eley, *Reshaping the German Right*, and a wider perspective in "The German Right: How It Changed," *idem, From Unification to Nazism*, 231–53; and Chickering, *We Men Who Feel Most German*.

[18] See Nipperdey, *Deutsche Geschichte, 1866–1914*, 2:301–3, and an earlier but, as far as I can see, more balanced view, in "1933 und die Kontinuität der deutschen Geschichte," in his *Nachdenken über die deutsche Geschichte*, 186–205. Also compare Zmarzlik, "Anti-Semitismus im Deutschen Kaiserreich," 249–70.

[19] I am thankful to Gideon Reuveni for providing me with a copy of his as yet unpublished paper, ""Productivist" and "Consumerist" Narratives regarding Jews in German History."

[20] Still very useful is Leuschen-Seppel, *Sozialdemokratie und Anti-Semitismus*. See also Wistrich, *Socialism and the Jews*.

[21] See Sterling, "Anti-Jewish Riots in Germany in 1819," and Katz, *Die Hep-Hep Verfolgungen des Jahres 1819*, especially 71–88. This is a translation of an article that had appeared in Hebrew almost 20 years earlier, in *Zion* 38 (1973): 62–115.

References

Birnbaum, Pierre. *The Anti-Semitic Moment: A Tour of France in 1898*. New York: Hill and Wang, 2003.

Chickering, Roger. *We Men Who Feel Most German: A Cultural Study of the Pan-German League*. Boston: Allen and Unwin, 1984.

Eley, Geoff. *Reshaping the German Right: Radical Nationalism and Political Change after Bismarck*. New Haven: Yale University Press, 1980.

———. *From Unification to Nazism: Reinterpreting the German Past*. Boston: Allen and Unwin, 1986.

———, and David Blackbourn. *The Peculiarities of German History: Bourgeois Society and Politics in Nineteenth-Century Germany*. Oxford: Oxford University Press, 1984.

Furet, François, ed. *Unanswered Questions: Nazi Germany and the Genocide of the Jews*. New York: Schocken, 1989.

Geertz, Clifford. *The Interpretation of Cultures: Selected Essays*. New York: Basic Books, 1973.

Katz, Jakob. *Die Hep-Hep Verfolgungen des Jahres 1819*. Berlin: Metropol, 1994.

Leuschen-Seppel, Rosemarie. *Sozialdemokratie und Anti-Semitismus im Kaiserreich: Die Auseinandersetzungen der partei mit den konservativen und völkischen Strömungen des Antisemitismus, 1871–1914*. Bonn: Neue Gesellschaft, 1978.

Na'aman, Shlomo. *Marxismus und Zionismus*. Gerlingen: Bleicher Verlag, 1997.

Nipperdey, Thomas. *Nachdenken über die deutsche Geschichte*. Munich: C. H. Beck, 1986.

———. *Deutsche Geschichte, 1866–1914*. Vol. 2. Munich: C. H. Beck, 1992.

Silberner, Edmund. *Sozialisten zur Judenfrage: Ein Beitrag zur Geschichte des Soialismus vom Anfang des 19. Jahrhunderts bis 1914*. Berlin: Colloquium, 1962.

Sterling, Eleonora. "Anti-Jewish Riots in Germany in 1819: A Displacement of Social Protest." *Historia Judaica* 2 (1950): 105–42.

Volkov, Shulamit. "The Immunization of Social Democracy against Anti-Semitism in Imperial Germany." In *Juden und jüdische Aspekte in der deutschen Arbeiterbewegung, 1848–1918*. Vol. 2 of *Jahrbuch des Instituts für deutsche Geschichte*. Tel Aviv, 1977: 63–81.

———. "Anti-Semitism as a Cultural Code: Reflections on the History and Historiography of Anti-Semitism in Imperial Germany." *Yearbook of the Leo Baeck Institute* 23 (1978): 25–46.

———. *The Rise of Popular Antimodernism in Germany: The Urban Master Artisans, 1873–1896*. Princeton: Princeton University Press, 1978.

———. "Le Texte et la Parole: De l'anti-Sémitisme d'avant 1914 à l'anti-Sémitisme nazi." In *L'Allemagne Nazie et le génocide Juif*, edited by François Furet. Paris: Gallimard, 1982.

———. *Anti-Semitismus als kultureller Code: Zehn Essays*. Munich: C. H. Beck, 2000.

———. "Anti-Semitismus und Antifeminismus: Soziale Norm oder kultureller Code". In *Das jüdische Projekt der Moderne: Zehn Essays*. Munich: C. H. Beck, 2001.

Wistrich, Robert. *Socialism and the Jews: The Dilemmas of Assimilation in Germany and Austria-Hungary*. New Brunswick, NJ: Associated University Press of America, 1982.

Zmarzlik, Hans-Günter. "Anti-Semitismus im Deutschen Kaiserreich, 1871–1918." In *Die Juden als Minderheit in der Geschichte*, edited by Bernd Martin and Ernst Schulin. Munich: Deutscher Taschenbuch Verlag, 1981.

Convergence: The Classic Case
Nazi Germany, Anti-Semitism
and Anti-Zionism during World War II
Jeffrey Herf

In order to understand what divergence of anti-Zionism from anti-Semitism means, it is important to examine what convergence looked like. That, in turn, calls for a look at the most obvious case of convergence—namely, Nazi Germany during World War II and the Holocaust. Understanding the convergence of Jew hatred with rejection of the idea of a Jewish state in this limited case is important both because there remains much confusion about the Nazi attitude towards Zionism and because clarity is essential if we are to understand those other instances when anti-Zionism diverged from anti-Semitism. During the Cold War, the Soviet Union and its Warsaw Pact allies asserted that there was collaboration between Nazi Germany and Zionist leaders and that therefore the origins of the Jewish state were rooted in Nazi-Zionist cooperation.

In fact, in Nazism's entire history, though the Nazi regime allowed limited Jewish emigration to Palestine between 1933 and 1939, neither Hitler nor any other significant figure ever supported the Zionist goal of a Jewish state in Palestine or anywhere else.[1]

Hitler's hostility to the idea of a Jewish state in Palestine was long-standing and consistent. In *Mein Kampf* he contemptuously rejected the "lie" that Zionism was primarily a movement focused only on a homeland for the Jews in Palestine.

> For while the Zionists try to make the rest of the world believe that the national consciousness of the Jew finds its satisfaction in the creation of a Palestinian state, the Jews again slyly dupe the dumb *Goyim*. It doesn't even enter their heads to build up a Jewish state in Palestine for the purpose of living there; all they want is a central organization for their international world swindle, endowed with its sovereign right and removed from the intervention of other states: a haven for convicted scoundrels and a university for budding crooks.[2]

In the 1930s, Nazi support for emigration by German Jews to Palestine stemmed from the anti-Semitic motivation of removing Jews from Germany, not from a desire to see them found their own new state in Palestine. Under the terms of the *Ha'avarah* (Transfer) Agreement concluded in 1933 between the German Ministry of the Economy and Zionist representatives, Jewish emigrants were allowed to transfer part of their assets, and the export of goods from Germany to Palestine was facilitated. Between 1933 and 1939, about one hundred million marks were transferred to Palestine, and most of the 60,000 Jews who arrived there had some economic resources.[3] Yet Nazi support for emigration to Palestine was not the same as support for the establishment of a Jewish state there. These and other measures described below were never intended to lead to the establishment of a Jewish state. The Third Reich was never pro-Zionist in that sense. With the coming of war, Nazi ideological postulates about the existence of an international Jewish conspiracy converged with the strategic demands of gaining support for the Arabs in the war against the Allies. This convergence in both ideology and policy comprised the classic case of convergence of anti-Semitism and anti-Zionism. Francis R. Nicosia has demonstrated that Nazi anti-Semitism was compatible with support for limited Jewish emigration to Palestine in the 1930s in the context of the transfer agreement.[4]

Ambiguities before World War II

While Nazi ideology and policy never supported the idea of a Jewish state in Palestine, there was a dualism in the Nazi approach to the idea of supporting Zionist efforts to encourage Jews in Germany to emigrate there. The distinction was important, though often blurred. The anti-Semitic ideologue Alfred Rosenberg exerted a significant impact on Hitler's and Nazism's views about Zionism. His key text on the subject was *Der Staatsfeindliche Zionismus* (Zionism hostile to the state), which he published in 1921 and which the main Nazi publishing house published again in 1938.[5] Rosenberg both favored Zionist efforts as a means of removing Jews from Germany and feared that such a gathering could evolve into a "Jewish Vatican" in the Middle East that would become part of an international Jewish conspiracy.[6] Yet he took reassurance from skepticism that the Jews were capable of forming a state at all.[7] The text echoes the bitterness of Germany's defeat in World War I and connects Zionism to England, to hostility to Germany and to Bolshevism.[8] Though the Zionists had opted to work with the British empire, Rosenberg surmised that as the empire crumbled, "the Jews would turn to a new patron"—namely, the United States. There follows reference to the 3.5 million Jews in the United States, their heavy concentration in New York and, as Henry Ford had explained in *The International Jew*, their presumed control over the press, film, government and business.[9]

Yet, Rosenberg's central point—hence the title of the booklet—was that the Jews were incapable of statecraft. If a Jewish state in Palestine were established, it would collapse and the Jews would again be an "international nation." Zionism, he wrote, was "the powerless effort of an incapable people to engage in productive activity. Mostly it was a means for ambitious speculators to establish a new area for receiving usurious interests on a global scale."[10] A Jewish state was a terrible idea but not a dangerous one. This was so because it was doomed to failure given Jewish incapacity for engaging in power politics. Francis Nicosia writes that "the dual nature of the National Socialist approach to Zionism"—that is, a wavering between rejection due to the conspiracy theory and support as a possible way of expelling Jews from Germany—"was clearly established by Hitler and Rosenberg during the early 1920s, and became the basis of the regimes's policy on Zionism after 1933."[11] Actually, the evidence Nicosia and others offer demonstrates that the dualism to which he refers applied to a policy of encouraging Jewish emigration to Palestine rather than to the idea of a Jewish state there.

Nicosia documents that two sections in the German Foreign Office, the *Referat Deutschland* and the *Orient Abteilung*, "supported the Zionist objective of promoting Jewish emigration to Palestine" between 1934 and 1937. He further examines the evolution of the *Ha'avarah* Agreement which promoted Jewish emigration from Germany to Palestine until 1939, which he describes as "a rather uneven six-year process whereby the Zionist movement was utilized by the Hitler regime to solve the so-called Jewish question in Germany."[12] He points to contacts between the SS and Revisionist Zionists based on shared support for Jewish emigration to Palestine at the same time, and to permission of Zionist organizations in Germany to continue functioning while the regime was restricting or dissolving Jewish organizations devoted to defending the place and rights of Jews *within* Germany.

Yet Nicosia's argument and evidence from the archives of the Foreign Ministry do not support the conclusion that all of the above amounted to the Nazi regime's support for Zionism's goal of a sovereign Jewish state. Indeed, he notes that in response to the British government's Peel Commission Report on Palestine of July 1937, which recommended partition of Palestine into independent Jewish and Arab states, "the idea of an independent Jewish state revived [among officials of the Nazi regime] the specter of an international Jewish conspiracy operating from its own power base in Palestine" and of Zionism's role in that conspiracy.[13] In June 1937, Foreign Minister Konstantin von Neurath sent guidelines to the German embassies in London, Cairo and Jerusalem which stressed Germany's opposition to the creation of an independent Jewish state, a state, he said, that would serve as a political base for international Jewry just as the Vatican did for Catholicism and Moscow for the Comintern. Another Foreign Ministry memo sent to all German embassies later than month argued that Jewish emigration to Palestine could adversely affect Germany's strategic position by contributing to Jewish strength in Palestine. Nevertheless, in accordance with his vision of a racial reordering of Europe, Hitler himself continued to encourage emigration of the Jews in Germany to Palestine in 1937 and 1938. Nicosia plausibly concludes that the "removal" of Jews from Germany and Europe, not their mass murder, "was the only fixed aim of German Jewish policy prior to the war, and this is evident in the Nazi support for Zionist emigration to Palestine."[14] As war approached, the anti-Semitic conspiracy theory, which focused on the dangers such a state would pose to Germany, increasingly supplanted the view of Palestine as a place in which Germany could dump its unwanted Jews. With German aggression and expansion, Germany now had many millions of Jews in its grasp, rather than only Germany's 500,000. Palestine was too small and now too inaccessible to offer a solution through deportation. War also meant a search for allies among the Arabs. The hostility to the goal of a Jewish state, which had been there from the outset and was now reinforced by a search for Arab allies, led to a pristine moment of convergence of anti-Semitism with antagonism both towards Zionism's end goal and to any further emigration to Palestine.

War and the Ideologues of Convergence

On 28 March 1941 Rosenberg, then the publisher of the *Völkischer Beobachter*, the official daily paper of the Nazi regime, director of political education of the Nazi Party and founder of the Institute for Research on the Jewish Question (Institut zur Erforschung der Judenfrage) in Frankfurt/Main, spoke on "The Jewish Question as a World Problem." He did so at a conference to mark the opening of this government-financed anti-Semitic think tank. The speech was broadcast on national radio and published the following day on the first page of the *Völkischer Beobachter*.[15] It was evidence of the preeminence of the conspiracy theory over the view of Palestine between 1933 and 1939 as a welcome destination of Jewish emigration. He began with an attack on the "encirclement policy of Jewish-British high-finance" in World War I, denounced connections between Britain and Zionism and asserted that the roots of the Balfour Declaration lay in Jewish promises to place money and political influence in the service of Britain. "The Jewish world press" and "British-Jewish high-finance" from the Rothschild house had worked together with "[J. P.] Morgan" and a group of Jews around Woodrow Wilson led by Bernard Baruch (who "controlled all of industry in the United States") to support the Allies in World War I. At home in Germany, Jewish leftists such as Paul Levi and the industrialist Walter Rathenau had joined Jews in "England, France and New York" to undermine Germany. Fortunately though, 1933 made possible "world-historical, revolutionary" developments such as the Nuremberg Laws which completed the destruction of "Jewish rule in Germany" and thus prevented a repetition of 9 November 1918.[16]

Having painted this grim picture, Rosenberg then reassured his audience about the Jews' prospects in Palestine. The Jews only knew how to engage in trade. Palestine was too small to house the world's "15 to 16 million Jews" and thus could not serve as a solution to the world's and Europe's Jewish problem. Zionism, he argued, did not emerge to solve the Jewish question. Rather, it sought a Jewish state in Palestine to be able to participate in international diplomatic conferences, to form an "economic jumping-off point" for the economic penetration of the Middle East, and to offer refuge to "Jewish adventurers" who had been expelled from their own countries. There they could be provided with new names and passports to engage in new subversive activities. So the solution of the Jewish question was not a Zionist one but a "Jewish reservation" under police observation.[17] He did not add, as he might have, that such a "reservation" would be in Europe, not in Palestine. Whether or not Rosenberg thought the Jews capable of actually establishing and sustaining a state, he continued to view it as part of a threatening international Jewish conspiracy and opposed it on those grounds as well.

Before and during the war, the Nazi Propaganda Ministry controlled the press through secret daily and weekly directives to newspaper and magazine editors. The *Presseanweisungen* (press directives) were known as the "word of the day" (*Parole des Tages*) or "word of the week" (*Parole der Woche*). They came primarily from the Reich Press Office directed by Otto Dietrich, with occasional input from Propaganda Minister Joseph Goebbels, and were sent to several thousand newspapers daily. Dietrich consulted with Hitler each workday morning, then passed on the Führer's suggestions to his staff in Berlin.[18] The directives concerned political themes as well as instructions about political vocabulary. A weekly *Zeitschriften-Dienst* (magazine service) gave similar instructions to editors of periodicals. On 13 June 1939 the Press Office instructed editors not to use the term "anti-Semitism" because doing so undermined efforts to establish friendly relations with the Arab world. Instead, the appropriate terms to describe Nazi policy were "defense against the Jews" or "hostility to the Jews" (*Judengegnerschaft*).[19] Five years later, Dietrich's staff again voiced concern that the term "anti-Semitism" was appearing with great frequency in the German press. This was to be avoided because its appearance there "could destroy our relationships with non-Jewish Semites, namely the pan-Arab world that is so important for us." Therefore, the press was to replace the words "anti-Semitism" and "anti-Semitic" with expressions such as "opposition to Jews," "hostility to Jews," "anti-Judaism" and "antagonistic to Jews" or "anti-Jewish."[20] The linguistic turn was part of a broad strategic effort to woo the Arabs to the side of the Axis powers.

Nazi propagandists and anti-Semitic writers based in Nazi "research" institutions published an impressive array of works in which the convergence of anti-Semitism and anti-Zionism was apparent. A Propaganda Ministry directive in the *Zeitschriften-Dienst* of 26 August 1939 brought Heinrich Hest's *Palästina: Judenstaat?* (the second volume of his *Weltjude ohne Maske* [World Jew without a mask]) to journalists" attention and strongly urged them to review it favorably. Hest was a pseudonym for Herman Erich Seifert, the author of several essays published by the Nazi Party (NSDAP), including *Der Aufbruch in der arabischen Welt* (Revolt in the Arab world) in 1941.[21] The service praised the "excellent mastery" of material which allowed "Hest" to "clearly analyze the real line of Jewish politics, namely the striving for a new, perhaps decisive base for Jewish world power" in Palestine, accomplished with the use of terror against the Arab population. The journalists were further advised that the work was important not only for its information about the Palestine conflict. It also provided "new material about the fateful role of world Jewry" and about the "community of interests between England and Jewry."[22] Seifert's *Palästina: Judenstaat?* linked anti-Zionism to Nazi Germany's propaganda offensive against England. "English colonial policy" had become a "tool of world Jewry." Confronting it was "the Arab's heroic war of defense." England was using "brutal power" and "terror" to secure rule in Palestine. The Arabs were defending themselves "against England's terrorist mandate policy" and "against the attack by world Jewry" (*Weltjudentums*).[23]

Seifert offered a quick overview of 5,000 years of Jewish history to demonstrate that the Jews were incapable of organizing a state. Plans for a Jewish state in Palestine were a basis of "striving for world power." Like other Nazi propagandists, Seifert favorably quoted the opposition of the Grand Mufti of Jerusalem, Mohammed Amin al-Husseini, to a Jewish state, and his assertion that English policy was dominated by the Jews and that there was no possibility for a compromise between Arabs and Zionists.[24] He claimed that the confrontation between "world Jewry" and the Arabs in the 1930s was due to Jewish pressure on the English government to support the establishment of a Jewish homeland. The armed conflict of the late 1930s in Palestine was the result of England's broken promises to the Arabs, which in turn had deepened Arab resistance to the Jews. "Today the colonial striving of the 'humane' democracies and the striving for power of world Jewry confront a united Arab population. . . ."[25] The driving force of British policy in the Middle East was the desire to secure oil and control of the Suez Canal (more important, as Spain and Italy threatened to control the Mediterranean). England tolerated Jewish immigration to Palestine because the Jews would be "the best guarantee against a successful Arab freedom struggle" and because England was "now under the pressure of the financial power of world Jewry and had long ago ceased to be free in its decisions. As a result of its policy in Palestine, it had become an instrument of world Jewry, the previously proud Albion!"[26]

The Nazi Party publishing house published Seifert's *Der Aufbruch in der arabischen Welt* in 1941. It presented Nazi Germany and fascist Italy as partisans for the Arabs in their struggle against British and French colonialism. Seifert presented Mohammed and Islam as antagonistic to the Jews. In the modern world, where the Jews struggled for dominance in the capitalist world, it was no accident that the Arab-Jewish conflict was sharpest where the Arabs were "dominated by the democratic, liberal states where the Jews are the unchecked beneficiaries of the plutocracies to which they closely linked."[27] He rejected the notion that there were any racial affinities between Arabs and Jews. Hence the gap between them could not be bridged. In French colonial North Africa, Seifert spoke of an "inner bond between Jews and the French since the beginning of the conquest of Algeria ... because France's victory rested not only on its weapons but even more on the secret but therefore all the more effective support of its campaign by the Jews."[28] The French repaid the debt by defending the Jews against attacks from Arabs and putting them in dominant positions in the colonial economy and administration. "The newspapers and public opinion of the Arab countries" were controlled by the Jews. Yet as serious as France's "guilt" was for supporting Jewish "exploitation of the Arabs by the Jews," England's guilt was far greater for it had broken promises to the Arabs, imposed its rule with violence and "unleashed world Jewry" on the Palestinian Arabs. Seifert wrote that "the last mask fell" in England's policy towards the Palestinians when, upon the outbreak of war in Europe, Chaim Weizmann wrote to Neville Chamberlain that the Jews in Britain "stand and fight on the side of the democracies" and Chamberlain replied to affirm shared goals. He viewed Weizmann's statement as yet more evidence of "the clear bond between the English government and Zionists."[29] Nazi propaganda made a great deal of Weizmann's affirmation of Jewish support for the Allies as evidence confirming the reality of an international conspiracy and of Jewish partisanship for England and France. The Arabs, however, were prepared "for a decisive struggle for freedom" and had learned that "English order is nothing but slavery. The Arabs want to be free!"[30]

Giselher Wirsing was another of the Nazi propagandists who examined Zionism through the lens of Nazi ideology on the eve of World War II. He did so in *Engländer, Juden, Araber in Palästina* (The English, Jews and Arabs in Palestine), also published in 1939. The Zionist goal in Palestine, he wrote, was the "establishment of a Vatican of world Jewry. A firm base is to be built on which in later years Jewish world policy can rest." A Jewish state in Palestine would not offer a "solution to the world Jewish question" (*Weltjudenfrage*) because at most a third of the Jews in the world could live there. Instead it would foster cooperation between the Jews in Palestine and the assimilated Jews in finance and banking in Western Europe and the United States. Since most Jews would not be living in Palestine, the real goal of a Jewish state was to establish a "Vatican of world Jewry, whose most important branches would build and strengthen their political and economic power in Western Europe and the United States."[31] The prevention of the formation of a Jewish state in Palestine was, from the Nazi perspective, an act of national security against a spreading international foe.

On 8 November 1940 a directive of the *Zeitschriften-Dienst* requested that "all magazines that reviewed political books" should review Wolf Meyer-Christian's *Die englisch-jüdische Allianz* (The English-Jewish alliance). The officials wrote that "the book shows the wide-ranging identification between the English and the Jews and presents the essential presuppositions for understanding the deeper reasons for the current war, one that is simultaneously an English and a Jewish war." It offered an "intellectual framework for the definitive confrontation with the English-Jewish world power."[32] Meyer-Christian's work came equipped with full scholarly apparatus. He explained England's opposition to German foreign policy in 1939 as well its support for a Jewish homeland as the result of what he saw as the inordinate influence of Jews in English history: Germany was threatened not by the English people but by British imperialism and a small upper class. "This stratum is as English as it is Jewish and Jewish as it is English!" While in Germany Jewry was "on the side of the fight against the existing order," in England, "it supported the rule of the upper class, was part of it" and "as an inseparable part of this caste led the battle for its interests for wealth and for power over Europe." *Der englische-jüdische Allianz* was devoted to exploring "this historically unique special case (*dieser geschichtlich einmalige Sonderfall*) of the process of the mixture (*Vermischung*) of the English leadership groups with those groups of the Jewish people in which the idea of Jewish world domination is alive and at work." The Jewish question in Europe and in Germany would only be solved if it was first solved in England—that is, "if the alliance between the traditional English upper class and the leadership of world Jewry is broken once and for all. For this alliance is Europe's deadly enemy."[33]

Meyer-Christian first examined "the Jewification (*die Verjudung*) of the English people," which he saw as stemming from several factors. English individualism of the English upper classes led parents to allow their sons and daughters to marry Jews, indicative of their failure to understand the threat that "Jewry" as a group posed to England. As a result, by 1939 "no decision of the British government is possible which is not approved by the Jews participating in the leadership of the government." Family ties and business links alone would not have produced the power position of Jews in England. "Puritanism, the specific English form of Christianity" was the deepest reason for the emergence of this alliance. It would not have come about without "the basic preexisting similarity of both peoples consisting in the capitalist way of thinking and the claim to world domination." Indeed, "no one other than the Christian dictator, Oliver Cromwell, had first recognized this and made it the foundation of his politics. At their center was his decision to recall the previously banned Jews back to England in order to insure their help in the founding of today's British Empire."[34] Meyer-Christian then offered stories of connections between Edward VII, Queen Victoria and Winston Churchill with English Jews including Disraeli and the Rothschild, Montefiore, Goldsschmidt and Sassoon families. All of this led to English support in the twentieth century for Zionism and the "arming of the Jews and expulsion of the Arabs." It accounted for Churchill's support as well.[35] The "degeneration of the English upper stratum" was not the result of "accidental bonds of love." Rather, it was due to a carefully planned effort by the Jews who "made the British aristocracy a fifth column of world Jewry."[36]

Meyer-Christian's attack on Zionism was the longest part of the book. In the chapter entitled "Politics and Money in Palestine" he wrote that the expectation that England would bring about the Jewish state "forged the connections between the leading English statesmen and individual powerful Jews finally into a bond between world Jewry and English leadership."[37] By the end of the nineteenth century, Jewry in

England had more prestige and power than in any other country. Hence, it was no surprise that London became the center of Zionism. Meyer-Christian's narrative of the 1920s and 1930s was one of Jewish immigration to Palestine combined with forceful expulsion of the Arab population.

He rejected the idea of common interests between Zionism and those who wished a Europe free of Jews. National Socialism, he noted, had opposed the creation of a Jewish state precisely because "the Jewish intentions clearly are not aimed at a state which can incorporate all of Jewry or even its essential part. Even the Jewish leadership appears to understand that this goal is not realizable but also undesirable. This is so because the majority of the assimilated, less religious Jews will never move to Palestine but also because the Jewish state, in contrast to the German, Italian or other state founded on the totality of the people" was of a completely different nature. He quoted Moses Hess to the effect that the Jews in Europe would not give up their place in Europe should a Jewish state be established. Therefore a Jewish state would be "nothing other than an international power center over non-Jewish peoples, a state whose citizens did not live within its borders but rather were all over the world."[38] A Jewish state would be "only a key base for world Jewry" which would enjoy citizenship in this state without giving up citizenship rights in their states in Europe and the United States. There would be no "abandonment of the internationality of Jewry" or of the "positions of power it had gained in the past fifty years." A "völkischer Staat" that encompassed the majority of world Jewry was not the goal. Rather, the mass of Jewry was to remain in other states "and in cooperation with the false state help to strengthen the power of Jewry as a world power." A Jewish state "would not in any way offer a solution to the Jewish question. It would do just the opposite. Each of the 17 million Jews in the world would retain the positions they had conquered in England, France or America" in and outside government. Meyer-Christian interpreted Chaim Weizmann's statement in 1919 that the Zionist movement would be recognized in the world as a political factor as evidence that a "Jewish state would be the power center of world Jewry."[39]

With the combination of faulty causal reasoning, leaps from bits of evidence to large generalizations and apparent detailed empiricism that characterizes conspiratorial explanations, Meyer-Christian offered his readers lists of actual persons and organizations. A section on "the Jewish Agency as the government of world Jewry" featured the increasingly familiar names of Weizmann, Rothschild, Warburg, Herbert Samuel and Albert Einstein, all of whom supposedly gave weight to the combined efforts of "17 million Jews" around the world favoring a Jewish state. The Jewish Agency, he continued, "encompassed for the first time in Jewish history all of world Jewry in a single, tightly ordered organization. It was in this way that the Zionist organization became a world power which no longer appeared to need England for a push for power."[40]

Meyer-Christian viewed the beginning of World War II as confirming his analysis. The "same clique" in Britain that was linked to "world Jewry" and was waging war against Germany now tilted toward the Zionists. In what may have been the first reference to a "Jewish war" from a Nazi propagandist, Meyer-Christian wrote in 1939 that "the English war is a Jewish war, a preventive war of the English-Jewish upper strata against the strengthening Reich and the *völkische* idea to which the Reich owes its strength. For the Arabs, Germany is the second common enemy of the English-Jewish alliance."[41] Weizmann's statements of support for Britain in the first week of the war, as well as British Cabinet Minister Duff Cooper's speech in Washington, DC on 6 January 1940, which revealed an English turn in favor of the Jews in Palestine, were taken as yet further evidence of the "English-Jewish alliance." British efforts in 1940 to limit land purchases by Jewish organizations in Palestine and to restrict Jewish immigration were simply tricks to deceive the Arabs. The more Jewish leaders and organizations expressed support for British, and later American, efforts in the war, the more Meyer-Christian would be confirmed in his view that the "English war is a Jewish war."

Meyer-Christian offered a kind of cultural historical element to his examination of the English-Jewish alliance. It rested not only on a transient convergence of interest but on a long-standing elective affinity between Puritanism and the Jews in England, what he called the "deeper connection between English and Jewish mentality ... an intellectual affinity that bonds the English people with Jewry." He found the answer to "the riddle of these mutual feelings of affiliation" in the argument that there was "a close connection between English Christianity and the Jewish religion." First, both were outspokenly "capitalist religions. They affirm the accumulation of wealth as God's command. Both are religiously articulated egoism." Second, both "rest on the idea of a chosen people. Among Jews and the English, political superiority and unscrupulousness are grounded in this kind of religion."[42] Meyer-Christian's interpretation of the links between the Jews and capitalism drew directly from Werner Sombart's *Die Juden und das Wirtschaftsleben* (The Jews and economic life).[43] English imperialism drew its power and lack of scruples from its Puritan religious grounds, which in turn were "Jewish." In its orientation to the Old Testament, Calvinism had distanced itself from Christianity and opted instead for a this-worldly life similar to rules required in Judaism. "Puritanism and Judaism are identical." Political England in 1939 was "nothing other than a modernized Jewry" which "carries within itself the will to dominate the world." The urgent conclusion "for the whole world must therefore be the equation of hostility to the Jews with hostility to England. Only if this is done can Europe be freed from the English-Jewish alliance."[44]

Works such as those of Seifert and Meyer-Christian clearly articulated the convergence of anti-Semitism and anti-Zionism in the Nazi regime in both ideology and policy in 1939. Despite willingness to allow modest Jewish emigration to Palestine up to 1939, the Nazi regime never publicly expressed support for creation of a Jewish state. With the publication of works such as those by Seifert and Meyer-Christian, the regime's propagandists elaborated the anti-Semitic conspiracy theory at Nazism's ideological core and applied it to an attack on Zionism. Though Britain was restricting the numbers of Jews it would allow to emigrate to Palestine before and during the war and the Holocaust, Nazi propagandists interpreted the fact that England was at war with Nazi Germany and gave any support at all to the idea of a Jewish state in part of

Palestine as evidence of Jewish power in London. These policy choices were, for Meyer-Christian, the outcome of the several-century-long alleged affinity of Puritanism and Judaism. This explained the otherwise perplexing "riddle" of the emergence of Oliver Cromwell's successor, Winston Churchill. With such an analysis, Meyer-Christian connected Nazi anti-Zionism both to anti-Semitism and to wartime enmity with England.

The Grand Mufti, Amin al-Husseini and Nazi Propaganda

Wartime pressures to gain support from the Arabs reinforced a perspective based on long-standing ideological postulates. The 26 February 1943 issue of the *Zeitschriften-Dienst* included a comment on "the British, helpers of Bolshevism" which presented them as being in league with Bolshevism from the days of the Spanish Civil War to the present, and a note on the United States in the Middle East, which discussed its plan to establish a "large Jewish state in Palestine under its leadership." It instructed editors to remember that the Americans "did not have to take Islamic subordinates into account," in contrast to the British, who were concerned about Islam in still colonial India. "Therefore they represented exclusively the interests of the Jews in Asia." They wanted to exploit the region's wealth and "enslave the native population, a policy that corresponds to their hostility to Islam as a religion. ... In stressing the hostility to Islam of the United States, which is a consequence of Jewish domination, we must avoid giving the impression that English domination of the Near East would be better."[45]

As these directives suggest, the Nazi regime was making firm efforts to connect its interests not only to Arabs but to followers of Islam as well. A directive from the *Zeitschriften-Dienst* of 11 September 1942 urged deeper and sympathetic under-standing for "the Islamic world as a cultural factor."[46] The Reich Press Office directives warned against the danger of underestimating the Orient's cultural contributions. "Superficial discussions" due to "linguistic similarities between Arabs and Jews" had led to conflating them. Much of the discussion of Islam in Germany was out of date or inspired by church polemics. The editors must

> strengthen and deepen existing [Nazi] sympathies in the Islamic world. We must draw this great cultural power, which in its essence is sharply anti-Bolshevik and anti-Jewish, closer to us. Through friendly, but not obsequious presentation, we must convince the Muslims of the world that they have no better friend than the Germans. In the treatment of this theme, the words semitism and anti-Semitism must be avoided.[47]

Zionism and the conflict in Palestine were not frequent themes of front-page headlines in the *Völkischer Beobachter*, though when they appeared, in the midst of an anti-Semitic propaganda campaign of spring to autumn 1943, the narrative was familiar. On 20 March 1943 the paper led with "Appeal of the Grand Mufti against the deadly enemies of Islam, Arabs will fight for their freedom on the side of the Axis," a report on a lecture delivered the previous evening by Amin al-Husseini, the Grand Mufti of Jerusalem, in a Berlin mosque on the occasion of Mohammed's birthday.[48] The bonds between the Nazis and the Grand Mufti began in 1937 and remained firm throughout the war and the Holocaust. They drew on a convergence of anti-Semitic ideology, antagonism to Britain and opposition to Jewish emigration to Palestine.[49] The report sympathetically described his appeal to the Islamic and Arab world and its fight against "occupation and cruelties by enemy oppressors." He said it was "the duty of all Muslims to lead and conduct the fight against the enemy by all means. ... With the help of the Jews, the enemies of Islam envisage the complete domination of the Holy Lands" in order to establish a base for exploiting the neighboring Arab countries. "Arabs and Muslims had the duty to defeat Jewish greed and insatiability." The paper described the Grand Mufti as "one of the great personalities of the Islamic world who had led the struggle of the Palestinian Arabs against onrushing Jewry." In the face of "the English and American promises to world Jewry to make Palestine into Jewry's exclusive property and to expel the Arabs," Palestine had become "a symbol of the Arab freedom struggle" against "British betrayal" and "the Atlantic swindle."[50]

The *Völkischer Beobachter* published several more lead stories about the Middle East in autumn 1943. On 6 October, in response to reports of Jewish brigades in the British 8th army, the paper led with "English-American conflicts in the Middle East, Jews present a change, Palestine, Egypt and Iraq are supposed to become Jewish-American colonies."[51] Illustrating the diffusion of the work of Nazi propagandists and anti-Semitic think tanks to a broader audience, the article expressed no surprise at this latest sign of British-Jewish cooperation. Churchill "his whole life long had been dependent on the Jews." Now Churchill was returning the favor as he gave in to Jewish demands concerning Palestine and broke promises to the Arabs. In the United States, the article continued, the Jews were preparing to drive the Arabs out of Palestine. "Here is the truth of Jewish-American imperialism at work which hopes to gain important bases in the far and middle Orient to aid in future world domination."[52]

This article signaled a greater focus of attacks on Zionism's links to the United States. From the earliest days of World War II the supposed power of the Jews in the Roosevelt administration was a central theme of Nazi propaganda. As American involvement in the Middle East grew in the course of the war and British power waned, German propaganda began to turn its fire at "USA imperialism" in the Middle East. The article was a typical, and failed, effort to use anti-Semitism to stir up tensions between the United States and Britain. The *Völkischer Beobachter* asserted that expansion of American involvement in Cairo, Beirut, Baghdad, Teheran, Istanbul, Algiers and Tunis was a policy "openly directed against England, which world Jewry had long since written off as a decisive factor in future world politics." Roosevelt, "a tool" of the Jews, now viewed and treated England as a "kind of colony of the USA-Jewish state."[53] The outlines of a postwar convergence of anti-Semitism and anti-Zionism were also evident from this article. "World Jewry," now having gained power in New York and in the Roosevelt administration, used the American government to support the establishment of a Jewish state in Palestine. The state of Israel would become the base for the penetration of the Middle East as a whole by "Jewish-American imperialism." The expansion of American power in the region would, for those who accepted this framework, appear to confirm the basic anti-Semitic conspiracy which conflated the growth of American power with that of Jewish power, just as earlier the existence of the British Empire had been linked to "world Jewry."

Husseini's connections to the Nazi regime led to private meetings with Hitler and Himmler and correspondence with Foreign Minister Joachim von Ribbentrop. On 18 December 1942, when Husseini gave the above-mentioned speech at the opening of the Islamic Institute in Berlin, Joseph Goebbels was in the audience. The text had been shown to and approved by von Ribbentrop.[54] Before the event Husseini wrote to Hitler to express his

> friendship and sympathy to your excellency and to the German people. We are firmly convinced of the close cooperation between the millions of Mohammedans in the world and Germany and its allies in the Three Power Pact which is directed against the common enemies, Jews, Bolsheviks and Anglo-Saxons, and which, with God's help, will lead to a victorious outcome of this war for the Axis powers. This victory will bring happiness and good fortune to the Axis powers, the Muslims and all of humanity.[55]

His speech included the following extended attack on the Jews: "The Jews were the bitterest enemies of the Muslims. They had always expressed their antagonism with cunning and deception. Every Muslim knows how, from the first days of young Islam, the Jews have assaulted him and his beliefs and how much hatred ... intrigues ... conspiracies" the Jews directed at the Muslims. The Koran, he continued, was full of stories of Jewish lack of character, their lies and deceptions. Just as had been full of hatred against Muslims in the days of the prophet, so they were in modern times in Palestine which they sought to establish as "a base from which to extend their power over neighboring Islamic countries." More generally, the Jews were "a destructive element on earth." Citing Ranke, he accused the Jews of unleashing wars and playing nations off against one another. Husseini went further, however, and made clear that he shared Nazism's anti-Semitic outlook on world politics.

> The Jews' essence, in this war as well, is to keep the world in turbulence. Their leader Weizmann said that this war was a Jewish war. ... In fact, today world Jewry leads the allied enemies into the abyss of depravity and ruin, just as it did in the age of the Prophet. In England as well as in America, only Jewish influence is dominant. It's the same Jewish influence that stands behind godless Communism. ... It is Jewry who drove the nations into this war of attrition and from its tragic destiny only the Jews will benefit. The Muslims' bitter enemies are the Jews and their allied English, Americans and Bolsheviks. Their British allies for example, who are directed by world Jewry and its capital, and whose history is filled with antagonism to the Muslims, today continue their persecution and oppression of Muslims in all countries. ...

The Allied attacks in North Africa demonstrated that the Jews, Americans, English and the Bolsheviks were all an "irreconcilable enemy of Islam" and had "oppressed and persecuted 40 million Muslims. ... This war which was unleashed by world Jewry offers the Muslims the best opportunity to free themselves from these instances of persecution and oppression if they will use this opportunity." He concluded with a religious appeal to Muslims that God would help them to victory if they displayed sufficient willingness to sacrifice.[56]

In a speech on 19 March 1943 in Berlin, Husseini repeated his view of the threat posed by Zionism. The Jews in England and America were driving the effort to dominate Palestine. The fact that a majority of the members of the House and Senate had urged Roosevelt to allow unlimited Jewish emigration to Palestine and support the establishment of a Jewish state was evidence of the great influence of the Jews in the United States. This "evil intention of the Allies" was directed "against Arabs and Muslims" and corresponded to the aims of the Jews. He spoke of "the Jewish danger, not only for the Arab countries but also for the other Muslim areas of the Magreb." The Jews wanted to establish "a Jewish bridge between New York and Jerusalem" and posed a danger for the whole Muslim world by seeking to annex the Aksa Mosque and the Solomon Temple. The Arabs and Muslims in general should swear before God to "destroy this Jewish greed and insatiability and destroy the planned bridge [between Jerusalem and New York]. The Arabs should show evidence that the power of faith is more powerful than that of unjustly attained interest, yes, stronger than the despicable and devilish intrigues which world Jewry pursues." He concluded by expressing the hope that "God will show Arabs and Muslims the correct path and endow them with the strength for united endurance against the arch enemies, the Jews and the Allies, until God helps us to victory. Then the Arabs and Muslims will be free in their own countries. "He who fights for God, also receives victory from him!"[57]

The Grand Mufti's cooperation with the Nazis extended beyond making speeches. He urged the Foreign Ministry as well as Adolf Eichmann not to allow Jews from Bulgaria, Romania and Hungary to escape to Palestine and urged instead that they be sent to Poland. He worked with Himmler to establish an SS division of Muslims from Bosnia, appealed to the Germans to bomb Tel Aviv and Jerusalem, and received financial support from the Nazi regime. On 10 June 1943, he wrote to Ribbentrop that the Jews wished to go to Palestine as part of a plan to dominate the world and were thus "a dangerous influence for the outcome of the war."[58] In working against Jewish emigration, he made a direct contribution to the Holocaust. On 27 July 1944, he wrote to Himmler to urge him "to do what was necessary to prevent the wandering of Jews to Palestine." Doing so would be a "practical example of the natural allied and friendly stance of Germany to Arabs and Muslims."[59]

In his study of Husseini in Nazi Germany, the German historian Klaus Gensicke offers a detailed account of Husseini's cooperation with Himmler to establish an SS division of Bosnian Muslim volunteers in 1943.[60] In a speech to officers and Imams in the division, Husseini stressed that the "parallels" of National Socialism and Islam had become ever closer. These included: monotheism, defined as obedience to one spiritual, political and military authority; a stress on obedience and discipline; a view of battle as one of the most important expressions of faith; preeminence of community over individual self-interest; and praise for work. "Regarding fighting Jewry, Islam and National Socialism have moved very close to one another." In the Second World War, "a victory for the allies would constitute a victory for Jewry and thus a great danger for the Muslims and for Islam in general. ... Cooperation of 400 million Muslims with their real friends, the Germans, can have a great influence on the war. It is very useful for both."[61]

The Grand Mufti also broadcast radio addresses to the Arab world from Berlin. On 2 July 1942 he addressed "the Egyptian people" in the wake of Rommel's initial victories in North Africa. They had "filled all Arabs in the whole Orient with joy" because the Axis powers had "common enemies, the English and the Jews" and defended against the Bolshevik danger. The address connected the Egyptian struggle against British imperialism with the struggle of the Palestinians against the "concentrated British power and its alliance with the Jews."[62] On 11 November 1942 he spoke over German radio to "the Arabs" about martyrdom. Before the war broke out, the Arabs had been fighting for twenty years against "the English and the Jews who were always hidden behind them." The Arab peoples had shed "noble blood" for the freedom and independence of Palestine, Egypt, Syria, Iraq and the Arabian peninsula. "The spilled blood of martyrs is the water of life. It has revived Arab heroism, as water revives dry ground. The martyr's death is the protective tree in whose shadows marvelous plants again bloom." The goal of "English-Jewish policy" was to divide Palestine and then to dominate the remainder of the Arab countries. "We Arabs" who have fought the English, he continued, "clearly should join the Axis powers and their allies in common struggle against the common enemy. Doing so for us means the continuation of the fight we have fought alone for the past twenty years. Today the powerful enemies of our enemies stand on our side." Yet if England and her allies "God, forbid," were to win the war "Israel would rule the whole world, the Arabian fatherland would suffer an unholy blow and the Arab countries would be torn apart and turned into Jewish colonies." The Jews would seek Jordan, Lebanon, Syria, Iraq, and the border areas of Egypt. But if England and her allies were defeated, "the Jewish danger" for the Arab countries would be defeated. Millions of Arabs would be freed and millions more Muslims would be saved. A defeat of the Soviet Union would also liberate millions more Muslims suffering under Soviet rule. America offered nothing to the Arabs as it too "was subject to Jewish will."[63] His efforts in Berlin combined short-term political alliances based on shared enemies with longer-term ideological affinities.

Later that month, on 26 November, in a radio speech over German radio aimed at North Africa, Husseini attacked the United States following the American landings there. It was a striking example of the translation of Nazi propaganda into Arabic and the idioms of the Arab world:

> The strength of Jewish influence in America has clearly come to the fore in this war.
> Jews and capitalists have pushed the United States to expand this war in order to

expand their influence in new and wealthy areas. The North Africans know very well what unhappiness the Jews have brought to them. They know that the Jews are the vanguard fighters of imperialism who mistreated North Africa for so long. They also know the extent to which the Jews served the imperialists as spies and agents and how they seek the energy resources of North African territories to expand their wealth . . . . The American intervention in North Africa strengthens the power of the Jews, increases their influence and doubles their misdeeds. America is the greatest agent of the Jews and the Jews are rulers in America.[64]

The Grand Mufti was one of those who translated National Socialist ideology into Arabic and into the idioms of fundamentalist Islam. This is a dimension of World War II in North Africa and the Middle East that still needs considerable research.

Conclusion

Throughout its history, beginning with Hitler's early speeches in 1920, Nazism was unequivocal in the ideological convergence of anti-Zionism and anti-Semitism. At no point did Hitler approve of the establishment of a Jewish state in Palestine. The Nazi regime's support for limited Jewish emigration to Palestine in the 1930s did not mean that Hitler or the leading officials of the government supported the idea of a sovereign Jewish state. As war approached, and then when Hitler started World War II, the convergence between anti-Zionism and anti-Semitism became even more pronounced. The theory of an international Jewish conspiracy aiming to establish a "Jewish Vatican" in Palestine completely subordinated limited efforts to allow Jewish emigration as a means of removing Jews from Germany. In the midst of this convergence an alliance borne of shared enemies and shared ideology emerged between the radical Islamist, the Grand Mufti of Jerusalem, and the Nazi regime.

In the aftermath of the terrorist attacks on the United States of 11 September 2001 and of the Palestinian terrorist campaign launched in autumn and winter 2000 and 2001 against Israel at the moment when a compromise peace seemed within reach, there has been a flurry of commentary noting parallels between the ideology of the Islamic fundamentalists and that of twentieth-century European fascism and Nazism.[65] For the first time since 1945, the idea of an international Jewish conspiracy is animating a significant political movement, that is, al-Qaeda and the various other groupings inspired by Islamic fundamentalism. It has been through this prism that the Islamists have understood the Allied victory in World War II, the founding of the State of Israel and its victories in the Arab-Israeli wars, the American and Western victory in the Cold War, and the wars with Iraq. Each was further demonstration of the validity of the paranoid conspiracy theory previously articulated by Hitler and the Nazi regime's propagandists according to which the power of international Jewry was a dominant force in world affairs. From the perspective of fascist and Nazi ideology and its aftereffects, the preeminence of the United States after the end of the Cold War and the continued existence of Israel were yet further evidence that the international Jewish conspiracy had emerged victorious after 1989/90 yet again.

The scholarly examination of the convergence of a religiously based Islamic anti-Semitism with the anti-Semitic conspiracy theory of National Socialism during World War II and the Holocaust remains in its early stages.[66] The emergence of Islamic fundamentalism and the terrorism it has inspired in recent years have fostered renewed interest in the similarities, differences and aftereffects of Europe's fascist, Nazi and totalitarian ideologies in the ideology and policy of the Muslim Brotherhood, Hizballah and Hamas, and aspects of secular Arab nationalism as well.[67] Though the differences in language, historical experience and political context should be kept in mind to avoid facile analogies, the comparative historical imagination should not shrink from comparisons when merited. Paul Berman has trenchantly noted, in his discussion of lineages between Europe's totalitarian past and radical Islam today, that "the world is full of exotic things; but not every exotic thing is a foreign thing."[68] More remains to be done on the paths and extent of such diffusion from the center and its reception, transformation and incorporation into wartime and postwar Islamic fundamentalism, and on the cultural and ideological aftermath of World War II in the Middle East. In the era of the fascist dictators, Germany, but also Italy and Japan, demonstrated that a "reactionary modernist" path to modernity, one in which modern technology was incorporated into an overall rejection of the values of liberal political institutions, was a theoretical and practical reality.[69] Both within and outside Israel today, lively debate about government policy, for example, regarding settlements, takes place without venturing into the realm of anti-Semitism. It would be naïve, however, to assume that anti-Semitism is playing no role in denunciations of Israel in recent years. Reflection on the classic case of the convergence of anti-Semitism and anti-Zionism serves as one starting point for examining what kind of residues and aftereffects it left behind and for a clearer understanding of when Jew hatred converges with and diverges from a rejection of the idea and reality of the Jewish state.

Notes

[1] This article draws partly on research from a larger project on the history of Nazi anti-Semitic propaganda during World War II and the Holocaust. See Herf, *The Jewish Enemy*. Also see Herf, "The 'Jewish War.'"

[2] Hitler, *Mein Kampf*, 324–25.

[3] Friedländer, *Nazi Germany and the Jews*, vol. 1, *The Years of Persecution*.

[4] See Nicosia, *The Third Reich and the Palestine Question*, "Zionism and Palestine," "Ein Nützlicher Feind," and "Zionism in National Socialist Jewish Policy."

[5] Rosenberg, *Der Staatsfeindliche Zionismus* (1938).

[6] See Rosenberg, *Der Staatsfeindliche Zionismus* (1922), 62–63; and Nicosia, "Zionism in National Socialist Jewish Policy," 1256–57.

[7] Rosenberg, *Schriften aus den Jahren 1917–1921*. See in particular his discussions of the Jews and the Free Masons, Zionism, Jewish world rule and the consequences. Also see the Nazi publication of the *Protocols of the Elders of Zion* with Rosenberg's foreword and introduction, Rosenberg, *Die Protokolle der Weissen von Zion*. By this 4th edition in 1933, the press had published 25,000 copies.

[8] See Rosenberg, "Deutschfeindliche Auslassungen, Zionismus und Bolschewismus," in *idem, Der Staatsfeindliche Zionismus* (1938), 50–64.

[9] Ibid., 73–78.

[10] Ibid., 86.

[11] Nicosia, "Zionism in National Socialist Jewish Policy," 1259.

[12] Ibid., 1262–63.

[13] Ibid., 1267.

[14] Ibid., 1281.

[15] Rosenberg, "Die Judenfrage als Weltproblem," 64–72; also in *Völkischer Beobachter* (hereafter *VB*), 29 March 1941, 1–2; also see the radio transcript of the speech, "28.3.1941, Alfred Rosenberg, Rundfunkvortrag in Berlin im Anschluß an die erste Arbeitstagung des "Instituts zur Erforschung der Judenfrage" in Frankfurt am Main über "Die Judenfrage als Weltproblem","" in Roller, ed., *Judenverfolgung und jüdisches Leben*, 1:181–87.

[16] Rosenberg, "Die Judenfrage als Weltproblem," 64–65.

[17] Ibid., 70–71.

[18] The following draws on my forthcoming book, *The Jewish Enemy.*

[19] "Antisemitismus," *Zeitschriften-Dienst*, no. 6 (13 June 1939), Nr. 222.

[20] Sammlung Oberheitmann, Bundesarchiv Koblenz, VIdRMVP, V.I., Nr. 215/44, 30 September 1944, Zsg 109/51.

[21] Hest, *Palästina: Judenstaat?* and *Der Aufbruch in der arabischen Welt.*

[22] "Bucher: Juden, Engländer, Araber," *Zeitschriften-Dienst*, no. 17 (26 August 1939), Nr. 656, p. 18. See Hest, *Palästina: Judenstaat?*

[23] Hest, *Palästina: Judenstaat?*

[24] Cited in ibid., 49–50.

[25] Ibid., 98.

[26] Ibid., 101.

[27] Hest, *Der Aufbruch in der arabischen Welt.*

[28] Ibid., 38.

[29] Ibid., 80.

[30] Ibid., 91.

[31] Wirsing, *Engländer, Juden, Araber in Palästina*, 120. The book sold 10,000 copies in four editions.

[32] "Die englisch-jüdische Allianz," in *Zeitschriften-Dienst*, (8 November 1940), Nr. 3504. See Meyer-Christian, *Die englisch-jüdische Allianz*. By this 3rd edition in 1942, 20,000 copies had been printed. See also the sequel to *Mein Kampf* that Hitler wrote in 1928 but did not publish. Discovered by the historian Gerhard Weinberg in 1958 in American archives of captured German documents, it was first published in German in 1961 and in English in 2003. Hitler argued that England would be amenable to German plans for expansion to the East and domination of the continent unless the Jews would stand in the way: "But another important factor for England's attitude toward Germany appeared as well: world Jewry, which also exerts a controlling influence in England." While "the English people" could "overcome the war psychosis vis-à-vis Germany ... world Jewry will leave nothing undone to keep the old enmities alive, to prevent a pacification of Europe, and to enable—in the confusion of general turbulence—full expression of its disruptive Bolshevik tendencies .... One cannot speak of world politics without taking this most terrible power into account" (Weinberg, ed., *Hitler's Second Book,* 174). Hitler's views about the role of world Jewry in England and elsewhere found ample expression in Nazi propaganda by Meyer-Christian and others.

[33] Meyer-Christian, *Die englisch-jüdische Allianz*, 10–11.

[34] Ibid., 18.

[35] Ibid., 20–26.

68 J. Herf

[36] Ibid., 78.

[37] Ibid., 89.

[38] Ibid., 141.

[39] Ibid., 142–45.

[40] Ibid., 153.

[41] Ibid., 185 and 188.

[42] Ibid., 200.

[43] The literature on Sombart is extensive. See Herf, *Reactionary Modernism*, 130–51; and Muller, *The Mind and the Market*.

[44] Meyer-Christian, *Die englisch-jüdische Allianz*, 207–8.

[45] "Die Briten–Helfer des Bolschewismus," and "USA auch in Vorderasien," *Zeitschriften-Dienst*, no. 199/68, 26 February 1943, Nr. 8433, and Nr. 8435, p. 2.

[46] "Die islamische Welt als Kulturfaktor," *Zeitschriften-Dienst*, no. 175/44, 11 September 1942, Nr. 7514, p. 2.

[47] Ibid.

[48] "Aufruf des Großmufti gegen die Todfeinde des Islams, Araber werden für ihre Freiheit an der Seite der Achse kämpfen," *VB*, 20 March 1943, 1. The Nazi regime published a sympathetic book about the Grand Mufti. See Fischer-Weth, *Amin Al-Husseini*.

[49] On the Grand Mufti in wartime Berlin, see the valuable study by Gensicke, *Der Mufti von Jerusalem*. On contact beginning in 1937, see 45–55. For a very early and quite detailed account of Husseini's cooperation with the Nazis, and criticism of the failure to bring him to justice, see Wiesenthal, *Großmufti–Großagent der Achse*.

[50] "Aufruf des Großmufti gegen die Todfeinde des Islams," *VB*, 20 March 1943, 1.

[51] "Englisch-amerikanischer Gegensatz im Nahen-Osten, Juda präsentiert den Wechsel, Palästina, Ägypten und Irak sollen jüdisch-amerikanische Kolonien werden," *VB*, 6 October 1943, 1; also see "Englands Polizistenrolle für das Weltjudentum, Britische militärmacht soll für Ordnung und Sicherheit in Palestine sorgen," *VB*, 11 October 1943, 1.

[52] "Englisch-amerikanischer Gegensatz."

[53] Ibid.

[54] Gensicke, *Der Mufti von Jerusalem*, 134–39.

[55] Cited in Ibid., 155, from the Politisches Archiv Auswärtiges Amt, "handakten Ettel 3," no date, 304371.

[56] Amin al-Husseini, "Nr. 55: Rede zur Eröffnung des Islamischen Zentral-Instituts in Berlin, 18.12.1942," in Höpp, *Mufti-Papiere*, 123–26.

[57] Amin al-Husseini, "Nr. 73: Rede zum Maulid, 19.3.1943," in ibid., 152–55.

[58] On these contacts and activities, see Gensicke, *Der Mufti von Jerusalem*, 149–212 and 225–51. On the letter to Ribbentrop, see 160–61.

[59] Amin al-Husseini, "Nr. 101: An Himmler, 27.7.1944," in Höpp, ed., *Mufti-Papiere*, 216.

[60] On the Bosnian and Muslim SS volunteer division, see Gensicke, *Der Mufti von Jerusalem*, 167–212.

[61] Amin al-Husseini, "Nr. 104: Rede vor den Imamen der bosnischen SS-Division, 4.10.1944," in Höpp, ed., *Mufti-Papiere*, 224–25.

[62] Amin al-Husseini, "Nr. 18a: Rundfunkerklärung an das agyptische Volk, 3.7.1942," in ibid., 45–46.

[63] Amin al Husseini, "Nr. 42: Rundfunkrede an die Araber ("Märtyrerrede"), 11.11.1942," in ibid., 103–5.

[64] Amin al-Husseini, "Nr. 45a: Rundfunkrede an die Nordafrikaner, 25/26.11.1942," in ibid., 115.

[65] See Herf, "What Is Old and What Is New," 25–32.

[66] See Hirszowicz, *The Third Reich and the Arab East*; Kedourie, *Arabic Political Memoirs*; Cao-Van-Hoa, *"Der Feind meines Feindes..."*; and Schwanitz, ed., *Jenseits der Legenden*. For the

most comprehensive synthesis of the global dimensions of World War II, see Weinberg, *A World at Arms.*

[67] Berman, *Terror and Liberalism*; Küntzel, *Djihad und Judenhaß.*

[68] Berman, *Terror and Liberalism*, 21.

[69] See Herf, *Reactionary Modernism.*

References

Berman, Paul. *Terror and Liberalism.* New York: Knopf, 2003.

Cao-Van-Hoa, Edmund. *"Der Feind meines Feindes...": Darstellungen des national-sozialistischen Deutschland in ägyptischen Schriften.* Frankfurt/Main: Peter Lang, 1990.

Fischer-Weth, Kurt. *Amin Al-Husseini: Grossmufti von Palästina.* Berlin-Friedenau: Walter Titz Verlag, 1943.

Friedländer, Saul. *Nazi Germany and the Jews.* Vol. 1, *The Years of Persecution, 1933–1939.* New York: HarperCollins, 1997.

Gensicke, Klaus. *Der Mufti von Jerusalem, Amin el-Husseini und die Nationalsozialisten.* Frankfurt/Main: Verlag Peter Lang, 1988.

Herf, Jeffrey. *Reactionary Modernism: Technology, Culture and Politics in Weimar and the Third Reich.* New York: Cambridge University Press, 1984.

———. "What Is Old and What Is New about the Terrorism of Islamic Fundamentalism." *Partisan Review* 69, no. 1 (winter 2002): 25–32.

———. "The "Jewish War": Goebbels and the Antisemitic Campaigns of the Nazi Propaganda Ministry." *Holocaust and Genocide Studies* 19, no. 1 (spring 2005): 51–80.

———. "Der Krieg und die Juden." In *Das Deutsche Reich und der Zweite Weltkrieg, Band 9/2: Die Deutsche Kriegsgesellschaft 1939 bis 1945*, edited by Jörg Echternkamp. Stuttgart: Deutsche Verlagsanstalt, 2005.

———. *Nazi Ideology and Propaganda During World War II and the Holocaust.* Cambridge, MA: Harvard University Press, forthcoming, 2006.

———. *The Jewish Enemy: Nazi Propaganda during World War II and the Holocaust.* Cambridge, MA: Harvard University Press, forthcoming, Spring 2006.

Hest, Heinrich [Herman Erich Seifert]. *Der Aufbruch in der arabischen Welt.* Berlin: Zentralverlag der NSDAP, Franz Eher Nachf., 1941.

———. *Palästina: Judenstaat? England als Handlanger des Weltjudentums.* Vol. 2 of *Weltjuda ohne Maske.* Berlin: Joh. Kasper and Co., 1939.

Hirszowicz, Lukasz. *The Third Reich and the Arab East.* London and Toronto: University of Toronto Press, 1966.

Hitler, Adolf. *Mein Kampf.* Translated by Ralph Mannheim. 1943: Boston: Houghton-Mifflin, 1971.

Höpp, Gerhard, ed. *Mufti-Papiere: Briefe, memoranden, Reden und Aufrufe Amin al-Husainis aus dem Exil, 1940–1945.* Berlin: Klaus Schwarz Verlag, 2001.

Kedourie, Elie. *Arab Political Memoirs and Other Studies.* London: Frank Cass, 1974.

Küntzel, Matthias. *Djihad und Judenhaß: Über den neuen antijüdischen Krieg.* Freiburg: ça ira Verlag, 2003.

Meyer-Christian, Wolf. *Die englisch-jüdische Allianz: Werden und Wirken der kapitalistischen Weltherrschaft.* 3rd ed. Berlin-Leipzig: Nibelungen-Verlag, 1942.

Muller, Jerry Z. *The Mind and the Market: Capitalism in Modern European Thought.* New York: Knopf, 2003.

Nicosia, Francis R. "Zionism in National Socialist Jewish Policy in Germany, 1933–39." *Journal of Modern History* 50, no. 4 (1978): 1253–82.

———. "Ein Nützlicher Feind: Zionismus im Nationalsozialistischen Deutschland 1933–1939." *Vierteljahrshefte für Zeitgeschichte* 37, no. 3 (1989): 367–400.

————. "Zionism and Palestine in Anti-Semitic Thought in Imperial Germany." *Studies in Zionism* 13, no. 2 (1992): 115–31.

————. *The Third Reich and the Palestine Question.* 2nd ed. New Brunswick, NJ: Transaction, 1999.

Roller, Walter, ed. *Judenverfolgung und jüdisches Leben unter den Bedingungen der nationalsozialistischen Gewaltherrschaft.* Vol. 1, *Tondokumente und Runkfunksendungen, 1930–1946.* Potsdam: Verlag für Berlin-Brandenburg, 1996.

Rosenberg, Alfred. *Die Protokolle der Weissen von Zion und die jüdische Weltpolitik.* Munich: Deutscher Volksverlag, 1933.

————. *Der Staatsfeindliche Zionismus.* Munich: Zentralverlag der NSDAP, Franz Eher Verlag, 1938.

————. "Die Judenfrage als Weltproblem." In *Weltkampf: Die Judenfrage in Geschichte und Gegenwart.* Frankfurt/Main, 1941.

————.*Schriften aus den Jahren 1917–1921.* Munich: Hoheneichen Verlag, 1943.

Schwanitz, Wolfgang, ed. *Jenseits der Legenden: Araber, Juden, Deutsche.* Berlin: Dietz, 1994.

Shils, Edward. *The Constitution of Society.* Chicago: University of Chicago Press, 1982.

Weinberg, Gerhard L. *A World at Arms: A Global History of World War II.* New York: Cambridge University Press, 1994.

————., ed. *Hitler's Second Book: The Unpublished Sequel to* Mein Kampf *by Adolf Hitler.* New York: Enigma Books, 2003.

Wiesenthal, Simon. *Großmufti–Großagent der Achse.* Salzburg-Vienna: Ried Verlag, 1946.

Wirsing, Giselher. *Engländer, Juden, Araber in Palästina.* Jena: Eugen Diederichs Verlaag, 1939.

An Inseparable Tandem of European Identity? Anti-Americanism and Anti-Semitism in the Short and Long Run

Andrei S. Markovits

Introduction

One need not be a diligent student of survey research to know that antipathy towards America and Americans has become a worldwide phenomenon. By any measure, American-European relations have reached a nadir over the past few years. Regardless of the issue involved, the tone of the dialogue has been fraught with irritation, anger and condescension. This article argues that a growing dislike of the United States and most things American has permeated European discourse since the fall of the Soviet Union in 1991. Moreover, it also maintains that Europe's deep antipathy towards America hails from a fertile history. Anti-Americanism in Europe has long preceded George W. Bush and will persist long after his departure. Furthermore, the article will briefly discuss anti-Semitism, one of anti-Americanism's most consistent conceptual companions, perhaps even one of its constitutive features. To be sure, European anti-Semitism preceded anti-Americanism by centuries. And the two did not emerge as the inseparable tandem that they have now become until the nineteenth century. The most important difference between the two is the fact that European anti-Semitism killed millions of innocent people whereas, even in its most virulent form, European anti-Americanism rarely went beyond the prolific burning of American flags and/or the destruction of property. However, today anti-Semitism and anti-Americanism have become inseparable both conceptually and empirically.

Anti-Americanism is a murky concept because it merges antipathy towards what America *does* with what America *is*. Thus, it has characteristics like any other prejudice in that its holder "pre-judges" the object and its activities apart from what actually transpires in reality. And just like in the case of any prejudice, anti-Americanism, too, says much more about those that hold it than it does about the object of its ire and contempt. But where it differs so markedly from "classical" prejudices such as anti-Semitism, homophobia, misogyny and racism is the fact that unlike in these latter cases—where Jews, gays and lesbians, women and ethnic minorities rarely, if ever, have any actual power in and over the majority of populations in most countries—the real existing United States most certainly does have power. And because of this unique paradox, the separation between what America *is* and what America *does* will forever be murky and impossible to disentangle. It is precisely because of this fact that—unlike these other prejudices which, as a fine testimony to progress and tolerance over the past forty years, have by and large become publicly illegitimate in most advanced industrial democracies—anti-Americanism remains not only acceptable in many public circles, it has even become commendable, indeed a badge of honor, and perhaps one of the most distinct icons of being a progressive these days. After all, by being anti-American, one adheres to a prejudice that ipso facto also opposes a truly powerful force in the world. Thus, in the case of anti-Americanism, one's prejudice partially assumes an antinomian purpose thereby attaining a legitimacy in progressive circles that other prejudices—with the exception of anti-Zionism and anti-Semitism, as discussed below—do not have anymore.

Anti-Americanism, just like any other prejudice, is an acquired set of beliefs, an attitude, an ideology, not an ascribed trait. Thus, it is completely independent of the national origins of its particular holder. Indeed, many Americans can be, and are, anti-American, just like Jews can be, and are, anti-Semitic, blacks can, and do, hold racist views, and women misogynist ones. It is not a matter of the holder's citizenship or birthplace that ought to be the appropriate criterion but rather her/his set of acquired beliefs about a particular collective. But here, too, context means everything. Delighting in Michael Moore's *Bowling for Columbine* or *Fahrenheit 9/11* in an artsy movie theater in an American college town has a vastly different meaning from having this film become far and away the most successful documentary movie of any kind in most European countries. Michael Moore's books grace Europe's bestseller lists, even before they are translated into the local languages. Thousands thronged his lectures on his European tour in December 2003, when he was received like a rock star by an adoring public. And his adoring public was not confined to members of the radical left. Instead, to take Bavaria as an example, many sympathizers of the conservative Bavarian party, the Christian Social Union (CSU)who would otherwise have nothing but contempt for Michael Moore's views and social entourage, flocked to his films and lectures, bought his book, and delighted in his put-downs of the United States.[1] Clearly, the context of the admiration bestowed upon Moore by these adoring Europeans hails from something much deeper than their disagreements over policy or even the dislikes of a particular American president. Whereas in the United States Moore's popularity bespeaks his humorous depiction of a conservative establishment, in Europe Moore embodies little more than a legitimating foil behind which one can safely voice one's anti-Americanism without being accused of harboring prejudicial antipathies since, after all, Michael Moore, an American, says the same things. The passion for Moore bespeaks an emotional enthusiasm not an intellectual one.[2]

To be sure, just like an imagined America served all kinds of purposes to Europeans, not least of which was to delineate a clear "other" to themselves, the exact obverse pertained to Americans as well who, throughout their history, created all kinds of imagined Europes that fulfilled an "othering" function. However, there always was a difference: whereas in the United States the carriers of prejudice and antipathy towards Europe have predominated in the lower social strata, American elites—particularly cultural ones— have consistently extolled Europe, and continue to do so. This love for and emulation of European tastes, mores, fashions and habits remained a staple of American elite culture even during the country's most nativist and isolationist periods. Virtually all of America's highbrow culture continues to be European. In massive contrast to the outright negative and pejorative—at best ambivalent—notions that the word "American" conjures up in Europe, "European" invariably invokes positive images among American elites and masses alike. "European" to Americans invariably connotes "quality," "class," "taste," "elegance," "style." Any resentment of Europe by American mass opinion is of a different order of magnitude than anti-Americanism's presence in Europe.

Also, there are huge differences by social class and status. Ordinary Europeans have never exhibited the aversion and disdain towards America that their elites have. Indeed, as demonstrated by regular public opinion surveys since the 1950s, a solid majority of Europeans have expressed positive views of America, with only about 30 percent holding negative ones. Tellingly, the higher one proceeds on the social scale of the respondents, the greater the quantity of negative attitudes towards America becomes. As such, anti-Americanism is arguably one of the very few prejudices in post-1945 Europe that correlates positively with education and social status: the higher the education, the greater the prejudice. Until the mid-1960s, this was also the case with anti-Semitism in Austria and Germany where, since the nineteenth century, the most virulent anti-Semites were to be found at universities and among their graduates—for example, doctors, lawyers and engineers. In the course of the past four decades, conventional anti-Semitism in these two countries has assumed the pattern of other kinds of collective prejudices and hatreds: the lesser the respondent's education, the greater his prejudices. This has never been the case with anti-Americanism and might yet again change with anti-Semitism, as will be discussed. Thus, an inverted mirror image has characterized European-American perceptions of each other: European masses have by and large liked America while European elites have certainly not, whereas American elites have liked Europe, with American masses less so.

Perhaps what differentiates the current level and quality of European anti-Americanism from that of all its predecessors is the fact that for the very first time a solid majority of European publics also bear negative attitudes towards the United States, thus establishing a complete congruity with their elites on this topic. There can be no doubt that the current Bush administration's actions, tone and demeanor have contributed to this unprecedented one-dimensionality between European publics and elites in terms of their jointly felt and politically mobilized anti-Americanism.

Lest there be any misunderstandings and conceptual uncertainties as to what exactly I mean by anti-Americanism, here is the definition offered by Paul Hollander in his definitive book on the subject:

> Anti-Americanism is *a predisposition to hostility* toward the United States and American society, a relentless critical impulse toward American social, economic, and political institutions, traditions, and values; it entails an aversion to American culture in particular and its influence abroad, often also contempt for the American national character (or what is presumed to be such a character) and dislike of American people, manners, behavior, dress, and so on; rejection of American foreign policy and a firm belief in the malignity of American influence and presence anywhere in the world. (emphasis in original)[3]

While some of current anti-Americanism's manifestations might indeed be unique, it is also quite clear that there never was a "golden age" in which European elites genuinely liked America. To be more precise still, there never existed an era in which European intellectuals and literati viewed the United States without much *ressentiment*. Well before America had any power, and well before it was an independent country, tropes emerged in its perception that were to become mainstays of European anti-Americanism to this day: venality, vulgarity, mediocrity, inauthenticity, but also a clear sense of danger in its undefinable but clearly evident attraction. Thus, the argument that it has been America's disproportionate power when compared with Europe's alleged powerlessness that lies at the heart of European *ressentiment* towards the United States and things American simply does not hold up. For clearly, even when the United States had virtually no power as compared to the big European players, Europeans bore hostility towards this new entity. From the very beginning until today, European elites have continued to view America as this threatening parvenu. European *ressentiment* towards America bespoke a fear of losing control on the part of the Europeans which rested partly in America's potential as a powerful country but also in its undeniable—almost irresistible—attraction to Europe's masses, surely not the aristocracy's friends. From the very outset, there was something eerily attractive about the place well beyond the new life that it offered to millions of Europe's masses. It was similar, yet different; weak, yet powerful; repellent, yet attractive. In notable contrast to any other country, from the very beginning the enemy for European elites was not "America the Conqueror—not the 'Imperial Republic'—but America the Beguiling."[4]

European Anti-Semitism as a Constitutive Companion to European Anti-Americanism

It was not until the middle of the nineteenth century that anti-Semitism began to accompany European anti-Americanism in a systematic manner. It was the fear and critique of capitalist modernity that brought these two *ressentiments* together. European elites saw America and the Jews as paragons of modernity: money-driven, profit-hungry, urban, universalistic, individualistic, mobile, rootless, hostile to established traditions and values and thus profoundly inauthentic and artificial. It was never the real *existierende* United States and its Jews that were feared and disdained but the combination of Judaism and Americanism as concepts and social trends. After World War I, the Jews as rulers of America became pronounced. It was at this juncture that the notions of Jewish Wall Street, Jewish Hollywood, Jewish Jazz, a thoroughly "Jewified" America became commonplace. It was at this time that all the forerunners for current codes such as "certain East Coast circles" were established. Jews and America became inextricably intertwined, not only as representatives of modernity but also as holders of power. One of the standard staples of European anti-Semitism has always been to impute much more power to Jews than they actually have. Moreover, what makes this putative power even more potent is that it is believed to be clandestine and cliquish. With America's real power massively growing after World War I, power as a unifying notion between Jews and America became more pronounced and also more lasting. The hostile perception of this alleged link became integral to National Socialism.

Things appeared to change after the end of World War II, the Holocaust, the establishment of Israel and the Cold War. American power, though still massively resented by Europeans, also became a much-needed protector against the Soviet Union, its allies and communism. Probably for the first time in over 900 years, the Holocaust rendered overt anti-Semitism socially unacceptable among Europe's elites.[5] And Jews for the very first time in nearly 2,000 years actually attained real power by dint of running a state. While these structural changes substantially altered the tone and the substance of the discourse about Jews and America in Europe, the two remained as intertwined as ever. By the late 1960s, Israel became little more than an extension of American power to many on Europe's political left. Israel was disliked not so much because it was Jewish but because it was de facto American, thus powerful. It is by virtue of this shift in power that contemporary Europeans dislike Israel so intensely and why their current anti-Semitism assumes a different veneer from the traditional one that dominated Europe for 1,000 years. Contemporary Europe's allegedly postnational elites pretend to dislike states that behave the way European states used to before 1945: assertively, unilaterally, particularistically, realpolitically, all of which pertain to Israel's conduct in the world, as well as to America's, most certainly under the aegis of the Bush administration. The fact that current European anti-Semitism has changed is best demonstrated by the fact that the very people who are allegedly appalled by anti-Semitic incidents in their own countries are most certainly Israel's unforgiving critics. That they then often resort to characterizations of Israel's essence and its very existence—as opposed to its policies—in eerily similar terms and tone to the old-fashioned European anti-Semitism of yore attests not to the end of European anti-Semitism but merely to its mutation from what Daniel Goldhagen so aptly calls the Shylock Jew to the Rambo Jew.[6] And we all know how much Rambo has become a synonym for America and Americans in European discourse of the past two decades. The tough Jew in the form of the omnipotent Israeli has led to a new twist of the longstanding interaction between anti-Semitism and anti-Americanism: if in former times it was the powerful United States that used powerful Israel as its puppet in its "imperialist" and "neocolonial" designs, then we have witnessed a reversal, especially in the context of the Iraq War of 2003, in which it is all-powerful Israel and its East Coast minions that have co-opted American power for their own purposes. As already noted above, anti-Americanism had been perhaps the only prejudice in Europe that correlated positively with the respondents" level of education and social position. One could legitimately voice this prejudice because it inevitably also expressed overt opposition to a powerful actor. Being prejudiced against the powerful has an entirely different social acceptability than being prejudiced against the weak. And this is the position to which the new European anti-Semitism has mutated. While it has become illegitimate in the post-Holocaust world to openly express hatred for powerless Jews—meaning Jews currently living in Europe—it has become all the more acceptable to express antipathy towards powerful Jews. The former is unadulterated anti-Semitism which one can only express in the pub, the *Stammtisch* or on the Internet, in other words apart from acceptable public discourse. The latter has become a badge of honor and very much forms acceptable public discourse.

Jews in Europe have once again become objects of controversy and contestation by dint of the following developments:

1. The disappearance of communism as an enemy and a perceived threat and thus the need to accord absolute primacy to the task of containing, even defeating, this perceived ill.
2. On account of communism's defeat, the decreased need for the United States as a protector. This fostered the resurgence of an already present anti-Americanism of which the intellectuals and the political classes have been the most avid carriers. With manifest anti-Americanism, anti-Semitism has been rarely far behind.
3. What makes them so related is their being perceived as the quintessential expressions of modernity. With a massive critique of modernity afoot in Europe there emerged yet another piece in the puzzle that explains a necessary, albeit not a sufficient, reason for the rise in anti-Semitism in Europe.
4. Everything about "Europe" and the worries associated with this state-building process pertains a fortiori to the process of "globalization" as well. This development is nothing new and has been with us most certainly since the advent of capitalism and

the discovery of the Americas in the sixteenth century. Moreover, it has witnessed many greater leaps in its history than the one that we are currently experiencing. But objective factors have never been a true match to subjective perceptions. And those currently dictate an intellectual climate that associates only calamities with globalization and thus—even if inadvertently—assumes an antimodernist strain that easily lends itself to a revival of anti-Semitic tropes.

5. Multiculturalism in Europe initially fostered little more than a welcome culinary diversity for the increasingly cosmopolitan palate of its inhabitants. But by the 1970s this mutated into a nasty contest over identity, citizenship, permanence, language, ethnicity, religion—the hot buttons of politics. The empirical reality has been that a large number of Europe's new immigrants hail from the Muslim world. The presence of these immigrants awakened first and foremost a nasty strain of xenophobia and overt racism in all European countries, which led to severe and frequent acts of violence by members of the indigenous population against these minorities. How shocking it must have been to the ever-noble and virtuous Europeans to discover that they, too, were assaulting and killing their dark-skinned minorities and were just as racist as they had always accused the Americans of being. Oddly, this influx of ethnically (and religiously) different immigrants to Europe had a twofold effect on anti-Semitism: first, it offered yet another—and actually related—object of hatred to those who loathed these newcomers and wished them ill. This represents the European anti-Semitism of old, the conventional anti-Semitism with all its well-known tropes. But second, it introduced a hitherto unknown subject of anti-Semitism in Europe by making its carriers those who continue to remain targets of racism and xenophobia on the part of the European majorities who hate them. I am speaking, of course, of the large Muslim minorities in Europe who have become major carriers of anti-Semitism largely, though not exclusively, on account of the Israeli-Palestinian conflict.

6. Surely one needs to mention Israel's deeply problematic policies and objectionable actions in the occupied territories as irritants to most European publics, elite as well as mass. But here, too, the line between completely legitimate criticisms of policies and the much more worrisome questioning of Israel's very existence needs to be strictly delineated. Alas, it is increasingly less so in the commentaries of the European public.

Criticism of Israel has attained a tone in Europe's mainstream media which goes well beyond the country's policies, and questions the worth of its very existence. While such things are nothing new in the worlds of the extreme right and left in Europe and have been commonplace since the Six Day War in June of 1967, they were not part of Europe's accepted political discourse until the 1990s. After all, many people have been rightfully upset with many a country's policies. But in virtually no case that I can recall has this led to the questioning of the very worth of the country's existence. This development reinforces the conclusion that among the bevy of European prejudices and hatreds, anti-Semitism has constantly assumed a place all its own. It is related to racism, yet substantially different from it. And it is back with a vengeance in acceptable European discourse despite all the sanctimonious denials to the contrary. Seldom has this been clearer than in the case of contemporary Europe's irritation with Israel and Jews, which needs to be analyzed in a comparative context.

A new tone can be heard among European intellectuals in which criticizing Jews— not merely Israel and Israelis—has attained a certain urgency that reveals a particularly liberating dimension. One can almost hear the cries of relief: "Free at last, free at last, we are finally free of this damn Holocaust at last!" In this context Europeans posit that Jews, who created a culture of guilt and shame for Europeans, and kept them from speaking their minds as they wished, now behave just like they did. The lid is off: Jews are legitimate targets yet again. To be sure, anti-Zionism and anti-Semitism are distinguishable: one is a political position, the other a prejudice. Yet, as Mitchell Cohen has noted,

> the overlap between anti-Semitism and anti-Zionist discourses today is considerable, and it is especially striking at a time when many intellectuals, notably the post-modernist left and post-colonial theorists, base their work on the very notion of "discourse," contending that clusters of assumptions, embedded in our languages and cultures, pre-select how we think about the world, and mesh the production of knowledge and power.[7]

By constantly bringing up the truly warped and ill-willed analogy of the Israelis with the Nazis, Europeans absolve themselves from any remorse and shame and thus experience a sense of liberation from their centuries of murderous anti-Semitism. Especially since the second *Intifada*, which erupted in September 2000, there developed a discourse that equated Israelis with Nazis. To be sure, this equation is not new; it had been a staple of Soviet anti-Zionism and remains a persistent one in contemporary Arab propaganda and public discourse. Moreover, this mantra was common on the fringes of the far left in Western Europe from the early 1970s. But since September 2000 and then much reinforced by the attack on New York and Washington, DC, exactly one year later, this equation has moved from the political and social fringes of European discourse to its accepted middle. Indeed, as Melanie Phillips argued in a perceptive article in the *Observer*, the roots of this type of anti-Semitism rest less with its usual source—the far right—but with the "Sharon-hating" left.[8] In the course of my research, I collected over 500 cartoons from major mainstream newspapers in Germany, Italy, France, Britain and selected other countries from Europe's south and west. The analogizing of the Star of David with the Swastika, the depicting of Sharon as Hitler or some Nazi official, the usage of SS-type runes in denoting Israeli objects is decidedly noticeable since the autumn of 2000. One exception still pertains: in notable contrast to their Greek, British, French, Italian and Spanish counterparts, the depicting of Israelis as Nazis in cartoons is totally absent in German mainstream newspapers. The point here is simple: the source and driving force of this equation has not been the radical right but the socially acceptable liberal left.

With the discourse of Israelis = Nazis, one hurts the intended target by equating it with the very perpetrators that almost wiped it off the earth in the most brutal genocide imaginable. In particular, all of this needs to be viewed in a comparative context both in terms of its tone as well as its substance: as to the former, what is important here is that no other vaguely comparable conflict has attained anywhere near the shrillness and acuity as has the Israeli-Palestinian conflict. If one looks at two much more bloody, and geographically proximate, conflicts—the four succession wars following the dissolution of the former Yugoslavia and the Russian wars in Chechnya—neither of them have even vaguely created a tone of dismissal, bitterness and contempt of the respective aggressors (the Serbs, the Croats and the Russians) among Europe's intellectuals as have the Israelis. Oxford dons never even thought of banning Russian, Croatian or Serbian researchers from their laboratories, as actually happened with Israelis.[9] The editor of *The Translator* and *Translation Studies Abstracts* published in Britain did not dismiss colleagues from its editorial boards because they belonged to nationalities whose countries were engaged in some form of conflict and injustice. But two Israeli academics were summarily dismissed from this board merely for being Israeli citizens.[10] Examples abound. The tone in which the Israeli-Arab conflict has been reported by Europe's mainstream media shows a trend in which the Israelis and their actions were much more frequently couched in words with negative and pejorative connotations as compared to the actions by the Arab side that were conveyed in a much more neutral tone. Palestinian suicide bombers are "nationalists" who acted out of "desperation" whereas the Israelis' retaliation was inevitably "vengeful" and "brutal." Tellingly, the same media have without any hesitation depicted the Basque ETA's and the Irish IRA's actions in Spain and Britain, respectively, as "terrorist."[11] The passion against Israel is simply disproportionate in its tone and its shrillness when compared with other agents of violence and injustice.[12]

This noticeable change in European discourse hails much more from the left than from the right. The latter—mainly by dint of the continued illegitimacy and unacceptability of Nazism and fascism in European public opinion—has had a much more circumspect influence on how Jews and Israel are depicted than has the left. Because classical anti-Semitism, certainly in its praxis, was mostly associated with the European right, the left enjoyed a certain bonus when it came to discussing all matters relating to Jews and Israel. The left could take liberties with being anti-Israeli and anti-Semitic that the right could never have. This bonus enabled the left to employ anti-Israeli discourse that, in the meantime, has become completely common and acceptable parlance in Europe. Because of this general acceptability and overall legitimacy, left-wing anti-Semitism is much more relevant and disturbing than right-wing anti-Semitism, which has essentially remained the same. Today's neo-Nazis are ugly and unpleasant, but they continue to remain beyond the pale of acceptable European discourse. The *Guardian*, the BBC, the *Independent*—to use British examples that have their continental equivalents in every country—have not assumed their overly negative language and hostile attitude towards Israel, Jews and the United States under the influence of the National Front but reflect changes in British and European attitudes hailing from changes of the late 1960s. It is by dint of this left-liberal voice, not the right's old-style anti-Semitism, that 59 percent of Europeans view Israel as being the greatest threat to global peace, putting this country in first place ahead of countries such as Iran, North Korea, the United States, Iraq, Afghanistan and Pakistan, in that order. Not surprisingly, Europeans had the moral arrogance to list themselves as a distant last, congruent with their self-perception as the paragons of global peace.[13] Anybody following the European media's tone in covering the Israeli-Palestinian conflict since the second *Intifada* will not be surprised by these results. The origins of this hegemonic tone in Europe hail from the left not the right.

And this brings us to the difference in substance. It is rather evident that the European intellectuals and the political classes—as well as increasingly the general public—are not so much expressing their sympathies for suppressed Muslims or disadvantaged Arabs as they are expressing their antipathies towards Israel and (not so indirectly) the Jews. This is best demonstrated by the following paradox: precisely those who were the most silent during the Bosnian war and its massive slaughter of Bosnian Muslims at the hand of mainly Bosnian Serbs but also Bosnian Croats, and who only raised their voices in 1995, de facto in support of the (mainly Serbian) perpetrators, to protest against American intervention on behalf of the Bosnian Muslims, have also been the most vocal opponents of Israel. The link once again is the United States. If the United States intervenes on behalf of Muslims, then many European intellectuals rally to the side of people like Slobodan Milosevic who previously engaged in mass murder of such Muslims. Thus, the antipathy towards Israel and the accompanying anti-Semitism cannot be separated from a larger enmity towards the United States and what it represents. How else can one explain the attitude of Greek intellectuals, politicians, the clergy and public opinion all of whom were rabidly pro-Serbian and vehemently anti-Bosnian Muslim, while at the same time these very Greeks are among the most pro-Arab and pro-Palestinian Europeans? What drives the liberal left in Europe is dislike and hatred of Israel and America, and not a genuine sympathy for and identification with downtrodden Muslims. It was not the slaughter of innocent Muslim women and children that riled the European left. Instead, what mobilized thousands in the streets of Berlin, Paris and Athens once the much-belated step was taken to intervene on behalf of the brutalized Muslims was once again the American bogeyman. And once again, far right and far left meet on matters relating to America and Jews. No far right in Europe has a nastier anti-Serbian history than the German and Austrian, both of which have been long-time supporters of the most vicious anti-Serbian fascists in Croatia. Still, their hatred of Serbs could not compete with their hatred of Americans, and once the United States intervened against Serbs on behalf of the Bosnian Muslims and their Kosovar coreligionists, German and Austrian neo-Nazis and far rightists rallied to Milosevic's side in their unmitigated opposition to NATO's American-led interventions. "Les extrêmes se touchent" on matters related to Jews and American yet again, as they have so often throughout the twentieth century.

The common trope here, as elsewhere, is mobilized anti-Americanism. When José Bové, the French anti-globalization leader, joined the Palestinians in Ramallah in the spring of 2002 instead of traveling to Gujarat where many more Muslims were slain in multiple pogroms by Hindu mobs, his action was not primarily driven by the urge to express solidarity with a repressed people but rather by an enmity towards the United States and everything that it purportedly represents. It is by dint of America's proximity to Israel that the latter has become such a bogeyman to the anti-globalization movement. The vile expressions of anti-Semitism in Durban, Porto Alegre and Davos need no lengthy elaboration here. In all three instances, important— and justified—criticisms of and demonstrations against some of the ills of an unfettered market-driven globalization soon assumed anti-Semitic tropes of the vilest sort. At the gathering against racism in Durban in early September 2001, anti-Zionism and hostility to Israel not only became one of the congress's main themes, the tropes that were employed for this purpose hailed from the storied repertoire of conventional anti-Semitism. A few months later—in the winter of 2002—similar images and tone appeared in Porto Alegre, where an annual "Anti-Davos" gathering has attained some prominence. But at the core event itself—namely, at the much-coveted annual Davos conference which has become de rigueur for all leading politicians, business leaders, intellectuals, actors and "beautiful people"—there was a massive demonstration in the winter of 2003 in which demonstrators danced around a golden calf with one of the participants sporting a Donald Rumsfeld mask and featuring a yellow Jewish star on his chest with the word "Sheriff" on it. His comrade donned an Ariel Sharon mask and wielded a cudgel in his hand. Suffice it to say that anti-Semitism in the context of anti-globalization has furnished a fruitful meeting ground for right and left that has not existed in such a manifest way since the flourishing of National Bolshevism. Clearly, the intensity of the hatred borne towards Israel, which goes way beyond a legitimate criticism of its policies, derives in good part from the perception of Israel as a complete American proxy, as a de facto part of the United States. And as such, *any* tone can be used against Israel because it is powerful and part of an even larger power—that is, the United States. By definition, such tone cannot be anti-Semitic because anti-Semitism only exists in the accusation of weak Jews, which the Israelis clearly are not. But the question for the anti-globalization movements still remains: Why Israel, why not—say—Saudi Arabia, to which the United States is equally close and which, arguably, has a greater global role and influence than does Israel? The answer to this aspect of the puzzle lies not only in Israel's political proximity to the United States but also in the former's identity as a Jewish state and the Jews" relationship to Europeans and their history. For the surplus of enmity exhibited towards Israel by Europeans, the much greater coverage of Israel by the European media compared with that of any other conflict in the world, including those much closer to Europe, bespeaks a qualitative dimension to this sentiment and attitude that borders on an obsession which reaches way beyond conventional politics. Much deeper historical, cultural and psychological forces are at work. And thus we are back at the three standard pillars of classical anti-Semitism and anti-Americanism: Jews, America and modernity.

The substance and tone of public debates really matter. These debates create "frames" that influence political behavior and can also contribute to enduring elements of political cultures. Debates shift the boundaries of legitimate discursive space in politics since they define the realm of acceptable terms and sanction those who violate them. Debates shape language and create new code words for old ideas, including prejudices and antipathies. Above all, the ensuing changes in discursive space change how elites and ordinary citizens discuss and then think about a topic. Thus, the tone of these debates reflects broader ideological shifts in politics and society.[14]

Europe's Elite Voices on America, 1 January 1992–31 December 2002: Condescension, Ridicule, Irritation, *Ressentiment* and a new Sentiment— *Schadenfreude*

As part of a larger empirical project on European anti-Americanism, I collected 1,000 articles written on the United States in the four key European countries: Germany, France, Italy and Britain. In order to maximize America's "is" dimension as opposed to its "does" for my study, I consciously excluded articles and reports that dealt with overtly political questions, particularly all those related to American foreign policy broadly construed, since it is via its foreign policy that America "does" things most overtly to other countries. Moreover, I also consciously excluded events after 31 December 2002 precisely to avoid the excessively heated atmosphere in European-American relations caused by the Iraq crisis. I concentrated my research on articles about film, theater, food, travel and the weather, as well as human-interest pieces and descriptions of the iconography of particular events such as party conventions, car manufacturing, subway construction and the world of sports. My sample included more than twenty elite newspapers and periodicals in Britain, Germany, France and Italy. (Note the West European exclusivity of the study.)[15]

The world of soccer will offer a fine example for my point precisely because whatever one wants to argue about this sport and its culture, it is clear that the United States has been, at best, an also-ran in it throughout the twentieth century. America simply did not matter—and still matters very little. When it was decided that the World Cup would take place in the United States in the summer of 1994, much of the European press was appalled. Instead of rejoicing that the last important terra incognita for soccer was about to be conquered by the "beautiful game," the usual objections to American crassness, vulgarity, commercialism and ignorance were loudly voiced by Europeans—in notable contrast to Latin Americans who, if objective criteria and real injustices were to decide predilections and negative opinions, have had much more compelling reasons to dislike Americans than have Europeans. Many Europeans argued that giving the tournament to the Americans was tantamount to degrading the game and its tradition. The facilities were denigrated, the organization ridiculed, the whole endeavor treated with derision. When the stadia were filled like in no other World Cup tournament before and since, when the level of violence and arrests was far and away the lowest at any event of this size, the European press chalked this up to the stupidity and ignorance of Americans. Of course Americans came to the games, because they like events and pageantry, but did they really enjoy and understand the games? Could they ever learn to? When more than 60,000 people crowded into Giants

Stadium near New York City on a Wednesday afternoon to watch Saudi Arabia play Morocco (surely no powerhouses in the world of soccer), this, too, was attributed to the vast ignorance of Americans regarding soccer. Indeed, five articles proudly pointed to the fact that similar games in soccer-savvy Italy attracted fewer than 20,000 people in the 1990 World Cup held in that country. Those few European journalists who bothered to write anything about American sports such as baseball which, as always in the summer, was in full swing at the time, had nothing but contempt, derision and ridicule for the game: no attempt to engage its traditions, no endeavor to understand it on its own terms, merely yet another vehicle to have one's prejudices about America confirmed. Michel Platini, the former French soccer great of the 1980s and in charge of organizing the subsequent World Cup in France, summed up his feelings and judgments in the vernacular of current Europe: "The World Cup in the United States was outstanding, but it was like Coca Cola. Ours will be like sparkling champagne."[16] Surely Platini could not have meant to characterize the riots, the violence, the ticket scandals, the racial insults that occurred during the tournament in France as "sparkling champagne." And it is equally unclear what he meant by characterizing the American tournament as "Coca Cola." The code, however, is clear to all: regardless of its actual success and achievements, the American event was by definition crude and inauthentic (like Coca Cola), whereas the French—equally by definition—was inevitably going to be refined and profound (like champagne).

It was remarkable how differently the European press reported on the World Cup 2002 in Japan and South Korea, both newcomers to the world of soccer, just like the United States. Rave reviews were accorded to the facilities and organization in both countries. This contrasted sharply to the negative tone describing the equivalent structures in the United States in 1994 even though FIFA, for example, and soccer officials had nothing but praise for the American effort. What was viewed as kitsch in the American context (the opening ceremony, for example, and other pageantries accompanying the tournament) was lauded as artistic and innovative in the Japanese and South Korean equivalent. Lastly, the American team was first ridiculed as an incompetent group of players who barely deserved to be in the tournament. The huge upset over Portugal was attributed to sheer luck. When Team USA advanced to the second round and then defeated its archrival Mexico, the press corps that was vocally rooting for the Mexicans during the game remained stunned in silence at the press center. In notable contrast to the positive sentiment that was expressed towards Turkey, Senegal and South Korea, the other Cinderella teams of the tournament, nothing but bitterness and derision was voiced towards the American team. And when the mighty Germans narrowly (and luckily) beat the Americans in a quarterfinal, some European commentators became genuinely alarmed. Quipped one British journalist on a radio program: "This is terrible. Now they are getting good at this, too. They will steal our game. Imagine eleven Michael Jordans running onto the pitch at Wembley. That would be the end."[17] Damned if you do, damned if you don't, it could not be articulated more clearly: when the Americans play poorly, they are irritating merely by doing so. When they finally play well, they are disliked because they become threatening.

This underlying irritation was further confirmed during my many lectures on comparative sports in Germany, especially on my two book tours in support of the German edition of my book *Offside* (*Im Abseits* in its German translation). In literally every forum in which I presented my book and work—from university campuses to book stores; from rented public halls to semi-private settings; from Saarbrücken in the west to Potsdam in the east—at some point the question arose as to whether I did not find it arrogant that the Americans" sports culture centered on baseball, basketball and American football, and did not include soccer; whether indeed this was not yet another expression of America's self-anointed status as being better than the rest of the world. To many people my response that this development bespoke America's different history and its constructing its own modernity, which indeed entailed creating its own sports culture, did not allay their suspicions that underneath it all there lurked a normative dimension which somehow made America—in the Americans" eyes—better rather than just different. Fears along the lines that Americans might yet prove successful at soccer as well merely reinforced the constant malaise with and disdain for the United States, regardless of what it actually did or did not do.

The negative predisposition of European elites towards America ran so deep that even those few American innovations that one would expect European progressives to like were deformed into basically negative caricatures. Take affirmative action, multiculturalism, feminism and America's campaign against cigarette smoking. Rather than seeing these as impressive steps towards progressive reform, even left-wing European commentators decried these as merely mutated expressions of American puritanism, collective control and hysteria. They derided these reforms under the rubric of "political correctness." To them, American universities had been taken over by zealous feminists who dictated a moral code that forbade flirting and punished men for complimenting women.

European labor's anti-Americanism, usually confined to vocal opposition of American capitalism and foreign policy, also manifested itself in a clear disdain for American workers. In a detailed study of Daimler workers" attitudes in Stuttgart towards their presumed fraternal colleagues in the Daimler-Chrysler plants around Detroit, there were no attempts made to hide the contempt and disdain. Employees in Stuttgart characterized their colleagues in Detroit as lazy, incompetent and inferior. The Stuttgart crew did not want its allegedly superior products "contaminated" by the shoddy American ways of the Chrysler workers. The contempt did not remain confined to the factory gates. Chrysler workers" home milieus and recreational habits were also ridiculed and characterized as inferior.[18]

To Europeans, America had degenerated into a quasi-Orwellian society: following the dictates of a puritanical culture supervised by increasingly rigid governmental rules, on the one hand; and succumbing to the exigencies of an uncontrolled market with no social consciousness whatsoever, on the other. America the prudish and the prurient; home of unbridled individualism and collectivist conformity; progenitor of Harvard and Hollywood.

The overall conclusion from my survey of the European press is that virtually all aspects of American culture—including its highbrow variant—received at least one derisive or dismissive comment, even among the minority of articles that featured a positive view towards the issue reported. More than 75 percent of the articles were overwhelmingly negative in the presentation of their topic. Most of these exhibited what I have called "gratuitous" or "surplus" anti-Americanism, meaning that the objections lodged were not immanent criticisms of the issue at hand but rather catered to a pejorative generalization of America or Americans that had little bearing on the immediate topic. The term "Americanization" of whatever the subject may be (movies, theater, universities, business practices, habits, subway construction, car manufacturing, sports) was almost always invoked in a negative manner and conveyed a clearly undesirable situation. Even beyond the United States itself, many adversities in Europe are conveniently associated with America. When a crazed teenager gunned down his classmates and teachers in Erfurt, much of the subsequent German debate blamed an alleged "Americanization" of German youth, society and culture for this tragedy. When an extreme heat wave tormented Europeans, articles appeared decrying the "Americanization" of Europe's climate. Americans were to blame when the dollar was high, just as they were to blame when the dollar was low. Thus Gerhard Schroeder's constant invoking of "amerikanische Verhältnisse" as a negative icon for effective political mobilization made perfect sense for his successful electoral campaign in 2002. "Americanization" has in the meantime developed such a solid basis of pejorative connotations in Western Europe that it pays for politicians to use this sentiment as an agent of mobilization and legitimation. In Germany, the term "amerikanische Verhältnisse" connotes complete negativity, regardless of the content and context at hand.[19]

The events of 9/11 added a hitherto underdeveloped sentiment to this anti-American mix—that of *Schadenfreude*. While Europe's mass opinion was initially sympathetic towards Americans, Europe's elites, especially its cultural ones, were not. Ground Zero was still burning when the first reports in the quality media initiated all the arguments, objections, analyses, conjectures, conspiracy theories and open rejoicing that have become commonplace: that the Americans clearly had it coming to them; that this was justified payback for all American misdeeds of the past, from Vietnam to globalization, from exterminating the Native Americans to the firebombing of Dresden; that this was no big deal since many more Americans die in yearly traffic accidents; that, if anything, the destruction of the Twin Towers improved New York's skyline; that the Israeli Mossad was behind it all since many Jews stayed away from work that day lest they be killed; that it was all a ploy by the American government to obtain a carte blanche for its imperialist endeavors, very similar to the burning of the Reichstag in February of 1933 that led to the consolidation of the Nazi dictatorship; that George W. Bush and Osama bin Laden were identical in their mental makeup and their religious fanaticism, basically mirror images of each other, just like the United States in its religious revivalism was not a real democracy but in fact resembled the theocratic constructs of the Islamists. By year's end, bookstores in Paris, Berlin and London were full of publications that rejoiced at the tragedy of 9/11. Examples abound wherein a significant voice of Europe's intellectuals and elites expressed a virtually unveiled *Schadenfreude* in America's woes.[20]

Let us consider the following telling counterfactual: had the Air France Airbus A-300 Flight 8969 crashed into the Eiffel Tower in Paris on 24 December 1994, as the Groupe Armée Islamique wanted it to, I doubt very much that any—let alone many—American intellectuals would have written lengthy pieces in prestigious publications like the *New York Times* or the *Washington Post* by, say, 26 and 27 December all but exculpating this crime by invoking France's many military and political missteps as well as its atrocities, from the Vendée to the Paris Commune, from Indochina to Algeria. Nor would they have invoked all kinds of conspiracy theories involving the French government, the Israeli Mossad or any of the other agents so often mentioned in connection with 9/11. I doubt very much that books purporting that such a crime had actually been planned and executed by the French president—had this terrible tragedy become reality—would have been written by American intellectuals, let alone become bestsellers in the United States. But all of this has indeed happened in Europe, particularly among social groups from whom one would least expect it by dint of their intelligence and education. Clearly, antipathy, as has often been the case, trumps either and both.

It was payback time for Mr. Big's arrogant attitude and demeanor, for his general misdeeds like imperialism as well as specific ones like the bombing of Dresden, but above all simply for his being big. Everybody hates Mr. Big in any context, be it in politics or in the classroom, be it Bayern Munich, the New York Yankees or Harvard. *Schadenfreude* is a very human trait, which gains in respectability and legitimacy when it pertains to the suffering of a perceived giant. That the widely held and vocally expressed *Schadenfreude* and anger pertaining to 9/11 quickly shifted from Europe's intellectuals and elites to a significant percentage of the population is best demonstrated by opinion polls which clearly reveal that by the summer of 2003, for example, one third of Germans under the age of 30 believed that the US government had sponsored the 11 September 2001 attacks on New York and Washington. About 20 percent of the entire German population agreed with this view, according to the same survey.[21] The *Stammtisch* and the internet were brimming with delight about America's misery.

The Mobilizing Function of Anti-Americanism in Europe's State-Building Process

Whereas there still was a clear disconnection between elite and mass opinion in Europe following the 9/11 tragedy, there emerged a hitherto unprecedented congruence in opinion of all constituents concerning the war in Iraq. In no other instance in Europe's postwar development did such a complete convergence of views emerge between elites and masses, between government and opposition, among voices on the left and the right, as occurred during the build-up to the war with Iraq. A one-dimensionality occurred in most European countries that no previous issue had ever approximated. Everybody united in opposition to what America was about to do. While the thrust of this antagonism clearly focused on America's actions, its amazing passion was deeply anchored in what Europeans perceived as America's very core, its identity. To many Europeans, America had become the "un-Europe," a clear "other."

This othering was, of course, not totally new and had many precedents. Even under the aegis of Bill Clinton, whom European intellectuals embraced wholeheartedly as a kindred spirit, Europeans commenced the conscious construction of Europe as America's other. "Europe: The Un-America" proclaimed Michael Elliott in an article published in *Newsweek International* in which he dismissed any semblance of a common transatlantic civilization.[22] Many European intellectuals appropriated Samuel Huntington's controversial notion of the "clash of civilizations" with which they characterized what they perceived as the increasing divergence between Europe and the United States and not—pursuant to Huntington's original—a clash between the predominantly Christian West and the Islamic world. The widely voiced indictment accused America of being retrograde on three levels: moral (being the purveyor of the death penalty and of religious fundamentalism as opposed to Europe's having abolished the death penalty and adhering to an enlightened secularism); social (being the bastion of unbridled "predatory capitalism," to use the words of former German Chancellor Helmut Schmidt, and of punishment, as opposed to Europe's being the home of the considerate welfare state and of rehabilitation); and cultural (America the commodified, Europe the refined; America the prudish and prurient, Europe the savvy and wise).[23] It was well before George W. Bush that French Foreign Minister Hubert Védrine inveighed against the United States as a "hyperpuissance" which needed to be brought down by an "un-American" Europe obviously led by France. To Védrine the clarion call of Europe's rise against the United States centered on the following American ills that all good Europeans had to fight tooth and nail: "ultraliberal market economy, rejection of the state, nonrepublican individualism, unthinking strengthening of the universal and 'indispensable' role of the U.S.A., common law, *anglophonie*, Protestant rather than Catholic concepts."[24] Overt anti-Americanism had become a badge of honor for many European intellectuals in their *Kulturkampf* against the United States.[25]

A *Kulturkampf* by artists and intellectuals is one thing. Mass mobilization of publics is quite another. No mobilization around these European counter-values could have been more emphatic than the huge demonstrations on Saturday, 15 February 2003. Like never before in Europe's history did so many millions of Europeans unite in public on one day for one purpose. From London to Rome, from Paris to Madrid, from Athens to Helsinki, from Barcelona to Berlin, Europeans across most of the political spectrum united in their opposition to the impending American attack on Iraq. And sure enough, a number of European intellectuals proclaimed this day as the one that historians would someday view as the true birthday of a united Europe precisely because like no other day in European history it united Europeans emotionally and not only by fiat of a faceless bureaucracy issued in impenetrable language from Brussels.

The first and most emphatic interpretation of 15 February 2003 as Europe's nascent national holiday was offered by Dominique Strauss-Kahn in a lengthy article in *Le Monde*. Strauss-Kahn could not have been more explicit straight at the outset of his piece: "On Saturday, 15 February 2003, a nation was born on the streets. This nation is the European nation."[26] Every facet of Strauss-Kahn's article makes it unmistakably clear that the only commonality of this nascent nation lies in its opposition to the United States. Lest there be any misunderstanding that this pertains only to policy interpretations, political rivalries or differences in interest, Strauss-Kahn leaves absolutely no doubt that he sees the chasm between Europe and the United States as a matter of values, identity, essence. Unlike politics, the latter are irreconcilable and non-negotiable. On 31 May 2003 Jürgen Habermas entered the fray with a coordinated endeavor unparalleled in its reach and effect. He published an article coauthored with the late Jacques Derrida, often one of Habermas's main intellectual challengers and epistemological rivals, in Germany's newspaper of record, the *Frankfurter Allgemeine Zeitung*, in which these two leading minds invoke the political rebirth and moral superiority of Europe in the wake of America's war against Iraq. On the very same day, the French newspaper *Libération* published the Habermas-Derrida piece in French. But Habermas's Europe-wide journalistic effort did not end there. Also on 31 May 2003, Habermas's close friend, the American philosopher and intellectual Richard Rorty, published an article in agreement with Habermas and Derrida in the *Süddeutsche Zeitung*, the *Frankfurter Allgemeine Zeitung*'s fiercest rival in Germany. The Swiss author Adolf Muschg weighed in on the pages of the prestigious *Neue Zürcher Zeitung*, Gianni Vattimo in Italy's renowned *La Stampa*, the famous Italian author Umberto Ecco in *La Repubblica*, and the Spanish public intellectual Fernando Savater in Spain's leading newspaper *El País*. While the tenor varied among these pieces, all of them emphasized in one form or another that Europe was to use the Iraq War as an irreversible distancing and separation mechanism from the United States and that the time was right and auspicious to commence the construction of something best called a European nation which was to arise in opposition to the United States.[27] As many commentators remarked, only a man of Habermas's stature could have pulled off a Europe-wide publication event of this magnitude and gravity.

Conclusion

At the end of the day the debate about America and the various views of and attitudes towards America held by Europeans have little to do with the "real existing America" itself and everything to do with Europe. It is far from certain in which direction the anti-Americanism analyzed in this work will proceed since it remains equally uncertain where, how, perhaps even if and whether Europe will develop. But one thing remains quite telling: nobody ever spoke of Europe's birth with regard to the fall of the Berlin Wall or the dissolution of the Soviet Union and its communist rule over the eastern half of the continent. And true enough, none of those events attained nearly the popular enthusiasm that 15 February 2003 clearly did. Then, in 1989/90, while Berliners danced in the streets, Londoners and Parisians fretted in their homes. And nobody in Europe's West thronged to any public place in support of the celebrations in Warsaw and Prague. Whether Strauss-Kahn, Habermas and their friends will prove correct in that this day will indeed become Europe's national holiday, only future historians will be able to ascertain for certain. One thing is clear, though: the long tradition of a deep ambivalence towards and a constant preoccupation with America in Europe clearly set the intellectual stage for the powerful symbolic presence of this potentially fateful day. History teaches us that *any* entity—certainly in its developing stages—only attains consciousness and self-awareness by defining itself in opposition to another entity. All nationalisms arose in opposition to others. With the entity of "Europe" now being on the agenda, anti-Americanism may well serve as a useful mobilizing function for the establishment of this new entity and become a potent political force on the mass level way beyond the elites" antipathy and *ressentiment* that has been a staple of European intellectual life since 5 July 1776, if not before.

It is of course clear that George W. Bush and his very conservative policies have driven European anti-Americanism into overdrive. To continue with this metaphor, this article has tried to shed light on the road, the car, and all other structural conditions and prerequisites that have framed this white heat of anti-Americanism that has engulfed much of Western European opinion and sentiment at the elite as well as mass levels during his presidency. That these structures are much deeper is best demonstrated by the fact that recent European animosities towards the United States preceded the Bush presidency and were acute under Bill Clinton, whom many Europeans adored. And should Al Gore have ascended to the presidency in 2000—as arguably he did—European anti-Americanism might possibly have been somewhat muted in its tone though hardly in its intent. To millions of Europeans, Bush epitomizes the ugly American par excellence. Disdaining him has sparked a European consciousness that for the first time has real political valence. Indeed, I have argued elsewhere that Europe's political classes were perfectly content to see Bush defeat John Kerry, since had Kerry proved victorious Europe's elites would have been robbed of their needed bogeyman of choice.[28]

As for contemporary European anti-Semitism, much of its acuteness and acerbity are linked to anti-Americanism, with Israel playing a key intermediate role. The European irritation with Israel cannot be separated from the European irritation and rivalry with the United States. I would go so far as to argue that were American-Israeli relations to deteriorate for some reason, Europe's relations with Israel would improve markedly and thus diminish at least some of the anti-Semitism that has become embedded in the emotional topography of most West European countries. The post-Holocaust philo-Semitism that was hegemonic in Europe's discourse for nearly half a century is rapidly fading. Contested from many angles, not least the rapidly growing political importance of Europe's Muslims, this discourse simply offers no tangible benefits to Europeans. In the strict framework of rational choice theory, being cool to the Jews and critical of Israel has a greater payoff than the obverse.

Notes

[1] Steinmaier, "Wir sind wieder wer" (unpublished manuscript, 2004).

[2] Andrian Kreye, "Zugpferd des Antiamerikanismus: Schlecht recherchiert, ohne Kontext: Warum ist Michael Moore in Europa so erfolgreich?" *Süddeutsche Zeitung*, 11 October 2003, 15.

[3] Hollander, *Anti-Americanism*, 339.

[4] Joffe, "Who's Afraid of Mr. Big?"

[5] Landes, "What Happens When Jesus Doesn't Come," 1–2.

[6] Goldhagen, "Die Globalisierung des Antisemitismus," 93–100.

[7] Cohen, "Auto-Emancipation and Anti-Semitism," 69–77.

[8] Melanie Phillips, "Anti-Semitism Is on the Increase but Its Roots Are Not in the Right but in the Sharon-Hating Left," *Observer*, 22 February 2004.

[9] Lucy Ward, "Oxford Suspends Don Who Rejected Student for Being Israeli," *Guardian*, 28 October 2003.

[10] The Mona Baker Affair was amply discussed in Israel, Britain and the United States. Academics in these countries voiced their opinions in many fora. The two best articles, in my view, on this controversy were Ori Golan, "Boycott by Passport," *Jerusalem Post*, 17 January 2003, and Andy Beckett, "It's Water on Stone—in the End the Stone Wears out," *Guardian*, 12 December 2002.

[11] Antje Kraschinski, "Wenn der Präventivschlag zur Vergeltung wird," *Frankfurter Rundschau*, 2 July 2003.

[12] Behrens, *Raketen gegen Scheinwerfer*; and Duisburger Institut für Sprach- und Sozialforschung, *Die Nahost-Berichterstattung*.

[13] These data hail from a series of Eurobarometer surveys of 2002/2003 which have been summarized in greater detail in my book, *Amerika, dich hasst sich's besser*.

[14] Art, "Debating the Lessons of History."

[15] The list of papers includes: *The Guardian, The Observer, The Times, The Sunday Times, The Independent, The Scotsman, The Daily Mail, The Daily Express, The Daily Telegraph* and *The Sunday Telegraph* in Britain; *Le Monde, Le Figaro, Libération, L'Express* and *L'Equipe* in France; *Die Welt, Die Zeit, Frankfurter Rundschau, Frankfurter Allgemeine Zeitung, Süddeutsche Zeitung, Spiegel, Focus* and *taz* in Germany; and *Corriere della sera, La Stampa, Il Messagero, La Repubblica* and *La Gazetta dello Sport* in Italy.

[16] Markovits, "Reflections on the World Cup "98," 1.

[17] "It's Only a Game," WBUR, Boston, 7 July 2002.

[18] Markovits, "Deutscher Hochmut statt internationaler Solidarität," 186–88.

[19] For a detailed study of "amerikanische Verhältnisse" and its ubiquitously pejorative connotation, see Markovits, *Amerika, dich hasst sich's besser*.

[20] The evidence for this is vast. From the composer Karlheinz Stockhausen's extolling the destruction of the Twin Towers as the greatest imaginable piece of art in the cosmos, to the Nobel Laureate Dario Fo's applauding the loss of 20,000 lives as a mere pittance as compared with the impoverishing of tens of millions of people at the hands of those who died in the attacks (when Fo rejoiced it still seemed that 20,000 had died in the collapse of the Twin Towers); from major public intellectuals like Arundhati Roy and Slavoj Žižek, to the philosopher Jean Baudrillard's welcoming article in which he extolled the the terrorists" deed by stating that they had finally accomplished what all of us had always imagined and secretly wanted, the list goes on and on. Even the famous article by Jean-Marie Colombani in *Le Monde*, 13 September 2001, appropriately called "Nous sommes tous Américains," represents as much an indictment of American policy and hubris as it does a declaration of solidarity. And when the German SPD parliamentary leader Peter Struck declared in a special session of the Bundestag on 12 September 2001 that "today we are all Americans," a vast majority of Germany's left-liberal intelligentsia dismissed such talk as risible at best, but actually nothing more than submissive, obsequious and quite embarrassing. For a detailed summary of all these utterances and a list of the relevant literature, see Markovits, *Amerika, dich hasst sich's besser*, 159–64.

[21] Jochen Bittner, "Umfrage: Blackbox Weisses Haus—Je komplizierter die Weltlage, desto fester glauben die Deutschen an Verschwoerungstheorien," *Die Zeit*, 31 July 2003, 5.

[22] As cited in Joffe, "Who's Afraid of Mr. Big?"

[23] Ibid.

[24] Hubert Védrine in his book *La carte de la France à l'heure de la mondialisation*, as cited in ibid.

[25] Peter Zadek, "Kulturkampf? Ich bin dabei. Mir ist Amerika zutiefst zuwider," *Der Spiegel*, 14 July 2003, 140.

[26] Dominique Strauss-Kahn, "Die Geburt einer Nation," *Frankfurter Rundschau*, 11 March 2003, 7. This is a verbatim German translation of the French original.

[27] Jürgen Habermas and Jacques Derrida, "Unsere Erneuerung. Nach dem Krieg: Die Wiedergeburt Europas," *Frankfurte Allgemeine Zeitung*, 31 May 2003. For the best English-language exposé of all these writings and the debate that they generated, see Levy, Pensky and Torpey, eds., *Old Europe, New Europe, Core Europe*.

[28] Andrei S. Markovits, "Europäische Krokodilstränen," *Handelsblatt*, 4 November 2004.

References

Art, David. "Debating the Lessons of History: The Politics of the Nazi Past in Germany and Austria." Ph.D., diss. Massachusetts Institute of Technology, 2004.

Behrens, Rolf. *Raketen gegen Scheinwerfer: Das Bild Israels im "Spiegel*. Münster: LIT-Verlag, 2003.

Cohen, Mitchell. "Auto-Emancipation and Anti-Semitism: Homage to Bernard Lazare." *Jewish Social Studies* 10, no. 1 (2003): 69–77.

Duisburger Institut für Sozial- und Sprachforschung. *Die Nahost-Berichterstattungzur Zweiten Intifada in deutschen Printmedien unter besonderer Berücksichtigung des Israel-Bildes: Analyse diskursiver Ereignisse im Zeitraum von September 2000 bis August 2001*. Duisburg: Institut für Sozial- und Sprachforschung, 2002.

Goldhagen, Daniel Jonah. "Die Globalisierung des Antisemitismus." In *Neuer Antisemitismus: Eine globale Debatte*, edited by Doron Rabinovici, Ulrich Speck and Natan Sznaider. Frankfurt: Suhrkamp Verlag, 2004.

Hollander, Paul. *Anti-Americanism: Critiques at Home and Abroad, 1965–1990*. New York: Oxford University Press, 1992.

Joffe, Josef. "Who's Afraid of Mr. Big?" *The National Interest*, no. 64 (summer 2001): 43–52.

Landes, Richard. "What Happens When Jesus Doesn't Come: Jewish and Christian Relations in Apocalyptic Time." Unpublished paper. Center for Millennial Studies, Boston University, 2000.

Levy, Daniel, Max, Pensky, and John, Torpey, eds. *Old Europe, New Europe, Core Europe: Transatlantic Relations after the Iraq War*. London: Verso Press, 2005.

Markovits, Andrei S. "Reflections on the World Cup '98." *French Politics and Society* 16, no. 3 (Summer 1998): 1–29.

———. "Deutscher Hochmut statt internationaler Solidarität—ein trauriger Vorfall." *Gewerkschaftliche Monatshefte* 52, no. 3 (March 2001): 186–8.

———. *Amerika, dich hasst sich's besser: Antiamerikanismus und Antisemitismus in Europa*. Hamburg: Konkret-Literatur-Verlag, 2004.

Steinmaier, Georg. "Wir sind wieder wer." Unpublished manuscript, 2004.

From Cowards and Subversives to Aggressors and Questionable Allies: US Army Perceptions of Zionism since World War I

Joseph W. Bendersky

Subversive Jews: Anti-Semitism and Zionism after World War I

"Never Advance without Security." That was supposedly the motto of a "Hebraic outfit" known as the "Jordan Highlanders" recruited in Britain in World War I, whose dismal service in Palestine epitomized the non-military qualities inherent in Jews. It implied physical weakness, dishonor, selfishness and even cowardice. This story circulated among US army officers, including two future chiefs of military intelligence, between the world wars. Officers invoked it for amusement as well as a clinching argumentative example to discount the possibility of a Jewish fighting force.[1] The "Jordan Highlanders" canard did not indicate, however, that Jews were a passive, non-threatening group. Intermixed with the image of weak, unheroic Jews was one of Jews who, lacking the ability or will to fight, pursued or exercised power on their own behalf by means other than open confrontation or overt force. They could allegedly achieve their own goals by hidden influence, international intrigue or domestic subversion. Such notions reflected the pervasive, often extremist variant of anti-Semitism among US army officers in the first half of the twentieth century.[2] They affected not only the army's engagement with the "Jewish Question" at home and abroad generally but also its view of Zionism. The motives prompting the army's concern with Zionism, like the mental framework through which it assessed that movement, remained fairly consistent well into the post–World War II era. While Zionism might be a boon to Jews, it was, in the minds of officers, a serious burden to America. Zionism's very existence and growth reinforced suspicions of American Jews as being more loyal to world Jewry than to their own country. Indeed, a Jewish state would have to be imposed and defended by others even when it was not in their best interest.

The army first expressed an interest in Zionism towards the end of World War I. Initial responses ranged from beliefs that Zionism was a manifestation of various types of international Jewish power and goals to doubts that Jews could succeed in establishing a homeland (or state) in Palestine. During the summer and autumn of 1918, Secret Agent B-1 submitted alarmist reports to Military Intelligence (MID) in Washington regarding international Jewish intrigues to ultimately establish Jewish world domination. B-1 described an intimate web encompassing dangerous Bolsheviks, "Zionist organizations, headed by Justice [Louis] Brandeis, and the German-Jewish financial group headed by Jacob Schiff." Although certain non-career officers dismissed such claims as absolute nonsense, upper echelon officers, among them MID chief Marlborough Churchill, found them useful even though one conceded that B-1 was "somewhat biased in his opinions of Jews." Some of B-1's claims about powerful American Zionists received corroboration from other secret agents, while US military attachés in Europe and British intelligence informed MID that "clever and unscrupulous" international Jews were the motivating and controlling forces of Bolshevism. Convinced that international Jews were fomenting revolution in the West, British intelligence urged an investigation of American Zionism.[3]

MID's simultaneous secret acquisition of *The Protocols of the Elders of Zion* in the autumn of 1918, in the midst of postwar discontentment in Europe and America, heightened the sense of apprehension and suspicion. While initial skepticism existed as to their Jewish origins, most agreed that the plans this document embodied coincided with Bolshevism and recent world events. MID created a separate file (99-75) for the *Protocols* in which was also placed intelligence on Zionism, Palestine and prominent American Jews associated with Zionism.[4] In early 1919, MID made plans for the suppression of an anticipated Bolshevik uprising among Jews in New York. MID's "Ethnic Map of New York" had identified immigrant Jewish neighborhoods as those "most strongly permeated with the Bolshevik movement." In collaboration with the New York Guard, MID had developed "Plans for the Protection of New York in Case of Local Disturbances." Ten thousand troops with a special Machine Gun Battalion were to be deployed in the "congested districts chiefly inhabited by Russian Jews." Six thousand additional rifles had actually been shipped to troops in the city. Although the May revolution never occurred, by mid-1919 MID learned that the British had definite "proof of an international Jewish Bolshevik conspiracy."[5]

By August 1919, the State Department's Division of Russian Affairs, in conjunction with MID, proposed an elaborate Zionist-Bolshevist theory entitled "The Power and Aims of International Jewry." This extraordinary document, expanded the following month as "Judaism and the Present World Movement—A Study," significantly affected MID's approach to Jews for most of the 1920s. Many of its assumptions about Jews would, in fact, endure long thereafter. Among these was the notion that the Jewish-owned and -controlled press in the United States prevented the public from knowing the truth about this Jewish movement. Other aspects reflected the paranoid anti-Semitism of the time. To those constructing this theory, the *Protocols*, even if inauthentic, offered a window into the secret world of Jewish intrigues by exposing the "fundamental principles and ideals" of Zionism, whose ultimate goal was not Palestine but the world. An "abundance" of State Department and MID documents had confirmed that the similarities between the *Protocols*, the writing of Jewish leaders and world events were too close to be mere coincidences. The document compared long quotes from the *Protocols* with ones from Theodore Herzl's "Jewish State," "Congress Addresses" and lectures on "Social Zionism" and with statements of contemporary Jewish leaders such as Rabbi Judah Magnus.[6]

Essentially, according to this document, Jews, while undermining other nationalities, ardently protected their own common national and religious identity. "Once a Jew always a Jew. Neither conversion nor naturalization will change him." Jews everywhere acted in concert in their own interest without loyalty to the countries in which they were born. Intriguing American Zionists (Felix Frankfurter, Brandeis, Louis Marshall) secretly manipulated the Paris Peace negotiations to acquire special privileges for Polish Jews while endangering the survival of the new Polish state. Disloyal American Zionists thereby undermined American efforts to establish Poland as a bulwark against Bolshevik expansion. Indeed, it stated, "Judaism and Socialism are different expressions of the same movement." Jews were the forces of revolution in Germany, Hungary and Russia; Lower East Side Jews posed a similar threat to the USA. Resources for Zionism (in certain cases also Bolshevism) came clandestinely from interlocking, often intermarried, international Jewish financial families: Warburgs-Schiffs-Kuhn, Loeb-Guggenheim. With deceitful and dictatorial means, Jews were "now, with remarkable unity of action, exerting so powerful an influence upon world politics." Left unchecked, this Jewish movement "might approach an actual world control."[7]

Although it is impossible to determine how many army officers accepted the most extreme allegations of a Jewish world conspiracy, officers at home and abroad had clearly provided a good deal of the intelligence data substantiating "The Power and

Aims of International Jewry." And the inferences of that document clearly resonated widely among officers. By supposedly exaggerating pogroms and insisting on minority rights for Jews, Zionists pursued a strategy "inimical to American policy" in Poland. Urging an investigation, one officer asked, "Is a cabal of international Jews using American public opinion as a lever for pro-German, and pro-Bolshevik ends against Poland? ... [and] what Jewish interests in particular are encouraged in doing this?"[8] Throughout the early 1920s, the anti-Semitism of US military attachés across Europe reinforced and elaborated anti-Zionist tendencies within the army. Most attachés were racial anti-Semites who continually based their intelligence collection and analyses on the assumption of inherited problematic Jewish traits. Anti-Semitism, legal restrictions and pogroms were a response to Jewish activities detrimental to their host countries. Wealthy and clever Jews made insidious inroads into economies, while lower-class Jews subverted governments and society from below. Attachés emphasized in particular the "internationality" of Jews and their self-centered interests. The "history of Bolshevism" clearly showed that "the Jew where he comes into power is apt to wield it with his innate arrogance and cynicism." Attempts by countries to protect themselves against detrimental Jewish activities brought down upon them the economic and media power of "International Jewry."[9]

There was equal concern about Zionist intrigues within America. Colonel Charles Mason, a top intelligence officer, felt it was necessary to learn whether there would occur "a change in the present social order in America to one of Bolshevism, or of socialism, or of Jewish Despotism." In response, MID developed a policy in mid-1920 for the close surveillance of dangerous international intrigues, including "International-Jewry." The "International Jew" was described as "a generally brilliant, egotistical radical, sometimes an idealist dreaming of ultimate world domination by the Jews, but more frequently a thorough-going rascal, using his keen wits for purely personal gain." The latter type controlled the Soviet Union. A revised version of this policy later exempted "high-class" conservative Jews and even Zionist Jews from such condemnation. Nonetheless, MID continued to approach Zionism as a dangerous movement associated with Bolshevism.[10]

MID paid particular attention to Brandeis, Frankfurter and Marshall. These prominent American Zionists were worthy of separate files, which, though not very extensive, convey a definite suspicion about their motives and activities. Classified under "Jewish International Movement" and "Zionist Movement," such intelligence highlighted their radicalism, association with foreign forces (especially Bolshevism) and Zionism. Officers worried that Justice Brandeis's Supreme Court decisions would advance Zionist or radical causes, while they deemed Frankfurter to be outright "dangerous." In investigating Frankfurter, MID worked closely with the State and Justice Departments. Two figures in this interdepartmental collaboration were J. Edgar Hoover, then surveilling radicals for the Justice Department, and Colonel Sherman Miles, MID chief in the first years of World War II. When Brandeis, Frankfurter and Marshall attended a Zionist conference in England in 1920, Hoover and Miles had the meeting secretly observed. The requested report on the conference, however, contained a fairly accurate description of the goals and difficulties of establishing a "new Jewish National Home" in Palestine. Nonetheless, the absence of anything subversive had not alleviated suspicion as Hoover and MID remained very interested in Zionism. Top intelligence officers on the general staff continued to inform other government agencies that certain Zionist leaders believed that "Russian Bolshevism is now the chief stronghold of Jewry in the world and that Zionism ought to make use of all the Jewish power embodied in the Soviet Government...."[11]

Neither had MID disregarded *The Protocols of the Elders of Zion*. Key intelligence officers in Washington continued to argue that "recent world developments would seem to bear out these protocols." Some defended Henry Ford's campaign against the "International Jew." Copies of the recently published English translation of the *Protocols* were sent to intelligence officers across the country and Europe to assist them in the "study and observation of the Jewish movement within our country." Colonel William Godson, the highly regarded military attaché in Switzerland, devoted himself zealously to such investigations because he was "thoroughly convinced of the reality of a Jewish movement to dominate the world." Although after the bogus nature of the *Protocols* was exposed MID ceased using them, some officers and attachés remained convinced into the 1930s that, whatever their origin or authenticity, they did reflect Jewish characteristics and motives.[12]

In the eyes of army officers, American Jews clearly revealed their disloyalty to America and solidarity with Jews internationally during the immigration debates of the 1920s. The army played an important role in promoting and justifying the necessity of completely ending Jewish immigration to the USA. Officers considered eastern European Jews to be a herd of racially inferior, disease-ridden, radical types threatening the country with racial degeneration and subversion. By facilitating the influx of Jews in total disregard of "the danger to our country from this scum of Europe," American Jews, Zionist or not, demonstrated their solidarity with Jews internationally at the expense of the welfare of the United States.[13]

Preoccupied with Jewish power and subversion worldwide, the army paid less attention to the true Zionist objective—Palestine. But here, too, it was a case of Jews arrogantly pursuing "Jewish interests before all others," as well as posing the same kinds of problems as elsewhere. Zionists sought establishment of a Jewish national homeland within the British Mandate of Palestine, which, through massive immigration, would ultimately embody three million Jews. These objectives required the dispossession of Arabs, who were already beginning to suffer economically and culturally under Zionist expansion. Commercially superior, supported by outside Jewish economic assistance, and contemptuous of Arab cultural sensibilities, Zionists created an anti-Semitic backlash, where prejudice against Jews had not previously existed. Indeed, the Zionists intended to "overawe Arabs" with force of arms and had already inflicted firearms injuries on them. American Jews financed this one-sided arming and many young Zionists had military training in European armies. Equally alarming, Arabs rightfully suspected that these arms went to Bolsheviks, as European socialists found Palestine a "potentially useful center of activity." With socialism increasingly prevalent in "Jewish minds and Zionist spirit," placid Palestine would eventually lapse into radical upheaval. It would be a crisis aggravated by the fact that the intended agricultural experiment would fail. Lack of sufficient land, together with the natural Jewish tendency towards cities and business, belied the Zionist promise.[14]

By the mid-1920s, officers believed the British had stabilized the situation by reasserting their control. Attempts by Zionists to establish a majority Jewish state under the protection of the Great Powers and drive out the Arabs had failed. So too would efforts by a Jewish minority to acquire economic hegemony and thus "political control." Both were undermined by Arab resistance and the unwillingness of "abler Jews" to return to Palestine. Neither officers nor Arabs objected to religious Zionism and a cultural home where old Jews could live in peace, while Jewish learning and intellectual creativity blossomed; they could even have some governmental representation. "But it is quite another matter for hordes of any race to be sent into a country and maintained there at the expense of their prosperous co-religionists until they are strong enough to get the native's substance and soil from him."[15] While still apprehensive about this Zionist intrusion into the Arab homeland, officers such as Colonel Robert Foy felt the British had finally recognized their "mistake" in acknowledging Zionist claims in Palestine. Foy's inference that the British, however, "do not dare" to reverse their decision presumed some Jewish influence over policy. But at least the British had removed the previous High Commissioner, "a Jew," and eliminated "preferential treatment" for the Jewish element. Foy conceded that Jewish settlements built with money from American and British Jews were "very respectable." The problem was that "the majority of the immigrants are Jews from Poland, Roumania, and Russia, the most repulsive form of humanity."[16]

It was presumed that not only the stability of the region depended upon the British but, as a permanent minority, Zionists would "need ample British military protection for many years." Zionists might exercise armed domination over disorganized local Arabs, but they could never hope to defend themselves against the region's numerically superior Arab populations. Moreover, Jews "are not conspicuously able soldiers."[17] And as the experience of the "Jordan Highlanders" suggested, Jews probably never would or even could be men of true military stature. Despite the service of Jews, often with distinction, in all of America's wars, the notion that one could not make soldiers out of Jews had deep roots in Western culture and US military thinking. Enduring into the second half of the twentieth century, such attitudes clearly colored the perspectives of officers on US policy towards Palestine.

Long-existing prejudices against Jewish military potential received significant theoretical substantiation through the racial literature read by officers in the early twentieth century. Among these were William Ripley's *The Races of Europe* and Major Charles Woodruff's *Expansion of Races* and "The Complexion of Jews." Ripley argued that Jews had evolved into such a degenerate condition that they had an inherited physical as well as mental aversion to exercise or exertion. Narrow chested, with limited lung capacity, they lacked the vitality of Christians. This "unalterable characteristic of this peculiar people" forced them to live by their brains and avoid agriculture, manual labor and, by inference, military life. To Woodruff, natural selection accounted not only for Jewish physical debility but also for behavioral characteristics such as cowardice and selfishness. With few exceptions, Jews could not be expected to share in national defense. In fact, "the Jew as a race will not fight for its existence, but demands that other races shall sacrifice themselves for him and preserve him. He now exists because he has been protected by the soldiers of the world from massacre." The Jew essentially "survives by spilling the blood of his protectors." Woodruff even interjected the sensationalist story of terror-stricken New York Jews fleeing inland at the announcement of war with Spain.[18]

Similar assumptions surfaced in officer attitudes towards Jewish immigrants and Jews in the army in World War I. One could hardly expect "to coax these people to die for a country which they regard only as a refuge against military duty." Even the *Army Manual of Instructions for Medical Advisory Boards* warned that "the foreign born, and especially Jews, are more apt to malinger than the native born." In the training of general staff officers in the 1920s, officers asserted that during the war Jews used political influence, medical exemptions or conscientious objection to escape the draft. Those drafted cleverly kept themselves out of combat. Entire units conscripted from "Semitic" districts were automatically suspect. Throughout the interwar period, officers also made similar claims about Jews in Europe, where, employing similar deceptive methods, "Jews habitually avoid military service." Such sentiments also reinforced the assessment drawn from the overall surveillance of Jews that, owing to their inherent adversity to anything military or their radicalism, they constituted a major source of anti-military political activity in the United States.[19]

Jewish vs. American Interests: Geopolitics and Wartime Security

After years of intense concern, Zionism suddenly disappeared as an issue for the army by the late 1920s. It remained basically ignored until World War II. Political and economic stabilization gradually defused the radical climate of the immediate post–World War I years. Passage of the restrictive immigration law of 1924 alleviated fears of hordes of racially inferior subversive Jews undermining America. A public backlash and ensuing strict legal restrictions on government surveillance, combined with draconian reductions in the size and funding of the military, ended the army's sweeping intelligence campaign. The intelligence and speculations about Zionist conspiracies rotted in the dustbin of history. Yet the underlying assumptions about Jews and their international solidarity vis-à-vis America had not likewise vanished from army thinking.

Instruction at the Army War College ensured the perpetuation of such views among officers into coming decades. The highly selective War College was one of the key institutions that cultivated officers for general staff positions of command and leadership. Part of its official instruction and assigned readings were by prominent racial theorists whose ideas were permeated with eugenics, geopolitical racial demography, Darwinian notions of struggle and biological anti-Semitism. Individual and committee reports by officers explicitly manifested this racial worldview and its corresponding political biology, including the characterization of Jews as a separate, usually problematic, racial group. Inherited peculiar mental traits differentiating Jews from others races explained why they were often economic parasites or Bolsheviks, without national loyalty except to other Jews. Some officers believed that Jewish characteristics could be eliminated through cultural assimilation; others seriously doubted that environmental influences could overcome biological destiny.[20] General William D. Connor, the War College commandant and later superintendent of West Point, belonged to the latter category. A vocal exponent of Darwinian political theory, he was an important mentor of Eisenhower and other top military leaders. After returning from the Middle East in the early 1950s, the retired officer complained that by pressuring the United States to support Israel, Jewish interest groups destroyed America's good relationship with the Arabs. To Connor, the same characteristics that made Jews a "menace" in the ancient world made them a threat in his own day. These were the same perceptions of Jews one also finds in the official and unofficial statements of many officers at home and abroad during the interwar years.[21]

Even assimilationist-minded officers, however, were among the most strident critics of the idea of Jews retaining any ethnic identity. The only assigned reading at the War College even marginally addressing Zionism warned that it would incite widespread anti-Semitism in Europe and America. Its author was a Wilsonian liberal, the Princeton Orientalist Herbert Adams Gibbons, who delivered annual lectures at the War College. One of the few to vigorously counteract the nativism of that institution, he believed that assimilation could transform Jews and others into true Americans. But Zionism would reverse all the progress of emancipation. He derided it as the final attempt "to preserve the Ghetto for those whose religion cannot thrive outside the Ghetto." Jews must have "one allegiance—to the Government of the United States." One officer committee echoed these sentiments in describing Judaism as the only "truly racial church" in America, which impedes the "amalgamation of the race with the native stock." Looking forward to the day when this chosen people would be "gathered in a great nation," Jews regarded gentiles as fit only for exploitation.[22]

It was not until the rise of Nazi Germany that the army again saw the "Jewish Question" as a serious policy issue. Although Zionism never entered the debate, the problem was usually framed in terms of American national interests vs. Jewish international solidarity. To many officers, American Jewish advocacy of increased immigration to solve the refugee crisis indicated the same disregard for the welfare of their country as it did in the 1920s. On behalf of foreign Jews, American Jews exposed the country to racial, economic and subversive dangers. Such long-standing army worries received continual reinforcement. At the War College, instructors and officers alike promoted immigration restrictions, pointing out how unassimilated minorities undermined the stability of nations. Meanwhile, military attachés abroad emphasized that Jewish refugees spread communism or socioeconomic discontentment wherever they migrated.[23]

Officers were equally wary of American Jewish pressure on the Roosevelt administration to counter repressive Nazi anti-Semitism. Jews disrupted important

US-German relations and might ultimately lead the country into a war contrary to its real interests. Some officers attributed this foreign policy blunder to the "Jewish-controlled press" or "Jewish money interests in the United States." Others claimed the alienation of Germany was especially effective "where banking and markets are strongly under Jewish influence, as in Great Britain and the United States." The Roosevelt administration was so sensitive to similar public suspicions it made a concerted effort to ensure that World War II would never be perceived as a war for Jews. The corresponding suspicion among officers and enlisted men with anti-Semitic proclivities was that even in a war against the Nazi oppressors of their fellow Jews, American Jews still evaded the draft and combat duty.[24]

During World War II the army confronted Zionism for the first time as a crucial political and military problem. The intimate, mutually reinforcing interrelationship that anti-Semitism and anti-Zionism had under these circumstances was most evident with an influential clique of high-ranking officers in military intelligence. This group extended from Chief of Staff George C. Marshall's German experts, Colonels Truman Smith and Percy Black, to the chief of MID, General George V. Strong, the most powerful intelligence figure in Washington. United States intelligence officers in the Middle East shared their attitudes. Together they significantly affected American policy on Palestine. As military attachés to Nazi Germany, Smith and Black had earlier favored accommodation with that country. Both spoke of the "power of international Jewry" and believed Jews in America, and earlier Germany, exercised great financial and political power. Smith even considered Houston Stewart Chamberlain's *The Foundations of the Nineteenth Century* authoritative on the "Jewish Question." Into the early 1930s, Strong found Jews a source of amusement in his correspondence; and in the midst of the Holocaust he privately acknowledged, "Arabs and Jews are of importance only in so far as security is concerned...."[25]

The powerful argument of national security in wartime could be invoked to override all other considerations, including that of Palestine as a potential refuge for those escaping extermination. With national survival and the lives of American soldiers at stake, Zionism could be made to appear more detrimental to America than ever before. Army policy on Palestine and subsequently that of Roosevelt began with decisions on North Africa in 1942 to maintain stability in the region by not disturbing the Arab population even if this meant the continuation of local anti-Semitic restrictions and closing the area to Jewish refugees. Eisenhower and the general staff posed the predicament in terms of granting "the comparatively few Jewish Semites a preferred status over the vastly more numerous Semites of Islam" and giving the impression that America was turning the area "over to the Jews." To the army, conceding to misguided public pressure to assist Jews would lead to Arab revolts, seriously endangering the military situation.[26]

It was also these "highly organized militant minorities" in the United States that Strong thought in 1943 seriously jeopardized not only the military situation in the Middle East but the entire prosecution of the war. To him, even Jewish rallies at Madison Square Garden urging Palestine as a refuge undercut "this war for national existence" and must be prevented by the government. Otherwise such political pressure would set the region aflame. It would endanger the North African campaign, supply lines to Russia, oil resources and naval operations. Strong received persistent support from intelligence officers in the Middle East. Relying heavily upon Arab elites and the British for their information, these officers were not only hostile to Zionists but quite mistrustful of Jews generally. To them, Herzl was a "crackpot" and Jewish expulsions humorous material. More important, they believed that to win votes Roosevelt backed the Zionist cause under "immense pressure" from influential Jews with significant financial and media power. The Middle East was destabilized as heavily armed Jews with great resources confronted disorganized and ill-armed Arabs without any United States lobby.[27]

These officers depicted Zionism as a psychological obsession, tinted with a "persecution complex" and mystic martyrdom, which fomented fanaticism and violence. Those who stood in the way of this "peculiar people" were regarded as the equivalent of its ancient oppressors. The objective of Zionism was not merely temporary refuge for European Jews but massive postwar immigration and the creation of a Jewish state. Given its own "totalitarian tendency" (extreme nationalism, youth groups, paramilitary units, and so on), Zionism was inherently contrary to the very democratic principles of the Allies. Jewish American soldiers in the region were suspected of working with the Jewish Agency to further the Zionist cause. To aid European Jews, Zionists collaborated even with the Nazis. Proof supposedly existed of Zionists "selling out allied contacts, agencies, and operations."[28]

Until the end of the war, Strong and his successor General Clayton Bissell used alarmist intelligence from the region to create a sense of a "powder mine" about to explode, as the "Jews want to drive the Arabs out and take possession." Arabs merely reacted to Jewish provocations but otherwise remained "satisfactorily passive." There was no validity to Jewish claims of either persecution or the need for arms to defend themselves against Arabs or the British. The situation was aggravated by unofficial endorsements by American politicians and government officials of Zionist aspirations, leading the Arabs to conclude that the United States' policy was "determined by a circle of Jewish advisors in the White House." Thus, the army wanted not only to postpone all discussions of Palestine until after the war, but furthermore to have the government declare it did not favor Zionist aims. Though unsuccessful in these efforts, the Army and State Departments convinced Roosevelt to prevent the reintroduction of the Wagner-Taft resolution supporting immigration to Palestine and creation of a Jewish commonwealth.[29]

At the time, such geopolitical and wartime security arguments appeared compelling when presented in such stark, pessimistic and inevitable terms. In retrospect, they certainly complicated efforts to discern the role of anti-Semitism vis-à-vis that of an anti-Zionism emerging from legitimate national security considerations. However, given the deeply embedded anti-Semitism in army culture it is difficult to imagine that such prejudice had little impact or that the confrontation with Zionism in a crucial theater of war did not confirm and enhance sentiments against Jews generally and suspicions of American Jews in particular. The very language used by officers often emitted anti-Jewish prejudice. For example, rumors spread among officers that wounded soldiers would be neglected because "all bed spaces in the American hospitals in North Africa would be turned over to Jewish refugees from Europe on their way to Palestine." The situation was also never as dire as the army insisted. Intelligence officers in the Middle East "agreed the Jew is too smart to risk any action before the end of the war."[30] Indeed, army considerations extended beyond the wartime necessity into the postwar era.

While some officers denied that Jews had any right to immigrate or to territory, Strong and others thought in geopolitical, economic and ideological terms as well. Zionism, even after a total Allied military victory in Europe, remained antithetical to American interests. From the beginning, alarmist policy papers consistently emphasized that Zionism threatened the survival of the British Empire, American access to oil and containment of communism in the long run. Zionism would drive the Arabs into the Soviet camp, while the influx of Jewish Communists would simultaneously facilitate Soviet penetration of the Middle East. The continuity in army thinking about Jews and communist subversion itself implied anti-Semitism. And concern with Zionism led army intelligence once again to investigate and analyze "Jewish political power" in the United States. MID concluded that Jews, though currently not fully unified, could influence a presidential election, and some of their leaders in law and politics could "wield political power." Zionist "lobbying" might eventually manipulate most Jews and the misguided American public into supporting their aims. Long-term American national security dictated that the army must counterbalance sensationalist Zionist propaganda with fact.[31]

Oil and Anti-Communism: The Birth and Burden of Israel

Zionism reinvigorated and then sustained anti-Semitism among certain segments of the army at the very time that such prejudice had reached a turning point in the gradual, though momentous, decline of such sentiments within that institution. Within the army and American society, World War II produced significant changes in attitudes towards Jews. The multi-ethnic, multi-million-man armed forces had destroyed the homogeneity of the old officer corps. Despite claims to the contrary, Jews had proven themselves in battle. At all levels of the military there had been greater social interaction between Jews and non-Jews than ever before; more Jews had military careers. With racial theories discredited by the Holocaust and Nazism, racial anti-Semitism disappeared from the mental framework of future generations of officers. The growing number of military men who accepted Jews as true Americans were less tolerant of prejudices their predecessors had flaunted. But anti-Semitism had not disappeared, especially among top officers in crucial decision-making positions regarding the Middle East. In addition, the reciprocal interaction of anti-Semitism and anti-Zionism can still be detected among other officers as well.

The period between the end of World War II and the early years of the State of Israel were ones in which the old attitudes, though no longer universal, prevailed in army policy positions. Military intelligence was hostile to Jews and Zionists, as were also the leaders in Plans and Operations (P&O). P&O Chief General Albert C. Wedemeyer was an extreme anti-Semite who believed that international Jewish power was manipulating Washington and blamed the Zionists and Roosevelt's Jewish advisers for getting the USA into World War II.[32] As in past decades, officer perspectives were often contradictory. Zionism supposedly reflected international Jewish solidarity and power; yet Zionists appeared as fanatics willing even to sacrifice Jews to achieve their ends. The Zionist experiment would fail because most Jews were not agriculturalists and many Jewish displaced persons retained their national identities and wanted to return to Europe.[33]

The army dismissed the very idea that a Jewish state might emerge as a democratic and militarily reliable ally. Zionists were not democratic, and Jews in America deceived the public about the true plight of Jews and their objectives. Militarily, Jews had not performed well in the recent war and their potential in the next was doubtful. The infiltration of Jewish Communists into Palestine continued, and the possibility that Israel would turn to the Soviet Union for military assistance remained strong. Although Zionists had created the crisis by their terrorism against the British and Arabs, their victory over poorly armed Arabs would be temporary. An outside force would be necessary "to prevent large scale massacres of Jews." On the eve of the 1948 war, the army predicted that the Arabs could eventually destroy Jewish resistance in two years.[34] Thus, the top secret reports from MID and P&O between 1946 and 1949 strenuously opposed partition plans, the establishment of Israel and aid to the new state. All were contrary to United States oil interests and containment of communism. Among the most ardent advocates of this army position was Secretary of State George C. Marshall, who aligned himself with his old generals in the internal struggles of the Truman administration over Palestine.[35]

As in the previous war, the army revived the old question of Jewish loyalty. Exploiting America's natural humanitarian impulses, "two non-Americanisms," Zionism and Jewish Nationalism' had deceived the American public into supporting a cause detrimental to the country's security. "United States Jewry" had with its money and political agitation created an unnecessary crisis in Palestine. It could result in another world war with the Soviet Union. Thus concerned with Jewish Americans, the army, often in cooperation with the FBI, conducted surveillance of Jewish activities dealing with Palestine or Zionism. They had particular interest in collections of money for Jewish relief or Palestine and attempts to recruit American veterans to train a Jewish army in Palestine.[36]

Such views, however, were no longer universally shared within the military, and the top echelons had access to far less prejudicial intelligence than that contained in their own policy papers. But residues of earlier notions about Jews persisted even in some of these alternative perspectives. A study on the relationship between communism and Jews commissioned in 1946 by the deputy director of intelligence concluded no such link could be proven.[37] That such a study had to be requested is telling; and the pursuit of Jewish Communists continued into the next decade. In that same year, the Pentagon also had at its disposal an incisive, reliable guide on Palestine produced by Royal Air Force intelligence for its own officers in the region. It was a judicious, balanced analysis of both Arab and Jewish positions without any of the suspicions or invectives about Jews that characterized some American intelligence. The RAF study examined forthrightly the salient issues of the ethnic conflict (including Jewish terrorists) without the predictions of dire geopolitical consequences or communist subversion. It referred not to international Jewish power but to "traditions of national solidarity and self-help." This solidarity, combined with realism and industriousness, was transforming an immigrant polyglot into a homogeneous unified whole.[38] Similarly, in late 1948, the American military attaché to the new State of Israel offered perhaps the most pro-Israeli military perspective to date.

In the "National Aims of the Israeli People," Colonel R. W. Van de Velde's vision of the current and future prospects for Israel contrasted starkly with that which the general staff presented to the government. Jews legitimately sought a national home for all Jews of the world. This required continual immigration, self-sufficiency and trade within a kind of mixed socialist-capitalist economy. Israelis sought peace and friendly relations with their neighbors. As westerners, they shared strong democratic principles with Americans and British; many had family relations in the USA. Educated Israelis favored the West over the East, but the government had to project neutrality in order to facilitate immigration of Jews out of Russia. Van de Velde conceded that the lower classes from eastern Europe tended more towards the USSR but argued that this problem could be readily rectified if the USA abandoned its vacillation and took a strong stand in favor of Israel at the United Nations and lifted the arms embargo. It was a question of which Great Power won them over first. While the Israelis sought modified defensible borders, they were not expansionists. It was not Israeli conquest that the Arab governments feared but the "presence of a democratic, progressive state" in their midst that would undermine their own autocratic power. Although the Israelis drove out those Arabs who fought against them, those who did not resist were well treated.[39]

Van de Velde recommended that the USA ignore the current facts overwhelmingly favoring a pro-Arab policy. A politically immature country along a narrow coast, without oil or a canal, Israel nonetheless was a democratic state in a strategic location. If permitted to develop in peace, it could become "the guiding power of the Middle East more rapidly than Turkey." Whereas other military intelligence often noted various inherent problems of Jews, Van de Velde saw their "advanced civilization and education" as the salvation of the region. In the long run, they could uplift the ignorant masses of the region and replace the traditional governing classes with democracy.[40]

Other attachés and officers in Washington insisted, however, that "there was no military advantage in American support for Israel." It was equally illogical to contain communism in Turkey, Greece and Iran, while allowing its penetration through Israel, whose military power was based upon Soviet support. Earlier pessimistic estimates of Israel's military ability to withstand an Arab onslaught in coming years gave way to concerns over that country's superiority over its neighbors. Marshall himself spoke of the "evident aggressive tendencies of the Israeli government" to exploit its "military advantages, real and anticipated." While no match for any serious power, Jews were apparently now quite willing to fight their local enemies, and capable of doing so. Israel had proven itself "unusually strong" defensively compared to "its actual size and power" due to its "intense nationalistic spirit" and realization that it "must fight to the end or be annihilated." Its air force, in fact, had the potential of becoming the "best and strongest" in the Middle East. But its rhetoric of self-defense was misleading. Israel sought only temporary peace with the Arabs. When its economy and armed forces developed, the enormous number of immigrants might force the country to expand for "more living space" and secure borders. The American public had been misled into thinking that Israel was the "underdog," as it had been deceived when it supported Japan in its war with Russia in 1904. America might now also learn that Israel was a "militaristic and aggressive state." The Israeli government had, in fact, a de facto policy of making "life unlivable for Arabs" in Israel. After driving the Arabs out, the Israelis ensured they did not return by destroying their property, vineyards and flocks and confiscating their possessions. Jewish immigrants replaced them.[41] In the minds of some officers, the image of the cowardly, anti-military Jew had, almost without comment, been swiftly supplanted by that of the Jew as oppressor and potential aggressor.

Nevertheless, the army felt itself on the defensive within the domestic political climate and the friendly stance of the Truman administration towards Israel. Despite recent revelations of Truman's own exasperation over Zionist pressure, he remained less persuaded by the pessimistic geopolitical and security rationalizations that had swayed Roosevelt. If top officers had worried about Jewish influence in the Roosevelt White House, they surely shared Marshall's opinion that, in recognizing Israel, Truman had compromised national security to "win a few votes." Marshall subsequently championed the Bernadotte Plan to alter the borders of Israel established in the 1948 war by making Israel part of a dual state joined with Jordan in which Jerusalem would be controlled by the latter and immigration restricted. Truman's stern intervention silenced Marshall's public support for Bernadotte, but no doubt hardened army sentiments against both Jews and Zionism. Unable to reverse the political decisions in favor of Israel, the army now defined its strategic interests as ensuring that Israel oriented itself towards the West rather than the Soviet Union. But this should not be achieved by alienating the Arabs. Thus, for the next several decades, the army consistently urged dealing with Israel and Arab states on an "impartial basis."[42]

The army's balanced approach included an arms embargo, which it succeeded in imposing on Israelis and Arabs during the Truman administration. The army offered "decided opposition" to Israeli efforts to acquire arms and access to military training. Officers complained about being "blackmailed" into concessions by Israeli manipulation of the press and politics. Neither could the Israelis be trusted in security or intelligence matters. For the next several decades, arms sales and the US-Israeli military relationship were barometers of the status of relations between the two countries.[43] Eisenhower's 1952 presidential election strengthened the army's stance against pressure from Israel and its Zionist allies in the USA. With one of its own in power, army views on Zionism would never again be as parallel as they were now to those of the administration.

No "Special Relationship": Eisenhower through the Cold War

Starting with the Eisenhower administration, however, it becomes quite difficult to discern the relative weight of anti-Semitism in motivating or affecting anti-Zionist postures of the military. Most of the easily identifiable anti-Semitic top officers had retired by the end of the Korean War. Wary of Jews and liberals in the government since the Roosevelt administration, and now of the increased number of Jews with military careers, biased officers had become cautious in revealing their positions to anyone except confidants who shared their attitudes. There were in the ranks significantly fewer anti-Semites than ever before; for some, anti-Semitism had been reduced to vague social or religious prejudice without political implications. It is not surprising, therefore, that so many Jewish American officers serving in coming decades attested that they never experienced any anti-Semitism. Lack of evidence impedes an accurate view of this increasingly complex and often hidden picture of army attitudes. The kind of documentation that has recently changed our perspectives on the army by disclosing its deeply entrenched and extremist anti-Semitism of earlier decades is not accessible for examination to determine the persistence or decline of such prejudice. Army records since the mid-1950s remain closed; a substantial number of those from even the postwar years have been kept classified by the CIA. Also unavailable are the kind of private correspondence and diaries that had likewise proven so illuminating in discovering earlier actual army attitudes as opposed to official public expressions. Neither does the army publish official records similar to the State Department's *Foreign Relations of the United States*. Most studies of US-Israeli relations also focus on the State Department, various administrations or arms sales. We know very little, if anything, about the significant real internal workings and attitudes within the military in the second half of the twentieth century.

The evidence that has come to light does suggest, nonetheless, that there might be more to the Eisenhower administration's antagonistic stance towards Israel than was previously thought. Not only had Eisenhower's career coincided with the years in which the anti-Semitic culture of the army flourished, but he had been mentored by one of the most vehement and conspiratorially minded anti-Semites within that institution—General George Van Horn Moseley. Eisenhower greatly respected Moseley—"his most intimate friend"—whom he hoped would become chief of staff in 1934. Even after Moseley's fanatical 1940s anti-Semitic political crusade, Eisenhower still considered him a misunderstood "patriotic American" who got "bad press." While Eisenhower never engaged in anti-Semitic banter, he did speak in those years of the need to free America from the "pernicious influence of noisy and selfish minorities." He displayed no concern for the plight of Holocaust survivors and defended the army's treatment of them until ordered by Truman to improve their conditions. As chief of staff, Eisenhower also defended UNRR (United Nations Relief and Rehabilitation Administration) Director Sir Frederick Morgan who had claimed that Jews had contrived stories about pogroms in postwar Poland and that refugees were healthy "with plenty of money." A fine officer, Eisenhower asserted, should not be removed merely because "he said something about the "Jewish migration" that doesn't sit well at all with the leaders of the Zionist movement." Into his presidential years, Eisenhower relied considerably upon the advice of his close friend General Alfred M. Gruenther, who had referred to a fellow officer as "a prosperous, fat, greasy, Kike." While on the Joint Chiefs of Staff (JCS), Gruenther provided the Truman administration with catastrophic predictions of what would happen if Palestine were partitioned. In the midst of these army battles with Truman, General Wedemeyer, a leading anti-Semite, had also provided Eisenhower with literature to "quickly clarify" his thinking on Judaism and Zionism.[44] And Eisenhower turned to Gruenther again during the Suez crisis. Eisenhower's secretary of state, John Foster Dulles, and others criticized the previous administration for succumbing to Zionist influence. Suspicious of such pro-Israel activity, the Eisenhower administration harassed various Zionist organizations in the United States. During a discussion of arms for Israel in 1956, Eisenhower, in reference to Zionist pressure, expressed his refusal to be influenced by "political considerations" as his predecessor had supposedly been. He also posed one of the pivotal questions affecting the interaction of anti-Semitism and anti-Zionism in the minds of officers when he stated: "We thought the American Jew was probably an American before he was a Jew."[45] Historians disagree, however, as to whether the Eisenhower administration was the low point in relations between Israel and the United States or whether the second Eisenhower term represented the beginnings of a convergence between the two countries that came to fruition in the Kennedy administration.[46]

Published documentation also indicates that while subsequent administrations gradually shifted closer to Israel, the military held steadfast to its existing perceptions of Israel and American Zionists as a burden rather than an advantage. The "special relationship" concept introduced by Kennedy eventually evolved into an understanding of the two countries as Cold War allies by the late Johnson years. Though motives are difficult to establish, there remained striking continuity not only in army resistance to both concepts but also in its rejection of the fundamental justifications for these relationships. The military generally worked to contain as much as possible these developing ties. Whether regarding arms sales, economic assistance or military cooperation, the military, with few concessions, consistently held that "there appears no valid military reason to accede... to Israel's request for military assistance ... or economic aid in lieu thereof." The military usually considered Washington's support for such assistance as politically driven rather than emanating from national security needs; to the army, such requests always complicated and often compromised the latter.[47]

Twenty years after the struggles by General Strong and Wedemeyer for an anti-Zionist Middle Eastern policy in the 1940s, published Pentagon and JCS policy papers, though completely lacking anti-Jewish invectives, made almost identical arguments. American security interests still involved strategic access to and stability in the region, communist containment and oil. These objectives were imperiled by American public sympathy for Israel that led Washington to abandon the necessary balanced approach to Israel and Arab states in favor of the former. "If the United States concedes to Israeli pressures, the Arab states would probably turn increasingly to the Soviet Union for support." The military remained equally concerned about Israeli aggression and territorial aggrandizement, as well as about the plight of Arab refugees. Security guarantees to Israel, joint contingency planning and new arms policies had to be rejected, even if "overriding political reasons" required some accommodation with the Israelis. Just months before the outbreak of the 1967 war, the JCS reiterated that such a shift "would be contrary to US interests in the Middle East." Additional military aid was not justified by external threats, its economic condition or even the need to ensure "Israel's pro-Western orientation."[48]

Nevertheless, the quick, decisive victory in the Six Day War demonstrated the importance of Israel's place in the Western camp and its real potential as a military ally. It had defeated Soviet surrogates, showed Western arms superiority and exposed the limits of Soviet intervention on behalf of Arab states. With few exceptions, most presidential administrations henceforth regarded Israel as a de facto strategic ally in the Cold War. The military, however, though definitely pleased with the strategic blow to the Soviet Union in 1967, felt its position vindicated as well. The outcome confirmed the military's insistence that Israel held arms superiority.[49] Moreover, the aftermath of the next Middle East war in 1973 revealed that for some crucial decision makers at the very top of the military hierarchy, geopolitical assessments of the US-Israeli relationship also rested upon deeply embedded anti-Semitic presumptions. The source of this revelation was the very American general credited with the quick, efficient resupply of Israeli forces during the Yom Kippur War.

After a lecture at Duke University Law School in October 1974, General George S. Brown, chairman of the JCS, complained that the strength of the Jewish lobby was a serious detriment to the national welfare of America. He resented the fact that Israelis—"somebody from another country"—bragged that they could manipulate Congress to get their desired arms and policies. They were "so strong, you wouldn't believe it." Most illuminating, however, were the factors to which he attributed this power. Making no distinction between Israelis and American Jews, he bluntly asserted that "they own, you know, the banks in this country, the newspapers, you just look at where the Jewish money is in this country." Brown called upon Americans "to get tough-minded enough to set down the Jewish influence in this country and break it." The general subsequently apologized and survived the minor uproar he had incited, retaining the JCS leadership. Two years later, the supposedly re-educated general rekindled the entire controversy. Before the Armed Services Committee, Brown again asserted that American Jews had "an undue influence" on Congress. In an interview released a few months later, he stated that Israel was not "an asset to the United States today" and from a military standpoint was, in fact, "a burden." Again, he survived the uproar.[50]

In both incidents, Brown had articulated not only suspicions of Jews identical to those held by earlier generations of officers but the essence of the political anti-Semitism that had characterized the Western world since the nineteenth century. It was a mentality of a "Jew is a Jew"—whether American or Israeli. Their loyalty was to each other; they acted in concert as a group with international identity and interests contrary to those of the United States. Through their hidden control of finance and media, they had the power to manipulate governments. America was being sacrificed for Israel. Yet after some initial chastisement of Brown for ignorance or ethnic slurs, public discussion quickly shifted to arms sales to Israel. The deeper implications of his remarks both for the military as an institution and for policy decisions never received the attention they warranted. These were overshadowed by leaks from the defense establishment defending the core of his arguments. All, of course, dismissed his epithets against Jews as nonsense and proclaimed their "admiration for Israeli valor." But he was articulating a serious complaint from most top military commanders that the United States' military support for Israel was draining American resources to a level endangering defense needs in more important areas of the globe at a time of greatly reduced military budgets. The Israeli lobby and its congressional allies had created this critical imbalance and diverted attention from the real enemy—the Soviet Union. The debate over the Middle East was further skewed by the one-sided domination of the Israeli lobby to the virtual exclusion of the Arabs. It was clear to the American Jewish Committee that Brown had "brought out into the open what previously was whispered in Washington—Pentagon fears that the quantity of military equipment sent to Israel has left America dangerously weak and depleted." That Brown's JCS predecessor, Admiral Thomas H. Moorer, had expressed similar complaints about America's commitment to Israel also points to widespread discontentment.[51]

Into the 1980s, when the Cold War ally argument was strongest, the military resisted increased arms and other concessions supposedly justified by this new geopolitical alignment. In fact, the military was quite "dismissive" of Israel's "positive value as an ally." The official JCS position remained that an American war in the Middle East was contrary to its national interests, would be precipitated only by the Arab-Israeli conflict, and in such combat Israeli military power would be negligible.[52] Nevertheless, the Cold War argument became mute with the fall of the Soviet Union.[53] With its disappearance also vanished any residue of the communist-Jewish link and concerns that Zionism was driving the Arabs into the Soviet camp. They were buried alongside discredited racial interpretations of Jews of earlier generations. Indeed, it was not, as the army had long feared, Israel that brought the United States into a Middle East war.

Had Cold War military assessments resulted from detached geopolitical and military analyses and calculations? Was General Brown (West Point class of 1937 and son of an army general) the last of a dying breed succeeded by officers without such biases? Clearly by this point in history the army was much different in makeup and attitudes from its predecessors of the 1940s. The completely revamped army of the 1980s that would fight the two Iraqi wars was more culturally diverse, tolerant, better educated and more professional than at any other time. Moreover, even while contesting Zionist pressure on Congress and the White House, the army always emphasized the need to maintain the security of Israel in conjunction with equally good relationships with the Arab states. Military men entirely free of anti-Semitism could quite reasonably argue against a "special relationship" as well as honestly doubt the benefits of any alliance. One could be an anti-Zionist without being an anti-Semite. Military men could sincerely believe that their attempt to restrain Israel enhanced the security of that country as well as that of the United States. In the absence of evidence to the contrary, can one assume that anti-Semitism among officers continued to decline to the point of insignificance towards the end of the twentieth century? Or had the struggle over American relations with Israel rekindled an anti-Semitism within the military that still affects its geopolitical views? All surface indications are that the military has a more positive view of Israel than ever before. Beyond that, any judgment on such questions must await the disclosure of relevant evidence.

Notes

[1] "Army Composed of Russian Jews," 19 February 1923, RG 165, MID 245-135 (1-8); Strong–Gibson Correspondence, Hugh Gibson Papers, Hoover Institution Archives, Stanford, CA, box 61.

[2] For a thorough examination of the army's engagement with the "Jewish Question," see Bendersky, The "Jewish Threat."

[3] RG 165, MID 10110-920; "Perils of Bolshevism," MID 2070-1073; 10058-309 (1).

[4] "Protocols of the Meeting of the Zionist Men of Wisdom," RG 165, MID 99-75; 245-18.

[5] RG 165, MID 10110-920; Office of the Counselor, RG 59, entry 538, 861.0-628.

[6] RG 165, MID 245-1, 15.

[7] ibid.

[8] "Suspected Jewish Propaganda against Poland," 1919, Weekly Intelligence Summary, in Challener, ed., United States Military Intelligence, 9: 1724-5.

[9] "Poland, Jewish Problem," RG 165, MID 10059-153 (3), 10059-90; "Jewism," 245-98; 245-40; 2656-GG-13/14; "The Jewish Question," 245-100; Bendersky, The "Jewish Threat", 92–120.

[10] "International Movements or "Isms"," RG 165, MID 10058-586 (1); 10110-2048 (1); 255-54 (1).

[11] "Justice Brandeis and the "Jewish International Movement"," "Zionist Movement," RG 165, MID 245 (18, 26, 87); 10110-1727; 10110-1194; 10110-4283; RG 59, entry 538, 000-1612, 800.11-97.

[12] RG 165, MID 99-75 (22, 41, 45); 245-48 (41); 10110-KK-8 (7-8); "Jewish Influences in Soviet Russia," 28 March 1931, MID 2657-D-999 (1).

[13] "Emigration of Undesirables to the United States," 7 February 1921, RG 165, MID 10058-972; "Jewism in Roumania," 21 February 1921, MID 245-8 (6); 245- 71 (2-6, 13); "Notes on Foreigners in the United States," 11 February 1921, MID 239-64.

[14] "Palestine," 3 July 1920, in Challener, ed., United States Military Intelligence, 14:4055–58; "Zionists Will Not Dominate," 12 August 1920, 5243; "Immigration into Palestine," "American

Jews and Palestine," "Smuggling of Arms into Palestine," "Vladimir Jabotinsky," "Socialism in Palestine," "Political Situation in Palestine," and MID marked copy of *Palestine: Disturbances in May, 1921; Report of the Commission of Inquiry*, 50–58, RG 165, MID 245-24, 92, 112, 114, 116, 123, 125.

[15] "Protests against British Administration in Palestine," 21 March–3 April 1925, in Challener, ed., *United States Military Intelligence*, 24:10591–6.

[16] "Special Report: Palestine," 10 December 1925, RG 165, MID 2568-83.

[17] "Palestine," in Challener, ed., *United States Military Intelligence*, 14:4057–58.

[18] Ripley, *Races of Europe*, 372–73; Woodruff, *Expansion of Races*, 379–87, and "Complexion of Jews," 327–33.

[19] "Aliens," Benjamin M. Bailey Papers, Atlantic Historical Society, Atlanta, GA, box 3; "Discrimination in Armed Forces;" American Jewish Committee Archives, New York (hereafter AJCA), General Correspondence, 1906–1932; RG 165, MID 2657-DD-475; 2657-DD-490 (2); 10314-556 (304); 10560-152 (88); 10560-328 (162); Smith, *Berlin Alert*, 11.

[20] Bendersky, "Biological Anti-Semitism," 331–53.

[21] Connor–Moseley Correspondence, April 1953, October 1954, George Van Horn Moseley Papers, Library of Congress, Washington, DC, vols. 19–20; RG 165, MID 245-71 (13); "Jews," 245-74 (1-4); "The Jew, the Left, and the Russian. Their Relative Roles in Soviet Russia," 2656-D-17; "Jewish Influences in Soviet Russia," 2657-D-999.

[22] Gibbons, *Reconstruction of Poland*, 52–53, 212–18, and *New Map of Asia*, 192–228; "Estimate of the United States," pt. 3, 5, Army War College Archives, US Military History Institute, Carlisle, Pennsylvania (hereafter AWCA), 57-31; "United States Political Situation," 35, AWCA 225-16; "Anti-War Societies," 6-7, AWCA 287-8; "United States Political Situation," 33-34; AWCA 225-16.

[23] Fairchild, "Population," Lecture, 29 October 1936, 1–14, Frank J. McSherry Papers, AWCA, box Army War College; "Internal Stability of Nations," 8, 19, 25, AWCA 17-A; "Internal Stability of Nations," 6, 11–12, 15, AWCA 6-1936-8; "Jewish Question" and "Anti-Jewish Legislation," RG 165, MID 2493-84 (4-6); "France: Jews," 2015-1049 (56).

[24] "Estimate of European Situation," 25, AWCA 2-1935-10; "Report of War Plans Group No. 4," 172-4, AWCA 5-1935-20; "Survey of Germany," 11, AWCA 2-1939-2; Commentary on Nazi Party Program, 3-4, AWCA 2-1935-6; RG 319, Project Decimal, MID 000.24, box 6; 091.412, box 25.

[25] Bendersky, *The "Jewish Threat"*, 301–8; Strong to Marshall, 5 August 1943, RG 319, Project Decimal, MID 092. Palestine.

[26] Handy to undersecretary of war, 13 December 1942, Robert P. Patterson Papers, Library of Congress, Washington, DC, box 154; Breitman and Kraut, *American Refugee Policy*, 170.

[27] "Jewish-Arab Situation in the Middle East," RG 319, Project Decimal, MID 092.Middle East, 3-4-43; "Jewish Political Aspirations in Palestine," 6 November 1943, RG 226, OSS, entry 120, box 31; "Current Events," 6 May 1942, RG 319, Project Decimal, MID 350.05 Palestine; Autobiography No. 5, 10–18, Autobiographies of Jewish American Soldiers in World War II, YIVO Institute for Jewish Research, New York.

[28] "Palestine-Jewish Psychology and Attitudes," 30 April 1944; "Palestine-Zionist Problem Today," 3 October 1943, RG 319, Project Decimal, MID 092.Middle East, box 885; "General Security" 1 September 1943, box 31; "Jewish Agency," 7 August 1944, RG 226, OSS, entry 190, box 172.

[29] Strong to Marshall, 5 August 1943, RG 319, Project Decimal, MID 092.Palestine; Stimson Diaries (microfilm), 14 February 1944, Henry L. Stimson Papers, Library of Congress, Washington, DC; Stimson to Connelly, 7 February 1944, George C. Marshall Papers, George C. Marshall Foundation, Lexington, VA, box 78, folder 15; McCloy Diaries, 11 December 1944, John J. McCloy Papers, Amherst College Library Archives, Amherst, MA.

[30] McLean Diaries, 25 March 1943, Henry C. McLean Papers, New York Historical Society, New York; "Palestine-Political," 8 December 1943, RG 319, Project Decimal, MID 092. Middle East, box 885.

[31] "British-Russian-American Interests in the Middle East," "Soviet Interests in the Middle East," 24 July 1944, RG 165, Project Decimal, entry 182, box 805; "Summary Report on Palestine," 14 September 1944, RG 226, OSS, entry 120, box 32; "The American Jewish Conference," RG 319, Project Decimal, MID 291.2. Jews; "Palestine-Zionist Propaganda Methods," "Palestine-Political," "Palestine-Jewish Claims," MID 092.Middle East, box 885.

[32] Wedemeyer to Smith, 19 April 1948, Albert C. Wedemeyer Papers, Hoover Institution Archives, Stanford, CA (hereafter Wedemeyer Papers), box 101; Wedemeyer, "Fragments: Notes on W.W.II," 14–15, ibid., box 6.

[33] RG 319, Document File, entry 85, 3161.0503; entry 85A, 21465, 30400, 176618; entry 47, 091.3 Israel, 350.05 Palestine.

[34] RG 319, P&O, entry 153, 091.Palestine (23 Jun 47) and (13 Jul 48); entry 47, 3906, 72591, 71497.

[35] "Study on Palestine Situation," 8 December 1947, RG 319, P&O, entry 154, 091.Palestine TS, box 24; Pogue, *George C. Marshall*, 4:345–58.

[36] "Estimate of the Palestine Situation in 1948," RG 319, P&O, entry 154, 091.Palestine TS, box 24; RG 319, Document File, entry 47, box 260; Army Service Forces, *Weekly Intelligence Summaries*, 1946, RG 46, Van Deman Collection, box 45.

[37] "Study Showing the Relationship Between Jews and Communism," Wedemeyer Papers, box 94.

[38] "Middle East Countries: Political Background and Current Problems; Section III, Palestine," August 1945, Intelligence Headquarters, Royal Air Force, Middle East, RG 319, Document File, entry 82, "P" File, 0192763, box 2299.

[39] Van de Velde to Director of Intelligence, 24 November 1948, RG 319, Document File, entry 85, 0513945.

[40] ibid.

[41] "Defense Relations with U.S.," RG 319, Document File, entry 85A, 515264; Grose, *Israel in the Mind of America*, 299; "Air Estimate of the Situation," RG 319, Document File, entry 85A, 65911; "Border Relations," and "Treatment of Arabs," 594111-594112.

[42] Pogue, *George C. Marshall*, 4:370–8; Grose, *Israel in the Mind of America*, 281–98; Gray, *General of the Army*, 657–62; Druks, *Uncertain Friendship*, 126–9; FRUS, 6:1009–12, 1087–9, 1339–41.

[43] "Training of Israeli or Arabian Students in U.S. Service Schools," 7 February 1950; and 350.2 Israel, 15 November 1949, RG 319, Document File, entry 47, 000114, box 234; FRUS, vol. 18 (1962–1963), 668–69. See also Gazit, "Israeli Military Procurement," 83–123.

[44] "Moseley," and entries 28 February and 29 October 1933, Eisenhower Diaries, Kevin McCann Papers, Dwight D. Eisenhower Library, Abilene, KS, box 1; Eisenhower, *At Ease*, 213; Gruenther to Palmer, 14 June 1935, Williston B. Palmer Papers, US Military Academy, West Point, NY, box 2; Eisenhower, *The Papers of Dwight D. Eisenhower*, 7:722–23; Wedemeyer to Eisenhower, 8 January 1948, Dwight D. Eisenhower Papers, PPP, Dwight D. Eisenhower Library, Abilene, KS, box 123.

[45] Ben-Zvi, *Decade of Transition*, 98; FRUS, 15:585; "The Reaction of U.S. Jewish Organizations," 31; Druks, *Uncertain Friendship*, 153.

[46] Ben-Zvi, *Decade of Transition*, 131–32, argues the case for an increasingly positive attitude towards Israel in the late Eisenhower years. For a critical assessment of both Eisenhower terms, see Druks, *Uncertain Friendship*, 153, 203–17; and Gazit, "Israeli Military Procurement," 89–95. All three studies were published before the extensive documentation on anti-Semitism in the army and Eisenhower's relationship to this was disclosed.

[47] Druks, *Uncertain Friendship*, 203, 217, 223, 228; Gazit, "Israeli Military Procurement," 94; *FRUS*, 13:336–37; 14:342.

[48] "Memorandum From the Joint Chiefs of Staff to Secretary of Defense McNamara," 7 August 1963, *FRUS*, vol. 18 (1962–1963), 667–79, 684–85; "Memorandum From the Joint Chiefs of Staff to Secretary of Defense McNamara," 18 January 1964 and 2 February 1967, *FRUS*, vol. 18 (1964–1967), 23–26, 756–57.

[49] Druks, *Uncertain Alliance*, 52; Gazit, "Israeli Military Procurement," 99–104.

[50] "Head of Joint Chiefs Criticizes Jewish Influence in the U.S.," *Washington Post* 13 November 1974, 1, 9; "Brown"s Remarks on Israel Stir a Wave of Criticism," and "Ford and Rumsfeld Endorse Brown to Continue as Joint Chiefs" Head," *New York Times*, 19 October 1976, 26. Two files on Brown in the Blaustein Library compiled by the American Jewish Committee in New York contain some of the most extensive documentation on the 1974 and 1976 controversies. No military or government documentation is available on what must have ignited significant discussions at various levels of these institutions.

[51] Rowland Evans and Robert Novak, "Behind the General's Outburst," *Washington Post*, 18 November 1974, A23; Milton Ellerin, "The Brown Affair—Reactions and Aftermath," American Jewish Committee Report, 20 December 1974, 8, AJCA; "Problem at the Pentagon," *The Atlantic Monthly*, February 1977, 6–8; "General Brown and "Burdens"," *New York Times*, 21 October 1976, 11.

[52] Luttwak, "Strategic Aspects of U.S.–Israeli Relations," 198–99; Schoenbaum, *The United States and the State of Israel*, 205; Gazit, "Israeli Military Procurement," 120.

[53] For some discussion of the uncertainty of the US–Israeli military alliance in the post–Cold War world, see Ben-Zvi, *United States and Israel*, and Gold, *Israel as an American Non-NATO Ally*.

References

Bendersky, Joseph W. "Biological Anti-Semitism in the U.S. Army Officer Corps, 1890–1950." *Militärgeschichtliche Zeitschrift* 62, no. 2 (2003): 331–53.

———. *The "Jewish Threat": Anti-Semitic Politics of the US Army*. New York: Basic Books, 2000.

Ben-Zvi, Abraham. *Decade of Transition: Eisenhower, Kennedy, and the Origins of the American-Israeli Alliance*. New York: Columbia University Press, 1998.

———. *The United States and Israel: The Limits of the Special Relationship*. New York: Columbia University Press, 1993.

Breitman, Richard, and Alan Kraut. *American Refugee Policy and European Jewry, 1933–1945*. Bloomington, IN: University of Indiana Press, 1987.

Challener, Richard D., ed. *United States Military Intelligence, 1917–1927*. 30 vols. New York: Garland, 1978.

———. *The Uncertain Friendship: The U.S. and Israel from Roosevelt to Kennedy*. Westport, CT: Greenwood Press, 2001.

Druks, Herbert *Uncertain Alliance: The U.S. and Israel from Kennedy to the Peace Process*. Westport, CT: Greenwood Press, 2001.

Eisenhower, Dwight D. *At Ease: Stories I Tell to Friends*. New York: Doubleday, 1967.

———. *The Papers of Dwight D. Eisenhower*, edited by Alfred Chandler. Vol. 7. Baltimore: Johns Hopkins Press, 1978.

FRUS (*Foreign Relations of the United States*) 1949. *The Near East, South Asia, and Africa*. Vol. 6. Washington, DC: US Government Printing Office, 1977.

——- 1950. *The Near East, South Asia, and Africa*. Vol. 5. Washington, DC: US Government Printing Office, 1978.

——- 1951. *The Near East and Africa*. Vol. 5. Washington, DC: US Government Printing Office, 1982.

————. *Arab-Israeli Dispute; United Arab Republic; North Africa.* Vol. 13. Washington, DC: US Government Printing Office, 1992.

————. *Arab-Israeli Dispute January 1–July 26, 1956.* Vol 15. Washington, DC: US Government Printing Office, 1989.

————. *Near East, 1961–1962.* Vol. 17. Washington, DC: US Government Printing Office, 1994.

————. *Near East, 1962–1963.* Vol. 18. Washington, DC: US Government Printing Office, 1995.

————. *Arab-Israeli Dispute, 1964–1967.* Vol. 18. Washington, DC: US Government Printing Office, 2000.

Gazit, Mordechai. "Israeli Military Procurement from the United States." In *Dynamics of Dependence: U.S.–Israeli Relations*, edited by Gabriel Sheffer. Boulder, CO: Westview Press, 1987.

Gibbons, Herbert Adams. *The Reconstruction of Poland and the Near East.* New York: The Century Co., 1917.

————. *The New Map of Asia (1900–1918).* Chautauqua, NY: The Century Co., 1919.

Gold, Dore. *Israel as an American Non-NATO Ally: Parameters of Defense Industrial Cooperation in a Post–Cold War Relationship.* Boulder, CO: Westview Press, 1993.

Gray, ed. *General of the Army: George C. Marshall, Soldier and Statesman.* New York: Norton, 1990.

Grose, Peter. *Israel in the Mind of America.* New York: Knopf, 1983.

Luttwak, Edward N. "Strategic Aspects of U.S.–Israeli Relations." In *U.S.–Israeli Relations at the Crossroads*, edited by Gabriel Sheffer. London: Frank Cass, 1997.

Pogue, Forrest C. *George C. Marshall: Statesman, 1945–1959.* New York: Viking, 1987.

"The Reaction of U.S. Jewish Organizations to the Sinai Campaign and Its Aftermath." *Forum on the Jewish People, Zionism, and Israel*, no. 40 (winter 1980/81): 29–38.

RG (Record Group) 46. Van Deman Collection, Investigative Files, Records of US Senate Internal Security Subcommittee of the Senate Judiciary Committee, 1951–1975. Washington, DC: US National Archives (hereafter USNA).

RG 59. Entry 538, Office of the Counselor, General Records of the Department of State. College Park, MD: USNA.

RG 165. Military Intelligence Division (MID), Records of the War Department and Special Staffs. College Park, MD: USNA.

RG 226. OSS, Research and Analysis Branch. Palestine. College Park, MD: USNA.

RG 319. Army Intelligence Document File. Entries 47, 82, 85, 85A. College Park, MD: USNA.

RG 319. Army Intelligence Project Decimal. ACSI-G-2 (1941-1945) (1941-1948). College Park, MD: USNA.

RG 319. Plans and Operations (P&O). Entries 152–154. College Park, MD: USNA.

Ripley, William Z. *The Races of Europe: A Sociological Study.* New York: D. Appleton, 1899.

Schoenbaum, David. *The United States and the State of Israel.* New York: Oxford University Press, 1993.

Smith, Truman. *Berlin Alert: The Memoirs and Reports of Truman Smith*, edited by Robert Hessen. Stanford, CA: Hoover Institution Press, 1984.

Woodruff, Charles E. *Expansion of Races.* New York: Rebman, 1905.

————. "The Complexion of Jews." *American Journal of Insanity* 62 (1905–1906): 327–33.

Anti-Zionism in Britain, 1922–2002: Continuities and Discontinuities

David Cesarani

Since Theodore Herzl advocated the Zionist cause to British parliamentarians in his testimony to the Royal Commission on Alien Immigration in 1902, Britain has probably had a longer continuous engagement with Zionism than any other country in the world. The longevity of this entanglement provides a singular opportunity to study the diachronically shifting patterns of anti-Zionism and to assess their relationship with equally shifting patterns of anti-Jewish discourse.

Of course, anti-Zionism did not occur in a static matrix. When Britain assumed the Mandate for Palestine in 1922, the country was at the height of its imperial power and prestige. Within a decade Britain was in retreat from the Mandate, a symptom of imperial decline that culminated in the first stage of decolonization in 1947–48. During the 1950s Britain's foreign policy in the Middle East was framed by its post-imperial aspirations and alliance with France. After Britain entered the European Economic Community in 1973 its foreign policy was increasingly meshed with that of Europe. Surprisingly, from the mid-1980s, it took a decidedly Atlanticist turn under the direction first of Margaret Thatcher and then of Tony Blair.

The internal social and political conditions changed as well. From the 1900s to the 1950s the Jews (after the Irish, who represent a special case) were the only significant immigrant ethnic-faith community in Britain. Since the 1960s the size of the Muslim population has grown exponentially. There are now about 300,000 Jews in Britain as against nearly two million Muslims. The last century, in which these demographic shifts occurred, also saw extensive political realignment. It began with the rise of the labor movement and ended with its waning. Midway, a New Left emerged, liberation movements took hold, and a politics of identity developed which empowered ethnic-faith communities as never before.[1]

Nevertheless, the British case offers striking continuities of geopolitical interest in the Middle East and political culture at home. The persistence of a Jewish population and its presence in politics is another, important constant. These continuities may enable us to detect fixed features of anti-Zionism and aspects that are fluid. The persistence of a certain geopolitical framework may also assist the separation of policy and discourse based on perceived national interest from the expression of free-floating ideologies.

In order to discern such continuities and discontinuities, this article will briefly and schematically examine several key moments in the unfolding relationship between Britain, or the British, and Zionism. First, it looks at the extended political attack between 1922 and 1924 on the principle of assuming the Mandate for Palestine. In many respects this is a crucial template for all subsequent anti-Zionism and the benchmark against which it can be measured. Second, it examines political discourse concerning Zionism during the conflict between Britain and the Zionist movement in 1930–31 and 1945–48. Third, it examines the attitude of the New Left in Britain towards Zionism and Israel in the 1960s, and the *Perdition* affair of 1986–87—a case of left-wing anti-Zionism. Finally, it discusses attacks on Israel since the collapse of Soviet power, during the second *Intifada*, and in the wake of 9/11. Each of these periods could be the subject for a major research paper. Indeed, very little detailed research has been carried out on discourses about Jews and Zionism in Britain since the 1950s. What follows should be treated as a preliminary exploration of a complex subject and a research agenda rather than a definitive statement on the convergence or divergence of anti-Jewish and anti-Zionist discourse.

It is necessary to add a word about the sources for this inquiry. Much of the material cited below comes from the press, including editorials, signed articles and special reports by named correspondents. This is a relatively convenient source to use, but unless the signed articles are by politicians or other public figures, they do not offer much insight into attitudes beyond Fleet Street. In certain cases it is possible to link newspaper proprietors to political parties and this is indicated where such coordination occurs. Articles by correspondents may explicitly represent wider viewpoints and can be assumed to replicate a certain, significant strand of thought. Otherwise, the opinions they present would not have any resonance and would not see print. However, it would be a mistake to assume that leading articles in the press represented the outlook of either the political classes or the populace at large. It is also as dangerous to assume that newspaper articles had a definite influence on opinion. There was a plethora of newspapers in the period covered here and only a few are mentioned. It would be possible to construct a very different narrative and reach other conclusions if different journals were consulted.

However, on the basis of wider research it is possible to state that this newspaper material was representative of broad currents of opinion. Where possible, contemporary comment is cited as evidence of this. Patterns of continuity from one period to another and from one newspaper to another also suggest that the press did shape opinion, creating a received wisdom that was replicated ad nauseam. The object of this investigation is to establish these patterns and indicate how they leaped across the decades despite massive political, social and economic transformations. It should not be read as evidence of attitudes permeating the whole of British society or indictment by press cutting. The point of it is to show how certain sections of the print media in conjunction with certain political circles evolved, deployed and perpetuated a way of understanding Zionism and seeing Zionist Jews. Regardless of any impact it may have had on the "real world"—be it domestic politics, British foreign policy or the Middle East—a pattern of attitudes was thereby created that has enjoyed extraordinary longevity and resilience.[2]

Another major source comprises speeches by members of parliament and other utterances by politicians. This has a double value. First, it substantiates the occurrence of stereotypical and negative thinking about Jews in society as a whole, and in a very important section of society at that. Second, where anti-Jewish rhetoric in political life echoes the press it can be taken as verification of the influence that the press wielded and its role in shaping discourse. Patterns appear in the realm of politics, too, suggesting a degree of transmission and a received wisdom about Zionism. However, it must be stressed that, as in the case of the press, the quotations presented here are selective. They could be balanced by pro-Zionist and pro-Jewish declarations by politicians, but in a limited study such as, this it is only possible to demarcate and chart one side. There is clearly much need for a comprehensive study of Zionism and anti-Zionism in British politics, society and culture. Hopefully the partial research presented here will stimulate further efforts in this direction.

Opposition to the Mandate

In its annual report to the 14th World Zionist Congress in 1923, the Executive of the World Zionist Organization reported that 1921 and 1922 had seen an unprecedented onslaught against Zionism in the British press and in parliament in the run-up to the decision to accept the League of Nations Mandate for Palestine. The campaign began with the arrival of a Palestinian Arab delegation in August 1921. "With the encouragement of a variety of anti-Zionist forces which gathered around it, the Delegation conducted propaganda which gained in volume and vigour as time went on, until it eventually swelled into a torrent of malignant misrepresentation." However, the report recognized that some of the opposition was principled:

Mingled with the prejudice was a widespread desire for the reduction of British Commitments in the east, in pursuance of the general demand for economy and a genuine anxiety on the part of those who were imperfectly informed and who were disposed in good faith to take tendentious statements at their face value, lest anything should be done in Palestine which was prejudicial to legitimate Arab rights or inconsistent with British pledges.[3]

The anti-Zionism of this period emanated almost wholly from the right wing of British politics, notably the so-called Die Hards of the Tory Party (the rump of Tory MPs who chose to stay outside the coalition government), and the mass-circulation right-wing press. This was largely because support for the creation of a Jewish National Home was the considered policy of the prime minister, David Lloyd George, and his coalition government (1917–22). Lloyd George was leader of the Liberal Party, which was perceived by the Die Hards to be the dominant and malign political force in Britain. Lloyd George was also increasingly at odds with the press barons, who included Lady Bathurst, the owner of the *Morning Post*, Lord Northcliffe, owner of the *Times* and the *Daily Mail* until 1922 when his brother Lord Rothermere purchased the latter, and Lord Beaverbrook, who controlled the Express Group. Their papers all became conduits for a vicious anti-Zionism that was shot through with anti-Jewish themes and tropes.[4]

At a time when stereotypes of Jews as foreign, powerful, wealthy, money grubbing, arrogant and pushy were common and frequently expressed in polite society, negative stereotypes of Jews cropped up even in the articulation of principled opposition to Zionism. Indeed, the ubiquity of anti-Jewish attitudes and discourse makes it hard to isolate an anti-Zionism that is rooted in antipathy towards Jews from an anti-Zionism that is principled but expressed in contemporary negative stereotypes of Jews. For this very reason it may not even be necessary to distinguish principled anti-Zionism that employed anti-Jewish tropes, or anti-Zionism that used anti-Semitism cynically and instrumentally, from anti-Zionism redolent with anti-Jewish imagery that clearly emanated from a visceral antagonism towards anything Jewish. It is virtually self-evident that the anti-Zionism of the early 1920s drew both on traditional anti-Jewish tropes and also on what were then *new* forms of anti-Jewish discourse.[5]

The government's Zionist policy was typically depicted as alien to British interests and the result of machinations by rich, powerful, foreign Jews. According to the *Morning Post*, British taxpayers were "compelled to pay for establishing a national home for Zionist Jews." The Zionist project was imposed on them by powerful Jews acting in the selfish interest of their people. The *Morning Post* singled out Sir Alfred Mond MP for attack. He was a minister in the government of Lloyd George, a rich industrialist, and one of Chaim Weizmann's supporters in England. The *Morning Post* believed that Jews like Mond had other loyalties. "That is the reason why, despite the many virtues and great abilities of Sir Alfred Mond, we would like to see purely British representatives in a purely British parliament." The paper purveyed the notion that as well as being fundamentally alien, Jews were powerful and conspiratorial. "We have frequently complained of the atmosphere of intrigue and secrecy in which they have worked, and we do not at all like the coincidence between a time of dire British necessity and the Balfour Declaration, a coincidence too suggestive of blackmail." Having been forced to make the promise of a Jewish National Home, Britain later had to seek the imprimatur of the League of Nations, a body of international governance that the right-wing *Morning Post* loathed. "We have always considered the League of Nations as a sort of Jewish pawnshop which holds the pledges of the British Government."[6]

After a visit to Palestine and the Middle East in February 1922, Lord Northcliffe complained in The Times that the Jews in Palestine were "pushful, grasping and domineering." The country had been at peace "before the arrival of the undesirable Jewish element." Northcliffe set the tone for the paper's subsequent coverage. It particularly disliked the Rutenberg concession, the agreement by which the mandatory authority granted Pinhas Rutenberg, a Russian Jewish engineer and entrepreneur, sole right to extract hydroelectric power from a dam on the River Jordan. "Why," inquired *The Times*, "is it that ideal Zionism has so soon been degraded by allowing itself to become the instrument of materialist aims and of a sordid type of international finance?"[7]

The right-wing *Spectator* magazine remarked of Rutenberg that "We take it that, like so many of his race what he wants is to make a big profit for himself and those concerned with him …. "[8] On the eve of the November 1922 General Election, in which ratification of the League of Nations Mandate for Palestine was a major issue, the *Evening News,* owned by Northcliffe's brother, Lord Rothermere, combined a traditional anti-Jewish stereotype with antisocialism. In a leading article headlined "Levy for Levi," it noted that the Labour Party was a supporter of Zionism. "Mr Arthur Henderson, secretary of the Labour Party, has made it plain that he would raise money from British sources by levy and give it to Levi." A few days before the poll, the *Evening News* carried a headline "Why Pay for the Jews" and underneath in smaller type, "National Home."[9] Pursuing the same theme in parliament during a debate on Zionism, the right-wing Tory MP N. Pemberton Billing asked if the government would "appeal to the Jewish population to raise funds for this purpose and so relieve the British taxpayer. They are very wealthy."[10]

One article in the *Sunday Express,* owned by Lord Beaverbrook, was couched in Biblical imagery and ran the gamut of traditional anti-Jewish discourse from the blood libel to accusations of Jewish avarice. The article was headlined in large type: 'The British Ass and the Zionist Jew. More Christians in Palestine than Hebrews. The Double Burden We Bear.' It continued: "At the expense of the British taxpayer a Zionist Government, with a Jewish Governor, has been established in Palestine. 'Judah has washed his garments and his clothes in the blood of grapes.' Out of the great wine-press of the Great War paid for by British blood and British treasure, has arisen a Jewish State in Palestine." British troops had died to establish a Jewish despotism over Christians and the "subsidised importation of Jews from Russia." For the *Sunday Express,* though, "the Jewish Palestine is an inverted pyramid precariously poised on British treasure and British bones." This was not acceptable.

The British ass may be strong, but he is tired of bowing his shoulder to bear the burden of Judah. He is sick of becoming a servant unto Jewish tribute. Yet, marvellous to relate, he is not an anti-Semite. He does not object to the hand of Judah being 'in the neck of his enemies.' But he does object to it being on the neck of his best friend in the whole world, the British taxpayer.[11]

The stereotype of Jews as wealthy and powerful coexisted happily with the newer trope of the Jew as Bolshevik and a potent agent of revolutionary upheaval. The equation of Jews with European revolutionary movements was rooted in anti-revolutionary propaganda in the Tsarist Empire and went back to the 1870s, if not earlier. But the specific equation of Jews with Bolshevism received a massive boost from anti-Bolshevik propaganda during the Russian Civil War.[12]

Both tropes coalesced in Rutenberg, the former Russian revolutionary turned Zionist and entrepreneur. "Who is this Mr Rutenberg," asked the *Morning Post*, "that he should supplant an honest British firm in this enterprise? Is he a communist or a capitalist now?" In a further comment that added traditional religious-based antipathy, the paper added "We see no 'honour and glory' in conquering Palestine in order to hand over the holy waters of the Jordan to a Rutenberg . . . ."[13] Indeed, to the right-wing press Zionism represented an invasion of the Holy Land by godless Bolsheviks. In *The Times* Lord Northcliffe asserted that "the recent importation of undesirable Jews, Bolsheviks, and others, was the partial cause of the regrettable troubles with the Arabs, who resented the general situation."[14] The *Daily Mail* asked, "Is it true that Jews of the most undesirable character are being imported into Palestine for the purposes of replacing the present inhabitants, and that these Jews caused the riots of last May and placarded the Holy City with Bolshevik appeals?"[15] In a debate on Zionism in the House of Commons in March 1922, Viscount Curzon MP asked Winston Churchill MP, the Colonial Secretary: "Is he aware that the large majority of the Jewish immigrants to Palestine have been released from the ghettos of East and South East Europe and are saturated with Bolshevist ideas?"[16]

The allegation that Jewish immigrants to Palestine were Bolsheviks cannot be disentangled from the belief that the Russian revolution was the result of a Jewish conspiracy. This conviction was nurtured by the *Protocols of the Elders of Zion*, which reached Britain in the context of anti-Bolshevik propaganda. But the *Protocols* came to inform, indeed to undergird, anti-Zionism independently of events in Russia. The forgery was published as *The Jewish Peril* in February 1920 and serialized in a new translation in the *Morning Post* in July 1920, subsequently published in book form as *The Causes of the World's Unrest*. The *Spectator* and *The Times* both devoted editorials to the English version soon after it appeared. We can see that analysis of Zionism in all these papers was profoundly influenced by the *Protocols of the Elders of Zion*.[17]

As we have seen, the *Morning Post* detected an 'atmosphere of intrigue and secrecy' about the origins of the Balfour Declaration. When several Labour Party leaders attended a fund-raising dinner of the Keren Hayesod, the paper asked:

How is it that this Zionist fund does honour to the most violent politicians of the Left? And why do politicians of the Left embrace with so much enthusiasm the

Zionist cause?... It is impossible not to ask what influence has induced the Labour Party to throw over thus all the zeal for imperial economy and self determination. What telegrams, we wonder, have passed between Eccleston Square [Labour Party HQ] and the Poale Zion.

In another editorial, the *Morning Post* argued that the British government wanted the League of Nations to debate the Mandate issue in London because "No doubt the Zionists feel that if they could only get the Council of the League within the orbit of the British Government the thing was done. For Jewry and the British Government have become interchangeable."[18]

When Sir Herbert Samuel was appointed by Lloyd George to become the first High Commissioner for Palestine in 1922, the *Spectator* warned that behind him the Arabs saw "the controlling hand of Eastern Europe." After the fall of Lloyd George in 1922, and the installation of a Conservative government, the *Spectator* called on the new Prime Minister, Andrew Bonar Law, to pull Britain out of the Middle East:

> We sincerely hope that the British Government will not follow the advice which is sure to be given by the world wise to beware of offending International Jewry. In the first place, a large part of International and British Jewry is immune to the Zionist bacillus, though it greatly dreads the disease. Next, we shall never get on satisfactory terms with Jewish financiers by showing ourselves afraid of them .... Besides, we are not financially dependent on International Jewish capital. We can paddle our own canoe in the hidden river of gold and paper.[19]

Alleged Jewish power could be exercised in other ways than those set out in the *Protocols*, although there was always an overlap between different representations of the potent Jew. After the Conservative government refused to pull out of Palestine, Lord Beaverbrook unleashed an extraordinary attack on Zionism in a front-page article in the *Daily Express* that cast Weizmann in the role of Svengali—the literary creation of George du Maurier in his 1895 novel *Trilby*. According to Daniel Pick, the character of Svengali "gave expression to fears of psychological invasion, showing the Jews' capacity to get inside—and even replace—the mental functioning of the gentile through mesmerism." The seductive, hypnotic power of the Jew animates the article. The expansive headline screamed: "Why We Are Still in Palestine. Mystery of the Great Chaim. Of the Foreigners Who Meddle with British Affairs. Palestine Morass. Genius That Lured and Keeps Us There. Holy Land under Mortgage." The article depicted Weizmann as "the most wonderful of the mystery men" who induced Britain to spend millions of pounds to enable Jews to take over the Holy Land. He had "a genius for exerting a hidden mastery over the minds of simple politicians." "Who is this man of mystery," the paper asked, "one of the minds who dominates the destinies of nations?" It outlined his career to the point at which "he has established his ascendancy in the heart of our Foreign Office and in the core of our Government." Melding varieties of Jewish power, the article described Weizmann as heading a vast political and financial empire that was so deeply embedded in Palestine that "gentiles wouldn't dare meddle with it."[20]

Indeed, the British right-wing press and politicians opposed to Zionism seemed unable or unwilling to appreciate the movement for what it was, denying its moral claims, rationality or utility. Taking another tack, they imposed a curious double standard on Zionism. They repeatedly claimed that it should be an ethereal, spiritual movement. *The Times*, for example, protested that the British were now defending "mainly a political movement, largely of an alien character."[21] This was a form of double standard because no other nationalist movement was treated this way. It was also a rhetorical device to delegitimize the presence of Jews in Palestine and invalidate their cause. By constructing Zionism as a purely spiritual movement and, conversely, denouncing the Jewish immigrants as East European, secular and left wing, the anti-Zionists undercut their relationship to the Holy Land and rendered them alien to it.

The alleged illegitimacy of Zionism was useful in explaining the much-remarked upsurge of anti-Jewish feeling. In a signed article in his paper, Lord Beaverbrook posed as a friend of the Jews and asked: "Why is there such a marked recrudescence of feeling against the Jews?" The answer: "Politics—a racial policy known as Zionism." Beaverbrook explained that Zionism set the Jew apart from the rest of the community. Worse, Zionism cost money. "The Palestine policy is the biggest stumbling block that the Jews of England have to face. It is interpreted by the taxpayer as an additional impost on the income tax." In the article Beaverbrook also pointed to Jews who were opposed to Zionism as evidence that anti-Zionism could not be anti-Jewish. This was a common tactic. These antagonists of Zionism were immune to the notion that deciding who was a "good Jew" and who a "bad Jew" was itself a form of anti-Jewish practice.[22]

The anti-Zionist movement in Britain in the early 1920s was populated by people like Sir William Joynson-Hicks, who had made a career out of impugning the loyalty of Jews and harrying their presence in England.[23] Many who embraced the Palestinian Arab delegation in London during 1921–22—such as Arnold White, author of *The Hidden Hand* (1917), or Nesta Webster, who popularized the *Protocols* in her books on the French Revolution and Freemasonry—wrote explicitly anti-Semitic tracts.[24] Throughout this period, although it is possible to disentangle principled opposition to Zionism from sheer antipathy to Jews, so much objective criticism was couched in anti-Jewish discourse that the differentiation is almost pointless. It was received wisdom that Jews were rich, powerful, international in character and influence, devious and avaricious. Much of this was traditional stereotyping, but Zionism also attracted the myth of the Jew as Bolshevik and was taken to be an emanation of, if not the very evidence for, a worldwide Jewish conspiracy.

Conflict over Palestine

The response to the anti-Jewish riots in Palestine in 1929 offers a window into attitudes and examples of rhetoric at the mid-point of the interwar years. In many respects, political and press responses to the turmoil of 1929 closely followed the patterns established in the early 1920s. But there were significant differences. Years of peace and prosperity in Palestine had habituated the public to possession of the Mandate and there was no great wave of anti-Jewish feeling for anti-Zionists to capitalize upon.

Reports and comments in *The Times* were objective and calm. The paper recounted the events leading up to the outbreak and the significance of the riots. Its editorial position was that order had to be restored as a top priority. "Our plain duty and our plain interest point the same way."[25] Coverage of the riots dominated the front page of the *Daily Express* from 26 to 29 August and then subsided. The reportage was quite balanced and it was the first national daily to get a special reporter to Jerusalem. C. J. Ketchum supplied the paper with vivid "Boys Own" copy in which the Arabs were the villains, the Jews the victims and the British the heroes.[26]

By contrast, the editorial comment was totally unbalanced. Beaverbrook's *Daily Express* and *Sunday Express* reverted to exactly the same editorial position they had held in 1920–22, when they had carried some of the most distorted reporting and vitriolic editorial attacks on Zionism to emanate from Fleet Street. In its first editorial declaration, the *Daily Express* noted the shock that the riots had caused around the world and protested against the lacklustre British military reaction. But the leader writer then restated the paper's traditional hostility to "expensive responsibilities without any adequate return" such as the Mandate. On 31 August, an editorial headlined "Still Paying for Our Folly" elaborated on this theme. It was necessary to restore order, but once this had been achieved it would be time to reassess Britain's role in Palestine. Millions of British people, it suggested, were wondering why their country was involved there at all. "What possible connections are there between Palestine and British interests? What do we stand to gain now or hereafter, directly or at second hand, for all the trouble and expense we have incurred in accepting the Mandate and living up to its responsibilities? It is not merely a thankless task—we are used to that: it is also a task that puts us on trial before the world over an issue that fundamentally is not a British concern at all."[27]

When, in the light of the riots, the Labor government reconsidered its obligations to the Zionist movement, it could therefore rely on approval from the Conservative press. Of these papers, the most vociferous was Lord Rothermere's *Daily Mail*, which revived the "bag and baggage" rhetoric of the early 1920s. In its first editorial on the riots, the paper complained that "bickering" over the Wailing Wall seemed to be "perennial." This time, however, it suspected that some "mysterious external influences may have been at work, inspired not so much by religious fanaticism as by strictly mundane calculations." This was a reference to the old Bolshevik bogey: within a week, the paper was blaming "Soviet agents" for stirring up the Arab population of Britain's Middle Eastern possessions.[28]

On 27 August, the *Daily Mail* returned to its attack on the Mandate with a fierce editorial entitled "That Foolish Mandate."

> The root of the whole trouble was planted when the Coalition Government embarked on the futile and perilous policy of attempting to make Palestine a 'national home' for the Jews. Against this stupid and mischievous enterprise the *Daily Mail* has protested for years .... We have shown from the outset that it was

unjust, dangerous, and dishonourable, besides imposing a superfluous and intolerable burden upon the British taxpayer; that it ran counter to our own pledge at the close of the war, to give Palestine a Government based 'on the free choice of the native population'; and that it was bound to be resented by the overwhelming majority of that population.

It then recited the established anti-Zionist argument: that there were only 75–80,000 Jews as against 750,000 Arabs; that British bayonets were needed to preserve the 'privileged position' of the 'recent immigrants.' The editorial urged that 'when order is restored the matter, in its larger aspect, must not be allowed to rest.' The British position derived from a 'casual declaration' made to 'a very unrepresentative Jewish group' and it should not be regarded as binding. The paper concluded: "We hope that Mr MacDonald [the Labor Prime Minister] and his colleagues will waste no time in re-opening the question, and that they will go closely into the whole outrageous folly of endeavouring—with British backing—to convert an old Arab state into a sham Jewish 'nation' at the expense of the British taxpayer."[29]

A few days later, another editorial demanded "Give Back the Mandate." As far as the *Daily Mail* was concerned, there was no point in restoring order only to see disturbances break out yet again. "There is now no excuse for going on with it." Like the Beaverbrook press it tapped the mood of isolationism amongst the British public. "We cannot afford these expensive mandates. We are getting out of Egypt and Germany and we hope the Government will lose no time in settling up affairs in Palestine and Mesopotamia and passing back the mandates to the League of Nations."[30]

For different reasons, the now influential Labour press was also less than sympathetic towards the continuation of the Mandate. This marked a shift in attitudes towards Zionism and the Jews. The Labour Party and the socialist press had played a marginal role during the controversies of the 1920s. When they did express themselves, as Josef Gorny has shown, Labour politicians and publicists were moderately pro-Zionist. They saw Jewish settlement in Palestine as the conduit for modernization of the region. They sympathized with the aspirations of left-Zionists working to create a socialist Jewish state that would help to end the plight of the Jewish masses in eastern Europe by providing them with a homeland and social justice at one and the same time. Arab opposition to Zionism increasingly bothered the British left, but it was usually dismissed as the forces of reaction opposed to the creation of a progressive Palestine. The contradictions between anti-imperialism and support for the Mandate were never fully resolved, but the issue was hardly acute while the Labour Party was in opposition.[31]

The position that the Labour Party and the left in Britain took towards Zionism was, however, not simply determined by its stand on imperialism. It was also informed by stereotypical attitudes towards the Jews and an ambivalence rooted in a century of progressive, liberal thinking on "the Jewish Question."[32] The British left, no less than other progressives, bifurcated Jews into "good" and "bad" varieties. The former were Jewish workers, the latter were Jewish capitalists. Thus the doctrinaire anti-imperialism of the British left was complemented by a no less ingrained antagonism towards rich Jews. When J. Ramsay MacDonald, a future Labor Prime Minister, visited Palestine in 1922 at the invitation of the Zionist movement, he reflected on the difference between the socialist pioneers in the settlements and the parasitic Jewish capitalists of the diaspora. MacDonald contrasted the pioneers to

> the rich plutocratic Jew, who is the true economic materialist. He is the person whose views upon life make one anti-Semitic. He has no country, no kindred. Whether as a sweater or a financier, he is an exploiter of everything he can squeeze. He is behind every evil that Governments do, and his political authority, always exercised in the dark, is greater than that of Parliamentary majorities. He is the keenest of brains and the bluntest of consciences. He detests Zionism because it revives the idealism of his race, and has political implications which threaten his economic interests.[33]

As this rather extraordinary statement shows, even well-informed progressive left-wing intellectuals such as MacDonald had been contaminated by the myth of Jewish parasitism, power and conspiracy. The pro-Zionist discourse of the left coexisted with anti-Semitism. More than that, it actually validated anti-Semitic notions and made it possible for socialists who thought themselves opposed to racialism to voice basic slurs about the Jews. All subsequent manifestations of left-wing anti-Zionism and anti-Semitism are latent in this moment. Implicitly for the left, Zionism was acceptable only if it was opposed to "Jewish capitalism." The fact that many wealthy Jews in Britain were also super-patriotic assimilationists who contested Zionism fortified the belief of non-Jewish left-wingers that as long as they espoused Zionism they could articulate what was, in effect, rich-Jew anti-Semitism. This trait pervaded the Labor Party from top to bottom, and from right (where MacDonald was located) to left. George Lansbury, who would succeed MacDonald as leader of the Labour Party and guardian of its socialist values, was also prone to juxtapose rich Jews and poor Jews. He lauded the Zionist movement for seeking a way to alleviate the suffering of the latter as against the anti-Zionist rich Jews who were content to exploit Jewish workers. These stereotypical and doctrinaire points of view proved to be remarkably persistent.[34]

The Palestine riots of August 1929 and the subsequent inquest harshly exposed the contradictions of the Labor position. The fact that the riots occurred while Labor was in office, having formed a minority government under MacDonald in October 1929, made this confrontation unavoidable. A commission of inquiry despatched by Colonial Secretary Lord Passfield reported that Palestinian Arabs were alarmed by the volume of Jewish immigration and the extent of Jewish land purchases. In 1930 Passfield issued a White Paper proposing the restriction of Jewish immigration and the curtailment of land buying for Jewish settlement.[35]

The socialist press as a whole was committed to the principle of native self-government, a commitment that inevitably conflicted with the notion of a Jewish National Home in Palestine. Fortunately, the terms of the Mandate allowed the party to circumvent the clash between its formal anti-imperialism and the perpetuation of British rule. Although an editorial in the *Daily Herald* on 27 August 1929 called for a re-examination of the Mandate, over the following months it loyally supported the government line, which was to mollify Arab opposition but maintain the Mandate and the corollary commitment to foster the Jewish National Home. The *New Statesman*, edited by Clifford Sharp, took a more independent stand. The journal was founded in 1913 and was held in high esteem within the labor movement. But a sharply worded editorial effectively calling for Britain to consider withdrawing from Palestine also revealed the continuity of deep-seated left-wing prejudices about Jewish wealth and power. The editorial maintained that the Mandate had become unworkable, but asserted that the true extent of the conflict was being concealed from the public by a world press that was under Jewish financial control.[36]

The crisis of 1929–31 crystallized a shift in thinking and rhetoric within the British left. Passfield tended to perceive the Zionists as well-resourced, white, European settlers who were prone to exploit the natives, in this case the Arabs, in the same way as European colonists exploited indigenous peoples. This view was not simply a reaction to the riots and the inquest into what caused them. It was embedded in the socialist doctrine that made it hard for him to accept that a nationalist movement could be simultaneously a socialist one. Whenever socialist Zionists tried to exploit fraternal ties with the Labor Party and the labour movement in Britain, Passfield and those who thought like him felt confronted by a paradox that violated the laws of development. Furthermore, the greater the pressure he experienced from Zionist lobbyists in Britain and the USA, the more he became convinced that he faced a wealthy and powerful international Jewish movement.[37]

If the right had been predominantly anti-Zionist and unselfconsciously anti-Jewish during the 1920s, the crisis of 1929–31 showed that the left was dogged by ambivalence. It denounced anti-Semitism ritually, yet bifurcated Jews into those that were good and those that were bad. Even good socialist Jews posed a problem for some on the left if they were also Zionists. The radical left saw Zionism as an adjunct of British imperialism that benefited from Britain's imperial potency even if it was not excessively powerful in and of itself. The very elements on the left that differentiated Jewish workers from Jewish capitalists also tended to highlight the power of Jewish finance and alleged Jewish control of the press. The Zionist campaign against the 1930 White Paper that was carried out from Warsaw to New York appeared to the left as evidence of international Jewry at work. While socialist politicians and pressmen carefully avoided the crude rhetoric of the anti-Semites, their language frequently paralleled that of the right.[38]

Nevertheless, once the storm over the White Paper had passed, the Labor Party settled down to a position that was overwhelmingly pro-Jewish and pro-Zionist, and that was constantly reinforced by a common dismay over the persecution of the Jews in Europe and a shared antifascism.[39] This shared agenda tended to mask the potential for conflict over Palestine and the persistence of negative attitudes despite even the horror of anti-Semitism on the continent. The vulnerability of some on the left to anti-Jewish discourse was laid bare by the behavior and rhetoric of key Labor politicians in the critical years 1945–48.

In July 1945 a Labor Government was elected by a huge landslide. Clement Attlee became Prime Minister and Ernest Bevin was appointed Foreign Secretary. Neither was warmly inclined towards Zionism even though Bevin had worked closely with Poale Zion during the 1929–30 controversy. They both believed that diaspora Jews were primarily a religious group and that their future lay in the achievement of progressive, tolerant regimes in the countries in which they lived, rather than in a Jewish state in Palestine.[40] Attlee and Bevin bridled at the strength of the pro-Zionist campaign, especially in America, to allow Jewish survivors of Nazi persecution and genocide to enter Palestine. They resented President Truman's support for Zionist demands and blamed this on the power of the American Jewish vote. Both tended to assume that pro-Zionist statements by politicians in the USA were the result of political calculation rather than an expression of principle or a response to felt needs. Bevin was also prone to accuse the Jews of fomenting anti-Jewish feeling by their impatience to achieve a Jewish state.[41]

Bevin was roundly criticized for his notorious statement to the Anglo-American Committee of Inquiry in November 1946 warning Jews not to "want to get too much to the head of the queue" in their eagerness to get out of Europe. The phrase, which tactlessly echoed the stereotypical description of Jews as "pushy", may have come from Attlee who had earlier used it in a cable to Truman.[42] But Bevin spoke in public and his views were amplified within the labor movement. The Birmingham *Town Crier*, a local Labor Party paper under Bevin's domination, occasionally employed blatant anti-Jewish rhetoric. An editorial on 31 August 1946 (following the attack on the King David Hotel by Jewish terrorists) was headlined "The Eternal Jew," echoing the title of the Nazi propaganda film. No less egregious, it quoted the words of Shylock and turned them against Jewish terrorists in Palestine, drawing on a deeply embedded stereotype of the merciless Jew. The *Town Crier* regularly adverted to the role and power of "international Jewish finance" in the Zionist campaign against the British Mandate. The paper, echoing Bevin's stated view that Zionists were antagonizing public opinion, warned that anti-British propaganda Britain in the USA, as well as terrorism in Palestine, would heighten anti-Semitism.[43]

At points the anti-Zionist discourse of the left overlapped with the immoderate statements emanating from the right. On 5 January 1947 an editorial in the *Sunday Times* challenged British Jews to denounce Jewish terrorism in Palestine. This was a classic ploy. The demand was premised on the notion that the Jews formed an international collectivity and that one part of it was responsible, or liable, for the actions of another part. British Jews were damned whatever they did: if they condemned the terror campaign they affirmed its existence and implied a measure of responsibility, but if they did not they stood accused of complicity and treachery. But, as we have seen, there was nothing new in the identification of Jews with dual loyalty or with the game of playing off "good Jews" against "bad Jews." Nor was it new to imply that Jewish behaviour justified anti-Jewish attacks, which was the obverse of calling on one set of Jews to disown the behaviour of another set.[44]

Diaries from this period kept by volunteers for Mass Observation (MO), a large-scale anthropological research project, show that the adverse publicity generated by the Palestine crisis and the rhetoric emanating from the center-right and -left leached into popular opinion. The evidence of anti-Semitic attitudes and language amongst the public at large (insofar as the MO reporters may be regarded as typical) is all the more remarkable given the recent torrent of news from Europe about the consequences of Nazi anti-Jewish propaganda and policy. For this reason it is worth dwelling on an unusual but striking convergence of anti-Zionism and anti-Semitism.

Maggie Joy Blunt was a diarist who worked in marketing for a metals company and lived near Slough, outside London. On 25 May 1945 she was already expressing anxiety that "The pledge to the Jews in respect of Palestine is especially dangerous" and feared that "more poor British tummies will die in a cause they profit not by."[45] In October, Edie Rutherford, a middle-aged housewife in Sheffield who consistently espoused anti-Jewish views, reflected on reports of the well-organized illegal immigration to Palestine and inquired archly, in a manner that suggests the impact of Bevin's accusations, "Now who is behind it all?"[46] Traditional anti-Jewish prejudice colored perceptions of Zionist Jews regardless of their actions. The elderly Herbert Brush, a former engineer in London, recorded walking by the headquarters of the Zionist Federation where he supposed the Jews were "cooking up something to say to the Government about Palestine. There was no mistaking the Jewish proboscis of the men. ..."[47]

As the conflict in Palestine intensified and casualties mounted, the tone of the diarists became harsher. Edie Rutherford wrote in December 1946, "As more and more lads are killed there, I begin to wish we had started the war a bit later, so that Hitler would have exterminated a few more Jews." Reflecting the pervasive dichotomy between good/bad Jews, she remarked, "All very well for good Jews to write to the papers saying ALL Jews aren't bad—oh yeah? Why don't the good Jews, then, use their influence with the bad Jews?"[48] Rutherford excoriated "rich" Jews and implicitly sympathized with the threat of "reprisals" they faced from local fascists.[49] The vituperation reached its climax after the hanging by the Irgun of two British NCOs in August 1947. The diarist B. Charles, a homosexual antiques dealer in Edinburgh, declared that "The Jews are a scourge to mankind. I should rejoice to know every Jew—man, woman and child—had been murdered! We ought to drop six atomic bombs on six different cities in Palestine and wipe out as many Jews as possible."[50] Edie Rutherford wrote "I am not surprised and quite glad that people are taking their revenge on Jews in this country." Jewish assertions of loyalty and condemnations of terrorism in Palestine cut no ice with her. "I don't accept as sincere the comments of Jews these last few days. In their hearts I believe all Jews are glad to hit us British—they are notoriously lacking in moral courage on the whole."[51]

During 1947, Sir Oswald Mosley revived the British Union of Fascists and took its campaign onto the streets, attempting to capitalize on the ill feeling generated by the events in Palestine. The attacks by Jews on British soldiers in Palestine were meat and drink to the British Union agitators. After the two British NCOs were killed in August 1947, Jewish communities throughout Britain were struck by riots: property was destroyed, synagogues damaged and cemeteries desecrated in London, Manchester, Liverpool and Glasgow. In this instance, anti-Zionism was crudely and instrumentally harnessed to an anti-Jewish campaign.[52]

These attacks were the first of what would become a characteristic of extreme anti-Zionism, connecting disturbances in the Middle East with cemetery desecrations in UK cities. Until today, damage to synagogues and Jewish cemeteries reflects spikes of tension in the region. However, the 1947 disturbances also represent the high-water mark of a popular right-wing anti-Zionist discourse that overlapped with or utilized anti-Jewish tropes. When British interests were uncoupled from the Zionist movement, right-wing anti-Zionism declined into a species of pro-Arab sentimentalism or remained an offspring of antipathy towards Jews. Hostility to Jews and Israel lingered on in society, and was quite common amongst the upper strata, but it was not the mobilizing issue it had once been. By contrast, the mass-based left adopted anti-Zionism as a "poster-issue." Socialist doctrine, more than perceived interests, became the generating station for anti-Zionism.

The New Left and Anti-Zionism

Between 1948 and 1956, British political attitudes to Zionism tended to echo perceived British interests in the Middle East as refracted through party doctrine and ideology. The Conservatives were cool about Zionism except when Israel was a useful tool in British Middle East policy, exemplified by the collusion with Israel at the time of the Suez Affair. The Labour Party condemned this dalliance because it was the parliamentary opposition and was obliged to do so, but also because it seemed a last reflex of British imperialism to which the party was opposed on doctrinal grounds. The Anglo-French military action in collusion with Israel sparked allegations of dual loyalty against Jewish MPs, but from an unexpected direction. Because the bulk of Jewish MPs were in the Labor Party and followed the party line, they were criticized for having a double allegiance by members of the Jewish community who thought their first loyalty should have been to their Jewishness and Israel.[53]

However, when Labour was in power during the 1960s its policy on Israel and Zionism was determined by a generation of politicians such as Harold Wilson, Richard Crossman and Michael Foot who had been strongly pro-Zionist in the 1940s. To them, Israel was a socialist country that offered a showcase for socialist development policies.[54] This fundamentally pro-Zionist, pro-Israel posture was undermined by the emergence of the New Left and the generation of 1968, a process that saw anti-Zionism migrate from the right to the left of politics. This historic shift was a response to new Middle Eastern realities. After 1967 Israel was perceived as a hegemonic regional power closely allied with the USA. The Palestinian cause naturally took its place alongside national liberation movements that were cast as antagonistic to American interests. The shift also reflected social change and ethnic politics in Britian. Throughout the diaspora, Jewish communities were increasingly middle class and Israel was installed as a central tenet of Jewish identity. Whereas the Jewish community had once been a social bedrock of the left, revolutionary Marxist, Trotskyist and Maoist groups now attempted to root themselves in Black and Asian immigrant populations. Since New Left leaders believed that these groups would identify with Third World struggles, they deployed anti-Zionism as a central element of their appeal.[55]

In the course of relocating from the right to the left, anti-Zionism took with it many traditional elements of anti-Jewish and anti-Zionist discourse. A typical article in the London *Socialist Leader* in October 1970 attacked "Zionism—Religious Fascism." According to the article, typical of its genre, Zionism was the product of Judaism:

> It was primarily in pursuance of, and for the eventual fulfilment of, such prophecies that Zionism was founded at the turn of the century, with the express purpose of restoring the 'Chosen Race' to Israel, the 'Holy Land,' Palestine, that Jehovah the God of the Jews had given to their remote ancestors but from which they had been expelled by Roman pagan invaders in AD 70 exactly 19 centuries ago.

Since religion was ephemeral and invalid, this was hardly a good reason to create a state.

> The real paradox inherent hitherto in the current state of Israel is that it was actually founded for a different purpose from which its present leaders advocate. Currently, we have the still further paradox of a Zionist racial state claiming the sympathy and support as a 'National Home' for the Jews ....[56]

The left denied that the Jews were a nation with any claim to an ancestral homeland, although they were happy to bolt onto that hoary allegation a contradictory claim that the Jews were a unified 'race' that sought to maintain a "racial state" in Israel.

The allegation that Zionism was racist was authorized when the United Nations (UN) pronounced Zionism a form of racism in 1975. This step greatly increased the value of anti-Zionism for ethnic politics in the UK. The UN resolution made it possible to link popular mass-based anti-racist campaigns at home with palpably less relevant anti-Zionism. When the right took power in Israel in 1977, the final elements to complete the realignment of anti-Zionism fell into place. Throughout the late 1970s in Britain, revolutionary Marxist, Trotskyite and Maoist student groups used the National Union of Students' "No platform for racists" policy to ban Jewish student societies that were branded Zionist and therefore racist. By the mid-1980s the cadres of the New Left were in positions of power within municipal government and anti-Zionism went from doctrine to policy. For example, the Greater London Council (GLC) under Ken Livingstone routinely espoused anti-Israel positions. This was also part of the GLC's ethnic politics and the attempt to engage Irish, Black and Asian Londoners by espousing anti-imperialist, Third World causes.[57]

For years, Soviet-inspired propaganda had depicted Zionism as a form of racism and asserted that, as such, it was no different from Nazism. The suggestion that an ideological affinity existed between Zionism and Nazism provided the groundwork for the accusation that Zionists and Nazis had collaborated. This was a gross distortion of history which was implicitly predicated on the malign (but hidden) activity of a vast worldwide Jewish conspiracy. During the 1980s this fantasy took hold in swathes of the left in Britain. Its centrality and tenacity was revealed by the controversy over the play *Perdition* written by the highly regarded and successful TV dramatist Jim Allen and directed by Ken Loach. *Perdition* used the convention of a dramatized court case, modeled on the Kasztner case in Israel in 1953–54, to lay out every aspect of the alleged Nazi-Zionist collaboration and the alleged conspiracy by Zionist Jews to deceive the world into believing their version of the European Jewish catastrophe so as to obtain recompense through the creation of Israel.[58]

Perdition was intended as anti-Zionist agitprop theatre. Allen, a veteran Trotskyite, said that "it does provide a subtext acutely aimed at discrediting Zionism." He described his play as "the most lethal attack on Zionism ever written, because it touches at the heart of the most abiding myth of modern history, the Holocaust. Because its says quite plainly that privileged Jewish leaders collaborated in the extermination of their own kind in order to help bring about a Zionist state, Israel, a state which is in itself racist." But it went far beyond rational anti-Zionism. The play purported to reveal a gigantic conspiracy by powerful Jews who cruelly and mercilessly sacrificed fellow Jews in order to gain political advantage and then conspired to cover up their genocidal malfeasance. The script was laced with anti-Jewish stereotypes and Christological tropes that may have originated in Allen's Roman Catholic upbringing. For example, one character declares that "Israel was coined in the blood and tears of Hungarian Jewry." The courtroom is described as a "confessional" in which the accuser says he aspires to "absolution." The legal speeches are replete with references to Pontius Pilate, Golgotha and crucifixion. The play ends with a climax similar to the *Merchant of Venice*: a Jew is humbled and confesses to his misdeeds. Yet, when *Perdition* was pulled by the management of the Royal Court Theatre, it became a cause célèbre for intellectuals and activists of the far left. On radio and TV, Loach and Allen repeatedly condemned the "Zionist lobby" for suppressing the truth about Nazi-Zionist collusion. Michael Ignatieff observed that the defenders of the play were "pandering to the latent anti-Semitism that is still a factor in the modern world."[59]

However "new" the New Left was and however "new" its anti-Zionism may have seemed, it embodied key structural continuities from previous forms of anti-Zionist and anti-Jewish discourse. True, anti-Zionism in the 1970s and 1980s inevitably reflected Israel's occupation of territory after the 1967 war and its emergence as a regional superpower. Other new elements flowed from anti-imperialist and anticolonial Third World struggles, such as the identification of Zionism as racist and Israel as a colonial settler state. Soviet anti-Zionism that featured the myth of Zionist-Nazi collaboration also fed into some propaganda in the United Kingdom. In essence, though, left-wing anti-Zionism was a development of Marxist and socialist dogma concerning Jews and nationalism in general and was shot through with all the ambivalences towards the continuation of the Jews as a collectivity that had bedeviled relations between the socialist left and the Jews since Marx and earlier.[60]

Anti-Zionism, Anti-Americanism and 9/11

During the years of the "Oslo Process", anti-Zionism in Britain went into remission. Anti-Semitism seemed to be, once again, the exclusive preserve of the far right. However, after the collapse of the peace process in late 2000 and the outbreak of the second *Intifada*, anti-Zionism in Britain and Europe experienced a sharp resurgence. Jewish communal organizations, institutions monitoring anti-Jewish currents, and various commentators now identified a "new anti-Semitism" that was organically linked to anti-Zionism and events in the Middle East. This antipathy reached new levels in the wake of the attack on America in September 2001. First, al-Qaeda's hatred of America was widely attributed to American support for Israel. Zionism was thus held partly responsible for the events of 9/11. Second, the subsequent American-led war on international terrorism was depicted as a "crusade" against Muslims who resisted American policy in the Middle East, a quasi-imperialistic adventure that was orchestrated by Jewish neoconservative policymakers in Washington who had intimate connections with Israel and Zionism. The concatenation of anti-Americanism, anti-Zionism and anti-Semitism reached its apogee in the opposition to military action against Iraq in 2003–4.[61]

While the "new anti-Semitism" in Britain and Europe is tightly meshed with antipathies towards Zionism and Israel, certain key ingredients do not seem very "new" at all. On the contrary, they evince continuity with traditional anti-Jewish and anti-Zionist themes. For example, it is commonly alleged that Jews possess enormous wealth that is translated into political power through control of the mass media and the funding of political parties in what amounts to buying influence and then retaining it by a form of blackmail. "Jewish power" is irresponsible, unaccountable and exercised behind the scenes: it is the work of a conspiracy or a cabal. This hidden international network embraces London, Washington, New York and Jerusalem. As a result of concealed influences, American and British foreign policy is driven not by national interests but by Jewish interests, notably the service of Israel.[62]

The chief themes and the types of continuity as well as convergence may be illustrated by several representative examples from the press and political statements. On 14 January 2002 the *New Statesman*, a political weekly that is virtually the house magazine of the Labor Party, appeared with a cover design depicting a golden Star of David piercing a Union flag. The illustration was meant to complement the cover story entitled "A Kosher Conspiracy." This article, by Denis Sewell, asserted:

> That there is a Zionist lobby and that it is rich, potent and effective goes largely unquestioned on the left. Big Jewry, like big tobacco, is seen as one of life's givens. Wealthy Jewish business leaders, acting in concert with establishment types and co-ordinated by the Israeli embassy, have supposedly nobbled newspaper editors and proprietors, and ensured that the pro-Palestinian position is marginalized both in news reporting and on the comment pages.

Sewell gave evidence of journalists apparently being "nobbled" by proprietors such as Conrad Black, who is "married to Barbara Amiel, the enthusiastic Zionist," *éminences grises* like Lord Weidenfeld, who breakfasts with Peter Hain MP, the Board of Deputies of British Jews, Bicom, a pro-Israel lobby group, and the Israeli embassy. He concluded ironically that "The truth is the 'Zionist lobby' does exist, but it is a clueless bunch." The following article, by John Pilger, stated that Prime Minster Tony Blair "shamelessly appointed a friend Michael Levy, a wealthy Jewish businessman who had fundraised for New Labor as his 'special envoy' in the Middle East, having first made him Lord Levy." Pilger listed Lord Levy's Jewish communal affiliations, mentioned his house and business in Israel, and the fact that his son worked for the Israeli Ministry of Justice. This "was the man assigned by Britain's prime minister to negotiate impartially with Palestinians and Israelis." Pilger compounded the picture of a lop-sided British policy by citing recent British arms sales to Israel and support for Israel's campaign against the Palestinians.[63]

The cover and the content of this *New Statesman* issue outraged many people. David Triesman, the general secretary of the Labour Party, condemned it in a letter to the weekly and the editor, Peter Wilby, subsequently admitted that he "got it wrong." "The cover," he said, "was not intended to be anti-Semitic; the *New Statesman* is vigorously opposed to racism in all its forms. But it used images and words in such a way as to unwittingly create the impression that the *New Statesman* was following an anti-Semitic tradition that sees the Jews as a conspiracy piercing the heart of the nation." And yet, a few weeks later, the *New Statesman* carried an article by Andrew Stephen on the power of the Jewish lobby in America, entitled "Why Israel Gets an Easy Ride." "The Jewish lobby," Stephen claimed, "is simply too strong for any US politician, Republican or Democrat, to ignore." Stephen recited some of the names of the donors to Clinton's election campaign and drew links from the pro-Israel lobby group AIPAC to the State Department. He concluded that "The Bush administration—even including Colin Powell—has been neatly coerced into justifying Israel's ever mounting aggression as part of the worldwide war against terrorism."[64]

The fantasy of Jewish power, global influence and conspiracy was echoed by Tam Dalyell, a veteran Labour Party MP, when he was interviewed about the Blair premiership for an article in the magazine *Vanity Fair* in Spring 2003. Dalyell was indirectly quoted by the writer David Margolick as saying that "he thinks Blair is unduly influenced by a cabal of Jewish advisers. He mentions Mandelson, Lord Levy (Blair's chief fundraiser) and Jack Straw.... " This aside drew the attention of other journalists who asked Dalyell if he stood by the claim that the prime minister was in the thrall of a "Jewish cabal." When offered the chance to backtrack or apologize, Dalyell repeated what he had been reported as saying and even enlarged on his comments by naming Jewish neoconservatives in Washington who he claimed were influencing President Bush and Blair. He told the *Jewish Chronicle*: "I am critical of Israel's extreme Likud agenda, and of certain people in Washington whose considerable influence got us into a war with Iraq that was a catastrophe. That does not make me anti-semitic."[65]

The notion that Zionist-orientated Jews comprise a powerful and coordinated international force was also expressed by Perry Anderson in his editorial article for the highly influential theoretical journal *New Left Review* in summer 2001. Anderson engaged in a standard *NLR* polemic against Zionism, but his argument strayed into territory that had nothing to do with criticism of Israel. He observed that whereas most colonial settler states originated when settlers left the motherland, this was not the case for Jews who emigrated to Palestine. The Jews had corrected this anomaly, though, by engaging in a process of reverse colonization.

> Entrenched in business, government and media, American Zionism has since the sixties acquired a firm grip on the levers of public opinion and official policy toward Israel, that has weakened only on the rarest of occasions. Taxonomically, the colonists have in this sense at length acquired something like the metropolitan state—or state within a state—they initially lacked.[66]

This astonishing comment is a miniaturized version of the *Protocols of the Elders of Zion*. It manages in just a few lines to combine several elements of anti-Jewish discourse. It rehashes the allegation leveled against Jews since the French Revolution that they form a "state within a state." According to Anderson, Jews are inordinately powerful and exert a malign influence via control of the press and government. America is reduced to a puppet of Israel.

Thanks partly to the political realignment of Jews in the USA and the emergence of Jewish figures in the ranks of the neoconservatives, the association of Jews with the right has become a routine stereotype in much the same way that Russian Jews were once tarred with Bolshevism. But the popularization of the stereotype owes much to anti-American and anti-globalization campaigners who routinely conflate the stated goals of "Jewish neo conservatives" in Washington with US and Israeli policy. This linkage was boosted by the US response to 9/11 and, particularly, the war in Iraq. In Britain, during 2003–4, the Stop the War Coalition, an organization dominated by cadres from the Communist Party of Britain, the Socialist Workers Party and the Muslim Association of Great Britain, ran a two-track campaign against the war and in support of Palestine. The campaign slogan, "Stop the invasion of Iraq—Free Palestine", tersely captured the coalescence of anti-Americanism and anti-Zionism.[67]

This linkage was clearly set out in a message of support from the Edinburgh Stop the War Coalition and Edinburgh Campaign for Nuclear Disarmament (CND) to the 2003 Cairo Conference of the International Campaign Against US and Zionist Occupations:

> We want to expose the lies of imperialism that justifies the oppression of our sisters and brothers in Iraq and Palestine. We aim to expose the US project for the "new American century" as a plan for imperialist domination, in particular through the "star wars" project. We want to remove brick by brick the fear that ties so many of our people to the imperialist war lords.[68]

However, as Naomi Klein has observed, when anti-American and anti-globalization polemicists depict US policy in Iraq as serving Israel's interests, or Israeli repression of the Palestinians as sanctioned by a Jewish-dominated Washington, they are transforming and rehabilitating the myth of a worldwide Jewish network operating with selfish and malignant intentions.[69]

The attack on Zionism as a form of racism allied to or identical with Nazism also resurfaced amongst left-wing intellectuals and parties after 2000. In April 2002, Professor Tom Paulin, a poet and Oxford academic, told the Egyptian paper *Al-Ahram* in an interview that American Jewish settlers on the West Bank "should be shot. I think they are Nazis, racists. I feel nothing but hate for them." This was not the first time Paulin had made this identification. He had earlier compared Israelis to Nazis in a poem "Killed in Crossfire," published in the *Observer*:

> We are fed this inert
> This lying phrase
> Like comfort food
> As another little Palestinian boy
> In trainers jeans and a white tee-shirt
> Is gunned down by the Zionist SS
> Whose initials we should
> —but we don't—dumb goys
> Clock in the weasel words
> Crossfire.

Paulin, who is a regular broadcaster on the BBC as well as being a professor of English literature at Oxford University, was never reprimanded for his poem or obiter dicta.[70]

Within mainstream politics, too, it has become possible to equate Zionists with Nazis and to draw parallels between Nazi policy and Israeli policy with impunity. After a visit to Gaza in June 2003, the Black Jewish Labor MP Oona King compared conditions there to the Warsaw ghetto. She wrote in the *Guardian*: "The original founders of the Jewish state could surely not imagine the irony facing Israel today: in escaping the ashes of the Holocaust, they have incarcerated another people in a hell similar in its nature— though not its extent—to the Warsaw ghetto."[71] In the demonstrations organized by the Stop the War Coalition against British military action against Iraq in 2003, protesters routinely carried placards juxtaposing the Star of David with the swastika.

One significant innovation has been added to anti-Zionism since 2000. Reviewing how interest in the history of the Nazi persecution of the Jews grew in America from the 1960s onwards, Peter Novick identified a "massive investment by Jewish communal organizations in promoting 'Holocaust consciousness.'" This "investment" was intended to solidify support for Israel, neutralize anti-Zionism, deter anti-Semitism and foster Jewish group solidarity. According to Novick: "Over the last quarter century American Jewish leadership, in response to a perception that needs had changed, has chosen to center the Holocaust—to combat what they saw as a 'new anti-semitism'; in support of an embattled Israel; as the basis of a revived ethnic consciousness."[72] The political scientist Norman Finkelstein takes Novick's argument even further. He claims that the mass murder of the Jews by the Nazis is only one genocide amongst many in the last century and deserves no privileged attention. On the contrary, 'the Holocaust' is a cultural construct fabricated by Jews to inculcate guilt in Western nations and extract reparations money for Israel, as well as to suppress criticism of Zionism.[73]

Novick and Finkelstein won considerable attention in the British media and both addressed audiences in the United Kingdom. They benefited anti-Zionists at a crucial juncture by depicting Holocaust memorialization as a Zionist scam. Indeed, their arguments had a multiplier effect. Whereas it was once possible to stigmatize anti-Zionism by warning that it shared a language with Nazi anti-Semitism, any reference to "the Holocaust" is now automatically deemed special pleading on behalf of Zionism and Israel. It was never very sensible to justify Israel as recompense for genocide or to defend Zionism as being merely the response to Nazi persecution, but Novick and Finkelstein have made this line of argument at best embarrassing and, at worst, almost untenable.

Academics in Britain made their own unique, practical contribution to anti-Zionism by successfully promoting the academic boycott of Israeli institutions of higher education. The boycott movement was started in Britain in April 2002 by Professors Steven Rose and Hilary Rose. An attempt to persuade the Association of University Teachers (AUT) to impose a blanket boycott on Israeli universities was repelled at the AUT annual council meeting in 2003.[74] However, a second attempt, tactically restricted to a boycott of three named universities for specific alleged offences, was made at the AUT annual gathering in April 2005. The promoter of the boycott resolution, Dr. Sue Blackwell, a member of the Socialist Workers Party, called on AUT members to support action against the "illegitimate state of Israel." This time the boycotters were successful, if only by a narrow margin.[75]

It was soon evident, however, that the anti-Zionist boycott had anti-Jewish implications. In effect it targeted only Jewish Israelis because the method of implementation relied on guidance from Palestinian organizations that depicted Arab Israelis as "victims" of discrimination and oppression. Furthermore, it excluded from the boycott any Israeli who agreed to condemn the occupation of the West Bank and Gaza Strip, a requirement that would be surely irrelevant in the case of Arab Israelis. Nevertheless, the passage of the AUT resolution was indicative of the degree to which Zionism and Israel have acquired negative connotations amongst the most highly educated sector of British society.[76]

Continuities and Discontinuities

In this survey of anti-Zionism in Britain certain remarkable convergences and continuities appear. Jews are consistently credited with great power and identified with international finance. The alleged financial power of world Jewry is deemed the source of their overweening political power. Jews are said to be installed at the heart of politics in Washington and London. Their power is exerted covertly and Jewish control of the press is used to mask it. Jews are blamed for anti-Semitism. Max Hastings, a former editor of the *Daily Telegraph* and *Evening Standard*, and once a vociferous supporter of Israel, recently wrote: "If Israel persists with its current policies, and Jewish lobbies around the world continue to express solidarity with repression of the Palestinians, then genuine anti-semitism is bound to increase."[77] The game of good Jew/bad Jew is still played. Writing in defence of Dalyell, the Trostkyite journalist Paul Foot observed that "he is wrong to complain about Jewish pressure. But that is a mistake that is constantly encouraged by the Zionists." Foot continued: "The most honourable and principled Jews here, and in Israel, are those who oppose the imperialist and racist policies of successive Israeli governments." He gave as an example Tony Cliff (Gluckstein), his mentor in the Socialist Workers Party.[78]

Certain stark discontinuities also appear, although on closer examination what at first appears to be a caesura seems more like a process of elision. Jews and Zionists are no longer identified with Marxism or subversive movements of the left. But the withering away of the Jewish left and the collapse of communism have not ended the political stereotyping of Jews and Zionism. Instead, they are ritualistically associated with the ideology and policies of the right, notably in the guise of neoconservatism. For the anti-globalization movement, Israel and Zionism represent agents of American capitalism and global hegemony in much the same way as for the right eighty years ago they were the agents of Bolshevism and world revolution.

Explicit religious references are largely absent from anti-Zionism amongst nominal Christians, as would be expected in a secular era. However, there have been instances when even these ancient tropes have been invoked. During the siege of the Church of the Nativity in Bethlehem by the IDF in spring 2002, religious images were sometimes employed by cartoonists, while journalists and politicians repeatedly, and gratuitously, invoked the sanctity of the place. One cartoon in the *Observer* showed three wise men heading past a signpost to the Church of the Nativity. Two wise men carry boxes marked gold and frankincense; but the third figure is an Israeli soldier carrying a gun inscribed "murder." It was at this time that an Episcopalian church in Edinburgh commissioned a mural that showed Israeli soldiers in place of the Roman soldiers at the foot of the cross.[79]

It may be farfetched to argue that a cartoon that appeared in the Independent on 27 January 2001 depicting Ariel Sharon biting off the head of a Palestinian baby is a deliberate evocation of the myth that Jews engage in the ritual slaughter of Christian children. But it is surely fair to question why such an offensive cartoon should have been printed on Britain's Holocaust Memorial Day. The cartoonist, Dave Brown, subsequently won a press industry award for this work.[80]

Amongst Muslims in Britain the use of religious imagery and rhetoric in the context of anti-Zionist discourse is widespread. But this is only one, small, aspect of the unprecedented situation created by the presence of a large, well-organized, media-savvy and politicized Muslim population in Britain. Anti-Zionism is now firmly established in the diverse Muslim communities of the United Kingdom: indeed, it is one of the few issues on which all Muslims can unite. A recent report of the European Monitoring Centre on Racism and Xenophobia demonstrated that there is a clear correlation between anti-Jewish violence and rhetoric and events in the Middle East. The report showed that Arab-speaking Muslims access crude anti-Semitic propaganda from Arab satellite TV stations while most members of the Muslim communities visit Internet sites purveying similar material from Islamist or right-wing groups.[81]

Several Muslim journalists, notably Faisal Bodi, have gained a platform in the mainstream press for disseminating their view that "Israel has no right to exist." In multicultural Britain this position is treated as a legitimate point of view and it is considered the right of Muslims—like any other ethnic-faith group pursuing its interests—to articulate its rage against Israel, Zionism and Jews who are Zionists. Hence, an impeccably liberal forum such as the *Guardian* newspaper can carry an article denying Israel's right to exist followed a few days later by another advocating Zionism. The genocidal implications of calling for the dismantling of Israel do not inhibit such Muslim writers or those who commission and publish their work. It is one alternative point of view and to express it is a perfect right.[82]

Indeed, many Muslims feel that the relatively benign history of Jewish-Muslim relations renders them immune to charges of anti-Semitism. They feel no responsibility for Nazi atrocities against the Jews and, on the contrary, feel aggrieved that with the creation of Israel in 1948 Palestinian Arabs paid the price for Christian aggression against the Jews of Europe. To many young Muslims in Britain the Jews seem to be part of a wealthy, powerful white establishment that excludes them, and they cannot imagine that Jews were once the victims of institutional racism. Reminders about the fate of Europe's Jews within living memory are dismissed as "the Holocaust industry." Muslim representative bodies in the United Kingdom, such as the Muslim Council of Britain and the Muslim Association of Britain, have boycotted the national Holocaust Memorial Day ceremony since its inception in January 2001. The sense that European anti-semitism has nothing to do with them Muslims insensitive to Jewish anxieties and vulnerabilities, and blunts of the counter arguments that once gave anti-Zionists pause for thought.

The death of the character of Muslim anti-Zionism was illustrated in the course of the 2005 General Election. In the constituency of Bethnal Green and Bow, where Muslims comprise 40 percent of the electorate, George Galloway, leader of a small single-issue party dedicated to opposing the war in Iraq and championing the Palestinians, challenged the sitting Labour MP Oona King, who is black and Jewish. Three weeks before the poll young Muslim protesters violently disrupted the 60th anniversary memorial service to the mainly Jewish victims of a German V-2 (rocket bomb) attack on the East End which Ms. King attended. She protested that throughout the campaign Galloway's supporters referred to her color, her gender and her father's religion in slighting terms. Galloway succeeded in overturning King's majority and will enter Parliament as the sole MP for his party, Respect.[83]

However, mass-based anti-Zionism in Britain's Muslim communities is the only manifestation of its power to mobilize people on a large scale. To this extent it reveals the starkest discontinuity in the history of anti-Zionism in Britain. In the early 1920s anti-Zionism was on a massive scale. It was blared from the headlines of a dozen influential and mass-circulation newspapers; it employed crude anti-Jewish rhetoric; it was used routinely in electoral politics; and it was hardly contested. Today, outside the Muslim population, anti-Zionism is not a mass phenomenon. Doctrinaire hostility to Israel is confined to niche publications of the left, such as the *New Statesman*, and the relatively small-circulation papers of the liberal-left such as the *Guardian* and the *Independent*. The more popular the paper, the more pro-Israel it tends to be. When left-of-center papers do publish anti-Israel diatribes or when a politician attacks Zionism they are met with a barrage of criticism.[84] To that extent the situation is transformed—for the better. Yet it is disturbing to see mythic and stereotypical discourse recycled within the "chattering classes" with less and less self-restraint. Israel has always been the victim of double standards and the object of a special asperity. But the expression of a belief in Jewish power, conspiracy, treachery and malice that was once confined to a lunatic fringe has re-entered public discourse via anti-Zionism. Similarly, the denigration of Holocaust memorialization and the relativization of Jewish suffering that was previously a preserve of right-wing revisionists has moved to the core of "respectable" conversation about Israel and Zionism. While it is hard to define exactly what is afoot and to disentangle it from rational and understandable rage against the policies of Israel's current government, there is a convergence of anti-Zionism and anti-Jewish discourse, and it is occurring not at the fringes but at the center of British political and cultural life.

Notes

[1] For a useful summary of these developments, see Clarke, *Hope and Glory*.

[2] I would like to thank the participants in the conference, "Convergence and Divergence: Anti-Semitism and Anti-Zionism in Historical Perspective," held at Brandeis University, on 24 and 25 March 2004, for their insightful comments on an earlier version of this article which these remarks are intended to address. For a helpful guide to the news media, see Hartley, *Understanding the News*.

[3] See Cesarani, "Anti-Zionist Politics," 28.

[4] See Defries, *Conservative Party Attitudes to Jews*, 98–118.

[5] For an overview, consult Cesarani, "The Study of Anti-Semitism in Britain," 249–75. For detailed research on the 1920s, see Lebzelter, *Political Anti-Semitism*; Holmes, *Anti-Semitism in British Society*; Cheyette, *Constructions of "the Jew"*.

[6] *Morning Post*, 2 November 1921, 16 October 1922, 6 November 1922. (Unless otherwise stated, such references are to leading articles.)

[7] *The Times*, 8 February 1922. Pound and Harmsworth, *Northcliffe*, 462.

[8] *Spectator*, 11 November 1922.

[9] *Evening News*, 2 and 7 November 1922.

[10] House of Commons Debates, 5th series, vol. 136, col. 1352, 21 December 1920.

[11] *Sunday Express*, 11 February 1923.

[12] See Haberer, *Jews and Revolution*; Kadish, *Bolsheviks and British Jews*.

[13] *Morning Post*, 22 April 1921.

[14] *The Times*, 8 February 1922.

[15] *Daily Mail*, 17 February 1922.

[16] House of Commons Debates, 5th series, vol. 151, col. 1942, 14 March 1922.

[17] Wilson, "The Protocols of the Elders of Zion"; Kadish, *Bolsheviks and British Jews*, 30–8. For a good, recent analysis of the *Protocols*, see Bronner, *A Rumour about The Jews*.

[18] *Morning Post*, 16 and 18 November 1922.

[19] *Spectator*, 11 and 18 November 1922.

[20] *Daily Express*, 28 October 1922. Svengali was an 'alien' Jew: see Cheyette, *Constructions of "the Jew"*, 52, 151; and Pick, "Powers of Suggestion," 105–25.

[21] *The Times*, 23 June 1922.

[22] Signed article, *Sunday Express*, 15 February 1922.

[23] Cesarani, "The Anti-Jewish Career of Sir William Joynson-Hicks."

[24] Cesarani, "Anti-Zionist Politics," 40–42.

[25] *The Times*, 26 August 1929, 12, and leading article, 13; 27 August 1929, 9, 10 and 11; 28 August 1929, 13.

[26] *Daily Express*, 26 August 1929–31 August 1929, 1 and 2.

[27] *Daily Express*, 27 August and 31 August 1929.

[28] *Daily Mail*, 26 August 1929 and 2 September 1929.

[29] *Daily Mail*, 27 August 1929.

[30] *Daily Mail*, 30 August 1929 and 3 September 1929.

[31] Gorny, *The British Labour Movement and Zionism*, 14–24.

[32] For a summary, see Cesarani, *The Left and the Jews*. More detailed treatment is provided in Hertzberg, *The French Enlightenment and the Jews*; Carlbach, *Karl Marx*; Jacobs, *On Socialists and the "Jewish Question"*; Traverso, *The Marxists and the Jewish Question*.

[33] MacDonald, *A Socialist in Palestine*, 6.

[34] Gorny, *The British Labour Movement and Zionism*, 21–24.

[35] Ibid., 91–95. Osmond, "British Jewry and Labour Politics," 55–70; and Collette, "The Utopian Visions of Labour Zionism," 71–92.

[36] Gorny, *The British Labour Movement and Zionism*, 62–66.

[37] Ibid., 57–81.

[38] On the ambivalence of the left, see Jacobs, *On Socialists and the "Jewish Question."* The lobbying of socialist Zionists is analyzed by Shimoni, "Poale Zion," 241–5.

[39] See Gorny, *The British Labour Movement and Zionism*, 164–80 and 186–88; Shimoni, "Poale Zion," 249–50.

[40] Gorny, *The British Labour Movement and Zionism*, 216–19.

[41] Bethell, *The Palestine Triangle*, 212–13, 216, 243–44; Harris, *Attlee*, 388–400; Bullock, *Ernest Bevin*, 164–69.

[42] Sykes, *Crossroads to Israel*, 284; Harris, *Attlee*, 391–92.

[43] Gorny, *The British Labour Movement and Zionism*, 221–22.

[44] For this affair, see Cesarani, *The "Jewish Chronicle" and Anglo-Jewry*, 194.

[45] Garfield, *Our Hidden Lives*, 53.

[46] Ibid., 106.

[47] Ibid., 244.

[48] Ibid., 321.

[49] Ibid., 328–29.

[50] Ibid., 430, 432–33.

[51] Ibid., 432.

[52] Kushner, "Anti-Semitism and Austerity," 149–68. For an eyewitness account of fascist anti-Zionism, see Beckman, *The 43 Group*, 60–61.

[53] There is a large literature on Suez. For a balanced appraisal based on new documents, see Kyle, *Suez*. For the domestic repercussions, see Alderman, *The Jewish Community in British Politics*, 131–3.

[54] For typical manifestations of affection, see Crossman, *A Nation Reborn*, and Wilson, *Chariot of Israel*.

[55] Rubinstein, *The Left, the Right and the Jews*, 77–117. The Jewish community's drift to the right in England is documented in Alderman, *The Jewish Community in British Politics.* See also Wistrich, "Left-Wing Anti-Zionism in Western Societies," 46–52.

[56] *Socialist Leader*, 10 October 1970.

[57] See Wistrich, "Left-Wing Anti-Zionism in Western Societies." For the anti-Israel politics of the GLC, see Alderman, *London Jews and London Politics*, 117–38. S. Cohen, *That's Funny*, gives an analysis of left anti-Semitism of the period.

[58] Allen, *Perdition.*

[59] Cesarani, "The Perdition Affair," 53–60. It is noteworthy that the play was revived in London in June 1999 and actually enjoyed a run at the Gate Theatre. Yet it aroused little of the heat that accompanied its abortive debut.

[60] See Mendelsohn, ed., *Essential Papers on Jews and the Left*; Wistrich, *Revolutionary Jews* and *Socialism and the Jews.*

[61] Iganski and Kosmin, eds., *A New Anti-Semitism?* Rosenfeld, *Anti-Americanism and Anti-Semitism*, offers a rather partisan analysis. For an excellent critique from a left-wing standpoint, which nevertheless arrives at very similar conclusions, see N. Cohen, *Pretty Straight Guys*, 101–34 and 271–8.

[62] Rosenfeld, *Anti-Zionism in Great Britain and Beyond*; Pulzer, "The New Anti-Semitism," 79–101; Fraser, "Understanding Trades Union Hostility towards Israel," 58–66; Melanie Phillips, *Observer*, 22 February 2004; European Monitoring Centre on Racism and Xenophobia, *Report on Manifestations of Anti-Semitism in the European Union*, November 2003, 8.

[63] *New Statesman*, 14 January 2002.

[64] *New Statesman*, 8 April 2002.

[65] *Vanity Fair*, June 2003; Colin Brown and Chris Hastings, *Daily Telegraph*, 3 May 2003; *Jewish Chronicle*, 9 May 2003.

[66] *New Left Review*, July–August 2001, 5–30, quote on 15.

[67] See N. Cohen, *Pretty Straight Guys*, 131–3.

[68] 2003 Cairo Conference of the International Campaign against US and Zionist Occupations at http://www.cairo campaign.com/docs_e.htm.

[69] Naomi Klein, *Guardian*, 25 April 2002.

[70] Poem, *Observer*, 18 February 2001; Rod Liddell, *Guardian*, G2, 17 April 2002.

[71] *Guardian*, 12 June 2003. King was accompanied by a Liberal Democrat MP, Jenny Tonge, who shared her views. But Tonge was dismissed from her role as a party spokesman after stating publicly that she empathized with Palestinian suicide bombers.

[72] Novick, *The Holocaust in American Life*, 152, 170–90, 280.

[73] Finkelstein, *The Holocaust Industry.* The best-selling writer and journalist A. N. Wilson has repeatedly invoked the notion that the real Holocaust was suffered by the Palestinians and drawn on the propaganda of US Holocaust revisionists to support his case that Israel has no right to exist, least of all as a consequence of previous anti-Semitism; *Evening Standard*, 22 April 2001, 15 April 2001, 2 Feburary 2003.

[74] Levy, "The Academic Boycott and Antisemitism," 248–55.

[75] *Guardian Education*, 5 April 2005; *Guardian*, 22 April 2005; *Times Higher Education Supplement*, 29 April 2005.

[76] The boycott was reversed at a special conference of the AUT on 26 May 2005. The conference was convened at the demand of campaigners against the boycott within the AUT.

[77] *Guardian*, 11 March 2004.

[78] *Guardian*, 14 May 2003.

[79] *Observer*, 7 April 2002; *Daily Telegraph*, 5 April 2002. Cf. Melanie Phillips, "Christians Who Hate Jews," *Spectator*, 16 February 2002.

[80] *Independent*, 27 January 2001. See Pickett, "Nasty or Nazi?" 160.

[81] European Monitoring Centre on Racism and Xenophobia, *Report on Manifestations of anti-Semitism in the European Union*, November 2003. See also Wistrich, "Muslims, Jews and September 11," 169–91.

[82] *Guardian*, 3 January 2001.

[83] Michael Freedland, *Guardian*, 16 April 2005; Nick Cohen, *Observer*, 17 April 2005; Johann Hari, *Independent*, 22 April 2005. Oona King, BBC4 Radio, World at One, 11 May 2005.

[84] The *Guardian* has been so stung by the perpetual criticism that it commissioned a book to justify itself: Baram, *Disenchantment*. Witness also the storm over anti-Jewish remarks by Mayor of London Ken Livingstone in February 2005: even the *Guardian*, 16 February 2005, called on him to apologize.

References

Alderman, Geoffrey. *The Jewish Community in British Politics.* Oxford: Oxford University Press, 1983.
———. *London Jews and London Politics, 1889–1986.* London: Routledge, 131.
Allen, Jim. *Perdition: A Play in Two Acts.* London: Ithaca Press, 1987.
Baram, Daphna. *Disenchantment: The Guardian and Israel.* London: Guardian Books, 2004.
Beckman, Morris. *The 43 Group.* London: Centerprise, 1992.
Bethell, Nicholas. *The Palestine Triangle.* London: Andre Deutsch, 1979.
Bronner, Stephen Eric. *A Rumour about The Jews: Antisemitism, Conspiracy, and the Protocols of Zion.* New York: Oxford University Press, 2000.
Brown, M., ed. *Approaches to Antisemitism.* New York: International Center for the University Teaching of Jewish Civilization, 1994.
Bullock, Alan. *Ernest Bevin: Foreign Secetary.* London: Heinemann, 1984.
Carlbach, Julius. *Karl Marx and the Radical Critique of Judaism.* New Brunswick, NJ: Associated University Press of America, 1978.
Cesarani, David. "The Anti-Jewish Career of Sir William Joynson-Hicks, Cabinet Minister." *Journal of Contemporary History* 24, no. 4 (1989): 61–160.
———. "Anti-Zionist Politics and Political Anti-Semitism in England, 1920–1924." *Patterns of Prejudice* 23, no. 1 (1989): 28–45.
———. "The 'Perdition' Affair." In *Anti-Zionism and Anti-Semitism in the Contemporary World*, edited by Robert Wistrich. London: Macmillan, 1990.
———. *The "Jewish Chronicle" and Anglo-Jewry, 1840–1990.* Cambridge: Cambridge University Press, 1990.
———. "The Study of Anti-Semitism in Britain: Trends and Perspectives." In *Approaches to Antisemitism*, edited by M. Brown. New York: International Center for the University Teaching of Jewish Civilization, 1994.———. *The Left and the Jews/The Jews and the Left.* London: Profile Books, 2004.
Cheyette, Bryan. *Constructions of "the Jew" in English Literature and Society: Racial Representations, 1875–1945.* Cambridge: Cambridge University Press, 1993.
———, and Laura Marcus, eds. *Modernity, Culture and "the Jew".* Stanford: Stanford University Press, 1998.
Clarke, Peter. *Hope and Glory: Britain 1900–1990.* London: Penguin, 1997.
Cohen, Nick. *Pretty Straight Guys.* London: Faber, 2004.
Cohen, Steve. *That's Funny, You Don't Look Anti-Semitic.* Leeds: Beyond the Pale Collective, 1984.
Collette, Christine. "The Utopian Visions of Labour Zionism, British Labour and the Labour and Socialist International in the 1930s." In *Jews, Labour and the Left, 1918–48*, edited by Christine Collette and Stephen Bird. London: Ashgate, 2000.
Crossman, Richard. *A Nation Reborn.* London: Hamish Hamilton, 1960.

Defries, Harry. *Conservative Party Attitudes to Jews, 1900–1950.* London: Frank Cass, 2001.

Finkelstein, Norman. *The Holocaust Industry: Reflections on the Exploitation of Jewish Suffering.* London: Verso, 2000.

Fraser, Ronnie. "Understanding Trades Union Hostility towards Israel and Its Consequences for Anglo-Jewry." In *A New Anti-Semitism? Debating Judeophobia in 21st-Century Britain*, edited by Paul Iganski and Barry Kosmin. London: Profile Books, 2003.

Garfield, Simon. *Our Hidden Lives: The Remarkable Diaries of Post-War Britain.* London: Ebury Press, 2005.

Gorny, Josef. *The British Labour Movement and Zionism, 1917–1948.* London: Frank Cass, 1983.

Haberer, Eric. *Jews and Revolution in Nineteenth-Century Russia.* Cambridge: Cambridge University Press, 1995.

Harris, Kenneth. *Attlee.* Rev. ed. London: Weidenfeld and Nicolson, 1995.

Hartley, John. *Understanding the News.* 1995. London: Routledge, [1982] 1995.

Hertzberg, Arthur. *The French Enlightenment and the Jews.* Philadelphia: Jewish Publication Society of America, 1968.

Holmes, Colin. *Anti-Semitism in British Society, 1978–1939.* London: Edward Arnold, 1979.

Iganski, Paul and Barry, Kosmin, eds. *A New Anti-Semitism? Debating Judeophobia in 21st-Century Britain.* London: Profile Books, 2003.

Jacobs, Jack. *On Socialists and the "Jewish Question" after Marx.* New York: New York University Press, 1992.

Kadish, Sharman. *Bolsheviks and British Jews.* London: Frank Cass, 1992.

Kushner, Tony. "Anti-Semitism and Austerity: The August 1947 Riots in Britain." In *Racial Violence in Britain, 1840–1950*, edited by Panikos Panayi. Leicester: Leicester University Press, 1993.

Kyle, Keith. *Suez.* London: Weidenfeld and Nicolson, 1991.

Lebzelter, Gisela. *Political Anti-semitism in England, 1918–1939.* London: Macmillan, 1978.

Levy, John D. A. "The Academic Boycott and Antisemitism." In *A New Anti-Semitism? Debating Judeophobia in 21st-Century Britain*, edited by Paul Iganski and Barry Kosmin. London: Profile Books, 2003.

MacDonald, J. Ramsay. *A Socialist in Palestine.* London: English Zionist Federation, 1922.

Mendelsohn, Ezra, ed. *Essential Papers on Jews and the Left.* New York: New York University Press, 1997.

Novick, Peter. *The Holocaust in American Life.* New York: Houghton Mifflin, 1999.

Osmond, Deborah. "British Jewry and Labour Politics, 1918–1939." In *Jews, Labour and the Left, 1918–48*, edited by Christine Collette and Stephen Bird. London: Ashgate, 2000.

Pick, Daniel. "Powers of Suggestion: Svengali and the *Fin-de-Siècle*." In *Modernity, Culture and "the Jew,"* edited by Bryan Cheyette and Laura Marcus. Stanford: Stanford University Press, 1998.

Pickett, Winston. "Nasty or Nazi? The Use of Antisemitic Topoi by the Left-Liberal Media." In *A New Anti-Semitism? Debating Judeophobia in 21st-Century Britain*, edited by Paul Iganski and Barry Kosmin. London: Profile Books, 2003.

Pound, Reginald and Harmsworth Geoffrey. *Northcliffe.* London: Times Publishing, 1959.

Pulzer, Peter. "The New Anti-Semitism, or When Is a Taboo Not a Taboo." In *A New Anti-Semitism? Debating Judeophobia in 21st-Century Britain*, edited by Paul Iganski and Barry Kosmin. London: Profile Books, 2003.

Rosenfeld, Alvin H. *Anti-Americanism and Anti-Semitism: A New Frontier of Bigotry.* New York: American Jewish Committee, 2003.

———. *Anti-Zionism in Great Britain and Beyond: A "Respectable" Anti-Semitism?* New York: American Jewish Committee, 2004.

Rubinstein, W. D. *The Left, The Right and the Jews.* London: Croom Helm, 1982.

Shimoni, Gideon. "Poale Zion: A Zionist Transplant in Britain (1905–1945)." In *Studies in Contemporary Jewry*, edited by Peter Y. Medding. Vol. 2. Bloomington: Indiana University Press, 1986.

"The Study of Anti-Semitism in Britain: Trends and Perspectives." In *Approaches to Antisemitism*, edited by M. Brown. New York: International Center for the University Teaching of Jewish Civilization, 1994.

Sykes, Christopher. *Crossroads to Israel, 1917–1948*. Bloomington: Indiana University Press, 1973.

Traverso, Enzo. *The Marxists and the Jewish Question: The History of a Debate, 1843–1943*. Atlantic Highlands, NJ: Humanities Press, 1994.

Wilson, Harold. *Chariot of Israel: Britain, America and the State of Israel*. London: Weidenfeld and Nicolson, 1989.

Wilson, Keith. "The Protocols of the Elders of Zion and the Morning Post, 1919–1920." *Patterns of Prejudice* 19, no. 3 (1985): 5–14.

Wistrich, Robert. *Revolutionary Jews From Marx To Trotsky*. London: Harrap, 1976.

———. *Socialism and the Jews: The Dilemmas of Assimilation in Germany and Austria-Hungary*. New Brunswick NJ: Associated University Press of America, 1982.

———. "Left-wing Anti-Zionism in Western Societies." In *Anti-Zionism and Anti-Semitism in the Contemporary World*, edited by Robert Wistrich. London: Macmillan, 1990.

———. "Muslims, Jews and September 11: The British Case." In *A New Anti-Semitism? Debating Judeophobia in 21st-Century Britain*, edited by Paul Iganski and Barry Kosmin. London: Profile Books, 2003.

The French Radical Right: From Anti-Semitic Zionism to Anti-Semitic Anti-Zionism

Pierre Birnbaum

Anti-Semitic Zionism

The violently anti-Semitic French radical right has frequently endorsed Zionism as a solution that would facilitate the longed-for emigration of the Jews, their ardently hoped-for departure to that distant Palestine whence, above all, they must not return: Zionism as a miracle solution, bringing the Jewish presence in the diaspora to an end. As early as 1891, Edouard Drumont, the author of *La France juive*, suggested getting rid of the Jews, "sending them all back to Palestine,"[1] and, a little later, was highly complimentary about Theodor Herzl's recently published book, *Der Judenstaat*, stating at a conference: "Dr Herzl wishes to restore a Homeland to this people that is a people; and I see nothing wrong in this as long as this Homeland is not mine . . .. I have seen with great pleasure in the *Archives israélites* the full-page advertisement by the Jewish National Society...the Zionist movement represents the democratic element in Jewry."[2] By 1903 Drumont was congratulating Max Nordau on his nationalist arguments, writing: "The Jew who aspires to reestablish a homeland for himself is worthy of esteem. The Jew who wishes to have a flag is a decent Jew....Is not having a homeland the most critical of all duties? France for the French! Palestine for the Jews."[3] In this way, Drumont—the inventor of political anti-Semitism, the man who made anti-Semitism into an organized mass movement from which the Austrian and German anti-Semitic movements would draw their inspiration—pursued a formidable line of reasoning to its logical conclusion, declaring himself openly in favor of the Jews' departure for Palestine, which would restore France's authentic nature.

In 1898, when the Dreyfus Affair was at its height, a subscriber to the Monument Henry (a fund publicized by Drumont's *La Libre Parole* paper to finance the legal proceedings brought against Joseph Reinach by the widow of Lieutenant-Colonel Henry after the latter committed suicide) sent the following outspoken note with his contribution: "Let the Jews be treated like plague victims and sent packing to Palestine."[4] At the same time, Jules Soury, the inventor of racial anti-Semitism, wrote: "any man of the Aryan race, whether Christian or Buddhist, far from desiring the Jews' conversion, wishes only to buy wheat and dates from them after they have reverted to being farmers in their ancient land of Canaan."[5] Likewise, Urbain Gohier, Drumont's friend, issued the following call: "Palestine for the Jews! The Jews in Palestine! And France and its thousands of millions for the French!"[6]—a slogan that would frequently be heard in Algeria, where Drumont's ideas enjoyed great popularity and where crowds of "poor whites" (*petits blancs*) would frequently shout, "France for the French! The Jews in Palestine," both at the end of the nineteenth century and during the interwar period.[7] Innumerable statements in favor of Zionism were made by radical-right writers who, when espousing the slogan "France for the French," evinced an unexpected degree of Zionist fervor. In their eyes, Zionism would make it possible to re-establish a French cultural identity undiluted by outside influences. For Jean Drault, Drumont's friend and closest associate, "France is being poisoned by these indigestible Jews. The remedy for indigestion is a simple one: to take an emetic, a purgative. When it has sent them packing, back... to Palestine, France will soon recover."[8] In a similar vein, *La Vieille France* hoped for the advent of "Herzl's prophecy for the salvation of France, Europe, and the White Race."[9] The radical right had one concern only: to halt the process of assimilation of the Jews that had been taking place since the French Revolution, and to challenge their emancipation, which was adversely affecting France's identity. Understandably, for the opposite reasons those who advocated the model of Israelites integrated into French society opposed the Zionist enterprise as well as its unexpected allies, and hence Henri Prague, editor of the *Archives israélites*, wrote:

> Do you not consider suspect this patronage that our worst enemies are according an enterprise which is represented to us by its promoters as being designed to

contribute, not just to the Jews' moral recovery, but to their social and political reinstatement also?! One can understand the legitimate mistrust that is triggered by an agitation whose most ardent sycophants come from the ranks of Israel's mortal enemies. . ... Anti-Semitism championing Zionism, wishing for it to triumph—this is not the stuff that stirs the hearts of Israel.[10]

The Zionism of the radical-right anti-Semites thus constituted a threat to the Jews' integration in the French nation. Hence, curiously, the wholehearted commitment of the radical right to expelling the Jews coincided with the very heart of Zionist logic, which held that Jewish life in the diaspora inescapably implied the disappearance of an identity and a culture stretching back thousands of years.

This anti-Semitic Zionism is surprisingly constant. The following contribution comes from one René Gontier in 1939:

> The Zionism which seeks to reestablish a national homeland in the Holy Land is a most interesting undertaking. The racist wishes for the rebirth of an Israelite State where an out-and-out Jewish nationalism can develop, with its own language, its folklore, its customs, and its culture. The efforts that the Palestinian Jews have made along these lines are laudable. They have reinstated the use of Hebrew.[11]

Louis-Ferdinand Céline, an extreme anti-Semite, was in complete agreement with these sentiments, enthusiastically supporting the idea of sending the Jews back to Palestine: "If we were to stem the flow of all these Jews, to send them back to Palestine with their Freemason big shots, since that's what they love. We would no longer be "Untouchables." We would have no wars, no bankruptcies. And we would have far more room. . ... Instantly. Immediately . . . Truly the best development."[12] Céline took a broad view of the situation, and was prepared to give the Jews an enormous swathe of territory: "The Jews in Jerusalem, a bit lower down on the Niger, they don't bother me! I'll give them the entire Congo! the whole of their Africa."[13] Even after World War II, Céline was still writing the following: "A new man is coming into being over there . . . a builder . . . a grower . . . a warrior."[14] His friend Georges Montandon, who developed the theory of ethnic racism, likewise stated in his book *L'ethnie française*, "we think that the solution to the Jewish problem is as follows: to bring about a completely independent Palestine which will have its legations and its consuls in all countries. Those Israelites who opt for Palestine would be foreigners when not at home; the others would have no reason not to assimilate."[15] This physician, who would play a crucial role in the deportation of the Jews under Vichy by ruling whether or not they were circumcised, was an enthusiastic advocate of the idea: acknowledging the "cramped space available in Palestine," foreshadowing the extremist pro-transfer theories to be found in modern-day Israel, he considered that "the Arabs can all find a place somewhere in Arabia, and these transplanted Arabs will have to be compensated by the Jewish community."[16]

During the Occupation, tracts circulated in the streets of Paris, proclaiming, as at the turn of the century, "France for the French, and the Jew in Palestine."[17]

This pro-Zionism of right-wing nationalists was frequently to be found in a number of publications of the Vichy regime. An example of this can be seen in the famous issue entitled "Le Juif et la France," published by *Notre Combat*, which states:

> What is needed is a site-territory for the Jewish reality of this world. In what must be a vast territory, the inward moral revolution of the Jewish soul must be able to take place through the people coming into contact in a very real and direct fashion with its most distant past.... Only through total immersion can Zionism undertake this normalization of the Jewish people.... The entire Jewish people must set out in order to conquer.[18]

This form of Zionism enjoyed quasi-unanimous support at the time, so much so that even somebody like Pierre Drieu la Rochelle declared in his "will": "I die an anti-Semite (respectful of the Zionist Jews) ... I like races from elsewhere in their homelands; I would have sincerely liked the Jews in their homeland. They would be a fine people."[19] At this time, there were no sacrifices that people were not prepared to make in order to advance this solution; thus, "in order to repatriate Karfunkelstein, aka Léon Blum," the *Progrès de Seine-et-Oise* insisted that "Marianne offer the bogus great man of the Popular Front a free ticket for Tel Aviv, Palestine," a desire shared by *Le Franciste*, which had but one hope: that "Léon Blum and the entire tribe take the first boat for Palestine."[20] This unanimity was touching: André Chaumet and H. R. Bellanger considered that

> the solution of the Jewish problem is grounded in an all-inclusive form of Zionism, a one hundred per cent Zionism. And in a Zionism that is mandatory for this accursed people. If Zionism is not mandatory, the Jew will not submit to it. We dream of a world in which Jerusalem will be the capital of the new Kingdom of Judea. After an absence of two thousand years, Israel must direct its gaze to Palestine.[21]

Commenting on observations by Theodor Herzl or Chaim Weizmann, wholehearted endorsement was expressed of the revival of Hebrew, with statements such as the following: "Israel must return to the Promised Land and live there for good, occupying a territory that extends to Transjordan, the granary of ancient Palestine".[22]

Undoubtedly the most systematic presentation of this intransigent form of Zionism is provided by Herman de Vries de Heekelingen in a learned study intended to show that "Theodor Herzl, the initiator of modern Zionism, reached exactly the same conclusion as his"—namely, "the urgent necessity to revive the nationalist Jew, proud of his nationality, to replace the rampant Jew lurking in the guise of a bogus Frenchman."[23] In his view, there was but one possible solution, as suggested by Leon Pinsker in his brochure *Auto-Emancipation*, a solution that was "extraordinarily perceptive" and gave rise to an "all-inclusive Jewish nationalism." For him, "Jabotinsky represents the purest form of nationalist Zionism, a solution that would bring about the definitive solution to the Jewish problem."[24] An enthusiastic advocate of the agricultural methods implemented by the Zionist pioneers, he praised their efficiency compared with the archaic methods of the Arab peasants. If the latter failed to understand them, "there is no shortage of places if they want to emigrate .... All that must be done is to use strong-arm methods, after all whole populations have been transported, Greek and Armenians, for infinitely less important reasons than the solution of the excruciating Jewish problem." As de Heekelingen explained:

> Palestine will never be able to contain all of the world's Jews.... It will therefore be necessary to look at the other side of the Jordan, where there are vast expanses.... Palestine together with Transjordan could become a centre which will contain at least half, if not two-thirds of the Jews living in the Diaspora.... It is not impossible that part of Syria and Mesopotamia might be joined to the Jewish State.

As a self-confessed advocate of Greater Israel from the Nile to the Euphrates, de Heekelingen reiterated the point that it was necessary to "allow the Jews, and if necessary to force them, to set up a State similar to other states, in other words to eliminate the diaspora."[25]

Many more such declarations could be cited. They were intended to call a halt to the French Revolution by reverting to an ethnic conception of the French nation, by doing away with the universalist vision advocated by a theorist such as Ernest Renan and adopted by the secular, rationalist Third Republic. Gérard Verdeveine likewise held that "the Jews must be reinstated in their original homeland. This requires transferring the Arab populations to other parts of Asia Minor in return for generous compensation in terms of land, livestock, etc."[26] According to Georges Batault, "everything will change the day that a real Jewish State exists."[27] In a similar vein, Gabriel Malglaive called for the "recognition of a Jewish Nation, hand in hand with the naming of a territory to be granted to it. Henceforth, all the Jews in the world would legally, officially regain the Jewish nationality that their heart has always secretly chosen. Those wishing to remain in France or Germany would remain there with the status of aliens."[28] Having become citizens of the Hebrew State, those French Jews who for lack of room were unable to emigrate to Palestine, would in this way be excluded once and for all from the public space—a solution that would eliminate for ever the menacing presence of the "state within a state" denounced since the French Revolution by right-wing counterrevolutionaries. The loathsome "Jewish Republic" would disappear, insofar as this collective departure would bring to an end the Jewish presence in the midst of the French State—a presence responsible for so many measures adversely affecting Catholicism and the virtues of French identity, for its decadence, for the decline in its virility, its "feminization," a depravity introduced by the Jews who came from the Orient.[29]

After World War II, the successes of the Jewish state further strengthened this conviction as displayed by the leading lights of the radical right. In this spirit, Xavier Vallat, former Commissioner for Jewish Affairs under Vichy, made no effort to disguise his "reasons for being a Zionist" following the Six Day War, especially since Israel was thus taking revenge for France's 1962 defeat, the loss of Algeria. As far as he was concerned,

> How can this State within the State justify itself? Simply by restoring to the members of this ethnic group their affiliation with their nation—the Jewish nation—and

reinstating their status as aliens. That is why I am a Zionist. That is why I hope that Israel, at the end of this third war, will receive international guarantees for its historical borders, from the Sinai to the Hermon, and from the Mediterranean to the Jordan.[30]

Even somebody like the fascist writer Lucien Rebatet, who espoused an obscene form of anti-Semitism, realised that "over there, the cause of Israel is the cause of all Westerners. I would have been really surprised if in 1939 somebody had prophesied to me that one day I would be hoping that a Zionist army would be victorious. But today that's the only solution that seems reasonable to me."[31] At this stage, the Zionism of the radical right was fed by a political approach that was hostile to the Arabs who were responsible for the loss of Algeria. In this vein, another writer, Thierry Maulnier, celebrated the Israeli army's military victory which had enabled this "resurrection of Israel on the land that the Omnipotent Eternal One gave to His People."[32] Lastly, according to *Aspects de la France*, the nationalist monarchist weekly,

> Maurras' long-standing teaching about international and anonymous Jewish finances does not apply to Israel, because Israel is the complete opposite. Here we do not have men lurking in the corridors of enormous banks, influencing the policies of countries drained by their profits. What we have is a nationalist state, all of whose men have become rooted in an utterly natural fashion in the soil and the skies of which Maurice Barrès spoke.[33]

Anti-Semitism would inevitably lead to Zionism, through nationalist fervor vindicating the honor and credit associated with being Jewish—in Israel, proof, if such were required, of the need for a culturalist vision that binds every nation closely to its own, unique cultural code, in the tradition of Herder.

Anti-Semitic Anti-Zionism

However, this Zionist infatuation on the part of the radical right lasted for a while only, and at the end of the war in Algeria it took very little time for things to revert to a form of Semitism which, as in the past, was slanted towards the Arabs, an ideal perspective for the revival of a form of anti-Semitism which henceforth would go hand in hand with anti-Zionism. Straight out of Drumont's contradictory thinking (the desire to send the Jews back to Palestine versus admiration for Arab anti-Semitism and pride), from now on it would be the "proud Arab" who would enjoy the approval of the extreme right, the "noble Arab" as opposed to the timorous, treacherous, evil Jew. For the author of *La France juive*, the Arab was "temperate," "proud by nature," "honest and straight," whilst in Algeria the Jews constituted "an abject race that lives solely off disgraceful trafficking activities, pinching the poor wretches that fall into their clutches and squeezing them until they are bled dry."[34] Following this approach, the noble Catholic and the proud Arab must join forces in order to confront the depraved Jew, especially since the latter was the product of a cosmopolitan, rootless Anglo-Saxon form of capitalism. Indeed, the supporters of the radical right ultimately come to question the Zionist undertaking, which was in such stark contrast to the

Jews' real nature. According to Georges Saint-Bonnet, "Rather than their own resurrection, they prefer their comforting denials [of Christ] ... parasites do not live on parasites. The Jews need an Aryan to feed off. New Jerusalem is collapsing. The Wandering Jew remains the wandering Jew, Tel Aviv is not the gate through which he enters the Promised Land."[35] The facts had to be faced: in the nineteenth century, the Jews were no more interested in a Zionist revival than they were in a form of revival along the lines espoused by Abbé Grégoire during the French Revolution, since both implied going back to the land, to manual labor, to brute force, to normality. Becoming disillusioned, supporters of the radical right constantly put the situation prevailing in Palestine in the dock, excoriating the governing plutocracy that they saw as benefiting the ruling capitalism. For those holding these views, the Jews henceforth maintained the domination of the rootless Anglo-Saxon capitalism that had always been heartily loathed by France's counterrevolutionary Catholic right; hence the need to fight the Zionist enterprise, because it constituted part of the global strategy for world imperialist domination.

Without a doubt, Roger Lambelin was the radical-right pamphleteer who in the interwar period most systematically developed the thesis equating Zionism with the Anglo-Saxon powers—a thesis that would enjoy an extended period of success, down to the present day. Following World War I, he maintained,

> maneuvring those who hold power in the United States and Great Britain, the representatives of a race of thirteen or fourteen million individuals have managed to impose on the world a *pax judaica* and a super-government called the League of Nations, of which they are the masters. As a sign of victory, they have managed to install a National Homeland for their people in Palestine and, under the aegis of the British Empire, the flag is already flying over Jerusalem, the Christian world's holy city.

The Balfour Declaration, from this point of view, represented a genuine war machine against the interests of Christian France: according to Lambelin, "Zionism not only aims to establish a Jewish state; it is undertaking an even more important task, that of world domination, as revealed by the Protocols of the Elders of Zion."[36] Along the same lines, Georges Batault believed that "we are seeing the Zionist movement being taken over by the magnates of international Jewish finance to the benefit of England ... the Zionists want to make Palestine into an English dominion."[37] In this spirit, the counterrevolutionary French right, attached to defending traditional French geopolitical interests, and hostile to Anglo-Saxon capitalism which had always been considered corrupting, suddenly changed its views and condemned Zionism as a pure and simple instrument of cosmopolitan capitalism which was so powerful in New York and London alike. While Jewish nationalism was as respectable as any form of nationalism, Jewish imperialism in the service of Anglo-Saxon capitalism coordinated from Zion was henceforth generally looked upon as a fearsome threat.

Similarly—and this will be the ultimate argument in favor of a policy resolutely hostile to the Zionist movement, a policy that prevails to the present day among the radical right, distancing itself from a previously pro-Zionist position—Catholic France had as a matter of urgency to stand up for the Arab masses in their struggle against the Jewish immigrants. The argument was now completely stood on its head: having previously disdained the Arab world and ignored its inherent desire to maintain its presence in Palestine, the counterrevolutionary right, henceforth hostile to Zionism, proclaimed its support for the Arab population's resistance to Zionism. Very detailed plans, including travel costs, were now drawn up for how to organize the departure of the Jews of Palestine to French Guiana, where they would be required to perform forced labor like the convicts in Cayenne: "Since the Palestine Arabs cannot put up with the Jews in Palestine, there is no option other than to send the Jews to Guiana."[38] Since no viable solution could be seen, either in France, where assimilation was out of the question, or in Palestine, and Zionism was illegitimate because this time it was harming Arab interests, "let us leave them to the countries which are poor in them: Lapland, Patagonia, Tierra del Fuego, and so on."[39] Roger Lambelin, one of Zionism's most intractable foes in the name of the struggle against the Anglo-Saxon plutocracy, was one of the pamphleteers who paid most attention to the fate of Palestine's Arab populations, from the very beginning highlighting the shared destiny of Arabs and Christians when confronting the Jewish foe:

> Palestine's Arab populations, with their sweet and peaceful ways, took a while to be roused by the Zionist projects, which aim more or less directly at expropriating and expelling them. The Christian States should raise their voices, should defend against the British authority, which has been harnessed to serve Zionism, the rights and privileges of the old-established Islamic and Christian populations, which have lived there for centuries in peace and tranquility.[40]

Jean Drault himself, always faithful to Drumont, now modified his stance, which had previously supported Zionism as a strategy for expelling the Jews of France; henceforth, he too would take up the cudgels in favor of the Palestinian Arabs: "They are defending their hides, their country. They are doing what the French no longer do, providing them with a very instructive example of energy and tenacity."[41] And Céline himself now called a halt to his Zionist enthusiasm: "It is the Jews who have practiced racism for 2,000 years! Including in today's Palestine."[42]

What we can see, therefore, is a complete turnabout in alliances, reversing the previously pro-Zionist position of the radical right—a pro-Zionism that would reappear only occasionally, as during the Six Day War, as revenge exacted against the Algerian enemy but dissipating swiftly once this temporary alliance was forgotten. Henceforth, and as at the end of the nineteenth century from the perspective of a figure such as Drumont, anti-Semitism in France would be accompanied by a stance that was radically hostile to Israel and favorable to the noble Arab world, which was not dominated by money, to that austere people with its fighting spirit, which spurned rootless Anglo-Saxon capitalism. The powerful anti-Arab racism directed against the presence of immigrants in mainland France, a racism that is continuously expressed in violent terms among the French radical right, the incendiary declarations, the attacks and frequent physical threats for which responsibility is claimed by such people as National Front militants, the rejection of mosques in the French landscape, the overt desire to send back immigrants from North Africa who have often become

French—none of this prevents an open admiration for an Arab world that is preserving its culture against the Judeo-American domination that is sapping national identities. As long ago as 1963, *Défense de l'Occident* wrote: "Nothing can justify keeping Israel in the Arabs' racial geographic space."[43] Charles Saint-Prot, a dyed-in-the-wool anti-Semite, also strove to demonstrate his Arabophilia and his disdain for Israel, the lackey of Anglo-Saxon capitalism, when he waxed lyrical in praise of Saddam Hussein who, according to Saint-Prot, shared with de Gaulle a passion for national renewal. He lauded the merits of this "great fighter," who was seeking a "third way" between capitalism and communism, taking up the defense of this "proud fighter" from "the desert" who was standing up to the fearsome international cosmopolitan forces.[44] The Gulf War was considered to be a "Jewish war" and many of the posters put up by the weekly *Minute* in the streets of Paris denounced that "Jewish war" without upsetting anyone in the slightest. Pierre Sidos, the long-time driving force behind Occident, the extremist and anti-Semitic movement, and known to be consistent to a fault, did not even try in *Le Soleil* to conceal his enthusiastic admiration for the courage of Saddam Hussein, "the heir of Nebuchadnezzar, that King of Babylon who took the city of Jerusalem and destroyed the last State of Israel by deporting the Jews to Mesopotamia"; and in the same vein, he issued a clarion call: "The Golan Heights for the Syrians, Palestine for the Palestinians, and France for the French!"[45]—which left no home at all for the Jews, let alone the Israelis, who were supposed to vanish entirely from history. "No to the war for Israel," declared the *Tribune nationaliste*, contrasting in stark terms "George Bush, the Jews' lackey" and "Saddam Hussein, the Arab nationalist." In the same weekly publication, Claude Cornilleau, wishing to "defend our motherland and our race," vehemently denounced the "deceitfulness practiced by Israel," which preferred "to push the whites to do the dirty work in its stead."[46] The French nationalist volunteers who joined the Iraqi camp in order to take up arms and fight side by side with it also underscored with admiration the fact that "Iraq is fighting tooth-and-nail to defend its Arab race, its race."[47] In the National Front's paper, *National Hebdo*, there was fulsome praise for Saddam Hussein, "the Assyrian who is from the race of empire builders," noting that as "an ethnic Assyrian, nobody could be more terrifying to a Jew."[48]

All members of the radical right were unanimous in defending Saddam Hussein and lauding the heroism of Arab soldiers waging a desperate struggle against the "lobbies."[49] In the name of respect for local cultures, they protested against the cosmopolitan and materialist menace which was now besetting Arab nationalism, just as it had no qualms about attacking French society's Catholic identity in the name of an eternally Jewish and Anglo-Saxon cosmopolitan market. By passing himself off as the defender of both of these cultures—there Muslim and here Catholic—Jean-Marie Le Pen shared Saddam Hussein's struggle to protect those nations which were confronted by invasions that undermined their coherent identity. Anti-Semitism and anti-Zionism were now one. According to the National Front leader, whose anti-Semitism is undisguised and unwavering, and who does not mince his words in attacking the Jewish presence in France, Israel represents an "artificial State created for the oil interests of America and Great Britain."[50] In 1996, just as in November 1990, right in the middle of the Gulf War,

Jean-Marie Le Pen still wanted to go to Baghdad, asserting that "the Americans are entirely responsible for this matter because of their unconditional support for Israel's sordidly mercenary policy."[51] While increasingly using anti-Semitic insinuations of varying levels of explicitness (given new French legislation against anti-Semitism), Le Pen attacked Israel as well, flying to the assistance of the Jewish State's most intractable enemy, Saddam Hussein. During the traditional May 1 procession, National Front militants chanted, "France for the French!" "Zionists—racists, imperialists," "Israel is a murderer, Americans are accomplices," and shouted, "Deauville, Sentier, occupied territories."[52] When the National Front organizes happenings, the entertainment includes skinhead rock groups, one of whose songs is called, "One bullet for the Zionists, one bullet for the cosmopolitans, one bullet for the Yanks."[53] In April 2002, Jean-Marie Le Pen was still denouncing "the barbaric Anglo-Saxon behavior in Iraq," as well as Israel's deadly policies.

Today, it is in France of all places that bizarre and surprising conjunctions result from the pro-Arab positions that are expressed by some radical right leaders. A selective alliance against the Zionist enemy, and the Jews with their natural affinity for the latter, is developing between the National Front and certain minority Muslim circles. Contacts are being established between Muslim fundamentalists and right-wing extremists. As *Le Monde* reported in 2000, "from the first Gulf War onwards, the NF undertook activities in order to entice youngsters from the underprivileged suburbs into its ranks," spurred on by a profound anti-Semitism. In Paris, since the demonstrations against the Gulf War, cries can also be heard of "death to the Jews, death to Israel," often uttered by demonstrators with a North African background who shout the same slogans as the far-right militants.[54] Maurice Latrèche, who is head of the French Muslim Party and whose anti-Jewish views are well known, went to Iraq in February 2003 in order to organize a "human shield" operation there at the same time as far right militants, and in 2004, at a number of marches organized in Paris and Strasbourg by Muslim organizations opposing the law banning girls from wearing the Muslim headscarf at school, cries of "death to the Jews!" could be heard, while Palestinian flags were flown in the midst of the demonstrators.[55] Ties are being established between fundamentalist Muslims and far-right militants, both groups being hostile to the United States, the war in Iraq and the Jews in France.[56] Thus an anti-Semitic pamphlet called *Le Manifeste judéo-nazi d'Ariel Sharon,* which is being circulated in radical pro-Palestinian circles in France, attesting through its revisionist positions on the Holocaust to the shift from anti-Zionism to anti-Semitism, is published by the French Muslim Party and La Pierre et l'Olivier, a pro-Palestinian association close to both Third World circles and the radical right. These conjunctions also sometimes involve the Vert écologiste environmental movement, which became responsible for certain near-anti-Semitic gaffes in its opposition to Israel when one of its leaders, Jean Brière, published a diatribe in 1991 called "Israel's War-Mongering Role and the Zionist Lobby." According to Brière, Saddam Hussein's Ba'ath Party "professes a humanist and secular socialism, combined with an Arab nationalism," which is wrongly attacked by "Jewish journalists." He went on to argue that "the weight of the Jewish lobby was decisive in swinging the vote in favor of war" in Iraq. Drummed out of the Greens, Jean Brière triggered a major crisis which led to the resignation of militant ecologists for whom anti-Semitism was unacceptable even when used to condemn Israel. This crisis recurred in 2003 when some Greens marched side by side with pro-Palestinian militants, who violently attacked two young left-wing Jews.[57]

Incidents such as these speak volumes about unacceptable alliances. They are symbolized by the Abbé Pierre affair in 1996, concerning a most eminent figure in France who is renowned for his courageous fight to help the poor. When Roger Garaudy, a former thinker of the French Communist Party who converted to Islam, published his book *Les Mythes fondateurs de la politique israélienne*, issued by a revisionist publisher, indicating his "skepticism" about "the myth of six million Jews who were exterminated"—a work that would go on to become a major bestseller in the Arab countries—Abbé Pierre publicly expressed his support, also regarding the figure of four million exterminated Jews to be "exaggerated," while in the same breath condemning "the suffering inflicted on the Palestinians."[58] While the liberal left very much regretted these statements, the far-right press welcomed them greatly.[59] Henceforth, far-right anti-Semitism could cite the support of famous individuals with a far-left background or embodying the qualities of the downtrodden masses, thus joining forces with the anti-Israel and often anti-Semitic struggle of certain groups of radical Muslims who also admire Garaudy's works. Using the jargon of the far right, Abbé Pierre now denounced what he called "the international Zionist lobby"—a statement that pleased not only the National Front leaders and the French Fascists in the *Oeuvre française*,[60] but also the major newspapers in Egypt, Qatar and Syria, where rallies were held in defense of Garaudy, who was defending Palestine. *Al Ahram* even went so far as to compare the Garaudy Affair with the Dreyfus Affair, when a French court sentenced the writer to pay a fine.[61]

Thus Israel has become a perfect target for radical-right circles, heir to Edouard Drumont, in their desire to extend their anti-Semitic fight in France. On the one hand they continue to condemn the presence in France of North African immigrants—many of whom have become French; they are pleased that Muslim women wear the headscarf that so antagonizes the "real" French; but on the other hand—a token of the imminent danger at home—they join with part of the Arab world in denouncing Israel, a project with marked anti-Semitic overtones that finds unexpected allies among a number of thinkers from the far left. If one bears in mind the fact that in December 2003 about one in four of the French population supported Le Pen's ideas,[62] and that the latter came second in the first round of the 2002 presidential elections, one can estimate the popularity of anti-Zionist arguments in today's France. These arguments, drawing on all kinds of sources, lead to violent anti-Semitic acts which target synagogues (67 synagogues were attacked between 1 September 2000 and 31 January 2002), schools, and so on, almost on a daily basis, to the extent that nowadays anti-Semitic acts, according to the observations of France's Advisory Commission on Human Rights, constitute the lion's share of racist behavior. It would appear, however, that the French population is incapable of taking a decision to openly show its indignation at this state of affairs. The commission's latest report, published in 2004, noted that 588 anti-Semitic incidents took place in 2003, of which 125 were violent acts (physical attacks on individuals, arson attacks on synagogues or schools, and so on).[63]

This anti-Semitism is leading to the increasing isolation of France's Jewish citizens, who are desperately worried by the violence of these acts, for which responsibility is most frequently claimed by youngsters with a North African background, projecting the Palestinian *Intifada* onto French territory, attacking French Jews as symbols of Israelis: their growing Judeophobia impels them to attack all signs of Jewish presence in the public space.[64] This anti-Semitism of the poverty-stricken suburbs, which the French left does not always dare to condemn publicly, exacerbates the delicate situation of the Jews, who are practically bereft of organizations to defend them at a time when the state itself is in retreat, no longer clearly undertaking to protect them, thus calling into question their traditional vertical alliance with the state, the traditional royal alliance protecting them from the masses.[65] This hostility toward the Jews, who are regarded as Israelis, also emanates (albeit nowadays less visibly) from far-right militants who paint Nazi slogans on graves in Jewish cemeteries, even though the National Front, engaged in a process of integration within the French political system, shows itself anxious to officially limit anti-Semitic blunders. Anti-Zionism is now leading to an anti-Semitism with multifarious origins, but which can nonetheless be traced to Drumont's praise of the noble Arab warrior so long ago, which even then went hand in hand with a robust contempt for the cowardly Jews, the lackeys of Anglo-Saxon capitalism. Moreover, it should be recalled that Drumont's movement represented a populism that brought together far left and far right alike, in which white supremacists took part, along with Guedists and sometimes even socialists, who had no scruples about being involved in a large-scale anti-Semitic movement that overwhelmingly drew its inspiration from the far right.[66] Is history repeating itself at a delicate moment, when the Jews are less able than in the past to count on the protection of the state, and when they see themselves as more or less equated with a conquering Israel, allied to the Anglo-Saxon world which openly rejects French geostrategy?

Translated from French by Ruth Morris.

Notes

[1] Drumont, *Le testament d'un antisémite*, 45. See O'Brien, *The Siege*, 667.
[2] Drumont, *Le peuple juif*, 37 and 43.
[3] *La Libre Parole*, 24 December 1903.
[4] See Wilson, "Le Monument Henry," 285.
[5] Soury, *La Rédemption d'Israël*.
[6] *La Vieille France*, 12 December 1918.
[7] Ageron, *Histoire de l'Algérie contemporaine*, 2:368.
[8] Drault, *Youtes impudents*, 25.
[9] *La Vieille France*, 11 August 1921.
[10] *Archives israélites*, 2 September 1897.
[11] Gontier, *Vers un racisme français*, 240.
[12] Céline, *Bagatelles pour un massacre*, 182.

[13] Ibid., 192.

[14] In Ovaldia, "Quand j'ai rencontré Céline," 260.

[15] Montandon, *L'ethnie française*, 145.

[16] Archives of the Centre de documentation juive contemporaine (CDJCA), XCV, 120.

[17] Archives of the Centre de documentation et de vigilance, Alliance israélite universelle, Paris, no.15, folder (chemise) 51.

[18] *Notre Combat*, September 1943, CDJCA, XCIX, 43.

[19] Drieu la Rochelle, *Journal: 1939–1945*, 84 and 385.

[20] *Le Progrès de Seine-et-Oise*, 28 May 1938; *Le Franciste*, 21 November 1937.

[21] Chaumet and Bellanger, *Les Juifs et nous*, 28.

[22] *Notre Combat*, no. 4 (September 1941).

[23] De Vries de Heekelingen, *Israël, son passé, son avenir*, 8.

[24] Ibid., 69 and 128.

[25] Ibid., 220–30 and 242.

[26] Verdeveine, *Israël, nation sans territoire contre la nation française*, 31.

[27] Batault, *Le problème juif*, 230.

[28] Malglaive, *Juifs ou Français*, 214.

[29] Birnbaum, *Un mythe politique*.

[30] *Aspects de la France*, 15 June 1967.

[31] *Rivarol*, 8 June 1967.

[32] Maulnier, *L'honneur d'être juif*, 101.

[33] *Aspects de la France*, 15 June 1967.

[34] Drumont, *La France juive*, vol. 2, book 4.

[35] Saint-Bonnet, *Le Juif ou l'internationale du parasitisme*, 181–82.

[36] Lambelin, *Le péril juif*, 5 and 36.

[37] Batault, *Le problème juif*, 233–37.

[38] *Les raisons de l'antisémitisme*, 222.

[39] Viguier, *Les Juifs à travers Léon Blum*, 189.

[40] Lambelin, *Le péril juif*, 185–87.

[41] *Le Réveil du Peuple*, 15 June 1936.

[42] Letter to Albert Paraz, 9 November 1948, in Céline, *Lettres à Albert Paraz*, 111.

[43] *Défense de l'Occident*, May 1963.

[44] Saint-Prot, *Saddam Hussein, un nouveau de Gaulle*, 23 and 102. See also *idem, La France et le renouveau arabe*.

[45] *Le Soleil*, July 1990.

[46] *Tribune nationaliste*, December 1990.

[47] *Tribune nationaliste*, February 1991.

[48] *National Hebdo*, special issue, February 1991.

[49] See *Rivarol*, 25 January and 22 February 1991.

[50] *La Lettre de Jean-Marie Le Pen* (monthly publication), 1 September 1990.

[51] *Le Quotidien de Paris*, 8 June 1996.

[52] *Libération*, 2 May 1996. Deauville is a small resort town on the Channel coast where many French Jews spend their holidays; le Sentier is a Paris neighborhood where many Jewish businessmen have their stores.

[53] *Le Monde*, 15 November 1998.

[54] *Le Monde*, 11 October 2000.

[55] *Libération*, 18 January 2004.

[56] *Le Monde*, 13 June 2002.

[57] *Le Monde*, 18 April 1991; *Libération*, 2 April 2003.

[58] *Le Monde*, 20 and 22 April 1996.

[59] *National Hebdo,* 15 May 1996.
[60] *Libération,* 11 November 1996.
[61] *Le Monde,* 3 June 1996 and 13 January 1998; *Témoignage Chrétien,* 8 June 1996; *Le Figaro,* 6 February 1998.
[62] *Le Monde,* 10 December 2003.
[63] *Rapport annuel.*
[64] See Brenner, et al., *Les territoires perdus de la République.* See also *Les antifeujs.*
[65] See Birnbaum, "The End of the Vertical Alliance?"
[66] See Birnbaum, *The Anti-Semitic Moment.*

References

Ageron, Charles-Louis. *Histoire de l'Algérie contemporaine.* Paris: PUF, 1979.
Les antifeujs: Le livre bilan des violences antisémites en France. Paris: Calmann-Lévy, 2002.
Batault, Georges. *Le problème juif.* Paris: Plon, 1938.
Birnbaum, Pierre. *Un mythe politique: La "République juive": De Léon Blum à Pierre Mendès-France.* Paris: Fayard, 1988.
———. *The Anti-Semitic Moment: A Tour of France in 1898.* New York: Hill and Wang, 2003.
———. "The End of the Vertical Alliance? The Retreat of the Strong State and the New Antisemitic Mobilization in Contemporary France." In *The New Antisemitism,* edited by David Kertzer. New York: Holmes and Meir, 2005.
Brenner, Emmanuel, et al. *Les territoires perdus de la République: Antisémitisme, racisme et sexisme en milieu scolaire.* Paris: Mille et Une Nuits, 2002.
Céline, Louis-Ferdinand. *Bagatelles pour un massacre.* Paris: Denoël, 1936.
———. *Lettres à Albert Paraz (1947–1957). Collection Cahiers Céline.* no. 6. Paris: Gallimard, 1981.
Chaumet, André and H.-R. Bellanger. *Les Juifs et nous.* Paris: Jean-Renard, 1941.
Drault, Jean. *Youtres impudents.* Paris: A. Savine, 1890.
Drieu la Rochelle, Pierre. *Journal: 1939–1945.* Paris: Gallimard, 1992.
Drumont, Edouard. *La France juive.* Paris: Flammarion, 1886.
———. *Le testament d'un antisémite.* Paris: E. Dentu, 1891.
———. *Le peuple juif.* Paris: Librairie antisémite, 1900.
Gontier, René. *Vers un racisme français.* Paris: Denoël, 1939.
Lambelin, Roger. *Le péril juif: Le règne d'Israël chez les Anglo-Saxons.* Paris: Grasset, 1921.
Malglaive, Gabriel. *Juifs ou Français.* Paris: CPRN, 1942.
Maulnier, Thierry. *L'honneur d'être juif.* Paris: Laffont, 1971.
Montandon, Georges. *L'ethnie française.* Paris: Payot, 1935.
O'Brien, Conor Cruise. *The Siege. The Saga of Israel and Zionism.* New York: Touchstone Books, 1986.
Ovaldia, Jacques. "Quand j'ai rencontré Céline." *Levant,* July 1991.
Les raisons de l'antisémitisme. Paris: Documents contemporains, 1942.
Rapport annuel de la Commission consultative nationale sur les droits humains. Paris: La Documentation française, 2004.
Saint-Bonnet, Georges. *Le Juif ou l'internationale du parasitisme.* Paris: Vita, 1932.
Saint-Prot, Charles. *La France et le renouveau arabe.* Paris: Copernic, 1980.
———. *Saddam Hussein, un nouveau de Gaulle.* Paris: Albin Michel, 1987.
Soury, Jules. *La Rédemption d'Israël.* Paris: Bureau de l'Action française, 1901.
Verdeveine, Gérard. *Israël, nation sans territoire contre la nation française.* N.p., 1937.
Viguier, Laurent. *Les Juifs à travers Léon Blum.* Paris: Baudinière, 1938.
Vries de Heekelingen, Herman de. *Israël, son passé, son avenir.* Paris: Perrin, 1937.
Wilson, Stephen. "Le Monument Henry: La structure de l'antisémitisme en France, 1898–1899." *Annales* 32, no. 2 (March–April 1977): 265–91.

Anti-Zionism as a Multipurpose Policy Instrument: The Anti-Zionist Campaign in Poland, 1967–1968

Dariusz Stola

Introduction: Anti-Zionism in Communist Poland before 1967

The noisy hate campaign that erupted in Poland in March 1968, known as "the anti-Zionist campaign," became the symbol of communist Poland's attitude towards the Jews and Israel.[1] However, before the campaign, the Polish communist regime had not displayed greater anti-Jewish or anti-Israel tendencies than other Soviet satellites; it had appeared even friendlier (or less hostile) than most of the regimes in the Soviet bloc, the Soviet one in particular.[2]

In the early postwar years, the new Polish government tolerated semi-legal Jewish emigration channels and acted favorably in the international arena; it even provided military training for Zionist organizations. In 1949–50 the Polish Politburo agreed to a request to allow an emigration scheme, which brought almost thirty thousand people to the new State of Israel.[3] The scheme was a favor (especially in the eyes of many non-Jews who wanted to leave but could not), but it also accorded well with the general drive of accelerated Sovietization that began at that time. This included centralizing and taking control of or liquidating Jewish institutions, restricting contacts with Jewish organizations in the West and diplomatic relations with Israel, and eventually discontinuing emigration under a broader non-exit policy.[4]

To many Polish Jews in the 1940s, the new regime was primarily a radical departure from the Polish regime of the 1930s, which had increasingly drifted towards the anti-Jewish positions of its opponents on the nationalist right. The Communists seemed to guarantee safety against Polish anti-Semitism. As Lucjan Blitt, a Jewish socialist, wrote: "One thing that every group of Jews who had decided to rebuild their lives in Poland [after World War II] was certain about was the conviction that as long as a communist regime was in power, official anti-Semitism would be out of the question."[5] While many of the regime's officials, especially at the lower level, shared some popular anti-Jewish prejudice, in the turbulent early postwar years the regime made efforts to combat (right-wing) anti-Semitism and to protect the Jews against attacks. Anti-Jewish resentment did not disappear from Polish society after the overwhelming majority of Polish Jewry perished in the Holocaust. Returning Jews often encountered hostility, whose bloody culmination was the Kielce pogrom in 1946.[6] The dark mystery of the hostility towards the Holocaust survivors requires further study and explanation, yet one of its factors was evident. This was the revival of the widespread stereotype of *Żydokomuna*, or Jewish communism: the conviction that Communists were mostly Jews, and vice versa. The conspicuous presence of Jews in the apparatus of the regime being brutally imposed on Poland, which was further exaggerated in popular perceptions, seemed to confirm the stereotype of *Żydokomuna*. The anti-Semitism of the time was largely tied to and symbiotic with anticommunism and anti-Sovietism; the new government fought against it quite sincerely.[7]

Obviously, Poland under the communist regime was not a paradise for the Jews. They were deprived of many basic rights and freedoms and exposed to terror, but as a rule not more so than others. This equality, although peculiar, was not unimportant, as Jews in prewar Poland (not to speak of the German occupation period) had felt acutely various forms of administrative and societal discrimination. A form of special discrimination against the Jews that marked the communist period was "thinning out comrades of Jewish origin"—that is, a kind of *numerus clausus* to avoid their "excessive concentration" in certain institutions such as the Foreign Service. This initially reflected the new rulers' desire to appear as a "genuine representative of the Polish people" and their awareness of the popularity of the *Żydokomuna* stereotype.[8] In practical terms, however, it was not so much these administrative measures that made the daily life of Polish Jews difficult as the persisting popular prejudice and resentment. These were, however, "relics of the past," believed to be destined to disappear in the process of building a new, Polish socialist society and culture.

The new regime's initial warm support for Israel did not last long. Israel soon became in the Soviet view an "agent of American imperialism in the Middle East"—that is, it took the wrong, Western side in the Cold War.[9] Consequently, pro-Israel attitudes among the inhabitants of the Soviet bloc became highly suspect. Zionism was not just bad as a form of nationalism but it now implied service to "imperialism" and "world capitalism," most likely in the form of espionage on behalf of the CIA. Spying for imperialists was the major crime against one's country, socialism and peace, clearly deserving the death penalty, as confirmed by the fate of eleven of the fourteen defendants at the 1952 show trial of Rudolf Slánský and other "Trotskyist-Titoist, Zionist and bourgeois-nationalist traitors" in communist Czechoslovakia. Moreover, the trial introduced "anti-Zionism" into the official vocabularies of communist regimes as a code name for any anti-Jewish speech and action. The terms *Zionism* and *Zionist* no longer denoted Jewish nationalism, which the Communists, including Jewish Communists, had long opposed, but became labels to be freely applied to any person of Jewish origin whom the regime targeted for attack. They became part of the communist Orwellian "newspeak," their meaning flexible and threatening, their application ritual and instrumental, both determined by the party leadership. (For this reason, I will place the terms *Zionist, Zionism* and *anti-Zionism* in quotation marks whenever they are used within this particular, totalitarian language.) To be sure, "Zionism" was not the only term that communist propaganda used freely for such labeling of enemies, real or imaginary. For example, the epithet "fascist" could be applied to any political opinion or group so defined, socialists and conservatives included.

The Slánský trial had relatively limited consequences in Poland. While the media reported on it extensively and propagated its hate speech, it did not generate any local mutation, arrests and executions.[10] Jewish Communists in high positions in the party, administration and security apparatus were not removed. Although their influence seems to have gradually weakened, legitimate fears of an approaching anti-Jewish purge did not materialize. Such a purge again appeared most likely when the Soviet media announced in early 1953 the discovery of the "doctors' plot" to kill Soviet leaders. Fortunately, Stalin's actual death in March 1953 discontinued the campaign against the doctors who, as the organ of the Polish party claimed, "had been recruited by the international, bourgeois-nationalist Jewish organization Joint, a branch of the American intelligence."[11] In the sphere of international relations Poland also differed from the rest of the Soviet bloc. While in December 1952, Polish authorities declared the Israeli envoy a *persona non grata*, they did not sever diplomatic relations altogether. Thus, since February 1953 Poland remained the only country of the bloc that maintained relations with Israel. This proved helpful later, when Polish diplomats assisted in the renewal of Soviet-Israeli relations.[12]

The relatively early change in party leadership in Poland may explain why the Polish regime did not follow the Czechoslovak example of struggle against "Zionism" in 1952. The Slánský trial was a late case of the bloc-wide pattern of replacing the communist leaderships installed in the early post–World War II years as part of the intensified Sovietization process and the Stalin-Tito rift. This change took place in Poland in 1948 under the slogans of fighting "the right-wing [Polish] nationalist deviation." The losers were marginalized, some of them arrested, and at the time of the Slánský trial they were still awaiting their own trial. Three aspects of the campaign against the "right-wing nationalist deviation" deserve a mention here. First, the group that emerged triumphant and then led the Sovietization drive in the early 1950s included many Communists who had spent the war in the Soviet Union. Among those

"Muscovites," prominent Jewish Communists were unsurprisingly overrepresented (those Polish Jews who had spent the war in the USSR, including deportees to Siberia, constituted the majority of Polish Holocaust survivors). Second, the Communists who were targeted as "right-wing nationalists," including their leader Władysław Gomułka, survived the campaign.[13] This point is not just to note the surprising leniency of the change of Polish leadership (elsewhere in the bloc the losers lost their lives, not just positions). Those accused of the "deviation" returned to the political scene in 1956, having acquired popular sympathy as victims of the regime and Polish patriots who had tried to resist Soviet pressure. In 1968 some prominent supporters of the "anti-Zionist" campaign traced its origins to the 1948 crisis, and the campaign's favorite targets were Jewish Stalinists who had contributed to Gomułka's fall in 1948.[14]

The "thaw," or the relaxation of terror, and the political shakeup in 1956 that ended the Stalinist period, temporarily destabilized the Polish regime and brought another change of leadership. Gomułka returned to the highest party position, that of first secretary of the Central Committee (CC) of the Polish United Workers Party (PZPR, i.e., the Communist Party). Upon his return he faced a party leadership divided into two factions: the relatively reformist group, called Puławy (since some of its leaders lived and met on Puławska Street in Warsaw), included leading Jewish Communists; the other faction, known as Natolin (a palace in Warsaw's suburbs where its leaders met), did not hesitate to exploit the ethnic argument against its rival, in particular blaming the Jews for the crimes of the Stalinist period.[15] What is interesting here is the pattern of two opposing programs for renewal of the regime that emerged in this rivalry. Puławians tended to call for structural reforms, while downplaying personal responsibility (i.e. they focused on how the regime operated rather than who operated it); Natolinians downplayed structural deficiencies of the regime and tended to stress personal responsibility (of their opponents). Both the proposed solutions were of course partial and insufficient, and their alternative false, yet by being expressed publicly at the top party level they undermined a major taboo, opening the door for public criticism of the regime's rules or its rulers respectively. In 1968, the "personalist" Natolin way of thinking would emerge again, together with the claims that Jews were responsible for the cruelties of the Stalinist period.

In 1956 Gomułka tactically cooperated with the Puławy group, but after a time he put his own people in key positions and, under the slogan of fighting against (Marxist) 'revisionism,' weakened his ex-allies. The broader context of the political games was reconsolidation of the regime after the shock of 1956, the smothering of reform tendencies within the party, the return of cultural and economic policies to their former course (but with the significant exception of collectivization), and Gomułka's increasing autocracy. In the 1960s a rising new force appeared on the political scene, the Partisans, a rather loose group of party leaders and lower-level activists united by similar political backgrounds (particularly their wartime experience in the communist underground, hence their name), unappeased ambitions and a worldview combining nationalism and communism, under the unquestioned leadership of General Mieczysław Moczar (one of the "right-wing nationalist" losers of 1948). Moczar's position consolidated as he gradually took full control of the Ministry of Internal Affairs (MSW) with its secret services, where he defeated his chief (Jewish) rival, Antoni Alster. Similar processes of gradual elimination of (alleged revisionist) Jewish Communists from important positions or their marginalization occurred in some other key institutions of the regime: certain sections of the party apparatus, the Main Political Administration (GZP) of the army, and the military secret services.[16]

The expressions of popular anti-Jewish attitudes, suppressed during the Stalinist period, reappeared in 1956. Archival evidence confirms grass-roots prejudice, often including the *Żydokomuna* stereotype, as well as exploitation and encouragement of the prejudice in the factional struggle.[17] When the regime restabilized in 1957–58, the particular "Jewish question" of communist Poland (including the sensitive topics of wartime Polish-Jewish relations, the role of Jewish Communists, and so on) was again censored out of the public discourse—until 1967. In the 1960s Poland maintained relatively good relations with Israel. In 1962 the countries upgraded their diplomatic missions to embassy status, and trade increased. In 1966 Polish Foreign Minister Adam Rapacki invited his Israeli counterpart, Abba Eban, to Warsaw. Israel repeatedly expressed support for Poland on a most important issue: Poland's new western border, questioned by the Federal Republic of Germany (FRG). Reportedly, Israeli assistance proved helpful in acquiring American credits, while for Israel Poland appeared to be a good bridgehead for improving relations with the rest of the Soviet bloc, the USSR in particular.[18] Nevertheless, the secret services of the MSW (the intelligence and the political police—SB [Security Service]) were increasingly suspicious towards both Israel and Polish Jews, clearly not without the influence of their Soviet partners/ masters.

The thaw of 1956 brought among other things a relaxation of the passport policy, resulting in a wave of emigration, which embraced more than half of the total number of Polish Jews. Notably, many of the Jewish emigrants had just repatriated from the USSR; this part of the "Gomułka wave" of emigration to Israel was an indirect migration from the Soviet Union. The authorities tightened the grip on emigration again in the late 1950s but the refusal rate among applicants for emigration permits to Israel was lower than to most Western countries. In 1966 as many as 67 percent of the applications were successful (78 percent in 1965), compared with 38 percent of the applications to France and the United States and just 19 percent to the FRG. Following the "Gomułka wave" and the limited emigration in the 1960s, on the eve of the Six Day War there remained probably some 25,000–30,000 Jews among Poland's more than 32 million inhabitants. The continuing outflow influenced the structure of the remaining Jewish population, as those less acculturated or adjusted to the sociopolitical regime were more prone to emigrate. Polish Jewry was thus decreasing in numbers, aging and assimilating, its younger cohorts tending to secular Polish identities. It had no qualified rabbi, but it had impressively developed secular institutions. However incomparable they were with the richness of the Jewish life before the war, these institutions were much more active and richer than the institutions of any other ethnic minority.[19] This was in large part the result of sizable foreign assistance, renewed after 1956, which other ethnic groups did not enjoy. From 1958 until 1966 the American Joint Distribution Committee (Joint) earmarked almost six million US dollars for the Jewish community in Poland (which the MSW saw as clear evidence of subversive Western penetration).

The above outline shows how in the Polish People's Republic (Polska Rzeczpospolita Ludowa, PRL) various elements gradually accumulated that would contribute to the "anti-Zionist" campaign in 1967–68, including popular anti-Jewish prejudice and resentment; Cold War hostility towards Israel and suspicion towards any sympathy for Israel; subordination to Moscow that was to make Poland take the Arab side in the distant conflict in the Middle East; a (Soviet) ready-made vocabulary of "anti-Zionism," which enabled the popular anti-Jewish resentment to be mobilized and exploited under an orthodox Marxist-Leninist camouflage, and the implicit tendency to extend the attack on Zionists to "Zionists"; and the legacy of the intra-party struggles and their Jewish aspect. The biggest factor, and easy to overlook because of its size, was the communist regime itself: the Leviathan of the centralized bureaucratic party-state, which controlled and monopolized the political sphere, the economy and media, with thousands of obedient apparatchiks, vigilant police officers, and activists (*aktiv*) ready to show devotion to any cause set by the party leaders, as well as non-party opportunists, conformists and ordinary loyal citizens.

In particular, this machinery had been well trained in running hate campaigns. Communist rulers and their propagandists had for years invested heavily in relevant institutions and training, and mastered their skills of inciting hatred. Aggressive propaganda and mobilization of the party and masses against real or imaginary enemies were such pervasive features of the Stalinist period that it can be seen as a permanent campaign with changing objects: the anticommunist opposition and Tito, the Roman Catholic Church and "right-wing nationalist deviation," kulaks and the Marshall Plan, and so forth. These hate campaigns were local mutations of the Soviet model, which had developed during the great purges and show trials of the 1930s, when communist hate speech had acquired its most elaborate and distinctive forms. Reading and listening to this hate speech was a necessary element of education of young party activists in pre-1956 Poland. After 1956 the campaigns were less frequent and intense yet they also bore the imprint of their Soviet forebears. Just a year prior to the anti-Israel campaign of 1967, a wave of protests and public condemnations was carefully prepared and carried out in earnest against the Catholic episcopate. In 1968 the "anti-Zionist" campaign had not yet come to an end before the propaganda machine targeted the reform movement in Czechoslovakia.

June 1967: The Anti-Israel Campaign, Intra-Party Conflict and the 'Zionist Threat'

The Israeli-Arab Six Day War in 1967 marked a turning point in the policy of the Polish authorities towards Israel and the Jews in Poland. For several years, besides rather routine criticism of Israel's cooperation with "imperialism," both anti-Zionism and "anti-Zionism" had been largely absent from the public discourse. Diplomatic representation was mutually raised to the embassy level, while Poland gave secret financial support to the Communist Party of Israel.[20] In June 1967 anti-Zionism openly returned, while "anti-Zionism" remained in the background for the time being.

Initially, the (party-controlled) media provided rather limited information about the war, and news commentary was cautious, thus not particularly aggressive towards Israel. On 6 June the Polish Politburo met to "exchange views about the events in the Middle East" and defined "directives for informational-propaganda work."[21] The next day the Polish government published a statement which, on behalf of the entire nation, condemned the perpetrators of the aggression and expressed complete support for the just struggle of the Arab countries. Immediately, the media filled with words of condemnation against the Israelis along with expressions of solidarity with the peace-loving Arab nations. Propaganda, although aggressive, still remained within the regular limits of presenting adversaries from the other side of the Iron Curtain and targeted the Israeli government, not the Jews in general.

On 9 June Gomułka and Prime Minister Józef Cyrankiewicz went to Moscow for a summit of communist leaders devoted to the Middle East crisis. The summit decided in favor of military and financial support for the Arab countries and the severance of diplomatic relations with Israel (which Romania rejected). One of the Polish eyewitnesses recalled this meeting as "very dramatic": "Everything took place in a somewhat morose atmosphere. There was the feeling that our camp had undergone, in a certain sense, a military and political failure, and lost prestige.... During the meeting unsettling information [on Arab defeats] reached us, which put everyone in a discouraged mood."[22] Soviet President Leonid Brezhnev's secret speech to the Soviet Central Committee on 20 June reveals much about the atmosphere in the Kremlin during those days:

> The caution of the moment, the speed with which the situation changed, the necessity of making decisions literally in the course of a few hours, important decisions regarding the vital interests of our country, the fate of war and peace, put all of us under great stress. I must tell you, Comrades, that the Politburo was working around the clock during those days.... After receiving the report from Cairo describing the dramatic situation on the Egypt-Israeli front, we members of the Politburo met at one o'clock in the morning. We analyzed the possible options for assistance to the defeated UAR [United Arab Republic] army. On 8 June, in light of the existing situation, the leaders of the parties and governments of the European socialist governments agreed to meet without delay to discuss together the joint measures required to be undertaken in the current conditions. All this occurred, Comrades, very quickly, decisions were made by means of personal telephone calls to Central Committee Secretaries and heads of governments.[23]

Having returned to Warsaw, Gomułka shared with other members of the Polish Politburo his mood of pessimism:

> The tense situation ... will continue and the possibility of new and more dangerous events cannot be excluded. A pretext for new aggression can always be found. That is why Romania's position is that much more shameful .... The appetites of imperialism grow on local wars in which they can count on successes .... We need

to be prepared for a variety of surprises. Nuclear war hangs in the air, since the situation is inching the world to war.[24]

Such dramatic thinking clearly contributed to Gomułka's angry reaction to the news of alleged pro-Israel attitudes among Polish Jews, which he was repeatedly receiving from the MSW. Already the MSW report of 6 June noted: "we observe expressions of support for Israel mainly among persons of Jewish origin." Other reports followed on the same note: "In the circles of the Jewish minority in Poland, and particularly among Jewish youth, there is a declared readiness to go to Israel to participate directly in the battle against the Arabs."[25] Indeed, in Poland one could hear opinions about the war that significantly departed from the official stance and tone conveyed by the media. Western journalists and other independent observers noted expressions of sympathy for Israel and praise of its military successes, not only on the part of Jews. One such well-known expression was the reported remark that "our Jews [from Poland] beat their [Soviet-backed] Arabs."[26]

Gomułka also learned that some Polish Jews had celebrated Israeli victories, sent greetings to the Israeli embassy and openly criticized the Polish and Soviet position on the conflict. His secretary recalled that this news greatly irritated the PZPR leader:

> I know that it hurt Wiesław [Gomułka] terribly, because he recognized that some of the comrades only formally [belonged] to our community in the sense of their feeling of [common] interest, threat, and the like.... That was very important for him, that certain comrades identified more with Israel than with the line of the party, in terms of international politics.[27]

His sensitivity to the issue probably also resulted from the fact that the groups and persons reported by the MSW as disloyal were often close to certain party leaders who had been increasingly irritating Gomułka for some time. Moreover, he learned that the news on disloyalty among Polish Jews had reached Moscow too. Thus, he had reasons of various kinds to react firmly.

After hearing Gomułka's account of the meeting in Moscow, the Polish Politburo confirmed the decision to sever relations with Israel and to give military assistance to the Arab countries.[28] When the Israeli ambassador left Warsaw several days later, a crowd of suspicious individuals, brought there undoubtedly by the MSW, made catcalls, which Polish radio described as "the spontaneous reaction of the people of Warsaw."[29] From then until the end of the communist period Poland kept in line with the general Soviet bloc's anti-Israel policy in the international arena, including in the United Nations. It was no longer Poland but Romania that was the liaison country between Israel and the bloc. This anti-Israel line was compatible with increasing political and economic cooperation with Arab countries. I do not know of any archival evidence of any discussion on the topic of Polish-Israeli relations, in either the party leadership or the Ministry of Foreign Affairs, not to speak of the Polish media. Clearly, since Moscow had decided on such a line, it seemed to be a topic outside their capacity—*Roma locuta causa finita*. It was only 23 years later, when Poland restored its sovereignty, that the first noncommunist government of Poland renewed diplomatic relations with Israel.

After the Politburo meeting, the media were evidently urged to intensify the anti-Israel campaign, as in a few days a new wave of aggressive articles reached the Polish public. The press emphasized the suffering of the Arab population and the alleged brutality of the Israeli army. A notable feature of many articles was their comparisons of the Israeli army to the Nazi German army and news of the FRG's support for Israel. Their authors evidently enjoyed implying a perverse Nazi-Jewish affinity. This was not as shocking as it might seem today, as comparing Western (especially American) governments and policies to Nazi ones was by no means unusual. Party officials responsible for the media were also fond of this theme, as their later documents repeat the directive to keep stressing the German-Israeli cooperation.[30]

The media accompanied the wave of anti-Israel public protests organized throughout the country. Factory workers and employees of various offices and other institutions gathered at such meetings to express feelings and opinions entirely in accord with the party guidelines. They used very similar or indeed the same words and expressions: "We condemn the criminal aggression of Israel against the Arab nations. We condemn the barbaric methods used by the Israeli army against the civilian population," declared Henryk Szaniawski, a worker at the Paris Commune Plant, speaking on behalf of his crew, "the Israeli government became the tool of subjugation of other nations through British-American and West German imperialists." One thousand miners from the Staszic mine passed a unanimous resolution demanding the immediate withdrawal of the Israeli forces from the Arab lands. The employees of the Mechanic Works and the Transformer Factory in Łódź expressed their cordial support for the Arab people. A female worker of the Uroda Soap Factory said to her colleagues, "As a mother it hurts me to see thousands of Arab women and children suffering from the misfortune brought by the Israeli aggression against the Arab people." Israel's aggression was also severely condemned by the workers at the Beton-Stal enterprise and the Radio Factory in Warsaw, the teachers of Rzeszów province, the employees of the truck factory in Starachowice, and tens of thousands of others.[31]

This wave of meetings resulted from party mobilization as practiced for years. Its chronology shows the party *modus operandi* and its chain of command. First, the secretaries of Voievodship (Provincial) Committees (VC) and directors of Central Committee departments gathered at a conference in Warsaw where they listened to Gomułka's speech on the Middle East crisis, in which he condemned Israel as the "outpost of imperialist interests" in the region. Gomułka claimed, however, that "contrary to Arab nationalists we support the existence of the Israeli state. We think that the slogan of liquidating Israel is wrong."[32] Next the VC apparatus transmitted instructions for action to the lower levels. This is how a party report presented this operation in Warsaw:

> On 14 June a meeting was held by the members of the Warsaw Committee, the executives of the District Committees, the Secretaries of the Workplace Committees, the employees of the party apparatus, as well as the leadership of the Warsaw National Council [i.e., City Council], the trade unions, and youth organizations. The first secretary of the VC, Stanisław Kociołek described the genesis and

development of the conflict, the position of the Polish government, and the political repercussions against Israel. Attention was called to the imperialist propaganda as well as the tasks of the party organizations. The present main task, resulting from the resolution of the 8th plenum of the Central Committee, is the summoning of meetings in party organizations, explaining the essence of the events in the Middle East, as well as the strengthening of active struggle with subversive propaganda and attempts to sow seeds of political chaos .... After conferences of secretaries of basic party organizations in the District Committees [that followed], meetings in the basic organizations began. Mass meetings take place in Warsaw workplaces and institutions, and provide a forum to express support for the PRL's position with regard to Israel's aggression in the Middle East and condemn Israel's aggressive, provocative, and imperialist policy in the Middle East, directed against the Arab countries.[33]

The party machine worked smoothly, producing the requested results, although a closer look at the photographs from the meetings reveals faces that are more tired or bored than angry.

The campaign's high point was Gomułka's appearance at the Trade Union Congress on 19 June. He delivered a twenty-page speech, mainly a lecture on the history of Israel and its entry into an "entente with British-American imperialists against the progressive Arab forces." This would have been just another of his long and boring speeches if it were not for a paragraph where he referred to the "fifth column"—a synonym for enemy infiltration:[34] "Israel's aggression in the Arab countries met with applause in Zionist circles of Jews—Polish citizens." The Polish authorities treat all citizens equally regardless of their ethnicity, he claimed, "but we do not want a fifth column to emerge in our country. We cannot remain indifferent towards people ... who support the aggressor." He also unambiguously urged that "those who feel that these words are addressed to them" should emigrate. The audience greeted these words with applause.[35]

A few of the Politburo members present—Edward Ochab, Eugeniusz Szyr, Stefan Jędrychowski and Adam Rapacki—were clearly surprised by and unhappy with precisely this fragment of the speech. Ochab put it bluntly: "You had no right to come forth with such a thesis, you had no right without the consent of the Politburo."[36] He was evoking an unwritten rule that the official speeches of the first secretary were passed among the members of the Politburo for their remarks. This was not a minor issue, as the rule expressed the "collective leadership" principle, which parties of the Soviet bloc had introduced following Nikita Khrushchev's critique of Stalin's rule, as a remedy against the "cult of the individual." The reason for departure from this rule, according to Gomułka himself and his secretary, was trivial and irrelevant to the controversial contents of the text: lack of time and the absence from Warsaw of the majority of the Politburo members before 19 June. Ochab did not believe this explanation, and there are good reasons to share his suspicion. He and other contenders must have been really angry, as under their pressure Gomułka agreed to alter the text of his speech for official publication. The sentence about the fifth column disappeared, while words moderating the tone of the fragment were added. This was quite unprecedented: the authoritarian first secretary had agreed to censor a speech he had already delivered! As participants in the congress and those who had listened to the speech on the radio knew the original version, this extraordinary fact could not pass ignored.

In Moscow the 19 June speech was well received. The Soviet press published it (the amended version) and Brezhnev himself personally praised Gomułka, confirming that his evaluation of the events was consonant with that of the Soviet Politburo.[37] A comment is in order here that the Soviets praised the Polish leaders for their correct approach to "the problem of Zionism" and their determined action in March 1968 afterwards, but there is no evidence that they had encouraged them to such action in advance. In the notes from several Polish-Soviet meetings at the highest level that took place between June 1967 and March 1968, the topic of the Middle East was raised several times, but no mention was made (or at least recorded) about the domestic "Zionists."[38]

The speech opened an essentially new phase of the campaign. These few sentences by the first secretary introduced the word "Zionism," that had augured ill for Jews since the 1950s. The anti-Israel campaign became anti-Zionist, possibly "anti-Zionist," and the Cold War crisis in the Middle East acquired a local Polish-Jewish dimension. At the same time the clash between Gomułka and the outraged Politburo members crystallized a serious division inside the party leadership, which was not limited to that single issue. "A very important tension appeared at that point within the leadership ... a very significant matter," as Gomułka's secretary later recalled.[39] What the issue was can only be surmised. The charisma that Gomułka had enjoyed in 1956 had long eroded. His authoritarian style of ruling and his economic and cultural policies had been increasingly difficult to accept for some members of the leadership. At the next Politburo session Gomułka defended his stance on the alleged disloyalty:

> Regarding the situation that existed in the country during the period of Israel's aggression and the dangerous symptoms, which were reported to us, I considered it appropriate to stand out against the germ of the fifth column. A very important problem has developed which we cannot overlook. These are matters that affect our entire country, our existence, and there must be clarity in these matters. With regard to people who have two souls and two fatherlands, conclusions must be drawn.[40]

In June 1967 the opposition in the Politburo prevented the unleashing of an open "anti-Zionist" campaign. The propaganda did not reproduce the sentence on the "fifth column" nor did it take up the theme of "Zionists in Poland." But behind the scenes, in fields and through channels outside the control of the opponents of the "anti-Zionism" theme, different messages started to circulate, which—as we know today—prepared the ground for a future campaign. Gomułka's words were a signal for those who had long been awaiting it, above all in General Moczar's Ministry of Internal Affairs. Having repeatedly provided party leaders with information on alleged Jewish disloyalty, they now received the desired feedback.

The MSW leadership had no doubts about the treacherous inclinations of Polish Jews. Some of its directors had for a long time pointed to the "Zionist threat." Their report, summarizing the reactions to the Six Day War in Poland, accused not only individual Jews but Jews in the most general terms: "Polish Jews show solidarity with the Israeli aggressors, praise the Israeli army and the policy of the Israeli government," and worst of all they "express themselves critically and often inimically about the policy of the party and authorities of the PRL, the Soviet Union and other socialist countries."[41] The Security Service reported that 81 Polish citizens had volunteered for the Israeli army, while others had transferred savings and sent greetings of solidarity to representatives of the Israeli embassy. Among the 382 Jews allegedly displaying pro-Israel attitudes were 76 journalists and writers, 51 individuals in upper managerial positions in the administration, 46 scholars and 36 lawyers. The reports visibly tended to contrast the attitudes of the Jews with the rest of society: "the working class, the peasants, and the intelligentsia, as well as the non-Jewish ethnic minorities almost universally expressed support for the position of the party and the government.... Polish society generally responded in favor of the Arab side, against the Israeli aggressor." The reports strongly denied it could be otherwise and claimed that information about the pro-Israel sympathies of Poles, "spread by Zionists and enemy foreign agencies," were deliberate misinformation.[42]

Fragmentary evidence shows that the theory of a Jewish threat had been ripening inside the MSW for a few years. One may suppose that Soviet influence had contributed to its development. Well before June 1967, Vice-Minister Franciszek Szlachcic claimed that the "USA exploits three forces against the socialist countries: [Roman Catholic] clergy, the FRG and Zionism." He saw a Jewish conspiracy behind the ferment among the intelligentsia—for example, behind such dissidents as Jacek Kuroń and Karol Modzelewski there was an alleged "conceiving and instigating group" entirely composed of Jewish intellectuals.[43] The paranoid thinking of the security officers appears most clearly in their expressed conviction that pro-Israel attitudes among Polish Jews could not appear spontaneously but "undoubtedly [had their] origins in the resolutions of the World Jewish Congress in Brussels and the World Zionist Organization in Jerusalem.... In recent years the Jewish minority was actively penetrated by representatives of the international Zionist organizations and the Israeli embassy."[44] In seeking sources for the paranoid vision of the "Zionists" in March 1968, we need to take into consideration not only anti-Semitic stereotypes but also the secret police's partiality for conspiracy theories and a more widespread "detectivist materialism," which had found fertile ground in Soviet-dominated communist parties.

After the Six Day War and the clash inside the Politburo, such thinking found political support at the top party level. General Kazimierz Witaszewski, a hard-liner who supervised the MSW on behalf of the party authorities, now encouraged its directors to "get to the party leadership in order to set forth these issues once again" (that is, to make the 'Zionist problem' a top political issue), in order to help "our party purge itself of incidental and undesirable elements."[45] Whether this was his own initiative or whether he spoke on behalf of some party leaders remains unclear. Certainly raising the topic would contribute to weakening the position of Ochab and other Politburo members who had opposed Gomułka on 19 June, as well as those critical of the growing power of Moczar and his men.

Summarizing the discussion of the MSW directors on 28 June, Moczar defined the Jews as infected with dangerous "Zionism," indicated them as a collective object for particular scrutiny and gave the priority to the struggle with "Zionism" thus understood. The anti-Israel campaign, which Gomułka transformed into an anti-Zionist one, through Moczar's guidelines acquired a secret and clearly anti-Jewish dimension. The Security Service followed his order for "in-depth investigation of certain fields of our administration and economy. It must be discovered, for example, who is planted in such fields as the state reserves, nuclear science, the Polish Press Agency... and pressure must be put on the executives in these departments to get rid of undesirable people."[46] This was a recommendation to prepare for a purge. In fact such preparations had already begun, as shown by an MSW document of 26 June, which calculated the number of Jews in key government agencies (putting the figure at 700 out of 3,500 employees).[47] The minister reminded those assembled of the subordinate role of the MSW vis-à-vis the party: "It is the party leadership which decides who gets to go to which post.... [Nevertheless] we need to convince the comrades, the employees of the MSW that their work cannot be in vain, that if results do not come today, then tomorrow."[48] These words had the power of a self-fulfilling prophecy.

The immediate consequence of the meeting in the MSW was the joint request of the MSW and the CC Administrative Department to the party authorities to block financial assistance from the Joint to Jewish organizations in Poland. The matter was quickly placed on the agenda of the CC Secretariat, which approved the recommendation with no objections.[49] The Jewish community lost its major source of income, which meant the inevitable elimination of a significant portion of its social, educational and cultural activity, and a serious blow to Jewish cooperatives. Simultaneously, a special party task force, supported by information from the MSW, evaluated the attitudes of a number of journalists with regard to the Middle East conflict. By 4 July it had examined 15 journalists in Warsaw and in the majority of cases recommended dismissals or party penalties.[50] The highest-ranking victim of this action was the executive editor of the party organ *Trybuna Ludu*, Leon Kasman, who most likely tried to protect his employees from charges of pro-Israel sympathy. In December 1967, when a special party delegation directly ordered him to fire his deputy and a few other employees, Kasman resigned.[51]

Yet the MSW's recommendations "to get rid of undesirable people" were not successful in every case. For example, the Ministry of Foreign Affairs, about which the MSW directors had spoken most critically, would not be purged until spring 1968. Another example of a "purge in suspension" was against the editors at the PWN publishing house, who were accused of downplaying wartime Polish suffering and disproportionate focus on the fate of the Jews in their *Great Universal Encyclopedia*. It may well have been the difficulties the MSW encountered in removing "Zionists" in some institutions in 1967 that contributed to its pressure for a general anti-Jewish purge in March 1968.

A separate current of the campaign in 1967 consisted of developments in the army. After the outbreak of the Six Day War, orders to increase political vigilance and the official condemnation of Israel as a US-sponsored aggressor, there was naturally increasing suspicion towards Jews in the army. As the head of the military Main Political Authority (GZP) later reported, "party organizations exhibited political maturity, vigilance and an uncompromising attitude, and excluded from their ranks those who were for imperialism, against socialism." Sixty-three party members were given party penalties for pro-Israel attitudes, and of these 41 were expelled.[52]

During the anti-Israel campaign in the armed forces, the GZP sent to the garrisons to lecture on the conflict a group of speakers, who clearly incited anti-Jewish emotions and openly or implicitly accused Polish Jewish officers of dual loyalty. The atmosphere at some party meetings in the army was simply hysterical. For example, at the meeting in the Modlin base, certain participants claimed that Israel had received 100 million dollars from Polish Jews and that some top-ranking officials and officers had committed state treason. They demanded that the "two-faced individuals" be removed from state and military positions, and even proposed to turn to the Soviet Union for help in rebuilding the Polish army.[53] After a series of such meetings in the Air Defense Forces (Wojska Obrony Powietrznej Kraju, WOPK), officers-party activists organized something close to a mutiny, demanding dismissals of the allegedly pro-Israel officers, including their commander, General Czesław Mankiewicz. Their accusation of Mankiewicz was based on sheer rumors and the fact that he had a Jewish wife.[54] Reacting to this discipline crisis, the GZP sent a special commission to the WOPK, but instead of chastening the insubordinate ranks, the commission supported their demands. The key moment in these incidents was a late-night conference on 6 July, when Minister of Defense Marian Spychalski agreed to dismiss Mankiewicz, who was one of his most loyal colleagues. Experts on relations in the army at that time agree that the main promoters of the WOPK purge were Generals Teodor Kufel and Józef Urbanowicz, heads of the military counter-intelligence and the GZP respectively. Both men were intriguers, proponents of the struggle against "revisionist-Zionist elements" (i.e. Jews and supporters of reforms) and trusted in Moscow. Urbanowicz had been a Soviet officer who acquired Polish citizenship only in 1954. It might be more than a coincidence that the two institutions most involved in initiating the purge in the army, the military counterintelligence and the GZP, were also the two most closely supervised and (most likely) infiltrated by the Soviets.[55]

Dismissals in the WOPK began a broader purge in the armed forces, targeting people "holding political opinions divergent from the position of the PRL government as well as the party line, and for the loss of the moral-political values required of an officer of the People's Polish Army." Jews constituted only a portion of those dismissed under this systematic "review of cadres," which was the culmination of a long-standing trend of removing officers unreliable from Moscow's point of view. In total, some 150 officers of Jewish origin were dismissed from service in 1967–68. This meant almost all of them, since according to Colonel Michał Checiński, the number of Jews in active service in 1967 was no more than 200, even according to the broadest criteria.[56]

The Campaign of March 1968

The full-scale "anti-Zionist" campaign began in March 1968. In Polish historiography the events of spring 1968 are often simply referred to as "March," and for many people the term is synonymous with an anti-Semitic witch-hunt.[57] The campaign that began in March included aggressive anti-Jewish propaganda, barely covered with the fig leaf of "anti-Zionism," mass mobilization against "the enemies of socialist Poland," and large-scale expulsion of Jews from the party, government posts and other positions. The campaign acquired these features in the course of just a few days, reaching its most intense period in two weeks, and continuing for the next few weeks, until the party leadership sought to restrain it and it began to lose impetus.

The "anti-Zionist" campaign was secondary to the main chapter of the March events, which consisted of a student rebellion and its pacification by the authorities. Street riots broke out when police and groups of the party *aktiv* armed with clubs brutally attacked a student rally at Warsaw University on 8 March. The students were protesting against the censoring of a drama by the great nineteenth-century Polish poet Adam Mickiewicz (some party hard-liners found the drama anti-Soviet), and in solidarity with their colleagues who had been dismissed from the university for initiating the protests a few weeks earlier. The brutal intervention at Warsaw University did not put an end to the rebellion but made it spread. In the following days in Warsaw and other academic centers, there were numerous protest meetings, student strikes and street riots, to which the authorities responded with police clubs, arrests, expulsions from the universities and conscription into the army. By 27 March the police had arrested 2,591 persons, including 597 students, while more than 600 students had been called up to the army and assigned to separate units in distant garrisons.[58] Repression continued for the next few months.

The "Zionists" appeared on the scene quite unexpectedly. Three days after the riots had begun, an article appeared in a minor newspaper accusing them of having instigated the rebellion.[59] From that point onwards the quantity and intensity of attacks against "Zionism" snowballed in the media and in public speeches. Of course no proof of any "Zionist conspiracy" behind the youth rebellion has been found. The claim was one of the factors endowing March with its murky, grotesque character. For its proponents, the undeniable proof was the relatively numerous participation of Jews, as defined by Nuremberg standards, among the leaders of the student protest. The opening of the MSW archives after 1989 has made it possible to trace this "Zionist explanation" to the Security Service. MSW reports evidently exaggerated the role of Jewish students and children of known party figures in the rebellion.[60] As in the case of the reports of June 1967, we cannot ascertain if this was an initiative of Moczar and his men, again intended to manipulate the party leaders against the "Zionists," or a manipulation requested by some members of the leadership. In any case, the reports provided a basis for decisions to launch a major hate campaign, with the "Zionists" among its principal targets. Propaganda connected them with "bankrupt politicians" who bore "the responsibility for errors and lawlessness of the Stalinist period" and were trying to return to power. To make it even more frightening and detestable, this Zionist-Stalinist conspiracy was depicted as having strong international backing in the Israeli-West German secret deal to cleanse the Germans of their criminal Nazi past and shift the responsibility for the extermination of six million Jews onto the Polish nation.[61]

Together with the eruption of the hate speech in the media, a wave of rallies started "in support of comrade Gomułka, against the instigators of riots," organized by every voievodship party secretary as well as by hundreds of party organizations at the lower levels. Thousands of such meetings sent resolutions and letters to the leadership in an increasingly radical tone: "We swear in memory of those who died for power to the people, that we will clean from Polish soil, with our workers' fists, all the instigators and leaders of the coup against the working class and peasant government. We will not permit revisionist and Zionists rioters to accuse us of anti-Semitism," declared the workers from the Polfer factories, while the workers from the Baildon steel works demanded a purge of Zionist elements from party ranks, their removal from their positions, and the expulsion of their children from the universities.[62] The largest rally gathered a crowd reportedly numbering 100,000 people, brought to Katowice from the entire Upper Silesia, with banners bearing slogans such as "Down with Zionism—the Agent of Imperialism," "Writers to Their Pens, Students to Their Studies," "Purge the Party of Zionists," "We'll Cut Off the Head of the Anti-Polish Hydra." Edward Gierek, the party boss of Silesia, thundered: "It's not difficult to figure out who's behind the organization of the brawls in Warsaw and elsewhere in our country. It's the same frustrated and disappointed enemies of People's Poland... revisionists, Zionists—servants of imperialism...."[63] The people he named as the enemies were a strange group made up of the Jewish Communists Roman Zambrowski and Stefan Staszewski, once powerful men in the party and vigorous Stalinists, and the Catholic writers Stefan Kisielewski and Paweł Jasienica, known for their independence and courage.

Gomułka appeared in public as late as 19 March at a meeting with a few thousand party activists in Warsaw, accompanied by all the Politburo members. Participants bore banners with slogans such as "Down with the Agents of Imperialism—Reactionary Zionism!" and "We Demand a Complete Unmasking and Punishment of the Political Instigators." Gomułka delivered a speech primarily attacking disobedient intellectuals, Kisielewski, Jasienica and Antoni Słonimski in particular; he devoted a relatively small fragment of his speech to the "Zionists" and denied that Zionism was a danger for Poland. He pointed to an alleged identity problem among Jews who were more attached to Israel than to Poland. "I presume that Jews in this category will sooner or later leave our country," he said. He also distinguished between cosmopolitans "who feel neither Poles nor Jews" and good "citizens of Jewish origin...for whom Poland is the only homeland." Gomułka reassured the audience that the party would "oppose with complete firmness every manifestation of anti-Semitism."[64] This declaration is of course difficult to square with so many hostile and openly anti-Jewish messages in the media and at the party-organized meetings. Clearly, in the spring of 1968 the party had other priorities than opposing anti-Semitism.

The massive verbal and symbolic attack in the media and at the meetings provided the background for a purge. Its first target was the most prominent member of the former Puławy faction, Roman Zambrowski, a man who had been a devoted Communist for forty years. A former key member of the Politburo, once serving as the Central Committee's powerful secretary, speaker of the Parliament and government minister, Zambrowski lost party membership and then his position by a decision (evidently inspired) of his local party cell, in his absence and following baseless accusations.[65] News of Zambrowski's dismissal sent a clear message: if such a prominent figure was defenseless, any "Zionist" could be attacked. Soon several other high-ranking Jewish officials lost their posts, and a nationwide purge of "Zionists," "revisionists" and other "alien elements" from the party and their positions quickly gathered momentum, descending from top government officials and editors-in-chief to university professors, bookkeepers in cooperatives, teachers in elementary schools and factory foremen. The unbearable atmosphere of a witch-hunt made many other Jews and Poles of Jewish origin decide to leave. Between 1968 and 1970, some 13,000 persons (i.e. half of the estimated total number of Jews) applied for emigration permits to Israel.[66] Gomułka's claim that "Zionists" would "sooner or later leave our country" was another self-fulfilling prophecy.

The "Zionist" was not the only enemy of the unfolding propaganda campaign, yet it appeared the primary one. As a distinguished analyst of the language of propaganda wrote: "Behind everything evil in the world, enemies of every kind, emerges the face of the Jew called a Zionist."[67] Notably, "Zionist" meant Jew even if the person so called was not Jewish by any standards; since the "anti-Zionist" campaign targeted some ethnic Poles as well, none could feel safe.

The "anti-Zionist" current of the campaign contained old anti-Semitic clichés, new 'socialist' charges or old ones recycled. The old accusations could have been (and sometimes actually were) copied from prewar anti-Semitic literature. As Mieczysław Rakowski, the editor of the relatively liberal weekly *Polityka*, noted in his diary: "If there is a hell, all Polish anti-Semites must be enjoying this moment. The Communists are doing what generations of Polish chauvinists had fought for."[68] The second kind of accusations reflected new types of crimes, such as Marxist revisionism or solidarity with a Cold War enemy. Muddy newspeak facilitated the translation of the old chauvinist charges against the Jews into new "socialist" accusations, for example by proving that "cosmopolitanism is not only anti-patriotism, but also and above all else, anti-socialism, since it opposes an explicitly classless society, in which there is no room for the bourgeoisie and ideological speculation."[69] In the absence of other good arguments, one could always be accused of lack of enthusiasm and insufficient support for the "anti-Zionist" campaign itself. Conspiracy theories spread freely and they seem to have found many receptive ears. "Zionist" plots in Poland were said to have some hidden connections with the Jewish conspiracy in the West, where the headquarters of the "World Zionist Mafia" was located. The Joint Distribution Committee, the World Jewish Congress and B'nai B'rith were in essence agents of the CIA, Israeli intelligence or the most secret "Zionist Center."

Paradoxically, probably the most powerful slogan of the March propaganda was the recycled claim of *Żydokomuna*—that is to say, accusing the Jews that they were zealous Communists, to blame for most, if not all, crimes and horrors of the Stalinist period. This accusation exploited and developed the popular stereotype: the Jews are not just Communists, they are the dark side of communism, responsible for whatever is wrong with communism. This claim both compromised the Jews and absolved other Communists from their crimes and misdeeds, as well as implying that ethnic cleansing of the party would make the regime better. Evidently, Jewish Communists were for the party the best scapegoat available. Externalizing evil onto the Jews was also a most welcome gift to all those who felt somehow uneasy serving the regime, which for many Poles (and maybe for themselves) was alien, imposed by the Soviets, atheist and stained with the blood of war heroes and innocent victims, or at least economically inefficient and full of absurdities.

Similarly, a most useful feature of the March enemy was his alleged elitist nature. He was presented as belonging to some kind of exclusive political, financial or cultural establishment; he was detached from the people and held the ordinary man in contempt. Clothing "anti-Zionism" in egalitarian costume, such accusations were instrumental in attracting to the campaign many such ordinary people, who had no special resentment against the Jews. In the March rituals that channeled discontent and aggression, the rulers let their subjects break certain taboos, which in ordinary times had been unthinkable. The Poles were permitted, even encouraged, to express loudly their dissatisfaction with and criticism of the regime and its functionaries, on condition, however, that they used the rhetoric of condemning "Zionists," revisionists, and so forth. This means that in 1968, after years of fearful silence, Poles were allowed to criticize the corruption and arrogance of the officials—not all of them, it is true, only the Jewish ones. They could even throw off submission to their superiors—but not all of them.... In this regard, the popularity of criticism of "Zionists" as members of the establishment seems to have been no accident. The egalitarian charges made against them, of alienation, arrogance, unjustified privileges and so on, were basically directed at the PRL establishment as a whole.

Therefore, the "anti-Zionism" of 1968 appears to have been more than a mere camouflage for attacking the Jews. Despite the brutal and unsophisticated methods of the campaign, "anti-Zionism" served as a complex and subtle code. Using its language was first of all a sign of obedience and loyalty to the party. Conspicuous "anti-Zionism" indicated a particular devotion or belonging to (or willingness to join) the victorious and hopefully rising group, as many observers in 1968 perceived the Partisans and their followers. At the same time, "anti-Zionism" could express frustration with and resentment against various features of the regime or the grim realities of everyday life in People's Poland. Furthermore, the favorite topic of "Zionist" plots and hidden Jewish agendas served, like other conspiracy theories, to alleviate the painful inability to understand the complex modern world.

The last but not least noteworthy feature of the image of the enemy was its chimeric quality, as Gavin Langmuir has observed in many demonic presentations of the Jews since the Middle Ages.[70] The March enemy possessed certain traits that to a rational mind were incompatible: "Jewish nationalists" could be simultaneously "rootless cosmopolitans," and "Stalinists" could act as "agents of American imperialism." The Chimera of Greek mythology was an impossible beast with the body of a goat, a lion's head and the tail of a serpent, rather like the Stalinist agents of American imperialism. Clearly, the propaganda exploited old and deep-rooted images of the Jew, but the presence of the Chimera in the 1968 campaign can be explained not only through reference to the rich Polish (and European) legacy of Judeophobia. The 'Zionist' was not the only enemy whom Communists endowed with the traits of an impossible beast. Soviet propaganda at least since the 1930s, and then communist propaganda in Poland, had constructed many more or less chimeric images of the enemy: Trotsky and Bukharin, who were "lackeys of capitalists" and counter-revolution; leaders of the Home Army (Polish anti-Nazi underground), who were chauvinists and agents of the Gestapo; "fascist" social democrats, and so on. In view of both the content of the hate speech and the patterns of the campaign, the March campaign appears to be more a return of the ghosts of Stalinism than of right-wing anti-Semitism.[71]

Handy and Effective

The feeling of revulsion, which many observers and historians of the campaign have expressed, should not prevent us from asking whether the campaign was effective. Did those who initiated and ran the campaign achieve their objectives? Was it cost effective? It seems that they mostly did, and that they found the costs acceptable, at least in the short term. Given their cynicism, which many of them proved, claims that the campaign was morally reprehensible, aesthetically repugnant and in some respects outright criminal probably would not count for much. The choice of an "anti-Zionist" campaign as a policy instrument was therefore rational.

The campaign served several goals. Crushing any real Zionists was probably among the least important. First, the campaign was a reaction to the student protests and dissent among intellectuals. It was a tool for fighting the youth rebellion, through compromising its alleged instigators, leaders and goals as alien and perverse. Second, "anti-Zionism" was used to prevent the youth rebellion from spreading beyond the universities to broader groups, industrial workers in particular. At least since the autumn of 1967, when a series of strikes and other industrial protests followed a rise in food prices, the party leaders had been seriously concerned about the possible eruption of popular unrest. This seems the most important motive for allowing and maintaining the aggressive and demagogic campaign. Portraying the dissident students and intellectuals as aliens—Jews, bloodstained Stalinists or their sons, arrogant members of the establishment, and so forth—certainly contributed to alienating them from the masses. Although quite a number of young workers joined the student riots (as the police data on arrests shows), the authorities managed to prevent a major explosion. (Today we know that they managed only to postpone it.

In December 1970 violent workers' protests against a new rise in food prices led to a bloody confrontation and serious political crisis that eventually ended Gomułka's rule.) Notably, while after the campaign "anti-Zionism" largely disappeared from the media and public discourse and did not return, the MSW archives show that the Security Service continued to focus on Jews and use some of the anti-Jewish claims tested in March to fight the democratic opposition throughout the 1970s and 1980s.

The third main objective of the campaign was to change the political balance in the party leadership. Those who decided on the campaign never revealed this explicitly, but their behavior confirms what the answer to the question *cui prodest?* suggests. The March attack on "Zionists" revitalized the conflict that had crystallized in the Politburo around Gomułka's speech of 19 June 1967. The new attack gave its proponents a strategic advantage over their adversaries, who were forced on the defensive and deprived of support from the *aktiv*. Within a few weeks, the latter realized their defeat. On 8 April the Politburo met for the first time since the beginning of the crisis, with the notable absence of Minister of Foreign Affairs Rapacki, who had requested release from his position after the anti-Jewish hunt began in his ministry, and the silent—that is, neutralized—presence of Marshal Spychalski, who had long been the object of intrigues (including anti-Semitic gossip). In the discussion on the campaign, Ochab, Jędrychowski and Szyr, who adopted a critical stance, faced Gomułka, Ignacy Loga-Sowiński, Ryszard Strzelecki, Zenon Kliszko, Gierek and Cyrankiewicz, who praised or justified it. The remainder supported the majority or refrained from taking a clear stand. In summarizing the discussion, which was the traditional way in which the first secretary expressed the party leadership's position, Gomułka could therefore legitimately approve the campaign thus far, with some minor reservations about its anti-Jewish excess.[72] Many years later, Edward Ochab published a short letter that he had handed to Gomułka in 1968:

> As a Pole and a Communist I protest with the deepest outrage against the anti-Semitic plot organized in Poland by various dark forces, yesterday's members of the Radical National Camp and their current mighty protectors. In the situation that has developed in our party, I am forced to convey my protest in the form of a resignation from my mandate as a member of the Political Bureau. Simultaneously I submit my resignation from the position of chairman of the Council of State, as well as chairman of the OK FJN [Front for National Unity].[73]

Thus, the March campaign enabled Gomułka to marginalize his opponents and reconsolidate the party leadership on his terms. In addition, the once powerful "bankrupt politicians" (Zambrowski in particular), who to some party leaders could still appear as potential challengers, were marginalized for good.

The hard work of Moczar's officers also proved to be not in vain. They had not only "helped the party," as they had been requested; they had also defeated their own political adversaries and muted their critics, as well as made thousands of Jews, whom they had so much resented and suspected, decide to leave Poland for ever. This article has focused on the political uses and abuses of the campaign—that is, its rationality—but we should not reduce participants and authors of the campaign to rational agents.

Poland in spring 1968 was the scene of innumerable expressions of the most irrational resentments and prejudices, which infused the words and deeds not only of the excited participants in the hate meetings but also of the officials and officers at the medium and upper levels of the state-party power structure. The pursuit of rationally defined political interests clearly combined with irrational impulses. Indeed, these different kinds of motivation combined well. Irrational anti-Jewish prejudice and resentment seem to have had a strange capacity to bring about quite rationally organized actions. Releasing and exploiting hateful emotions and opinions in 1968 obviously contributed to their invigoration and persistence well after 1968. Gomułka wanted to minimize this, a few times he warned against it, but clearly this was not the priority, and even less so for most of the party apparatchiks or police officers.

The above political objectives acquire greater weight in the context of developments in Czechoslovakia. As Gomułka claimed at the 8 April meeting of the Politburo, the radicalism of the campaign was well justified by the alleged preparations for counterrevolution in the neighboring country and its possible spread to Poland. If that was truly his perspective, then the brutal repression, the hate campaign and the mobilization of the party served as a preemptive strike against potential followers of the Czech path, as well as a means of consolidating the entire party, not just its leadership. A few months later the Polish army obediently participated in the Warsaw Pact forces' intervention in Czechoslovakia. Fresh memories of the March repression certainly contributed to intimidation of potential opponents to the intervention.

A result that the top decision-makers had not necessarily premeditated but accepted during the campaign was the beginning of a greater mobility of cadres, which enabled them to advance their own loyal people in particular. This was very important to many younger apparatchiks, whose frustration had been growing for several years at the old guard, who had held on to positions and blocked their career paths. To many such people, the purge offered a chance for upward mobility or at least a new hope for it. The personnel changes of 1968 began a major generational change that accelerated in the early 1970s, following the fall of Gomułka.

Playing the Jewish card was thus multifunctional and contributed to bringing about the desired or desirable effects. As for the costs, it is not clear to what extent the decision-makers could see or anticipate them at the time. Critics of the campaign warned Gomułka that it encouraged and rewarded immoral behavior and harmed innocent people, including devout party members, while promoting unscrupulous opportunists, and so forth. This was not pleasant to hear, but did not make Gomułka halt the campaign. Arguments that it was getting out of control and undermining the leaders' rule proved more important for the decision to end the campaign. For example, some high-ranking "non-Zionist" officials were dismissed without the required consent of the party authorities, which was a major breach of the principles of the *nomenklatura* system. Sometimes, excited participants in the hate meetings reached wrong conclusions (for example, if the "Zionists" had been responsible for economic shortages and rising food prices, the prices should decrease now...) or attacked the wrong people, such as Gomulka's right hand, Zenon Kliszko.

A costly consequence of the 1968 campaign, which the party leaders probably could not anticipate, was a profound disillusionment with the regime among those segments of the Polish intelligentsia who had sympathized with its socialist slogans. For many people who had dreamed of a "socialism with human face," the events of 1968—in Poland and in Czechoslovakia—were the final blow to such beliefs and left no doubts that the regime's officially declared ideology was dead. In particular, the experience of 1968 set many talented and courageous young people on a path towards open opposition. Later they significantly contributed to the development of dissident organizations in the 1970s and the Solidarity movement in the 1980s, and eventually to the regime's end.

None seem to have calculated the human capital loss due to the post-March emigration. It was the best-educated wave of emigrants from Poland ever. Several thousand members of the Polish intelligentsia, including many outstanding scientists, artists and writers, left the country. A long-lasting consequence of the campaign was its contribution to the image of Poland abroad as a country of incurable anti-Semitism, a problem that Poles and Polish governments were to face repeatedly, up to the present.

Notes

[1] For an extensive presentation and analysis of the "anti-Zionist" campaign of 1967–68, see Stola, *Kampania antysyjonistyczna*. The archival research for this study was made possible by a grant of the American Jewish Committee. On mass mobilization in the campaign, see Stola, "Fighting against the Shadows."

[2] On Jews in communist Poland, see Adelson, "W Polsce zwanej ludowę"; Cała, "Mniejszość żydowska"; Cała and Datner-Śpiewak, eds, *Dzieje Żydów*; Steinlauf, *Bondage to the Dead*, 46–52, 64–7; Chęciński, *Poland*; Grabski and Berend, *Między emigracje a trwaniem*; Lendvai, *Antisemitism*. On the early postwar years, see Szaynok, *Ludność żydowska*. On policies towards the Jews in the Soviet bloc, see Gitelman, "The Evolution"; Low, *Soviet Jewry*; Pinkus, *The Jews*.

[3] On Zionist activity in early communist Poland, see Aleksiun, *Dokęd dalej*; Adelson, "W Polsce zwanej ludowę," 412–17, 433–46; Cała and Datner-Śpiewak, eds, *Dzieje Żydów*. On early Polish-Israeli relations, see Chain, "Stosunek rzędów polskich"; Stankowski, "Poland and Israel."

[4] Adelson, "W Polsce zwanej ludowę," 476–77; Stola, "Zamknięcie granic."

[5] Lucjan Blitt, "Antyżydowska kampania we współczesnej Polsce," London 1968, Polish translation of a report for the Institute of Jewish Affairs, in the Archive of the PRL (Polish People's Republic), Warsaw (hereafter APRL), Starewicz collection.

[6] Adelson, "W Polsce," 400–4; Szaynok, *Pogrom*.

[7] Steinlauf, *Bondage*, 49–51; Kersten, *Polacy, Żydzi, Komunizm*, 76–88. Schatz, *The Generation*, 95–8, 150–2, 213–30. On the overrepresentation of Jews in the security apparatus, see Paczkowski "Jews in the Polish Security Service." Similar observations on the Ministry of Foreign Affairs appear in the "Notatka o stanie kadr MSZ" by Ostap Dłuski, 7 May 1953, in Archiwum Akt Nowych, collection of the Central Committee of the Communist Party (hereafter AAN, KC), file 237/XXII–41.

[8] Zaremba, *Komunizm*, 121–33.

[9] Kramer, *The Forgotten Friendship*; Gitelman, "The Evolution"; Low, *Soviet Jewry*.

[10] For a sample of the hate speech, see the brochure *Proces antypaństwowego ośrodka*. As Zaremba notes (*Komunizm*, 199–200), the anti-Jewish tone of the 1948 Soviet campaign against 'cosmpolitanism' had surprisingly no follow-up in Poland.

[11] *Trybuna Ludu*, 14 January 1953; other articles quoted by Cała and Datner-Śpiewak, eds, *Dzieje Żydów*, 136–41.

[12] Stankowski, "Zerwanie stosunków dyplomatycznych," 356.

[13] On changes in the party leadership in Poland and other Soviet satellites, see Paczkowski, *Pół wieku*, 219–22; Friszke, *Polska*, 160–1, 171; Zaremba, *Komunizm*, 180–90; Rothschild, *Return to Diversity*, 134–9.

[14] Werblan, "Przyczynek do genezy konfliktu"; interview with Gen. Moczar (12 April 1968) published by Osęka, in *Syjoniści*, 232.

[15] Paczkowski, *Pół wieku*, 298–303; Friszke, *Polska*, 214, 220–22, 225.

[16] Lesiakowski, *Mieczysław Moczar*, 218–35, 259–60; Zaremba, *Komunizm*, 287–99.

[17] Machcewicz, "Antisemitism."

[18] Stankowski, "Zerwanie stosunków dyplomatycznych," 357–58.

[19] Steinlauf, *Bondage to the Dead*; Cała, "Mniejszość żydowska"; Adelson, "W Polsce zwanej ludowę."

[20] Memorandum on financial assistance to the Poland-Israel Friendship League, 30 January 1962, AAN, KC 1721: 18–19.

[21] Politburo protocol, 6 June 1967, AAN, KC 1737.

[22] Interview with St. Trepczyński and W. Namiotkiewicz, 1983, APRL, K108: 61.

[23] Polish translation of Brezhnev's secret speech, "O polityce ZSRR w zwięzku z agresję Izraela na Bliskim Wschodzie," 20 June 1967, AAN, KC 2632: 358–408.

[24] Note of Gomułka's speech to the Politburo, 27 June 1967, AAN, KC 1738: 3–4.

[25] "Informacja nr 3 Departamentu III MSW o nastrojach w zwięzku z konfliktem na Bliskim Wschodzie," 7 June 1967, MSW Central Archive (hereafter CAMSW), MSW.II.3811.

[26] As confirmed by Professors Stefan Amsterdamski and Marcin Kula, eyewitnesses to the events. The MSW noted that in the city of Łódź there appeared leaflets proclaiming, 'We Support the Struggle of Israel against the Red Arabs'; see "Informacja Departamentu III MSW za okres 5.6–5.7.67," CAMSW, MSW.II.1976: 72.

[27] Interview with St. Trepczyński and W. Namiotkiewicz, 1983, APRL, K.108: 61–62.

[28] Politburo protocol, 10 June 1967, AAN, KC 1737.

[29] Eisler, *Marzec 1968*, 134.

[30] Tadeusz Walichnowski, an MSW officer who during the campaign advanced to the position of deputy director of MSW Department III, became the main expert on the Israeli-German conspiracy. In just 18 months his book *Izrael a NRF* (Israel and the FRG) ran into five Polish editions and eight in foreign languages, while his similar publications, *Israel-FRG and Poland* and *Around the Israeli Aggression*, were translated into seven and four languages respectively. See Podhorski and Majcher, *Bibliografia prac Tadeusza Walichnowskiego*. In spring 1968 the guidelines for the media campaign gave FRG-Israeli cooperation as one of the desired topics for publication ("Plan najbliższych publikacji w prasie", AAN, KC PZPR, 237/XIX-347: 3–9). See also Osęka, *Syjoniści*.

[31] *Trybuna Ludu*, 15, 16, 17 June 1967, etc.

[32] Minutes of Gomułka's speech at the conference, 12 June 1967, AAN, KC 237/V-706.

[33] "Informacja Wydziału Organizacyjnego KC," 20 June 1967, AAN, KC PZPR, 237/VII-5224.

[34] The term "fifth column" originated in Italy in 1922 to denote Mussolini's supporters in Rome when four columns of fascists marched towards the city for Mussolini's coup d'état. In Poland it was applied to disloyal ethnic Germans who supported the German invasion in 1939.

[35] Minutes of Gomułka's speech of 19 June 1967, Archiwum Ruchu Zawodowego (Trade Union Movement Archive), Warsaw, Wydział Organizacyjny CRZZ-file (no number).

[36] Torańska, *Oni*, 232. Of course the argument did not take place during the rally but immediately afterwards.

[37] Memorandum of conversation between Kliszko and Brezhnev, Moscow, 24 June 1967, AAN, KC 2642: 295.

[38] Minutes of the meetings of Gomułka, Cyrankiewicza and others with Brezhnev, Kosygin, Podgorny and others, 22 September and 7 December 1967, 12–14 January 1968, all in AAN, KC 6166.

[39] Interview with St. Trepczyński and W. Namiotkiewicz, 1983, APRL, K.108: 60; Torańska, *Oni*, 232.

[40] Note of Gomułka's speech to the Politburo, 27 June 1967, AAN, KC 1738: 5.

[41] "Ocena sytuacji w Polsce w związku z konfliktem na Bliskim Wschodzie" (with enclosures), June 1967, CAMSW, MSW.II.51.

[42] "Informacje Departamentu III o sytuacji w kraju w związku z konfliktem...," June–July 1967, CAMSW, MSW.II.1976.

[43] F. Szlachcic, "Tezy informacji dla aktywu Departamentu I," 27 November 1966; "Tezy informacji dla komendantów KW MO," 5 March 1966, APRL, Szlachcic collection, S.II.2.

[44] MSW Collegium protocol, 28 June 1967, CAMSW, MSW.II.51. An even stronger conspiracy theory is presented by a note of 1 July 1967, CAMSW, MSW.II.1976.

[45] MSW Collegium protocol, 28 June 1967, CAMSW, MSW.II.51.

[46] Ibid.

[47] "Zestawienie cyfrowe osób narodowości żydowskiej zatrudnionych w podstawowych resortach gospodarczych i innych instytucjach," quoted in Eisler, "Wydarzenia lat 1967–1968," 57.

[48] Ibid.

[49] "Notatka dot. zaprzestania przyjmowania środków Joint," 29 June 1967, and the protocol of CC Secretariat, AAN, KC 6522: 93, 108–13.

[50] "Sprawozdanie Zespołu Biura Prasy KC i KW PZPR," 4 June 1967, in Sołtysiak and Stępień, eds., *Marzec'68*, 29–34.

[51] "Notatka o zmianach w redakcji 'Trybuny Ludu,'" 4 December 1967, AAN, KC 2229: 415–17.

[52] Gen. Józef Urbanowicz's report on "events in certain military units in summer 1967," 12 December 1967, copy in author's files.

[53] Protocol of the party meeting in the military unit 2216, 14 July 1967. I am grateful to Leszek Gluchowski for a copy of this document.

[54] On events in WOPK, see Nalepa, "Rok 1967"; "Notatka służbowa GZP o naradach aktywu WOPK," 12 December 1967, copy in author's files.

[55] On 1967 in the army, see Chęciński, *Poland*; Pióro, "Czystki w wojsku." Notably, the classic books of Soviet 'anti-Zionism' (*The State of Israel* and *Danger: Zionism*) in the 1960s were published in Polish by the Ministry of Defense publishing house (Wydawnictwo MON), which the GZP supervised.

[56] Chęciński, "Ludowe Wojsko Polskie."

[57] On the events of spring 1968, see Kula, Osęka and Zaremba, eds., *Marzec 1968*; Eisler, *Marzec 1968*; Osęka, *Syjoniści, inspiratorzy, wichrzyciele*; Sołtysiak and Stępień, eds., *Marzec'68*; Rokicki and Stępień, eds., *Oblicza Marca 1968*; Fik, *Marcowa kultura*; Banas, *The Scapegoats*; Checinski, *Poland*; Rozenbaum, "The Background of the Anti-Zionist Campaign" and "The Anti-Zionist Campaign."

[58] "Dane statystyczne dot. osób zatrzymanych, ukaranych i wcielonych do służby wojskowej," supplement to the MSW Internal Bulletin 75/68, in Kula, Osęka and Zaremba, eds, *Marzec 1968*, 2:237–41.

[59] "Do studentów Uniwersytetu Warszawskiego," *Słowo Powszechne*, 11 March 1968.

[60] See a series of MSW "Internal Bulletins" (*Biuletyny Wewnętrzne*) from March 1968, in Kula, Osęka and Zaremba, eds., *Marzec 1968*, vol. 2.

[61] On the March 'anti-Zionist' propaganda, see Osęka, *Syjoniści*; interesting insights in Głowiński, *Marcowe gadanie*.

[62] Resolutions quoted in Mieszczanek, ed., *Krajobraz po szoku*, 43–46; Nowicki, "Mowi Warszawa": 116–17.

[63] Gierek's speech quoted in Andrzej Friszke, "Gwiazda Gomułki zgasła w marcu," *Gazeta Wyborcza*, 19 March 1994.

[64] Gomułka, *Stanowisko partii*; Eisler, *Marzec*: 360–63.

[65] "Listy R. Zambrowskiego," 75.

[66] "Notatka w sprawie wyjazdów emigracyjnych," 29 April 1969, AAN, KC 1742: 475–88; "Migracje zewnętrzne: Informacja statystyczna Biura Paszportów MSW," 1979; M. Glanz, "Niektóre problemy emigracji z Polskiw ostatnim ćwierćwieczu," June 1971, AAN, KC 3048. For a detailed description of the post-March emigration, see Stola, *Kampania antysyjonistyczna*.

[67] Głowiński, *Pismak*, 63.

[68] Rakowski, *Dzienniki polityczne, 1967–1968*, 218.

[69] "Kosmopolityzm polski," *Zycie Literackie*, 15 October 1967.

[70] Langmuir, "Toward a Definition of Antisemitism," 109; Smith, "The Social Construction of Enemies," 203–39.

[71] On the 1968 campaign's affinity with earlier Soviet campaigns, see Głowiński, *Nowomowa;* Jedlicki, *Źle urodzeni*, 56–70.

[72] Notes from the Politburo session of 8 April 1968, AAN, KC 1739.

[73] Torańska, *Oni*, p. 234; Ochab's letter to *Polityka*, 11 July 1981.

References

Adelson, Józef. "W Polsce zwanej ludowę." In *Najnowsze dzieje Żydów w Polsce*, edited by Jerzy Tomaszewski. Warsaw: Wydawnictwo Naukowe PWN, 1993.

Aleksiun, Natalia. *Dokęd dalej? Ruch syjonistyczny w Polsce (1944–1950)*. Warsaw: Trio, 2002.

Banas, Josef. *The Scapegoats: The Exodus of the Remnants of Polish Jewry*. London: Weidenfeld and Nicholson, 1979.

Cała, Alina. "Mniejszość żydowska." In *Mniejszości narodowe w Polsce: Państwo i społeczeństwo polskie a mniejszości narodowe w okresach przełomów politycznych (1944–1989)*, edited by Piotr Madajczyk. Warsaw: Instytut Studiów Politycznych PAN, 1998.

———, and Helena Datner-Śpiewak, eds. *Dzieje Żydów w Polsce 1944–1968: Teksty źródłowe*. Warsaw: Żydowski Instytut Historyczny, 1997.

Chęciński, Michał. "Ludowe Wojsko Polskie przed i po marcu 1968." *Zeszyty Historyczne*, no. 44 (1978): 36–52.

———. *Poland: Communism, Nationalism, Antisemitism*. New York: Karz-Cohl, 1982.

Eisler, Jerzy. *Marzec 1968: Geneza, przebieg, konsekwencje*. Warsaw: PWN, 1991.

———. "Wydarzenia lat 1967–1968 w materiałach archiwalnych Instytutu Pamięci Narodowej." In *Oblicza Marca 1968*, edited by Konrad Rokicki and Sławomir Stępień. Warsaw: Instytut Pamięci Narodowej, 2004.

Fik, Marta. *Marcowa kultura: Wokół "Dziadów": Literaci i władza. Kampania marcowa*. Warsaw: Wydawnictwo Wodnika, 1995.

Friszke, Andrzej. *Polska: Losy Państwa i narodu, 1939–1989*. Warsaw: Iskry, 2003.

Gitelman, Zvi. "The Evolution of Soviet Anti-Zionism." In *Anti-Zionism and Antisemitism in the Contemporary World*, edited by Robert S. Wistrich. London: Institute of Jewish Affairs, 1990.

Głowiński, Michał. *Nowomowa po polsku*. Warsaw: Pomost, 1990.

———. *Marcowe gadanie: Komentarze do słów 1966–1971*. Warsaw: Pomost, 1991.

———. *Pismak 1863 i inne szkice o różnych brzydkich rzeczach*. Warsaw: Pomost, 1995.

Gomułka, Władysław. *Stanowisko partii—zgodne z wolę narodu: Przemówienie wygłoszone na spotkaniu z warszawskim aktywem partyjnym 19 marca 1968r*. Warsaw: Książka i Wiedza, 1968.

Grabski, August and Grzegorz Berend. *Między emigrację a trwaniem: Syjoniści i komuniści żydowscy w Polsce po Holocauście*. Warsaw: Żydowski Instytut Historyczny, 2003.

Jedlicki, Jerzy. *Źle urodzeni czyli o doświadczeniu historycznym: Scripta i postscripta*. London and Warsaw: Puls, 1993.

Kersten, Krystyna. *Polacy, Żydzi, komunizm. Anatomia półprawd 1939–68*. Warsaw: Niezależna Oficyna Wydawnicza, 1992.

Kramer, Arnold. *The Forgotten Friendship: Israel and the Soviet Block, 1947–1953*. Urbana: University of Illinois Press, 1974.

Kula, Marcin, Piotr Osęka, and Marcin Zaremba, eds. *Marzec 1968: Trzydziesci lat później*. 2 vols. Warsaw: Wydawnictwo Naukowe PWN, 1998.

Langmuir, Gavin. "Toward a Definition of Antisemitism." In *The Persisting Question: Sociological Perspectives and Social Contexts of Modern Antisemitism*, edited by Helen Fein. Berlin and New York: Walter de Gruyter, 1987.

———. *Toward a Definition of Antisemitism*. Berkeley: University of California Press, 1990.

Lendvai, Paul. *Antisemitism without Jews: Communist Eastern Europe*. New York: 1971.

Lesiakowski, Krzysztof. *Mieczysław Moczar "Mietek": Biografia polityczna*. Warsaw: Rytm, 1998.

Low, Alfred. *Soviet Jewry and Soviet Policy*. New York: Columbia University Press, 1990.

Machcewicz, Paweł. "Antisemitism in Poland in 1956." *Polin: Studies in Polish Jewry*, no. 8 (1996): 170–83.

Mieszczanek Anna, ed. *Krajobraz po szoku*. Warsaw: Przedświt, 1989.

Nalepa, Edward J. "Rok 1967 w wojskach OPK." *Wojskowy Przegląd Historyczny*, nos. 1–2 (1997): 3–17.

———, ed. *Czystka w korpusie oficerskim: Wydarzenia 1967 roku w Wojsku Polskim w dokumentach*. Warsaw: Akademia Obrony Narodowej, 1999.

Osęka, Piotr. *Syjoniści, inspiratorzy, wichrzyciele: Obraz wroga w propagandzie Marca 1968*. Warsaw: Żydowski Instytut Historyczny, 1999.

Paczkowski, Andrzej. *Pół wieku dziejów Polski, 1939–1989*. Warsaw: Wydawnictwo Naukowe PWN, 1995.

———. "Jews in the Polish Security Apparatus: An Attempt to Test the Stereotype." *Polin: Studies in Polish Jewry*, no. 16 (2003): 453–66.

Pinkus, Benjamin. *The Jews of the Soviet Union: A Natural History of a National Minority*. Cambridge: Cambridge University Press, 1988.

Pióro, Tadeusz. "Czystki w wojsku polskim 1967–1968." *Biuletyn ŻIH*, no. 2 (1997): 74–80.

Podhorski, Kazimierz, and Krystyna, Majcher. *Bibliografia prac Tadeusza Walichnowskiego 1961–1985*. Warsaw: Akademia Spraw Wewnętrznych, 1986.

Proces antypaństwowego ośrodka spiskowego w Czechosłowacji. Warsaw: n.p., 1953.

Rakowski, Mieczysław. *Dzienniki polityczne, 1967–1968*. Warsaw: Iskry, 1999.

Rokicki Konrad, and Sławomir Stępień, eds. *Oblicza Marca 1968*. Warsaw: Instytut Pamięci Narodowej, 2004.

Rothschild, Joseph. *Return to Diversity: A Political History of East Central Europe since World War II*. New York and Oxford: Oxford University Press, 1993.

Rozenbaum, Wlodzimierz. "The Background of the Anti-Zionist Campaign of 1967–68 in Poland." *Essays in History*, no. 17 (1973): 71–95.

———. "The Anti-Zionist Campaign in Poland, June–December 1967." *Canadian Slavonic Papers*, no. 20 (1978): 218–36.

Schatz, Jaff. *The Generation: The Rise and Fall of the Jewish Communists of Poland*. Berkeley: University of California Press, 1991.

Smith, David Norman. "The Social Construction of Enemies: Jews and the Representations of Evil." *Sociological Theory*, no. 14 (November 1966): 203–40.

Sołtysiak Jerzy, and Jerzy Stępień, eds. *Marzec'68: Miedzy tragedię a podłością*. Warsaw: Profi, 1998.

Stankowski, Albert. "Poland and Israel: Bilateral Relations 1947–1953." *Jews in Eastern Europe*, no. 37 (1998): 5–23.

———. "Zerwanie stosuków dyplomatycznych z Izraelem przez Polskę w czerwcu 1967 roku." In *Rozdział wspólnej historii. Studia z dziejów Żydów w Polsce*, edited by Jolanta Żyndul and Marcin Kula. Warszawa: Wydawnictwo Cyklady, 2001.

Steinlauf, Michael. *Bondage to the Dead: Poland and the Memory of the Holocaust*. Syracuse, NY: Syracuse University Press, 1997.

Stola, Dariusz. *Kampania antysyjonistyczna w Polsce, 1967–1968*. Warsaw: Instytut Studiów Politycznych PAN, 2000.

———. "Zamknięcie Polski. Zniesienie swobody wyjazdu i uszczelnienie granic w latach 40. i 50." In *PRL. Trwanie i zmiana*, edited by Dariusz Stola and Marcin Zaremba. Warsaw: Wydawnictwo WSPiZ im. L. Koźminskiego, 2003.

———. "Fighting against the Shadows: The Anti-Zionist Campaign of 1968." In *Antisemitism and Its Opponents in Modern Poland*, edited by Robert Blobaum. Ithaca, NY: Cornell University Press, 2004.

Szaynok, Bożena. *Pogrom Żydów w Kielcach, 4 lipca 1946*. Warsaw: Bellona, 1992.

———. *Ludność żydowska na Dolnym Śląsku 1945–1950*. Wrocław: Wydawnictwo Uniwersytetu Wroclawskiego, 2000.

Tarniewski, Marek. [Jakub Karpiński]. *Krótkie spięcie (marzec 1968)*. Paris: Kultura, 1977.

Torańska, Teresa. *Oni*. Warsaw: Omnipress, 1990.

Werblan, Andrzej. "Przyczynek do genezy konfliktu." *Miesięcznik Literacki*, no. 6 (1968): 61–71.

Wydarzenia Marcowe. Paris: Kultura, 1968.

Zambrowski, Roman. "Listy R. Zambrowskiego do władz partyjnych." *Krytyka*, no. 6 (1980): 73–76.

Zaremba, Marcin. *Komunizm-legitymizacja-nacjonalizm. Nacjonalistyczna legitymizacja władzy w Polsce do 1980 r.* Warsaw: Trio, 2003.

Ideology and *Realpolitik*: East German Attitudes towards Zionism and Israel

Angelika Timm

The negative attitudes of the East German political elite towards Zionism, and their anti-Israel politics and propaganda, became part of academic and political discourse after the German Democratic Republic (GDR) was dissolved in 1990.[1] Using newly discovered archival material, historians and political scientists explored whether the GDR's one-sided Middle East policy and its failure to assume responsibility for the Holocaust should be labeled as anti-Semitic. This article seeks to portray a critical but complex and differentiated picture. It addresses the ideological and political background of anti-Zionist and anti-Israel positions, and highlights some changes in the image of Israel during the forty years of the GDR's existence.[2]

The Antifascist Legacy of the GDR

In order to understand the attitude of the GDR's political elite to Zionism and the State of Israel, one should first consider the context of political developments in East Germany. East Germany's foreign and domestic policy was shaped by the Cold War, the division of Germany and the GDR's membership in the Warsaw Pact and the Council for Mutual Economic Assistance (COMECON). From the very outset, East Germany viewed itself as the antithesis of West Germany. Thus, West German political and juridical claims to represent all of Germany were countered with the moral argument that the "antifascist democratic transformation" after 1945 and the establishment of the German Democratic Republic in 1949 had opened "a new chapter in German history" and become even "the turning point in European history."[3] By constructing a continuous tradition of revolutionary socialist and communist opposition to National Socialism, the existence of the East German state was legitimized. As a central element in the self-definition of the GDR, antifascism was instrumentalized from the very outset to justify the rise of the new communist elite and the Socialist Unity Party of Germany (SED). The communist opposition to Hitler was addressed in a special way because it embodied "the link between native antifascism, the Soviet Union as liberator and protector, and the first generation of political leaders in the GDR."[4]

Allied with the Soviet Union and represented by Communists, who had been persecuted under the Nazi regime, East Germans became increasingly convinced that they were among the victors in World War II. The fact that both East and West Germans had supported Hitler and only a few of them had actively resisted Nazism was ignored. The narrow ideological definition of National Socialism as fascism—that is, "the open terrorist rule of the most reactionary, most chauvinistic, most imperialist elements of finance capital"[5]—absolved most of the German population of Nazi complicity. Although members of the former military establishment, the upper strata and the middle class were categorized as fascist activists or supporters of the Nazi regime, the members of the working class were automatically assumed to be antifascist. During the first postwar years, the crimes of the Nazi era were debated in public, and a relatively broad denazification process ensued. Still, neither at that time nor later was there a general debate on personal guilt and responsibility.

The claim that "the legacy of antifascist resistance has been fulfilled in the German Democratic Republic" was repeated time and again.[6] In memorial ceremonies commemorating the victims of fascism at Buchenwald in 1958 and Sachsenhausen in 1961, Prime Minister Otto Grotewohl and SED leader Walter Ulbricht underscored the continuity of the antifascist struggle and political developments in East Germany. About three decades later, Ulbricht's successor, SED Secretary General Erich Honecker, declared: "As the GDR approaches the 40th anniversary of its founding, we can say with every justification that our people seized their historical opportunity by forging a socialist system that rests on unshakable antifascist foundations."[7]

The political leadership emphasized the importance of communist resistance to the Nazi regime in order to legitimize its dominant position in the newly established state. This point of view placed anti-Semitism and the Holocaust on the margins of the discussion and gave Communists a higher status than those who had been persecuted for religious or racial reasons, such as noncommunist Jews, as the latter were presumed to have refrained from active resistance against the Nazi regime. Although anti-Semitism, racism and xenophobia were prohibited by law, official restrictions were not sufficient to counteract them. The antifascist legacy lost its significance after the early postwar years as antifascism became more and more an aphorism that was never really accepted by most East Germans.

The Holocaust in Political Culture and History

The Holocaust was not ignored in East Germany, but for decades it played only a minor role in the GDR's historiography and political culture.[8] The writings and the speeches of party leaders were characterized by acceptance of the basic positions adopted by Marx, Engels and Lenin on the "Jewish question," and by endorsement of communist doctrine on the nature of fascism and the parallel concept of antifascism. Anti-Jewish pogroms were thus regarded as none other than a weapon used by the ruling class to enslave the German working class and destroy other peoples. The Holocaust was woven into the communist narratives because it symbolized and illustrated the cruelty of the Nazi regime. At the same time, anticommunism and anti-Bolshevism were viewed as central or defining features of German National Socialism.

High school and university students in East Germany were taught about *Kristallnacht* and the racist Nuremberg laws. *The Diary of Anne Frank* was published and made into a film in 1950, several movies on Jewish life and death during the Nazi period were made, and memoirs of Jewish survivors were published. Nonetheless, the full magnitude of the Holocaust was not addressed. The memorials in Buchenwald and Sachsenhausen did not mention Jewish inmates of the concentration camps. The collective memory also excluded Roma and Sinti, homosexuals and others persecuted by the Nazi regime who did not fit into "Aryan" society.

It was mainly Jewish communities, Christian religious groups and the Association of Victims of Nazi Persecution (VVN) that commemorated the Holocaust and organized memorial events.[9] Apart from the 40th and 50th anniversaries of *Kristallnacht* in 1978 and 1988, when the government organized official commemoration ceremonies, the annual celebrations of the Bolshevik revolution of 1917 and the German revolution of November 1918 overshadowed the remembrance of the Nazi pogroms.

Only during the early postwar years did some Communists emphasize the suffering of Jews during the Nazi era as a focal issue of antifascism. They argued in favor of restitution of Jewish property and compensation for Jewish victims, in addition to promoting close relations with Israel. Paul Merker, member of the SED Politburo, and Leo Zuckermann, secretary of the Presidential Chancellery, should be mentioned in particular. Zuckermann, for instance, stressed in an article in *Die Weltbühne* on 27 April 1948 that the Germans should pay global recompense to the Jews after the establishment of a Jewish state.[10]

Academic publications dealing with the Holocaust were very rare in East Germany until the Eichmann trial in 1960–61. Only when world attention focused once again on the annihilation of European Jewry did the issue gain priority in the GDR. However, the trial in Jerusalem did not serve primarily to publicize the Holocaust but rather to attack the political elite in the Federal Republic of Germany (FRG) and to unmask former Nazis in high-ranking positions there. The SED used the international attention that Eichmann and the Holocaust received as a means of linking the "Hitlers" and "Eichmanns" with the political elite in West Germany. Friedrich Karl Kaul, a Jewish-German lawyer, was sent to Jerusalem to present documents on State Secretary Hans Globke of West Germany, a former official for Jewish Affairs in the Nazi Ministry of the Interior who had written a commentary on the Nuremberg race laws. The Committee for German Unity, under the auspices of the Central Committee of the SED, published several brochures on this issue.[11] Furthermore, an international conference of historians was held in East Berlin in order "to scientifically prove the antidemocratic and barbarous nature of German imperialism," with the Eichmann trial as a starting point.[12]

In addition to dozens of propaganda brochures, a collection of documents was published in 1960 entitled "The Struggle of the Revolutionary German Labor Movement against anti-Semitism and the Persecution of Jews."[13] Three years later, documents on the persecution of Jews in Leipzig (Saxony) were published. By 1966, after years of bitter fighting against the propagandists in the SED, Helmut Eschwege, a historian from Dresden, succeeded in publishing a comprehensive study on the persecution and annihilation of German Jews.[14] A number of other scholarly publications followed in the 1970s.

It was only in the 1980s that GDR historians began to deal with the Nazi regime in a more complex fashion. New topics such as the bourgeois opposition and the persecution of Jews became feasible. It was admitted that "no group was hit [as] hard as the Jews."[15] Newspapers and journals published interviews with representatives of Jewish communities and articles on Jewish history in East Germany. The 50th anniversary of *Kristallnacht* on 9 November 1988 was commemorated by the government and the SED leaders. Jewish guests from all over the world, including Israel, were invited to memorial ceremonies. On that occasion, the president of the East German parliament, the Volkskammer, portrayed anti-Semitism as "the lynchpin of the fascist racial ideology," and quoted Wilhelm Pieck, the first president of the GDR, who in 1938 had called for "solidarity with the persecuted Jewish population."[16]

This new approach was mainly pragmatic. In 1985, after US President Ronald Reagan and Federal Chancellor Helmut Kohl had laid wreaths at a cemetery in Bitburg where Wehrmacht soldiers and SS officers were buried, GDR leaders sought to use critical statements by Jews as a means of improving the international prestige of their regime. Deriving legitimacy from the distinction between their approach to National Socialism and the approach of the Federal Republic, the political representatives of the GDR sought an opportunity to prove that a better German state had been set up in the east. Towards that end, Honecker planned to visit the United States as an official guest of the White House. He expected the World Jewish Congress to help him receive an official invitation, and hoped that the visit would broaden economic relations with the United States.[17]

Despite these efforts, the general approach of the GDR to the Holocaust did not change. In a speech delivered on the 50th anniversary of *Kristallnacht*, Honecker stated that "the burning synagogues were a plea to the conscience of people and nations. After all, the aim of the hideous crimes perpetrated during that night was to deal a blow to all antifascists, to threaten all those who opposed the impending savage war of annexation, and to leave them in a crippling mood of resignation."[18] Although Israeli guests were invited to East Berlin, any reference to the State of Israel, where thousands of European Jews had found refuge, was avoided.

The Marxist-Leninist Approach to the So-Called Jewish Question

The attitude of the ruling East European communist parties—including the SED—towards anti-Semitism, Zionism and the State of Israel was based on the Marxist-Leninist approach to the so-called Jewish question. According to this ideological doctrine, Communists regarded anti-Semitism and the persecution of Jews as an economic and political problem that concerned feudal and capitalist societies, and which would be resolved more or less automatically in socialist society. Because that ideology viewed the path to social liberation as being open to all oppressed people, the participation of Jewish citizens in the establishment of a socialist society was regarded as quite normal. It was expected that the assimilation process, which started after the French Revolution in Europe and stopped with the Holocaust, would continue after World War II. This approach characterized Jews only as a religious group and ignored their history and tradition. Thus, condemnation of racist Nazi ideology was implicitly accompanied by rejection of Jewish national aspirations.

According to communist ideology, which propagated proletarian internationalism, the 'solution to the Jewish question' was assimilation and the elimination of the social roots of anti-Semitism by revolutionary means and through the establishment of a socialist society. However, this came into conflict with fundamental Zionist ideas, which aimed to ensure the survival of the Jewish people and saw Jewish mass emigration to Palestine and the establishment of a Jewish state there as the ultimate solution to the problem of persistent anti-Semitism. Hence, Zionism was not accepted as a reaction to anti-Semitic persecution or as an attempt to curtail the assimilation process and fight symptoms of decline in Jewish community life. Nor was it endorsed as a legitimate effort to achieve national self-determination in the Land of Israel. Rather, it was characterized as an effort to distract the Jewish working masses from a class struggle and divide the workers' movement.

Zionism and Marxism had vied for the soul of European Jewry at the end of the nineteenth century and during the first decades of the twentieth century, and remained in conflict even after European Jewry was annihilated in the Holocaust. In Eastern Europe, Zionism became a code word for imperialism and racism. Soviet authors consistently opposed Zionism as an ideology that conflicted with the interests of the Jewish working class and portrayed Israel as a dangerous "bridgehead of imperialism" in the Middle East.[19] They described Zionism as an ideology "based on the dogma of racial exclusiveness" that advocated "the expulsion of all non-Jews from the 'Promised Land.'"[20] These stereotypes drew a parallel between Judaism, Zionism and Israel, and perpetuated classic anti-Semitic stereotypes. The relevance of Jewish history and tradition to Jewish life in Europe was ignored, and the multifaceted political scene in the Zionist movement was overlooked.

Like other communist parties, the SED portrayed Zionism as upper-class nationalism and chauvinism. Its leaders followed the Communist Party of the Soviet Union (CPSU) without taking their specific responsibility as Germans into consideration. Convinced that the antifascist GDR bore no responsibility for the actions of the Third Reich, anti-Zionist and anti-Israel campaigns were sometimes even fiercer than the propaganda in other East European countries. As Jeffrey Herf concluded, "the more they remembered the Nazi era in their own ideological framework, the more convinced they were of the need to participate in the 'struggle against Zionism.'"[21]

East German politicians did not accept Israel as the representative of the Jewish people and denied its right to speak on behalf of Holocaust victims and survivors. After the establishment of diplomatic relations between the FRG and Israel, Head of State Walter Ulbricht stated, for instance, in an interview with the Egyptian newspaper *Akhbar il-Yom* on 21 August 1965:

> They [the Jews] were not the only victims of the Hitler regime. The fascists also murdered millions of non-Jewish citizens of Germany, Poland, the Soviet Union, Czechoslovakia, Yugoslavia, France, Belgium, Norway and many other countries. The State of Israel has nominated itself, so to speak, as the general heir of the Jewish citizens of all those countries murdered by Hitler. That is not justified by anything.[22]

East German Interests in the Middle East

Although the ideological approach towards anti-Semitism, Zionism and the Holocaust played an important role in political discourse, one cannot ignore the pragmatic interests that guided East German policy in the Middle East. The most important factor that shaped attitudes towards the Arabs and Israel was the integration of the GDR's foreign policy with the foreign policy of the Soviet Union and the Warsaw Pact. The East German government had limited power for independent decision making. During the Cold War, it more or less identified with the approach of the Soviet leadership to international affairs and, thus, with the Soviet position on the Middle East conflict. Nuances in official and semi-official statements had hardly any impact. It was not until the 1980s that the GDR attained some political latitude and, hence, was able to modify its foreign policy for its own ends, largely in order to achieve economic goals.

After World War II, the Middle East began to play a crucial role in the conflict between East and West. Having emerged as a superpower, the Soviet Union sought not only to weaken the West but also to lay the groundwork for expanding its influence to the region. The Cold War thus had a strong impact on the attitudes of East European countries towards Israel and the Arab world. In the hopes that the termination of the British Mandate would strengthen Soviet influence in the region, Stalin supported the partition of Palestine and the establishment of the State of Israel. Thus, some 200,000 Jews were able to emigrate from Eastern Europe, and Israel was provided with weapons during the War of Independence in 1948/49. Several developments within the Soviet Union and among its allies influenced the policy of the Warsaw Pact countries towards the Jewish state in subsequent decades. This policy was also affected by developments in the Middle East, and especially by Israel's integration into the Western world.[23]

The pro-Arab and anti-Israel foreign policy of the GDR should be viewed, above all, in the context of the Middle East policy of the Warsaw Pact countries. At the same time, East German politicians looked after their own interests. They were eager to undermine the West German Hallstein doctrine of 1955, which declared that the Federal Republic would cut off diplomatic relations with any country establishing relations with the GDR. In an effort to be recognized as an independent and sovereign state, the GDR sought and obtained support in the Third World, especially in some Arab countries. This aim strongly influenced its approach towards the Middle East conflict. The East German government took advantage of a temporary dispute that arose between the FRG and Arab states due to West German relations with Israel. It sided with the Arabs and attacked Israel as a 'spearhead of imperialism' in the region. Ulbricht's visit to Egypt in 1965 and the establishment of diplomatic relations with Iraq, Sudan, Syria, South Yemen and Egypt in 1969 were the first steps towards worldwide recognition of the GDR. Over the two decades that followed, East Germany strengthened its political, economic, military and cultural ties with those countries and with other Arab states, in addition to improving relations with the Palestine Liberation Organization (PLO). As of the 1970s, the GDR provided military support and opened training bases for the PLO. The first official agreement between the SED and the PLO, signed in 1973 in East Berlin, included the supply of non-civilian goods to Palestinians.[24] By 1989, the East German state maintained full diplomatic relations with thirteen Arab countries and the PLO, but never established diplomatic relations with Israel.

In addition to political interests, it is important to mention the economic considerations that favored the expansion of relations with Arab states. Notably, those countries were rich in oil and had an interest in importing services and industrial goods. According to official views, improvement in relations with Israel would have endangered contact with the Arab states and possibly led them to place strong economic pressure on East Germany. By the end of the 1980s, the Arab countries— above all Iraq and Syria—had a debt of DM 2 billion to the GDR.[25] As a result of its perpetual economic weakness and the need for this income, the GDR adopted a kind of pragmatism in its foreign policy that was only partially veiled in its ideology.

Last but not least, the domestic policy of the SED should be taken into consideration. The leaders of the GDR, as in other East European countries, tried to convince their own people that it was necessary to fight the "imperialist enemy" throughout the world in order to prove the legitimacy of the communist regime. As a country that identified with the Western world and cooperated with the United States, Western European countries and South Africa, Israel was considered "an imperialist outpost in the Arab region."[26] At the same time, politicians in the GDR confirmed that their country 'supports the struggle of the peoples of all continents for political and economic liberation from imperialist oppression and exploitation in many ways.'[27] Thus, they declared their solidarity with the Vietnamese people, the Arab national movement and the PLO. From the "class point of view," the East German leadership condemned any kind of cooperation between "imperialist powers" and the Israeli government (and later with the Arab reactionaries) as being directed against peace and progress in the region. Its ideological offensive was based on the general principle of "the joint struggle" of all progressive forces "against imperialism, colonialism, neocolonialism, and Zionism."[28] For ideological and political reasons, the German shadow over Israel was permanently ignored.

The Attitude to Zionism and Israel among the GDR's Political Elite

Although there were no fundamental changes in internal and external circumstances during the four decades of the GDR's existence, some modifications in actual policy did occur. Several phases can be distinguished. During the first brief phase, which lasted from 1947 until the early 1950s, the foreign policy of the GDR was largely pro-Israel. At that time, the Soviet Union's support for the partition of Palestine and the establishment of the State of Israel was clearly the main determinant. Moreover, many East German antifascists—Communists and non-Communists—articulated strong feelings of guilt towards Jews in the wake of the Holocaust. In early 1948, the Central Committee of the ruling SED officially announced: "We consider the foundation of a Jewish state an essential contribution that makes it possible for thousands of people who suffered a great deal under Hitler's fascism to build a new life."[29] Politburo member Paul Merker wrote in the SED daily *Neues Deutschland*: "The Jewish population has the sympathy and active assistance of all progressive forces. In particular, the democratic forces in Germany are compelled to show their sympathy and readiness to help."[30]

Even after the publication of anti-Zionist articles in the Soviet press in autumn of 1948, newspapers and journals in the Soviet Occupation Zone continued to announce their support for the Jewish state. Several contacts between East German and Israeli representatives are documented for the years 1949 and 1950, when talks about trade relations and the delivery of archival material from East Berlin to the Central Jewish Archives in Jerusalem were held. In January 1950, the newly established East German Foreign Ministry launched an initiative requesting the establishment of an Israeli diplomatic outpost in Berlin, offering compensation to individuals and proposing direct commercial relations between the GDR and Israel.[31]

The second phase began in autumn 1952, when the anti-Semitic Slánský show trial was held in Prague. The campaign in East Germany was primarily aimed at people who had found refuge during World War II in Great Britain, the United States, Mexico and other Western countries. That group included many Jews who worked as officials in the SED party apparatus or belonged to the Association of Victims of Nazi Persecution (VVN), as well as Jewish community leaders. Jewish intellectuals were suspected of maintaining contacts with Jewish organizations abroad and betraying their country. Communist leaders like Walter Ulbricht adopted Stalin's advice to eliminate some opposition forces—which included Communists and non-Communists alike. In addition, compensation claims made by the Israeli government and Jewish organizations against both German states encouraged GDR politicians to follow Stalin's political line. The non-Jewish Communist Paul Merker, a strong opponent of Ulbricht, was accused of being the head of a Zionist spy ring, "defending the interests of Zionist monopoly capitalists," and of having arranged "the financing for Jewish capitalists to emigrate to Israel."[32] He was imprisoned from 1952 to 1956. Hundreds of Jews, among them many survivors of the death camps, escaped to the West for fear of possible arrest.

In 1952 East German politicians linked the compensation issue with their attitude towards Zionism and Israel for the first time. Not surprisingly, the first article published by the SED newspaper *Neues Deutschland* in response to the Luxembourg Agreement for reparations appeared only three days after excerpts from the indictment in the Slánský trial were printed. The article headlined "Reparations—For Whom?" referred to "a deal between big capitalists from West Germany and Israel."[33] In February 1953, the SED monthly *Einheit* published an editorial paper approved by the SED Central Committee, entitled "Lessons from the Trial against the Conspiracy Center of Slánský," which claimed that "the Zionist movement has nothing in common with the aims of humanity and true love of mankind. It is dominated, directed and commanded by US imperialism, and devotes itself exclusively to its own interests and the interests of the Jewish capitalists."[34]

After Stalin's death in March 1953, relations between the East European countries and Israel normalized to some extent. When the foreign ministers of the Allied powers met in Berlin in early 1954 to discuss the future of Germany, Israeli Prime Minister David Ben-Gurion again raised the reparations issue. In diplomatic correspondence dated 15 July 1955 and addressed to the Soviet deputy foreign minister, Israel once again demanded

> that the German people, who were responsible for all this misery and who maintain possession of the economic assets taken from the Jews, dead and alive, should be required to pay reparations to the survivors. On 10 September 1952, the German Federal Republic agreed to pay to the Government of Israel two-thirds of the estimated financial cost for the rehabilitation of victims of the Nazi regime. One-third of the cost remains a debt owed by the German Democratic Republic.[35]

However, the East German government had paid the Soviet Union reparations amounting to about $14 billion, and was eager to gain a foothold in some Arab countries. Hence, a response dated 28 December 1955 indicated that the government of the German Democratic Republic has done everything in its power to root out German Fascism and create conditions that preclude the possibility of another threat to the security and existence of other peoples—including the Jewish people—in Germany. The victims of Fascism residing in the territory of the German Democratic Republic were given generous support and aid. The government of the German Democratic Republic has thus fulfilled all of the requirements of the four Allied powers for reparations to compensate for the destruction wrought by German fascism.[36]

This statement was continually reiterated by GDR diplomats and politicians in subsequent decades. It also became a catch phrase used by East German journalists and scholars.

In the three decades that followed, the GDR was primarily interested in improving its relations with the Arab world, and adopted a policy of confrontation vis-à-vis Israel. Thus, the Foreign Ministry advised its diplomats in January 1963 not to risk the relatively good relations with some Arab states "by striving to establish official relations with Israel in the present stage of struggle for international recognition of the GDR."[37]

There was no real breakthrough in the GDR's foreign policy towards the Arab world until Walter Ulbricht visited Egypt in February/March 1965. In the joint communiqué signed in Cairo by Ulbricht and Nasser on 2 March 1965, both sides condemned "the aggressive imperialist plans that promoted the establishment of Israel as a spearhead of imperialism directed against the rights of Arab nations and their struggle for liberation and progress."[38] At a time when the other East European countries maintained simultaneous diplomatic relations with most of the Arab states and with Israel, an official declaration of this nature was rather unusual. The GDR ignored international protests, including strong criticism by the Communist Party of Israel, and showed no interest in a balanced Middle East policy. In their effort to thwart the Hallstein doctrine, East German politicians took advantage of every opportunity to mention that their country was a firm ally of the Arab countries at a time when West Germany was strengthening its cooperation with Israel.

The development of relations with some Arab countries was accompanied by anti-Israel statements. The East German government condemned "the imperialist aggression of Israel" in 1967, and named "the United States and West Germany [as] accomplices to the aggressor."[39] However, always fearing that harsh attacks against Israel might be understood as anti-Semitic, the GDR leadership attempted to use Jews for political purposes. On 11 June 1967, the daily *Neues Deutschland* published the following declaration by prominent Jewish citizens regarding the Six Day War:

As citizens of the German Democratic Republic of Jewish origin, we raise our voice in order to solemnly condemn the aggression, of which the ruling circles of Israel have made themselves guilty vis-à-vis the neighboring Arab states. We consider ourselves justified and obliged to raise our voice, because as citizens of the GDR, in which anti-Semitism has been extirpated and in which there is no room for

anti-Semites, who ourselves have suffered severely from the persecution of Hitler-
fascism, we mourn the loss of numerous family members who were murdered by the
German imperialists, even as many citizens of Israel do.

The declaration included the following sentence: "The very birth of Israel was already
marked with a breach of promise and annexation."[40] This was the reason why public
Jewish figures—including President of the Association of Jewish Communities in the
GDR Helmut Aris and the famous writer Arnold Zweig—were not willing to sign
the declaration, which had been prepared by Albert Norden, a member of the
SED Politburo. The *Nachrichtenblatt*, the official quarterly of the Association of
Jewish communities in the GDR, did not publish the declaration and made no
reference to it.

In the years that followed, resolutions of SED party congresses or conferences and
official statements of political representatives of the East German state reiterated the
"GDR's firm solidarity with the Arab states in the anti-imperialist struggle, especially
in counteracting Israeli aggression and overcoming its consequences."[41] For instance,
the Eighth Party Congress of the SED in 1971 "strongly denounced Israel's aggression
against the Arab countries and demanded that Israel withdraw its troops from all areas
occupied in violation of international law."[42] While the legitimate interests and rights
of the Arab Palestinian people were supported as "crucial to a lasting and just
settlement of all problems in the Middle East," Israel's right to exist was rarely
mentioned.[43] Sometimes East Germany adopted, both publicly and behind the scenes,
an even more virulent line than that of the Soviets. For example, in 1969 and 1970,
Walter Ulbricht wrote two letters to CPSU Secretary General Leonid Brezhnev, which
went so far as to suggest that volunteers be sent from socialist countries to liberate the
occupied Arab territories.[44]

The anti-Israel positions were well known to the Israeli government. Therefore, it
came as no surprise when Israel's Ambassador to the United Nations, Yosef Tekoah,
voted against admitting the GDR to the United Nations in September 1973. He placed
Israel's opposition on the record, and emphasized that the East German state 'has
ignored and continues to ignore Germany's historical responsibility for the Holocaust
and the moral obligations arising from it. It has compounded the gravity of that
attitude by giving support and practical assistance to the campaign of violence and
murder waged against Israel and the Jewish people by Arab terror organizations.'[45]
A few months earlier, Israel had renewed its claim for reparations from the GDR as a
partial successor to the Third Reich.[46] The SED continued to reject all Israeli demands
for reparations, declaring that the Jewish state had not come into existence until 1948
and was thus not a legitimate actor empowered to forward its claims to Germany.
Furthermore, the GDR refrained from establishing relations with Israel because of
"Israel's aggressive imperialist policy."[47]

As in 1952, the GDR government tried to justify its refusal to accept Israel's material
claims by labeling the Jewish state as "imperialist" and "Zionist." This time, however, the
possible reaction of Arab states played a more important role than it had twenty years

earlier. To avoid harming relations with Egypt, Syria, Iraq and other countries, the GDR Ministry of Foreign Affairs informed all of its embassies abroad about its position regarding reparations and compensation. The official documents issued by the *Kollegium* (leading board) of the Ministry stressed the traditional friendship with the Arab world and condemned "the foreign policy of Israel and imperialist Zionist organizations." Furthermore, the paper reiterated that the GDR would never pay reparations to Israel because the Jewish state had not existed during the period referred to in the reparations claims.[48]

In the mid-1970s a virulent anti-Zionist campaign was waged throughout Eastern Europe. Notably, at that time domestic issues were given more priority than foreign affairs. The campaign was initiated by the Soviet Union in response to a deluge of Jewish applications for emigration to Israel. The CPSU had already advised its East German counterpart to wage an all-out struggle against Zionism in 1971. Following this advice, the State Secretariat for Religious Affairs in East Berlin prepared a paper dealing with Zionist ideology and policy, and discussed it with leaders of the East German Jewish community.

The fifteen-page document portrayed Zionism as "a reactionary nationalistic ideology of the Jewish haute bourgeoisie" and as "anti-Arab racism." Moreover, the authors invoked the myth of a worldwide Jewish conspiracy, and claimed that the Zionists sought to control Jewish communities and people of Jewish origin in almost one hundred countries. Furthermore, they described the activities of the World Zionist Organization as "part of the ideological imperialist infiltration of the socialist countries."[49] As early as 1968 the GDR had used classic anti-Semitic stereotypes after the armies of the Warsaw Pact invaded Czechoslovakia. At that time, the press had published articles about Zionist attempts to change the political order in Czechoslovakia. The SED daily *Neues Deutschland* charged that "Zionist forces had taken over the leadership of the Czechoslovak Communist Party."[50]

East German representatives strongly supported the UN resolution on the elimination of all forms of racial discrimination, approved on 10 November 1975—a resolution that implicitly identified Zionism with racism and racist persecution. Additionally, the GDR press published many articles on this issue condemning "aggressive and chauvinist Zionism" as "a racist doctrine."[51] The biweekly *Deutsche Lehrerzeitung*, a journal for teachers and educators in East Germany, published the following statement: "One has to declare openly that Zionism and fascism have the same ideological platform—racism."[52]

Although the media did not challenge these statements and more or less followed the official party line, critical voices were heard in the Jewish communities and among some members of the churches. After a major dispute with leaders of the Jewish community, officials of the State Secretariat for Religious Affairs reported the following to the SED Central Committee: "The Jewish communities are unable to give serious consideration to Zionist ideology. They try to evade a clear condemnation of Zionism and the aggressive Israeli policy. Zionist tendencies among them should be exposed and strictly eliminated."[53] In a resolution adopted on 27 November 1975, the Conference of Protestant Bishops underscored the German responsibility for the Holocaust and called upon the government of the GDR to retract its vote in favor of the UN resolution.[54] The bishops' resolution was announced in Protestant churches, but it was not published in the East German media.

Another anti-Israel propaganda campaign was launched in the early 1980s. During the Lebanon War of 1982, the GDR press not only attacked Israel as an aggressor but compared its military actions with the practices of the Nazi German army.[55] Reports on the massacres in the Palestinian camps of Sabra and Shatila aimed primarily to depict the brutality of the imperialist enemy. However, it cannot be denied that anti-Jewish sentiments also played a role. Those sentiments were encouraged when the press kept silent about the role of the Lebanese militia in the massacres while emphasizing "the systematic extermination of the Palestinians by the Israeli army."[56] Not for the first time, but louder than before, anti-Semitic voices were heard in East Germany, as reflected in an anonymous letter addressing the Jewish Community of Berlin in August 1982: "We never thought that Jews are so bad. You told us that all the Germans are guilty. Now we are saying that you all are guilty.... You are a thousand times worse than the Nazis."[57]

It was only during the last five years of the GDR that some changes in the approach to Israel became evident. The new line of Soviet President Mikhail Gorbachev gave more latitude to the Soviet allies and, at the same time, fostered clear recognition of facts. For the first time, GDR leaders attempted to modify their Middle East policy and began to think about normalizing relations with Israel. Notably, what seemed to carry even more weight than Soviet foreign policy was the hope that the World Jewish Congress (WJC) would be involved in arranging an invitation for SED Secretary General Erich Honecker to visit the United States and obtain trade benefits.

When WJC President Edgar M. Bronfman visited the GDR in October 1988, he openly advocated the building of "bridges... between the GDR and the people and government of the Israeli state." At a press conference in East Berlin, he said he "had been given the impression that a certain renewal in the relations between the two countries is seriously being considered."[58] The commemoration ceremonies marking the 50th anniversary of *Kristallnacht* in 1988 were undoubtedly a turning point in the official East German approach to Israel. For the first time, official representatives of Israel were invited, such as Dr. Yitzhak Arad, director of the Yad Vashem Holocaust Memorial Authority, Dr. Yosef Burg, former minister of the interior and minister of religious affairs, and others.

In late January 1989, the GDR's State Secretary for Religious Affairs, Kurt Löffler, came on an official visit to Israel, leading a delegation that included two diplomats from the East German Foreign Ministry. At that time, Löffler met with Israeli Minister of Religious Affairs Zevulun Hammer in Jerusalem.[59] This was the first contact between government officials from the two countries. However, there were no follow-up visits, and no more formal talks were held between officials from the GDR and Israel before the political uprising in autumn 1989 because both sides insisted on certain preconditions. Despite their keen interest in intensifying contact with Israel, GDR politicians linked such progress with Israel's position on resolving the Middle East conflict. For its part, Israel claimed that East Germany had not accepted enough responsibility for the Holocaust and had not provided sufficient moral and material compensation. By contrast, Hungary and Poland had gradually begun to normalize relations with Israel, and meetings with the Soviet Union were under way at a consular level.

Another reason for the failure to develop the contact with Israel was the GDR's attempt to sustain and even to improve its friendly relations with the PLO. Yasser Arafat visited the GDR three times in 1988. On 15 November 1988, the East German government gave formal recognition to the Palestinian state proclaimed by the PLO, and in January 1989, the embassy of the PLO was renamed "the embassy of the State of Palestine in the GDR." Thus, it was clear that the Middle East policy of the GDR had not changed despite contacts with the World Jewish Congress and initial meetings with Israeli politicians. Essentially, it seems that the GDR's attempts to improve relations with Israel in 1988 and 1989 aimed to open doors to the leading country of the Western world, the United States of America. The leaders of the GDR believed that a direct line of influence existed between the US government and leaders of American Jewish organizations, who had criticized the continuation of East German anti-Israel and anti-Zionist propaganda.

It was only in January 1990, after the dramatic political changes in the GDR and the fall of the Berlin Wall, that negotiations began towards the establishment of diplomatic relations between the GDR and Israel. Two months later, during the second round of negotiations in Copenhagen, the GDR declared that it was ready to modify its position on Zionism and formally revise its previous position towards Israel. On 9 March 1990, a letter from the GDR's new Prime Minister Hans Modrow was delivered to Israeli Prime Minister Yitzhak Shamir, saying that

> the GDR recognizes that all German people are responsible for what happened in the past. This responsibility results from deep guilt for the crimes which the fascist regime under Hitler committed against the Jewish people in the name of the German people.... The GDR recognizes its humanitarian duty towards all Jewish people who survived Nazi oppression and have gone through immense suffering.... [We emphasize our] readiness to show solidarity and give material support to all Jewish victims of Nazi persecution.[60]

Many observers believed that the GDR was eager at that time to prove its legitimacy as an independent state. Others felt that the SED sought Jewish support for political and economic reasons. Beyond those considerations, however, it cannot be denied that the East German revolution, which began in the fall of 1989, also meant the discontinuation of former SED policies. The anticipated establishment of diplomatic relations with Israel and the end of anti-Zionist propaganda were understood by the public as an important signal of political changes. On 12 April 1990, the GDR parliament, the Volkskammer, unanimously accepted German historic responsibility for the Holocaust in a statement that went further than the declaration of West German Chancellor Konrad Adenauer had done in September 1951. This document was unique in that it asked "all Jews around the world for forgiveness."[61] On 22 July 1990—less than three months before the unification of both German states—the East German Parliament decided to retract the GDR vote in favor of the 1975 UN resolution that equated Zionism with racism.[62]

Conclusions

Over several decades, the East German stance towards Israel was marked by condemnation of Zionism, a unilateral position on the Arab-Israel conflict, and denial of reparations and restitution claims. The media did not shy away from comparing the Israeli army with the Nazi occupation forces in Poland and the Soviet Union. Hence it seems justified to examine whether the GDR policy towards Israel could be characterized as anti-Semitic. However, it would be too simple to give a short affirmative answer to this question.

Anti-Semitism obviously survived the Third Reich in both German states. Although officially taboo, undercurrents of anti-Semitism persisted in both societies. A survey sponsored by the American Jewish Committee in the immediate aftermath of German unification compared, for the first time, West and East German attitudes to Jews, Israel and remembrance of the Holocaust. The results speak for themselves: in October 1990, 44 percent of the East Germans and 65 percent of the West Germans believed that the time had come to put the memory of the Holocaust behind them; 45 percent of the West Germans and 20 percent of the East Germans agreed that "Jews are exploiting the Holocaust for their own purposes." Considering that the East Germans received one-sided information on the Middle East conflict, Israel and Zionism, it is surprising that 33 percent of both East and West Germans agreed that "Zionism is racism," although 41 percent of the West Germans and 38 percent of the East Germans disagreed with that statement.[63] Even if we take into consideration that in 1990 West Germans were more likely than East Germans to openly express their opinions, the figures do not show that anti-Semitic sentiments were stronger in the East than in the West. On the contrary, later surveys confirmed the findings of 1990—although the evidence indicates that general xenophobic tendencies were more prevalent in the East.

In order to determine whether the GDR policy was anti-Semitic, several points need to be addressed:

First, the official policy towards Israel was not anti-Semitic from the outset, but evolved out of pragmatic interests. The Cold War between the two superpowers, and the GDR's membership in the Warsaw Pact, as well as Israel's affiliation with the Western world, influenced the relationship between Israel and East Germany. When the GDR leaders sided with the Arab states and the Palestinians in the Middle East conflict, they followed the Soviet Union and their own political interests in the region. Israel's right to exist was not denied, and many journalists and academics tried to differentiate between the Israeli government and the Israeli people. However, when the GDR media reported on the wars between Israel and the Arab states or on Israeli policy in the territories that were occupied in 1967, they drew a one-sided and undifferentiated picture of the events in the region. Attacks against Israel as an imperialist enemy, as well as the characterization of Zionism as racism and the comparison of the Israeli army with the Nazi Wehrmacht, promoted anti-Semitic stereotypes and kept them alive.

Second, the psychological and political impact of the Holocaust on Israel was ignored. The East German political elite denied Germany's direct responsibility to the Jewish state. Their approach to the issue of reparations and compensation was based on a general approach to world history and German history, which argued that German capitalists were responsible for the Nazi crimes. Accordingly, the lesson to be learned from the past was that since capitalism was the basis for fascism, racism and militarism, it should be eliminated. Public debate on the Third Reich focused on the persecution of political opponents and the war against the Soviet Union, while the Holocaust was marginalized. East Germany rejected the material claims of Jewish organizations and the State of Israel, on the grounds that such payments would strengthen imperialism. This approach prevented a critical debate on German responsibility for the Holocaust. The attempt to confront the Holocaust in 1987 and 1988, in preparation for the 50th anniversary of *Kristallnacht*, exposed philo-Semitic tendencies that ultimately strengthened anti-Semitic opinions.

Third, the observation that the domestic policy of the vanguard SED was not anti-Semitic excludes 1952 and 1953, when Jews were dismissed from political and academic positions, discriminated against, and sometimes even arrested. Ulbricht used Stalin's anti-Semitic policies for his own political purposes, and even maintained those policies for several months after Stalin's death. The political campaign against emigrants who had returned to the eastern part of Germany from Western Europe or America was directed largely against Jews. Focusing on Zionism and the "imperialist" State of Israel, it weakened and destroyed the anti-fascist sympathy that Germans had voiced during the early postwar years. The political leadership of the GDR did not shy away from using anti-Semitic stereotypes, which remained alive even after the end of the Third Reich.

Fourth, the declaration that fascism and anti-Semitism should be rooted out, and the continual reiteration of this declaration precluded a systematic discussion of anti-Semitism and xenophobia. It was naturally assumed that everyone had learned a lesson from the past, and that "the bad Nazis" remained on the other side of the Wall. Hence, there was no need to look for them or their followers inside East Germany. Anti-Semitic propaganda was banned, but efforts to eliminate it were insufficient. On the assumption that anti-Semitism would automatically disappear after the socialist revolution, anti-Semitic incidents were mostly ignored or denied. This approach prevented society from recognizing the dangers involved in the recurrence of such incidents.

Following German unification, a revival of anti-Semitism in East and West Germany became evident. For example, in 1992 a Holocaust memorial for Berlin Jews who had been deported to the death camps was bombed. In addition, the "Jewish barracks" in the former Sachsenhausen concentration camp near Berlin were burned down, and there was an increase in the number of anti-Semitic crimes registered in Germany in the mid-1990s. Especially since the outbreak of the second *Intifada* in 2000, criticism of Israel has often been based on anti-Semitic stereotypes. Notably, Germans have not hesitated to compare the actions of Israeli Prime Minister Ariel Sharon to those of the Nazis. Furthermore, some statements made by German Members of Parliament in 2002 and 2003 suggest that there may be increasing tolerance of public expressions of anti-Semitism.[64]

In recent years, anti-Israel sentiment has been heard in both parts of united Germany. This sentiment comes very close to anti-Semitism when it denies Israel's right to exist and holds Jews throughout the world accountable for Israeli policy in the Palestinian territories. In East Germany its roots can certainly be traced to what amounted to the demonization of Zionism and Israel during the GDR's existence. Nonetheless, an explanation that focuses exclusively on historical antecedents and on the failures of East Germany cannot fully reflect reality. It should also be sought in the political developments within united Germany.

Notes

[1] See Herf, *Divided Memory*; Illichmann, *Die DDR und die Juden*; Kessler, *Die SED und die Juden*; Mertens, *Davidstern unter Hammer und Zirkel*; Offenberg, "Seid vorsichtig gegen die Machthaber"; Wolffsohn, *Deutschland-Akte*.

[2] See also Timm, *Hammer, Zirkel, Davidstern*; *Jewish Claims against East Germany*; and "Views on Zionism and Israel in East Germany," 93–109.

[3] Badstübner, *Deutsche Geschichte*, 60.

[4] Rosenhaft, "The Uses of Remembrance," 371.

[5] Pieck, Dimitroff and Togliatti, *Die Offensive des Faschismus*, 87.

[6] *The GDR Fulfills the Legacy*, 9.

[7] Association of Jewish Communities in the GDR, ed., *Beware Lest the Nightmare Recur*, 12.

[8] For periodization see Kwiet, "Historians of the GDR on Anti-Semitism," 173–98; Gröhler, "Der Holocaust in der Geschichtsschreibung der DDR," 47–65.

[9] The Association of Victims of Nazi Persecution (VVN) existed until 1953, when it was replaced by the Committee of Antifascist Resistance Fighters.

[10] Zuckermann, "Restitution und Wiedergutmachung," 432.

[11] See *Neue Beweise* and *Eichmann. Henker. Handlanger, Hintermänner*.

[12] Heitzer, "Die Barbarei," 1632.

[13] Kahn, "Dokumente des Kampfes," 552–64.

[14] Eschwege, *Kennzeichen J*.

[15] Petzold, *Faschismus*, 35; see also Pätzold and Runge, *Pogromnacht, 1938*.

[16] *The Council of State and the People's Chamber of the GDR*, 20–21.

[17] Foundation for the Archives of GDR Parties and Mass Organizations within the Federal Archives, Berlin (hereafter SAPMO-BArch), DY 30/J IV 2/2/2300.

[18] *The Council of State and the People's Chamber of the GDR*, 4.

[19] See Nikitina, *The State of Israel*, 309; and Vatomina, "Izrail'," 94.

[20] Dadiani, "Zionism," 6.

[21] Herf, "The Holocaust and the Competition of Memories," 25.

[22] Cited in *Neues Deutschland*, 22 August 1965.

[23] See Gorodetsky, "The Soviet Union's Role", and Ro'i, "The Deterioration."

[24] "Vereinbarung zwischen der SED und der Palästinensischen Befreiungsorganisation (PLO) für die Jahre 1973/74 vom 2. August 1973," SAPMO-BArch, DY 30/IV B 2/20/309.

[25] Winter, "Bemerkungen zur DDR-Politik gegenüber Israel," 160.

[26] *Neues Deutschland*, 6 February 1965.

[27] Ibid., 24 February 1965.

[28] See Bator and Bator, eds, *Die DDR und die arabischen Staaten*, 142, 263, 290.

[29] Quoted in Eschwege, "Die jüdische Bevölkerung," 89.

[30] Merker, "Der neue Staat des jüdischen Volkes," *Neues Deutschland*, 24 February 1948.

[31] See Jelinek, *Zwischen Moral und Realpolitik*, 139–40.

[32] "Lehren aus dem Prozess gegen das Verschwörertum Slansky," 207

[33] *Neues Deutschland*, 25 November 1952.

[34] "Lehren aus dem Prozess gegen das Verschwörertum Slansky," 205.

[35] Israel State Archives/Foreign Ministry, Jerusalem (hereafter ISA/FM), 93.39/547/2.

[36] ISA/FM, 93.39/547/2. See also Archives of the former GDR Ministry of Foreign Affairs, Berlin (hereafter GDR/FM), A 13364.

[37] GDR/FM, A 12608, 22 January 1963.

[38] "Aus der Gemeinsamen Erklärung über den Freundschaftsbesuch des Vorsitzenden des Staatsrates der DDR, Walter Ulbricht, in der Vereinigten Arabischen Republik vom 24. Februar bis 2. Maerz 1965," in Bator and Bator, eds, *Die DDR und die arabischen Staaten*, 98.

[39] "Erklärung des Ministerrats der Deutschen Demokratischen Republik zur israelischen Aggression gegen die arabischen Staaten," in Ibid., 111.

[40] *Neues Deutschland*, 11 June 1967.

[41] *The GDR Fulfills the Legacy of the Antifascist Fighters*, 19.

[42] *Protokoll des achten Parteitages*, 2:524.

[43] *The GDR Fulfills the Legacy of the Antifascist Fighters*, 19.

[44] SAPMO-BArch, DY 30/J IV 2/202/387. The documents are published in Timm, *Hammer, Zirkel, Davidstern*, 535–56.

[45] *Official Records of the General Assembly Twenty-Eighth Session, Plenary Meetings*, vol. 1, *Verbatim Records of Meetings*, 2117th Plenary Meeting, 18 September 1973, A/PV 2117, 10.

[46] United States Holocaust Research Institute Archives, Washington, DC, DrW 7, Box 3 [BBF Reports to Claims Conference in GDR, 1973–82].

[47] *Junge Welt*, 7 March 1973.

[48] GDR/FM, C 6491.

[49] "Information zu Problemen der Einbeziehung des Zionismus und jüdischer Bewegungen in die imperialistische Politik," Federal Archives, Potsdam Branch (hereafter BArchP), DO 4, 460.

[50] *Neues Deutschland*, 25 August 1968. See also *The Use of Antisemitism*, 11.

[51] See Babing, *Gegen Rassismus, Apartheid und Kolonialismus*, 351; *Berliner Zeitung*, 20 November 1975; *Neues Deutschland*, 14 November 1975.

[52] *Deutsche Lehrerzeitung*, no. 49 (1975): 4.

[53] SAPMO-BArch, DY 30/IV B 2/14/174.

[54] Erklärung der Leitenden Geistlichen der Gliedkirchen des Bundes der Evangelischen Kirchen in der DDR vom 27 November 1975, BArchP, DO 4, 1371; see Timm, *Hammer, Zirkel, Davidstern*, 546–57.

[55] *Neues Deutschland*, 16 August and 20 September 1982; *horizont*, 15, no. 34 (1982): 5; *Volksarmee*, 16 August 1982, 6; "Erklärung des Solidaritätskomitees der DDR, 24. September 1982," In Bator and Bator, eds, *Die DDR und die arabischen Staaten*, 414.

[56] *Neues Deutschland*, 20 September 1982.

[57] BArchP, DO 4, 1548.

[58] *Neues Deutschland*, 9 October 1988.

[59] "Bericht über den Aufenthalt von Staatssekretär Kurt Löffler in Israel vom 4. Februar 1989," BArchP, DO 4, 998.

[60] BArchP, DC 20, 5046 and 4998.

[61] *Neues Deutschland*, Berlin, 14–15 April 1990.
[62] *Protocol of the People's Chamber Session on 22 July 1990*, 27/601.
[63] Jodice, *United Germany and Jewish Concerns*, 12, 18–19, 23.
[64] For the Möllemann affair and the Hohmann affair, see Wistrich, *The Politics of Ressentiment*, 11–15, 20–23.

References

Association of Jewish Communities in the GDR, ed. *Beware Lest the Nightmare Recur: Remembrance of the Nazi Pogrom in the night of 9 November 1938*. Berlin (GDR): Verlag Zeit im Bild, 1988.

Babing, Alfred, ed. *Gegen Rassismus, Apartheid und Kolonialismus: Dokumente der DDR 1949–1977*. Berlin (GDR): Staatsverlag der DDR, 1978.

Badstübner, Rolf, ed. *Deutsche Geschichte*. Vol. 9 (*Die antifaschistische Umwälzung, der Kampf gegen die Teilung Deutschlands und die Entwicklung der DDR von 1945 bis 1949*). Berlin (GDR): Deutscher Verlag der Wissenschaften, 1989.

Bator, Angelika, and Bator, Wolfgang, eds. *Die DDR und die arabischen Staaten*. Berlin (GDR): Staatsverlag der DDR, 1984.

The Council of State and the People's Chamber of the GDR Remember the Victims of the Nazi Pogrom of 9 November 1938. Berlin (GDR): Panorama, 1988.

Dadiani, Lionel. "Zionism: Ideology and Practice of Racial Discrimination." In *Zionism: Past and Present*, edited by A. Kochin. Moscow: USSR Academy of Sciences, 1976.

Eichmann, Henker. *Handlanger, Hintermänner*. Berlin (GDR): Ausschuss für Deutsche Einheit, 1961.

Eschwege, Helmut. *Kennzeichen J.: Bilder, Dokumente, Berichte zur Geschichte der Verbrechen des Hitlerfaschismus an den deutschen Juden*. Berlin (GDR): Dietz, 1966.

———."Die jüdische Bevölkerung der Jahre nach der Kapitulation Hitlerdeutschlands auf dem Gebiet der DDR bis zum Jahre 1953." In *Juden in der DDR: Geschichte. Probleme. Perspektive*, edited by Siegfried Theodor Arndt et al. Cologne: Brill, 1988.

The GDR Fulfills the Legacy of the Antifascist Fighters. Berlin (GDR): Panorama, 1974.

Gorodetsky, Gabriel. "The Soviet Union's Role in the Creation of the State of Israel." *Journal of Israeli History* 22, no. 1 (2003): 4–20.

Groehler, Olaf. "Der Holocaust in der Geschichtsschreibung der DDR." In *Erinnerung: Zur Gegenwart des Holocaust in Deutschland-West und Deutschland-Ost*, edited by Bernhard Moltman, Doron Kiesel, and Cilly Kugelmann. Frankfurt a. M.: Haag und Herchen, 1993.

Heitzer, Heinz. "Die Barbarei—extremster Ausdruck der Monopolherrschaft in Deutschland." *Zeitschrift für Geschichtswissenschaft* 9, no. 7 (1961): 1632–38.

Herf, Jeffrey. *Divided Memory: The Nazi Past in the Two Germanys*. Cambridge, MA: Harvard University Press, 1997.

———. "The Holocaust and the Competition of Memories in Germany, 1945–1999." In *Remembering the Holocaust in Germany, 1945–2000*, edited by Dan Michman. New York: Peter Lang, 2002.

Illichmann, Jutta. *Die DDR und die Juden: Die deutschlandpolitische Instrumentalisierung von Juden und Judentum durch die Partei- und Staatsführung der SBZ/DDR von 1945 bis 1990*. Frankfurt: Peter Lang, 1997.

Jelinek, Yeshayahu A. *Zwischen Moral und Realpolitik: Eine Dokumentensammlung*. Gerlingen: Bleicher, 1997.

Jodice, David A. *United Germany and Jewish Concerns. Attitudes towards Jews, Israel, and the Holocaust*. New York: American Jewish Committee, 1991.

Kahn, Siegbert. "Dokumente des Kampfes der revolutionären deutschen Arbeiterbewegung gegen Antisemitismus und Judenverfolgung." *Beiträge zur Geschichte der deutschen Arbeiterbewegung* 2, no. 3 (1960): 552–64.

Kessler, Mario. *Die SED und die Juden—zwischen Repression und Toleranz: Politische Entwicklungen bis 1967*. Berlin: Akademie Verlag, 1995.

Kwiet, Konrad. "Historians of the GDR on anti-Semitism." *Yearbook of the Leo Baeck Institute* 21 (1976): 173–98.

"Lehren aus dem Prozess gegen das Verschwörertum Slansky." *Einheit* 8, no. 2 (1953): 203–16.

Mertens, Lothar. *Davidstern unter Hammer und Zirkel: Die jüdischen Gemeinden in der SBZ/DDR und ihre Behandlung durch Partei und Staat 1945–1990*. Hildesheim: Georg Olms Verlag, 1997.

Neue Beweise für Globkes Verbrechen gegen die Juden. Berlin (GDR): Ausschuss für Deutsche Einheit, 1960.

Nikitina, Galina. *The State of Israel: A Historical, Economic and Political Study*. Moscow: Progress Publishers, 1973.

Offenberg, Ulrike. *"Seid vorsichtig gegen die Machthaber": Die jüdischen Gemeinden in der SBZ und der DDR 1945 bis 1990*. Berlin: Aufbau Verlag, 1998.

Pätzold Kurt, and Irene Runge. *Pogromnacht 1938*. Berlin (GDR): Dietz, 1988.

Petzold, Joachim. *Faschismus, Regime des Verbrechens*. Berlin (GDR): Staatsverlag der DDR, 1984.

Pieck, Wilhelm, Georgi Dimitroff, and Palmiro Togliatti. *Die Offensive des Faschismus und die Aufgaben der Kommunisten für die Volksfront gegen Faschismus und Krieg: Referate auf dem VII. Kongress der Kommunistischen Internationale 1935*. Berlin (GDR): Dietz, 1957.

Protokoll des achten Parteitages der Sozialistischen Einheitspartei Deutschlands vom 15. bis 19. Juni 1971 in Berlin. Vol. 2. Berlin (GDR): Dietz, 1971.

Ro'i, Yaacov. "The Deterioration of Relations: From Support to Severance." *Journal of Israeli History* 22, no. 1 (2003): 21–36.

Rosenhaft, Eve. "The Uses of Remembrance: The Legacy of the Communist Resistance in the German Democratic Republic." In *Germans Against Nazism: Nonconformity, Opposition and Resistance in the Third Reich*, edited by Francis R. Nicosia and Lawrence D. Stokes. New York: Berg Publishers, 1990.

Timm, Angelika. *Hammer, Zirkel, Davidstern: Das gestörte Verhältnis der DDR zu Zionismus und Staat Israel*. Bonn: Bouvier, 1997.

———. *Jewish Claims Against East Germany: Moral Obligations and Pragmatic Policy*. Budapest: CEU Press, 1997.

———. "Views on Zionism and Israel in East Germany." *Shofar* 18, no. 3 (2000): 93–109.

The Use of Antisemitism against Czechoslovakia. London: Institute of Jewish Affairs, 1968.

Vatomina, L. "Izrail' – baza amerikanskogo imperializma na Blizhnem vostoke" (Israel: A base of American imperialism in the Middle East). *Voprosy ekonomiki*, no. 4 (1951): 94–105.

Winter, Heinz-Dieter. "Bemerkungen zur DDR-Politik gegenüber Israel." *asien. afrika. lateinamerika* 21, nos. 1–2 (1993): 153–63.

Wistrich, Robert S. *The Politics of Ressentiment: Israel, Jews, and the German Media*. Jerusalem: Hebrew University of Jerusalem, Vidal Sassoon International Center for the Study of Antisemitism, 2004.

Wolffsohn, Michael. *Die Deutschland-Akte: Juden und Deutsche in Ost und West. Tatsachen und Legenden*. Munich: edition ferenczy, 1995.

Zuckermann, Leon. "Restitution und Wiedergutmachung." *Die Weltbühne* 3, no. 17 (1948): 430–32.

Israel and the International Legal Arena

Arieh J. Kochavi

For years, Israel has had to contend with a plethora of anti-Israel resolutions passed in the United Nations General Assembly and its constituent organizations. The best known was Resolution 3379 of 10 November 1975, which concluded with the phrase: "Zionism is a form of racism and racial discrimination." The resolution also condemned Zionism "as a threat to world peace and security" and called "upon all countries to oppose this racist and imperialist ideology."[1] The automatic majority in favor of the Arabs in the United Nations (UN) has left Israel with little or no maneuvering space and dependent on an American veto in the UN Security Council. In 2002, Israel's apprehension in regard to its international standing further increased following the establishment of the International Criminal Court (ICC) at The Hague. Israel regarded the international legal arena as a means of threatening the country's legitimacy. This article follows the anti-Israel offensive in the international legal arena and analyzes Israel's counter actions.

World War II demonstrated the urgent need for an effective body of international law as well as a permanent International Criminal Court. In 1948, the UN approved the Convention on the Prevention and Punishment of the Crime of Genocide and, in 1950, the Convention for the Protection of Human Rights and Fundamental Freedoms. Efforts to set up a permanent International Criminal Court had begun in the early 1950s, but the escalation of the Cold War prevented any progress for almost forty years. In June 1998 a diplomatic conference was at last convened in Rome in order to finalize a statute for such a court.[2] In many respects, this conference turned out to be a milestone in the international legal arena; it also had a great impact on diplomatic relations. For the first time in history, the countries of the world decided to establish a permanent institution that "shall have the power to exercise its jurisdiction over persons for the most serious crimes of international concern... and shall be complementary to national criminal jurisdiction."[3] This Court, moreover, would be able to exercise its functions and powers not only on the territory of any party state, but also "on the territory of any other State."[4] The Rome Statute, as it became known, aimed "to entrench an effectively enforced international criminal law as an integral part of both national and international life."[5] The participation of so many NGOs as conference observers, furthermore, marked a new stage in international relations; several of these organizations had played a major role either directly or behind the scenes during the whole process of drafting and ratifying the statute.[6]

Israel and the ICC

Israel's then Attorney-General Elyakim Rubinstein (now a Supreme Court Justice) headed the country's delegation to the Rome Conference. In his speech on 17 June 1998, Rubinstein stated that although Israel "wholeheartedly supports the sacred mission of prosecuting war criminals," the involvement of political bodies in the decision-making process "presents built-in problematics." Rubinstein sought to frustrate the Arabs' intention to define Israel's settlements in the West Bank, Gaza Strip and Golan Heights as war crimes and to leave it to Israeli courts to deal with infringements of International Law. He did not conceal his fears that "the investigative procedure may be abused for political ends" and was wary of the "strong standing and independent position of the prosecutor," who would have the power to initiate *ex officio* investigations. Rubinstein also had reservations about including "crimes of aggression" within the statute of the Court. The clear lack of consensus with regard to an acceptable definition of this crime, together with the political sensitivity inherent in any attempt to reach such a definition, he argued, "gives us cause to fear that it [this item] would be too easily manipulated for political ends."[7]

The worry that the ICC would turn into another means of injuring Israel in the international arena continued to guide the Israeli delegation throughout the five weeks of the conference. Judge Eli Nathan, who replaced Rubinstein as delegation head, explained in his speech on the last day of the conference the reasons for Israel's negative vote on the Rome Statute. He stressed the paradox into which Israel had been placed as heir of the Jewish people, one third of whom had been exterminated during World War II, and as a country that fifty years ago had urged the UN to establish a permanent criminal court but now could not sign the Rome Statute. Israel, Nathan stated, had actively participated in all stages of the preparation of the Statute but never considered that it "would ultimately be blemished and abused as a potential tool in the political war against Israel." He referred to Article 8, Paragraph 2 (b), sub-paragraph viii, which the Egyptian delegation had introduced and which read as follows: "The transfer, directly or indirectly, by the Occupying Power of parts of its own civilian population into the territory it occupies, or the deportation or transfer of all or parts of the population of the occupied territory within or outside this territory."[8] Does such an action, the Israeli judge rhetorically asked, "really rank among the most heinous and serious war crimes, especially as compared to the other, genuinely heinous ones listed in Article 8 [War Crimes]? Or is it not clear that this has been inserted as a means of utilising and abusing the Statute of the International Criminal Court and the International Court itself as one more political tool in the Middle East conflict?" Nathan made it clear that had this sub-paragraph not been included, Israel would have voted for the Statute. He expressed regret at "being obliged here today to vote in a way that prevents us, as victims of genocide, founding fathers of the concept and idea of the International Court, to vote in favour of its Statute." Nathan concluded by expressing his hope that the ICC would "not become just one more political forum to be abused for political ends."[9]

Israel was emboldened to vote against the Rome Statute only after the United States had also voted negatively.[10] The United States and Israel were, in fact, the only democratic countries to refuse to sign the Statute. Article 125 of the statute, however, gave all states until 31 December 2000 to affix their signatures. The Israeli government now had time to reconsider its position.[11] Rubinstein continued to hold to his opposition to ratifying the Rome Statute because of its implication for Israeli settlement activity in the West Bank, Gaza and Golan Heights. The Americans, he explained in an article published in an Israeli newspaper, had for a time spoken of the Jewish settlements as illegal enterprises; however, since President Ronald Reagan's administration, "the formula that the settlements are not illegal but constitute an obstacle for peace, or are likely to constitute such an obstacle, has been adopted." According to the attorney-general, the settlements issue was part of the Israeli-Palestinian conflict and, as such, constituted a political question that should be resolved in the peace talks.[12]

A majority of Prime Minister Ehud Barak's government shared Rubinstein's principled stand: seven ministers voted against signing the treaty and four were in favor. The government, however, was to reverse its decision after learning that President Bill Clinton had decided, in spite of American reservations, to sign the treaty.[13] The Israeli Cabinet did not even try to conceal the fact that the reversal of its decision had been taken after consultation with the Americans.[14] On 31 December 2000, forty-five minutes after the United States had signed the Statute, Israel did so, too.[15]

The signing of the Rome Statute had mainly declarative significance. In order for the ICC to actually come into being, at least sixty countries had to ratify the convention. Very few in Israeli political and legal circles really believed that the proposed ICC would be guided by judicial principles and not influenced by political considerations. Yet, it was recognized that without the backing of the United States, the consequences of not ratifying the Statute could be detrimental to Israel's standing in the international arena, especially as the European Union (EU) was the driving force behind establishing the court. On 6 May 2002 the United States notified the UN of its refusal to ratify the Statute. Israel, now under the leadership of Prime Minister Ariel Sharon, followed suit and in June 2002 announced its own decision not to ratify. As it happened, Israel at this time found itself in the midst of two heated battles in the international legal and diplomatic arenas that only strengthened distrust of international forums.[16]

Obviously the United States and Israel had different motives for rejecting the Rome Statute; nevertheless, the two countries shared a fundamental common denominator: concern at politicization. Washington feared that different countries, motivated by political considerations, would take advantage of the ICC to harass US citizens and curtail freedom of action by Americans throughout the world. In particular, there was concern that American soldiers participating in UN missions, including those in Afghanistan and in Iraq, could be charged with committing war crimes.[17] Moreover, there was apprehension that top civilian and military leaders would be "the ones potentially at risk at the hands of the ICC's politically unaccountable Prosecutor, as part of an agenda to restrain American discretion, even when our actions are legitimated by the operation of our own constitutional system." American officials further stressed the marginalization of the UN Security Council's role in the ICC, warning that this "will have a tangible and highly detrimental impact on the conduct of US foreign policy." The Americans also questioned the contention that the ICC would have a substantial deterrent effect on the perpetration of crimes against humanity. Washington preferred national judicial systems and, if necessary, ad hoc tribunals, such as those that were constituted for Yugoslavia and Rwanda. "Unlike the ICC," it was argued, "these are created and overseen by the UN Security Council, under a UN Charter to which virtually all nations have agreed."[18]

The United States was not satisfied just with refusing to ratify the Rome Statute; it also took preventive counter-measures, including legislation. "The American Service Members' Protection Act" (known as The Hague Invasion Act) was signed by President George W. Bush on 2 August 2002. The act includes provisions prohibiting American cooperation with the ICC; restricting American participation in UN peacekeeping missions; forbidding the sharing of American intelligence with the ICC; and halting military assistance to most countries that ratified the ICC Statute. The act also authorizes the president to take "all means necessary and appropriate" to free from captivity any American or allied personnel held by or on behalf of the ICC.[19] On the basis of Article 98 of the Rome Statue ("Cooperation with respect to waiver of immunity and consent to surrender"), the United States began to sign bilateral agreements with individual states that required them to agree, either reciprocally or non-reciprocally, not to surrender American citizens to the ICC, not to transfer persons extradited to a country of persecution, and not to assist other parties in their efforts to send American citizens to stand trial before the ICC.[20]

The American decision not to ratify the Rome Statute disturbed the European Union, an ardent supporter of the ICC. In a forceful announcement published on 14 May 2002, the EU criticized the unilateral action taken by the United States, since it "may have undesirable consequences on multilateral treaty-making and generally on the rule of law in international relations." The EU dismissed Washington's anxieties with regard to the future activities of the ICC as unfounded, maintaining that "the Rome Statute provides all necessary safeguards against the misuse of the Court for politically motivated purposes."[21] Fighting back, the EU pressured countries seeking to join the EU to apply restrictive conditions on bilateral agreements with the United States.[22] The EU's strong reaction provided a hint of the risks that Israel had taken by refusing to ratify the Rome Statute.

Jerusalem had made its decision in full knowledge that the consequences could be detrimental to the country's already difficult position in the international arena. At the same time, however, the government expected that, with American backing, it could withstand international criticism and the pressure of standing aloof from the rest of the democratic world. Knowing of Washington's profound distrust of the ICC, Israel expected that the Americans would defend Israel's decision not to become a party to the ICC or to be bound by the Statute's obligations; and further, that the United States would protect Israel's interests in this context as it had often done in the UN and other international forums. And indeed, in his remarks on the ICC in November 2002, John R. Bolton, Under-Secretary for Arms Control and International Security, cited the example of the crime of "aggression," which was included in the Statute but not defined, as he described how "Israel justifiably feared in Rome that certain actions, such as its initial use of force in the Six Day War, would be perceived as illegitimate preemptive strikes that almost certainly would have provoked proceedings against top Israeli officials." He went on to predict that "there seems little doubt that Israel will be the target of a complaint in the ICC concerning conditions and practices by the Israeli military in the West Bank and Gaza."[23]

When explaining the government's decision not to ratify the treaty to members of the Knesset's Constitution, Law, and Justice Committee (CLJC), Attorney-General Rubinstein laid great stress on the clause in the Statute implying that Jewish settlement activity, including in Jerusalem, was a "war crime." However, he also called attention to the Statute's complementarity regime, which gave the ICC authority to intervene when a national court was unwilling or unable to genuinely carry out an investigation or a prosecution.[24] Rubinstein foresaw the possibility that the ICC would decide that Israel was unwilling to undertake an investigation and subsequent prosecution of an act that it considered defense and that others regarded as aggression—a war crime. He pointed to the battle in Jenin (3–11 April 2002), surmising that had it taken place after the ICC had started to function (1 July 2002), Israel could have been charged with perpetrating a massacre and brought to court, despite the fact that its government was convinced that it had acted upon its responsibility to defend the country's citizens and had been guided by humanitarian considerations.[25] Rubinstein further saw a circumstance in which Israel would have to defend its activities before the ICC without having the shield of an American veto. The danger, in his opinion, was not only the particular legal process with which the ICC was empowered, it was also the headlines that could be expected to follow in the world media accusing Israel of perpetrating a massacre. Rubinstein admitted that by not ratifying the Statute, Israel had eliminated only some of the risks, but certainly not all of them. He did not rule out the possibility that IDF officers could be arrested while abroad.[26] The attorney-general also attributed much importance to the question of who would be the prosecutor and the judges.[27]

Like Rubinstein, Rachel Sucar, the deputy state attorney who headed the Ministry of Justice team that dealt with the ICC, also feared politicization. Her past experience in the international legal arena had taught her to be suspicious. At the CLJC meeting, she recommended following the ICC's conduct, in particular the interpretations that the court would give to many of the legal terms, before Israel took a final decision on whether to ratify the Statute. While recognizing the drawbacks of not ratifying, she also saw several advantages to not being a party to the Rome Statute, among them the exemption from the obligation to surrender "wanted" persons to the ICC or to hand over all documents, even those that could prejudice national security interests.[28]

Alan Baker, the legal adviser to the Ministry of Foreign Affairs, called attention to the fact that the concept of the ICC was regarded throughout the world as the most important development since the United Nations Charter. The ICC, according to Baker, was part of an international desire to bring to trial the worst war criminals. When asked by MK Ofir Paz-Pines, chair of the CLJC, how it happened that Israel had failed to prevent the inclusion of Paragraph 2 (b, viii) in Article 8 of the Statute, Baker referred to the difficult international circumstances in which Israel had to operate. An illustration was the Durban Conference (31 August–9 September 2001), which had been supposed to denounce racism. Instead, it had transmogrified into a "festival" of anti-Semitism and racism against the State of Israel.[29] Durban "had lit a red light for us," Baker stated succinctly. Within the international community, he argued, there was a tendency to carefully follow every act that Israel committed and to present it as a war crime or a serious breach of humanitarian law.[30]

On 1 July 2002 the Rome Statute establishing the ICC came into effect after sixty-nine countries had ratified it. The ICC, which sits in The Hague, was the first permanent international judicial body capable of trying individuals for genocide, crimes against humanity and war crimes. The setting up of the court not only affected the international legal arena but also introduced a new factor into the sphere of international relations.[31] In the discussion at the CLJC, government jurists had pointed to the episodes of Durban, Jenin and the "Sharon case" in Belgium as clear manifestations of the dangers Israel faced on the international scene. In fact, when the government made its decision in June 2002 not to ratify the Rome Statute, Israel had been in the midst of a legal and political struggle with Belgium over efforts to put Prime Minister Ariel Sharon on trial.

The Sharon Case

On 18 June 2001, 15 Palestinians resident in Lebanon and 8 Lebanese of Palestinian origin filed a complaint alleging that Ariel Sharon, who had been Minister of Defense during Israel's Lebanon war in 1982, and Brigadier General Amos Yaron, then commander of Israeli forces in Lebanon, had been responsible for perpetrating war crimes, crimes against humanity, and genocide in two Palestinian refugee camps, Sabra and Shatilla, in the course of the Lebanon war.[32] The timing of the complaint was not accidental. Three months earlier, in March 2001, Sharon had been elected prime minister. One of the Palestinian plaintiffs admitted that besides the desire to call world attention once again to the infamous event, the timing of the complaint was related to the *Intifada.*[33] Coincidentally, one day before the filing of the complaint against Sharon, the BBC had broadcast a program charging the Israeli prime minister with war crimes in Sabra and Shatilla.[34]

The complaint against Sharon was based on the Belgian Law of 16 June 1993—Act Concerning the Punishment of Grave Breaches of International Law, as amended on 10 February 1999 to the Act Concerning the Punishment of Grave Breaches of International Humanitarian Law.[35] The timing of the amendment had to do with the success of the Rome Conference, as well as with growing interest in Belgium over the massacres in Rwanda and criticism in that African country that Belgium had become a safe haven for perpetrators of genocide. As it happened, Belgium was the first country to adjust its domestic law to the Rome Statute.[36]

Although believing that the Belgians were motivated mainly by political, not legal or moral, considerations, let alone justice, Israel decided to fight back in the legal arena. Belgium's political considerations probably had been influenced by the fact that it's Prime Minister had begun to serve, for a term of six months, as president of the EU in July 2001. The complaint against Sharon, which intermingled with strong anti-Israel sentiment in Europe in general and in Belgium in particular, enjoyed overriding support on the part of the local press and Belgian NGOs. Israel's defense team was led by Irit Kohn, director of the Ministry of Justice's International Department, and Michèle Hirsch, a Belgian attorney. On 7 September 2001 the Investigating Magistrate (*juge d'instruction*) Patrick Collignon accepted the main arguments of Sharon's defense team and refused to order the start of an investigation. The defense team had contended that Sharon was immune from prosecution in Belgium for several reasons: a prosecution would be contrary to the principle of *ne bis in idem*—prohibiting a second prosecution for the same conduct;[37] the Belgian legislation violated the principle in criminal law of non-retroactivity; and there were no links between the suspect and Belgium.[38]

Belgium's acting attorney-general, Pierre Morlet, however, refused to accept the magistrate's decision and took advantage of a provision in Belgian criminal procedure permitting pre-trial discussions of issues that may have a bearing on the admissibility of a case. He referred the complaint against Sharon to the Prosecution Chamber of the Court of Appeal of Brussels.[39] This was a novel move and, according to Attorney Hirsch, the first time in the history of the law of "universal jurisdiction" that such an action had been taken. A series of pre-trial hearings took place; nonetheless, the Court of Appeal on 26 June 2002 decided to accept the magistrate's ruling and held that the complaint against Sharon was inadmissible because he was not resident in Belgium on the filing date of the complaints. The Court of Appeal announced similar decisions at the time with regard to complaints against the leaders of the Democratic Republic of Congo and against the president of the Ivory Coast.[40]

Nonetheless, strong political motivation led a few Belgian politicians, with the support of several NGOs, not to concede and to try to bypass the Court of Appeal's decision by introducing laws that would strengthen the supremacy of Belgian courts in the world. The day after the Court of Appeal handed down its decision, four senators filed two draft bills for urgent adoption. The first, an interpretive bill, stated that the concept of universal jurisdiction established by the 1993 law was applicable even if the offender was not present on Belgian soil. The second, an amendment bill, aimed at harmonizing the 1993 law with the Rome Statute, since the ICC could try international crimes committed only on or after 1 July 2002. The new law stipulated, according to Hirsch, "that Belgium would remain the judge of all crimes of the world, of the past and of the future, even in the absence of a link to Belgium." The drafters of the bill, she continued, "wished to secure the jurisdiction of Belgian courts over acts which did not come under the jurisdiction of the International Court of Justice (ICJ), as well as over offences committed by citizens of a state which was not party to the Statute of Rome, in a state which was not a party to the [Rome] Statute, or offences committed before the Statute came into force."[41]

According to Israeli officials, the timing and the scope of the two bills left little doubt as to their aims: to influence the decision of the Court of Cassation (Belgium's Supreme Court) in the appeal filed by the 23 Lebanese plaintiffs to continue with the proceedings against Sharon. The two bills enjoyed wide support among the public, the media and a majority of government ministers in Belgium. Prime Minister Guy Verhofstadt even went public with his support, hoping to win political dividends in the forthcoming elections (May 2003). Not surprisingly, the Belgian Senate on 31 January 2003 approved the interpretive law, by a vote of 34 to 6, with 6 abstentions.[42]

Less than two weeks later, on 12 February 2003, the Court of Cassation heard the appeal by the Lebanese plaintiffs. The Public Prosecutor (*Procureur général*) Jean du Jardin argued that the case should not be heard because the defendants were not on Belgian soil, the court would have no means of truly investigating and determining the facts, and it would be virtually impossible to collect verifiable, admissible evidence. In contrast to the overwhelming majority of cases in which the Court of Cassation tended to adopt the position of the Public Prosecutor, the court decided in this case to accept the Lebanese plaintiffs' appeal. Rejecting du Jardin's premise that a *sine qua non* condition for a case must be the presence of the subject of investigation on Belgian soil, it reversed the Court of Appeal's decision of 26 June 2002, thus sending the case back to an Appeal Court. This meant that the whole process would have to start anew, with one exception: the Court of Cassation dismissed the charges against Sharon on the basis of customary international law regarding immunity for incumbent heads of government. The investigation against Yaron, though, could proceed.[43]

Israel denounced the Court of Cassation decision as having been influenced by political considerations and went as far as recalling its ambassador, Yehudi Kenar, "for consultations." Foreign Minister Benjamin Netanyahu attacked the decision of the Belgian court as scandalous and as legitimating terror. He also summoned Belgium's ambassador to Israel, lecturing him that Belgium was hurting not only Israel but the entire free world. Israel's response, Netanyahu threatened, would be stern.[44] This forceful reaction demonstrated the government's decision not to confine its campaign to the legal arena but to conduct a diplomatic and political offensive as well.

Israel's firm diplomatic stance seemed to have concerned Belgium's government. Foreign Minister Louis Michel denied publicly the allegations of politicization. In an open letter in the Belgian press addressed to "my Israeli friends," he expressed regret that Israel refused to accept the ethics of the law of 1993 and reiterated the claim that the law was not aimed specifically against Jerusalem. "At this stage," he wrote, "the complaint [against Sharon] has not been judged on its merits, nor even on the issue of its eventual validity, but only on the technical issue of its admissibility.... It is clearly wrong to portray the complaint as a politically inspired act by the Belgian government aimed at the state of Israel and its Prime Minister."[45]

In an effort to convince the Israelis that Belgium was not motivated by anti-Israel or anti-Semitic sentiments, Michel pointed to his efforts at the Conference against Racism at Durban, where he had served as chairperson of the EU delegation, to expunge any anti-Semitic remark from the final declaration; he had even succeeded in inserting an explicit reference to the Holocaust. Anxious to persuade the Israelis that Belgium had nothing against the Jewish state and was certainly not motivated by anti-Semitism, Michel introduced a theme that in actuality was out of context: he praised the important role that the Jewish community played in Belgium and assured his "Israeli friends" that "anti-Semitism is not tolerated" in Belgium; furthermore should any sign of it occur, he would "fight it with all the means at my disposal."[46] Michel's decision to bind the Jewish community in Belgium and anti-Semitism together with the dispute over the Sharon case reflected a growing tendency in Europe not to differentiate between Israel and the continent's Jewish communities. This approach was effectively a setback for these communities, which were being automatically associated with Israel's actions. The assaults that some communities suffered in due course may be tied to this linkage.[47]

Sharon's attorneys also criticized the Court of Cassation. According to Kohn, "the content of the decision, the alacrity with which it was reached, and the extraordinary appearance of the President of the Court to read it out rather than to deposit the text in the Court Secretariat—all these elements gave the occasion a strange, unusual character."[48] Hirsch, the Belgian attorney, held a low opinion of the way in which the Belgian legal system had handled the matter; she warned that the Sharon case "showed the extent to which a complaint could be used by the media, with the support of non-governmental organizations; how victims could be manipulated and exhibited for political aims, and how the law could be exploited and diverted from its true objectives."[49] Adrien Masset, a professor of criminal and procedural law at the University of Liège who had represented Sharon and Yaron in the Court of Appeal, concluded, after analyzing the judgment, that the Court of Cassation "did not take into account the legal arguments put by the General Prosecutor, did not refer to them, and did not answer them."[50]

When the Court of Cassation recognized Sharon's immunity, the judges may have been guided by a precedent: just one year earlier, on 14 February 2002, the ICJ had ruled that Belgium had violated international law by circulating an arrest warrant (on 11 April 2000) against the then foreign minister of the Democratic Republic of the Congo, Abdulaye Yerodia Ndombasi, who was accused of committing crimes against humanity.[51] In the Congo case, the ICJ had ruled that incumbent foreign ministers, prime ministers and heads of state charged with war crimes and crimes against humanity were immune from arrest by foreign courts. The idea was to protect those in office at the highest government levels from any act by another state that would hinder such individuals from carrying out their duties.[52]

The situation, however, became much more complicated for the Belgians when on 19 March 2003 seven Iraqi families filed charges of war crimes committed during the first Gulf War against former US President George Bush, General Colin Powell, Secretary of Defense Dick Cheney (now the US Vice President) and General Norman Schwarzkopf. Powell had been chairman of the Joint Chiefs of Staff and Schwarzkopf commander-in-chief of US forces during the 1991 war ("Desert Shield"). The accusation referred specifically to a US air attack on a Baghdad shelter that had left more than 400 civilians dead. The timing of the filing of this complaint, like that against Sharon, was probably not coincidental—it came at the height of tension over another, forthcoming American strike on Iraq (which in the event was launched the next day, 20 March 2003). The list of defendants was also not unintentional—two continued to hold key positions in the US government, while the incumbent president was the son of former President Bush, who had led the campaign resulting in the first Gulf War. Recognizing the serious consequences, including economic and diplomatic retaliation that could be expected—for example, losing Brussels' status as host to NATO headquarters—if the particular legal process continued, Belgian authorities quickly reacted.[53] Several amendments to the new interpretive law were introduced in a desperate effort to appease the Americans and to dissociate Belgium from the senseless effort to become the world's judge of crimes against humanity.

In early April, both the Senate and the Chamber of the Belgian Parliament approved the amendments, according to which the 1993 law would apply only to war crimes committed in countries lacking democratic credentials and unable to cope with fair trials. Otherwise, the complaints would be passed on to the countries concerned. The new law gave the government the power to intervene and refer pending cases to an accused person's home country or to the country in which the accused was present if that country upheld the right to a fair trial. Another amendment provided that if the victim were not Belgian, the government could transfer the case to the accused person's home country, so long as it upheld the right to a fair trial and had laws that criminalized the grave human-rights violations covered by Belgian law. The case would be dismissed if the other state decided not to act on the complaint.[54] The Belgian government's new authority to interfere in pending cases imparted to it wide maneuvering space.

The amendments also recognized state immunity and, in fact, were designed to harmonize Belgian law with the ICC statute. They also limited the ability of victims with no connection to Belgium to directly file cases. In order to file suits, non-Belgians had to prove a link between the crime and Belgium; that is to say, they had to prove that the suspect was presently on Belgian soil or that the crime had taken place in Belgium or that the victim was Belgian or had lived in Belgium for at least three years at the time the crimes had been committed. If such a link did not exist, a case could be brought only to the state prosecutor, but the government could decide to transfer it to another country.[55] Both Prime Minister Verhofstadt and Foreign Minister Michel of the Liberal Party supported the amendments, which were passed by a majority, with 63 votes for, 48 against, and 9 abstentions.[56]

The new amendments were clearly aimed at extricating Belgium from the legal and diplomatic morass in which it found itself. Belgian authorities recognized that their attempt to play a meaningful role in the international arena and to gain international prestige had boomeranged. As long as Belgian courts dealt with "leper" states—such as Israel—the country could win some points in world politics and "applause" from several domestic and international NGOs.[57] However, when Belgium found itself dragged into a confrontation with the United States, Brussels got cold feet and quickly revised the laws. The interplay of politics, domestic and international, and jurisprudence became clearer than ever in May 2003 when, shortly before the Belgian prosecutor made a final decision regarding another accusation by Iraqi citizens, this one against US General Tommy Franks, commander of Allied forces in Iraq, and other US military officials for alleged war crimes in the second Gulf War, Brussels rushed to announce that the case would be sent to the United States for judicial handling. The basis for this decision was the amendment passed in April.[58]

Meanwhile, the Court of Appeal decided on 10 June 2003 to reopen the investigation of Sabra and Shatilla and to examine the charges against Yaron. This development placed Brussels in a complicated situation, not only because of its consequences for Israeli-Belgian bilateral relations, but also because it meant applying different legal rulings to the Israeli and American cases. However, less than two months later, on 1 August, Belgium's last retreat from the 1993 law occurred, when the Senate gave final approval to a new version that dropped the "universal jurisdiction" claim. Before the vote, Foreign Minister Michel told the Senate members: "Unhappily, the noble cause that prompted the Parliament to adopt this law was hit with abuse and manipulated for political ends." The resulting cases, Michel continued, damaged relations with countries with which Belgium traditionally had excellent rapport and "which have nothing to learn from us about democracy."[59] Christine Defraigne, leader of Michel's party in the Senate, was more specific, accusing some left-wing law-makers of "politicizing" the law by interfering in the cases against Sharon and the American officials. Following the approval of the revised law, Michel's spokesman, Didier Seeuws, stated that the government expected the law "to resolve the unfortunate problems we have had with the abuse of filing politically motivated cases."[60] On the basis of this new law, a Belgian court on 24 September dismissed war-crimes charges against President George Bush and Prime Minister Sharon.[61] In many respects, the legal and diplomatic battle that Israel had been conducting in Belgium for more than two years had now come to an end.

The Security Fence

The conclusion of the Sharon and Yaron cases, though, hardly afforded Israel any respite in its struggle in the international legal arena. On 8 December 2003, the UN General Assembly adopted Resolution ES-10/14 requesting an advisory opinion from the International Court of Justice (ICJ): "What are the legal consequences arising from the construction of the wall [security fence] being built by Israel, the Occupying Power, in the Occupied Palestinian Territory, including in and around East Jerusalem, as described in the report of the Geneva Convention of 1949, and relevant Security Council and General Assembly resolutions?"[62]

Israel's efforts to quash this initiative failed, given the automatic majority that the Arabs enjoyed in the General Assembly (90 of the 191 UN members voted for the resolution). In the debate in the General Assembly, Dan Gillerman, Israel's ambassador to the UN, argued that the security fence "is a temporary, proven, necessary, and non-violent measure, adopted in accordance with international and local law, to defend the people of Israel from a continuing and vicious campaign of terrorism that has killed hundred of innocent civilians and will kill thousands more if not prevented." Referring to the Palestinian claim that the wall was designed to determine borders unilaterally, Gillerman maintained that "the fence is not a border, and has no political significance. It does not change the legal status of the territory in any way." Israel, the ambassador emphasized, "remains committed to determining the final status of the West Bank and Gaza Strip, including the issue of borders, through negotiations as has been agreed by the parties."[63]

Knowing that he had no chance to influence the voting results, Gillerman took the occasion to attack the double standard and hypocrisy of the General Assembly, charging that "the ridiculous nature of the resolution presented today is highlighted by the fact that the draft resolution pretends to seek guidance from the ICJ on the very issues on which the General Assembly has already determined its response." He went on to criticize the General Assembly's abuse of the ICJ and of the Advisory Opinion procedure, warning that it would constitute a dangerous precedent for all states. "The politically biased text, rife with supposed legal conclusions," he stated undiplomatically, "makes a mockery of the Court and threatens to undermine its status." Gillerman also left little doubt about Israel's opinion of the UN: "Peace, prosperity, and security for both the Palestinian and Israeli people will not be found in this Hall or in any other organ of the United Nations." Calling for a rejection of "this cynical resolution," Gillerman vigorously stressed: "No one-sided resolution, no ill-conceived and harmful attempt to request an advisory opinion, and no report can substitute" for the need to put an end to the "morally bankrupt strategy of terror."[64]

While belittling the importance of UN decisions, the Israeli government recognized that this move by the UN General Assembly's Tenth Emergency Special Session could set into motion a new stage in the campaign against Israel in the international diplomatic arena. The Arab initiative aimed at circumventing a probable US veto in the Security Council. The Palestinians' tactic was first to win ICJ support for their cause, then the support of the General Assembly, while at the same time conducting an extensive propaganda campaign whose objective was to gain public support worldwide that could influence the United States' stand when the issue of the security fence reached the Security Council.[65]

The United States and, unexpectedly, also the EU, including Belgium,[66] refrained from joining this legal-political move by the Arab countries. Europe's decision, of course, was not an expression of any support for Israel's arguments but concern that this process could boomerang. Probably, too, it thought that adopting the ICJ track would undermine the so-called Road Map, an initiative to settle the Israeli-Palestinian conflict.[67] As a result, representatives of only twelve states, most of them Arab countries, participated in the hearings at the ICJ that began on 23 February 2004.[68] Israel puzzled over the question of participating in the hearings, but in the end decided not to send representatives. Instead, Jerusalem presented the 15 ICJ judges with an extensive document explaining why the court did not have jurisdiction to discuss the matter and also listing the acts of terror conducted by the Palestinians against Israel. Forty-four of the United Nations Member States, as well as the Palestinian Authority, the League of Arab States, and the Organization of the Islamic Conference, also transmitted written statements.[69]

The Palestinian delegation dominated the first day of hearings. Nasser al-Kidwa, the Palestinian Authority permanent observer at the UN who headed the Palestinian delegation, argued that the "Wall is not about security: it is about entrenching the occupation and the *de facto* annexation of large areas of the Palestinian land. This Wall, if completed, will leave the Palestinian people with only half of the West Bank within isolated, non-contiguous, walled enclaves. It will render the two-State solution to the Israeli-Palestinian conflict practically impossible."[70] Al-Kidwa indirectly revealed the reason for bringing the "Wall" issue to the ICJ when he spoke of the use of the veto by one of the council's permanent members: "In the 30 years between 1973 and 2003, 27 vetoes have been cast on the Palestinian issue. The most recent was cast on 14 October 2003, when the issue of the construction of the Wall in the Occupied Palestinian

Territory was brought before the Council and it failed to act." Al-Kidwa, furthermore, did not hide the Palestinians' agenda when he spoke of their firm belief that an advisory opinion by the ICJ "can lead to positive developments and perhaps even a chain of events similar to that resulting from the Court's Advisory Opinion on Namibia."[71] He hoped that a ruling against the fence would then pave the way for international sanctions against Israel, similar to the actions taken against South Africa.[72]

Meanwhile, on 30 June 2004, the Israeli Supreme Court, sitting as the High Court of Justice, ruled on a petition by the Beit Sourik Village Council against the Government of Israel and the Israeli Defense Forces in the West Bank, who had issued orders "to take possession of plots of land in the area of Judea and Samaria [in order] to erect a separation fence on the land." The issue before the Court, in Court President Aharon Barak's words, was "whether the orders and the fence are legal." The key question, according to the judges, was "whether the route of the separation fence is proportionate." In other words, "is the injury caused to local inhabitants by the separation fence proportionate, or is it possible to satisfy the central security considerations while establishing a fence route whose injury to the local inhabitants is lesser and, as such, proportionate?"[73]

In their judgment, the three Supreme Court Justices who headed the case—Barak, Court Vice-President E. Mazza, and M. Cheshin—wrote that they were impressed by the sincere desire of the military commander to find a balance between security needs and the needs of the local inhabitants; however, the justices were of the opinion that the balance determined by the military commander was not proportionate and there was no escaping from "a renewed examination of the route of the fence, according to the standards of proportionality that we have set out." Recognizing the army's right to build a fence in order "to defend the country and its citizens against the wounds inflicted by terror," the three justices acknowledged that their judgment would in the short term not make the state's struggle easier. They believed, however, that a struggle waged according to the rules of law would strengthen Israel's power and spirit in the long run.[74]

For its part, the ICJ ruled in its advisory opinion, issued on 9 July 2004, that "the construction of the wall being built by Israel, the occupying Power, in the Occupied Palestinian Territory, including in and around East Jerusalem, and in associated régime, are contrary to international law." Only one of the fifteen judges—the American Thomas Burgenthal—voted against this ruling. The same fourteen judges also called on Israel to "terminate its breaches of international law" and "to cease forthwith the works of construction of the wall being built in the Occupied Palestinian Territory, including in and around East Jerusalem." The ICJ ruling demanded that Israel "dismantle forthwith the structure therein situated" and "make reparations for all damage caused by the construction of the wall in the Occupied Palestinian Territory, including in and around East Jerusalem." The judges, furthermore, asked the UN General Assembly and the Security Council to consider "what further action is required to bring to an end the illegal situation resulting from the construction of the wall and the associated régime, taking due account of the Advisory Opinion."[75]

Israel's sharp reaction to the ICJ advisory opinion demonstrated both extreme frustration and surprise. Although there had been little expectation that the ICJ would accede to the route of the fence, officials had expected the ICJ to accept Israel's justification for such a fence and to condemn Palestinian terror attacks. Prime Minister Sharon set the tone of reaction when he described the ruling as a "slap in the face" in the global fight against terrorism. He stated categorically that "Israel completely rejects the ICJ's one-sided ruling, which was purely political in nature." Justice Minister Yosef Lapid followed Sharon's line, asserting that Israel would not follow the ICJ ruling on the fence but would abide by the ruling of Israel's High Court of Justice. A Foreign Ministry spokesman charged that the ICJ had failed to address "the essence of the problem and the very reason for building the fence—the Palestinian terror."[76]

Reactions around the world to the ICJ ruling matched respective traditional positions. The White House belittled the significance of the ICJ ruling, arguing that the Court was not the right forum to "resolve what is a political issue" and that the United States "certainly recognizes the need for Israel to defend itself and protect the people of Israel." However, it continued, "it's also important that they allow the Palestinian people to move freely within that region." For its part, the European Union urged Israel "to remove the barrier from inside the occupied Palestinian territories, including in and around East Jerusalem."[77]

Following their overwhelming success in the legal arena, the Palestinians quickly strove for another victory, this time in the diplomatic arena—at the General Assembly. Al-Kidwa, the Palestinian Authority's representative to that body, did not conceal the Palestinians aim of convincing the international community to impose sanctions on Israel. "If Israel does not comply with its obligations as determined in the (court) opinion," he advised, "it will become officially, judicially, an outlaw."[78] Following this agenda, Al-Kidwa systematically drew a direct line between South Africa and Israel, and in his public statements regularly termed the fence the "Apartheid Wall."[79]

Given the automatic majority that the Arab bloc enjoyed in the General Assembly, the important question for Israel was the stand that EU countries would adopt, as traditionally they tried to vote uniformly in such matters. Much effort was invested by both sides in influencing the EU. In the end, French pressure proved decisive: the EU decided to vote in favor of the draft resolution demanding that Israel comply with the ruling of the ICJ. All together, 150 countries voted in favor, 6 opposed (Australia, Federated States of Micronesia, Israel, Marshall Islands, Tuvalu and the United States), and 10 abstained. The representative of the Netherlands, speaking on behalf of the EU, opposed the route of the barrier. On the other hand, he did not conceal the EU's disagreement with some of the elements of the Advisory Opinion and declared that Israel had the right to act in self-defense. He ended his statement by urging all sides to desist from further violence. Al-Kidwa described the ICJ opinion as the most important development since the 1947 partition plan (which the Arabs, in fact, had not accepted). The connection he made between the two events is not coincidental.

Finally, Al-Kidwa expressed appreciation to the Assembly for the "magnificent results" and thanked, in addition to the Assembly president, the EU for their efforts to ensure wider acceptance of the resolution. For his part, Gillerman thanked God that the fate of Israel and the Jewish people was not left to the decision of the UN General Assembly.[80]

Conclusion

Israeli officials consider the international arena a battlefield, but one where the chances of succeeding without American support are limited. The Rome Statute, the "Sharon case" in Belgium, the Jenin episode, the conference in Durban, the advisory opinion of the ICJ regarding the "Wall," and the adoption of this ruling by the overwhelming majority of members of the General Assembly—all these episodes strengthen the view in Israel that an overall campaign was and is being conducted to delegitimize the state in the world community. The long-held suspicion of the UN and its organs has now expanded to the international legal arena. Not only Israeli politicians but government legal advisers, too, have come to believe that political considerations dominate the international legal process and that judges sitting on international tribunals are guided by the policies of their respective governments no less than by international law.

Israel's decision not to ratify the Rome Statute on the establishment of the ICC derived mainly from the inclusion of an article defining as a war crime the transfer by an occupying power of parts of its own civilian population into territory it occupies. Jerusalem apprehended that the ICC would serve the political agenda of Israel's opponents. The fact that the United States, the world's only superpower, was so troubled at the probable politicization of the ICC only reinforced Israel's concerns about the international legal arena.

The developments in the Sharon case in Belgium strengthened the Israeli government's conviction that an anti-Israel agenda could percolate into the legal process. Enjoying little popularity in Europe in any case, Sharon was considered an almost ideal candidate for an effort to brand Israel as a state that regularly perpetrated war crimes. The determination of several political groups in Belgium to convict Sharon became transparent when the legal process continued even after both that country's Investigating Magistrate and its Court of Appeal had ruled that the complaint against Sharon was inadmissible. The public admission by Belgian politicians, including Foreign Minister Michel, that an anti-Sharon political agenda had interfered in the legal process was not made until some two years after the case had begun. Had the Iraqi families not filed a complaint against leading American political figures, the law may not have been revised. As it turned out, the most convincing "legal" argument proved to be the US warning that it would remove NATO headquarters from Belgium.

Although Israel may have won the battle in the legal arena in Belgium, Jerusalem has apparently lost the contest for public opinion. For two long years, the intensive, critical media coverage of the slaughter in Sabra and Shatilla, which had been executed by

Lebanese militias, intermingled with reports of a "massacre" in Jenin and "atrocities" committed by Israel during the *Intifida*. The net effect was to portray Israel as a state that perpetrated war crimes. Indeed, Ariel Sharon serves as the connecting thread through all these cases.

With the support of international legal courts, world public opinion and the UN General Assembly, several Arab countries are striving to convince the United States to limit the use of its veto in the Security Council when anti-Israel resolutions are proposed. The most recent manifestation of this campaign was the ICJ's recommendation that the UN take action against Jerusalem if Israel did not dismantle the security fence. Israel regards the legal campaign against it as one more component in the Arabs" overall strategy not only at portraying Israel as a pariah state that should be boycotted as South Africa had been, but also, and more disturbingly, at undermining the very legitimacy of Israel as a Jewish nation-state.

Notes

[1] United Nations General Assembly Resolution 3379, http://www.un.org/documents/ga/res/30/ares30.htm. On 16 December 1991 the UN General Assembly revoked Resolution 3379, following a diplomatic battle that began when Israel conditioned its participation in the Madrid Peace Conference on the revocation of this resolution.

[2] Bassiouni, *The Statute of the International Criminal Court*, 100–3.

[3] "Rome Statute of the International Criminal Court," 1998, Article 1. On the complementarity issue, see Morris, "Complementarity and its Discontents."

[4] "Rome Statute of the International Criminal Court," 1998, Article 4. See also Crawford, "The Drafting of the Rome Statute"; Robertson QC, *Crimes against Humanity*, 352–92; Lee, "The Rome Conference."

[5] Broomhall, *International Justice*, 63.

[6] For a list of the NGOs represented at the Conference by an observer, see Bassiouni, *The Statute of the International Criminal Court*, 108–12.

[7] Statement by Ambassador Elyakin Rubinstein, 17 June 1998, http://www.un.org/icc/speeches/617isr.htm.

[8] "Rome Statute of the International Criminal Court," 1998; see also Dörmann, *Elements of War Crimes*, 208–14; Triffterer, ed., *Commentary on the Rome Statute*, 209–14.

[9] Statement by Judge Eli Nathan, 17 July 1998, http://www.un.org/icc/speeches/ 717isr.htm.

[10] See, for example, Scheffer, "The United States and the ICC," 203–6; Broomhall, *International Justice*, 163–68.

[11] The other No votes were cast by China, Iraq, Libya, Qatar and Yemen. In contrast, 120 of the 148 nations in attendance voted in favor of the adoption of the Rome Statute; 21 countries abstained. Lee, "The Rome Conference," 26.

[12] "Politics in Court," analysis by Elyakim Rubinstein, 21 July 1998, *Yed'iot Aharonot*, 21 July 1998; Notes from the Inter Disciplinary Center (IDC), Herzliya conference entitled "Israel and the International Criminal Court," 13 March 2003, http://www.iccnow.org/conferencesmeetings/reportsdeclarations/northafricamdreports/2003/Israel_Summary13 March03.pdf; see also *Globes*, 19 June 2001; and *Ha'aretz*, 17 December 2000.

[13] Broomhall, *International Justice*, 168–78.

[14] Blumenthal, "Recent Developments," 603–9.

[15] "Background memorandum on the ICC" presented to the CLJC, 7 June 2002 by Dan Lahav, paragraph 11 (Hebrew).

[16] See following section, "The Sharon Case." The other one was the conflict with UN Secretary-General Kofi Annan over the fact-finding team appointed to investigate the battle in Jenin. UN News Center, 20 April 2002, http://www.un.org/apps/news/ storyAr.asp?NewsID=3447& Cr=palestin&Cr1=&Kw1=jenin&Kw2=&Kw3; Report of the Secretary-General prepared pursuant to General Assembly resolution ES-10/10, 1 August 2002, http://domino.un.org/ UNISPAL.NSF/22f431edb91c6f548525678a0051be1d/fd7bde7666e04f5c85256c08004e63ed! OpenDocument; see also Gross, "Ma'avakah shel Yisrael."

[17] Remarks of Marc Grossman, Under-Secretary for Political Affairs, to the Center of Strategic and International Studies, 6 May 2002, Washington, DC, http://www.state.gov/p/9949.htm; see also interview by Maurizio Molinari of *La Stampa* with Grossman, 29 August 2002, http://www. iccnow.org/documents/statements/governments/UDGrossman29Aug02.doc; Real Audio of Briefing with Pierre-Richard Prosper, US ambassador for War Crimes Issues Foreign Press Center Briefing, 6 May 2002, http://www.iccnow.org/documents/statements/governments/ USProsperUnsigning 6May02.doc; statement by Stephen M. Minikes, US ambassador to the Organization for Security and Cooperation in Europe, 4 July 2002, http://www.state.gov/p/eur/ rls/rm/2002/11726.htm; Broomhall, *International Justice*, 178–81.

[18] Remarks to the Federalist Society by John R. Bolton, Under-Secretary for Arms Control and International Security, 14 November 2002, http://www.iccnow.org/resourcestools/ statements/-governments/USBoltonFedSociety14Nov02.doc.

[19] "The American Service Members' Protection Act," 2 August 2002, http://www.amicc.org/ docs/ASPA_2002.pdf.

[20] Remarks by Bolton, 14 November 2002; see also Matias and Sharon, "The International Criminal Court," 14, 23–25.

[21] Statement of the European Union on the position of the United States of America towards the International Criminal Court, 14 May 2002, http://ue.eu.int/uedocs/cmsUpload/ICC20EN.pdf.

[22] Remarks at the American Enterprise Institute by Bolton, 3 November 2003, http://www.iccnow. org/documents/statements/governments/USBoltonAE13Nov03.pdf.

[23] Remarks by Bolton, 14 November 2002.

[24] See, for example, "Rome Statute of the International Criminal Court," 1998, Article 17; Matias and Sharon, "The International Criminal Court," 15–21.

[25] See press release, Report of Secretary-General on recent events in Jenin, other Palestinian cities, 1 August 2002, http://www.un.org/News/Press/docs/2002/SG2077.doc.htm.

[26] See, for example, *Ma'ariv*, 14 January 2002; *Ha'aretz*, 30 October 2002.

[27] Meanwhile on 21 April 2003, Luis Moreno Ocampo of Argentina was elected ICC prosecutor. Seventy-eight states participated in the voting of the eighteen judges in February 2003. The elected judges were from Ireland, Mali, United Kingdom, Trinidad and Tobago, France, Costa Rica, Cyprus, Samoa, Republic of Korea, Brazil, Bolivia, Germany, Canada, Finland, Ghana, South Africa, Italy and Latvia.

[28] Minute no. 485 of a Meeting of the CLJC, 11 June 2002, 9–10, http://www.knesset.gov.il/ protocols/data/html/huka/2002-06-11.html.

[29] For the Durban conference, see Porat, "Durban."

[30] Minute of the CLJC, 11 June 2002, 11–12.

[31] Schabas, *An Introductory*.

[32] The complaint against Ariel Sharon for his involvement in the massacres at Sabra and Shatila, official translation from the French, http://www.mallat.com/articles/comp.htm; see also Report of the Commission of Inquiry into the Events at the Refugee Camps in Beirut (the Kahan Commission), 8 February 1983, http://www.us-israel.org/jsource/History/kahan.html. The Kahan Commission determined that the massacre at Sabra and Shatilla was carried out by a

Phalangist unit acting on its own but that its entry was known to Israel. No Israeli was directly responsible for what occurred in the camps. But the commission asserted that Israel had indirect responsibility for the massacre since the IDF held the area. Sharon was found responsible for ignoring the probability of bloodshed and acts of revenge when he approved the entry of the Phalangists into the camps, as well as for not taking appropriate measures to prevent bloodshed. See also Gelber. "The Lawsuit Submitted against Ariel Sharon in Belgium."

[33] *Ha'aretz*, 24 January 2004. The second *Intifida* broke out at the end of September 2000.

[34] *Yed'iot Aharonot*, 19 June 2001; *Ha'aretz*, 19 June 2001; *Ma'ariv*, 19 June 2001. A spokesperson for the Israeli Foreign Ministry called the program "unfair," "biased" and "intentionally hostile," contending that it provided "only partial and distorted information." The BBC's producers were accused "of a lack of good faith and an attempt to tarnish Israel and its leader." Quoted in the *Jerusalem Post*, 27 June 2001.

[35] Stefaan Smis and Kim Van der Borght, "Belgian Law concerning the Punishment of Grave Breaches of International Humanitarian Law: A Contested Law with Uncontested Objectives," *The American Society of International Law*, July 2003, http://www.asil.org/insights/insigh 112.htm; see also Broomhall, *International Justice*, pt. 4; Reydams, *Universal Jurisdiction*, pt.1; Zilbershats. "Universal Jurisdiction."

[36] Weitz, "'Ariel be-gov ha-arayot.'"

[37] See n. 32 above.

[38] Hirsch and Kumps. "The Belgian Law"; *Ha'aretz*, 8, 10 August 2001.

[39] Interview with Morlet, *Yed'iot Aharonot*, 15 February 2002.

[40] Hirsch and Kumps, "The Belgian Law," 22; Masset. "The Supreme Court of Belgium," 29.

[41] Hirsch and Kumps, "The Belgian Law," 23.

[42] Belgian Senate Okays Law Interpretations Allowing Trial of Sharon, 31 January 2003, http://www.islam-online.net/english/news/2003-01/31/article09.shtml; Belgian Senate Justice Committee Passes International Justice Proposals, January 2003, http://www.hrw.org/update/2003/01.html. The Belgian Parliament consists of a Senate, with 71 members, and a House of Representatives (the Chamber), with 150 directly elected members.

[43] Sharon Trial: 12 February 2003 decision of Belgian Supreme Court explained, 19 February 2003, http://electronicintifada.net./v2/article1176.shtml; Masset, "The Supreme Court," 30; *Ha'aretz*, 13 February 2003.

[44] FM Netanyahu on Decision of the Supreme Court of Belgium, 12 February 2003, http://www.kokhavivpublications.com/2003/israel/02/0302132118.html; *Ha'aretz*, 13 February 2003. For Belgium's reaction, see *Ha'aretz*, 14 February 2003.

[45] "Open Letter to my Israeli Friends," 25 February 2003, http://diplobel.fgov.be/en/press/homedetails.asp?TEXTID=4469.

[46] Ibid. For anti-Semitism in Belgium, see *Antisemitism World Wide*, 1998/9, 2000/1, 2001/2.

[47] See, for example, Porat, "Ha'im Esar soneh le-ya'akov"; *Antisemitism World Wide*, 2002/3; *Fire and Broken Glass: The Rise of Antisemitism in Europe*, http://www.lchr.org/ pubs/antisemitism/antisemitism_report.pdf; Sarfaty, "Anti-Zionism."

[48] Lecture by Irit Kohn on universal jurisdiction, 17 November 2003 (not published; in author's possession).

[49] Hirsch and Kumps, "The Belgian Law," 23.

[50] Masset, "The Supreme Court," 30.

[51] The ICJ has a dual role: to settle legal disputes submitted to it by countries in accordance with international law, and to give advisory opinions on legal questions referred to it by duly authorized international organs and agencies. Muller, Raič and Thuránszky, eds, *The International Court of Justice*; Schabas, *An Introductory*, viii.

[52] Pieter H. F. Bekker, "World Court Orders Belgium to Cancel an Arrest Warrant Issued against the Congolese Foreign Minister," *The American Society of International Law* (February 2002), http://www.asil.org/insights/insigh82.htm; Broomhall, *International Justice*, 146–8.

[53] See, for example, press conference conducted at the State Department on 28 April 2003; "Belgium: Universal Jurisdiction Law Repealed," 1 August 2003, http://www.hrw.org/press/2003/08/belgium080103.htm.

[54] *Guardian*, 3 April 2003.

[55] Hirsch and Kumps, "The Belgian Law," 24; see also Stefaan Smis and Kim Van der Borght, "Belgian Law concerning the Punishment of Grave Breaches of International Humanitarian Law: A Contested Law with Uncontested Objectives," *The American Society of International Law* (July 2003), http://www.asil.org/insights/insigh112.htm.

[56] *Ha'aretz*, 3 April 2003.

[57] See also Steinberg and Lassman, "The Use and Abuse of International Law by NGOs." Trial Watch-Tommy Frankes, 15 January 2006, http://www.trial-ch.org/trialwatch/profiles/en/legal-procedures/p.359.html.

[58] *Washington Post*, 28 April 2003; *Washington Times*, 28 April 2003.

[59] "Belgium's Senate approves changes to war-crimes law that outraged Washington," *News Tribune*, 1 August 2003; see also "The Law on Universal Jurisdiction Reviewed," 24 June 2003, http://www.diplobel.fgov.be/enpress/ homedetails.asp?TEXTID = 5943.

[60] *News Tribune*, 1 August 2003.

[61] *New York Times*, 25 September 2003; Amos Yaron—The Belgian Judiciary dismissed the case on 24 September 2003, http://www.trial-ch.org/trialwatch/profiles/en/ legalprocedures/p277.html.

[62] Pieter H. F. Bekker, "The UN General Assembly Requests a World Court Advisory Opinion," December 2003, http://www.asil.org/insights/insigh121.htm; on the background of the events that led to the request by the General Assembly for the advisory opinion, see Dossier, Materials compiled pursuant to Article 65, Paragraph 2, of the Statute of the International Court of Justice, 19 January 2004, http://www.icj-cij.org/icjwww/idocket/imwp/imwppleadings/imw p_iIntroductoryNote_20040119.pdf; see also Zilbershats, "The Court Is Not Competent."

[63] Statement by Ambassador Dan Gillerman, 8 December 2003, http://www.israel-un.org/ gen_assembly/pal_issues/10ess_8dec2003.htm.

[64] Ibid.

[65] Israel's Reaction to the UN General Assembly resolution to request an 'advisory opinion' from the International Court of Justice in the Hague on the issue of security fence (Communication by the Israeli Foreign Ministry Spokesman), 8 December 2003, http://www.mfa.gov.il/ MFA/About + the + Ministry/MFA + Spokesman/2003/Israel-s + Reaction + to + the + UNGA+resolution + - + Dec + 8-.htm; Legal Aspects: Overview, 6 January 2004, http:// securityfence.mfa.gov.il/mfm/web/main/document.asp?SubjectID = 45665&Missio.

[66] Ironically, a Belgian Jewish lawyer was a member of the team representing the Palestinians in the ICJ. *Ha'aretz*, 11 January 2004.

[67] A roadmap to a final and comprehensive settlement of the Israeli-Palestinian conflict on the basis of permanent two-state solution under the auspices of the Quartet (the United States, the European Union, United Nations, and Russia), press statement of the US Department of State, 30 April 2003, http://www.state.gov/r/pa/prs/ps/2003/20062.htm.

[68] South Africa, Algeria, Saudi Arabia, Bangladesh, Belize, Cuba, Indonesia, Jordan, Madagascar, Malaysia, Senegal and Sudan. In addition, there was a large delegation from Palestine as well as from the League of Arab States and the Organization of the Islamic Conference. International Court of Justice, press release 2004/12, conclusion of public hearings, 25 February 2004, http:// www.icj-cij.org/icjwww/ipresscom/ipress2004/ipresscom2004-12_ mwp_20040225.htm; *Ha'aretz*, 22 February 2004.

[69] "ICJ Advisory Opinion: Israel's Written Submission," 7–9: press release: Legal Consequences of the Construction of a Wall in the Occupied Palestinian Territory (request of advisory opinion), filing of written statements, 22 February 2004, http://www.icj-cij.org/icjwww/ipresscom/ipress2004/ipresscom2004-08_mwp_20040216.htm.

[70] Introductory Statement by Nasser al-Kidwa at the Public Sitting of the ICJ, 23 February 2004, http://www.icj-cij.org/icjwww/idocket/imwp/imwpcrs/imwp_icr2004-01_20040223.PDF.

[71] Ibid.

[72] *Ha'aretz*, 24 February 2004; see also the Written Statement Submitted by Palestine to the International Court of Justice on Legal Consequences of the Construction of a Wall in the Occupied Palestinian Territory, 30 January 2004, http://www.icj-cij.org/icjwww/idocket/imwp/imwpframe.htm.

[73] Judgment of the Supreme Court Sitting as the High Court of Justice, 30 June 2004, http://elyon.court.gov.il/files_eng/04560/020/a28/04020560.a28.htm.

[74] Ibid.

[75] International Court of Justice, Advisory Opinion, 9 July 2004, http://www.icj-cij.org/icjwww/idocket/imwp/imwpframe.htm.

[76] *Ha'aretz*, 11 July 2004.

[77] Ibid.

[78] *Palestinian Chronicle Weekly Journal*, 13 July 2004; *Jerusalem Post*, 16 July 2004.

[79] Press conference of Al-Kidwa in New York, 12 July 2004, http://www.un.org/webcast/PC2004.html.

[80] Press Release GA/10248, General Assembly Plenary Tenth Emergency Special Session 27th Meeting, 20 July 2004, http://www.un.org/News/Press/docs/2004/ga10248.doc.htm; Press Release GA/10247, General Assembly Plenary Tenth Emergency Special Session 26th Meeting, 19 July 2004, http://www.un.org/News/Press/docs/2004/ga10247.doc.htm; *Ha'aretz*, 19, 21 July 2004.

References

Antisemitism World Wide. Tel Aviv University: The Stephen Roth Institute for the Study of Contemporary Anti-Semitism and Racism.

Bassiouni, Cherif, M. *The Statute of the International Criminal Court: A Documentary History.* New York: Transnational Publishers, 1998.

Blumenthal, Daniel A. "Recent Developments: The Politics of Justice: Why Israel Signed the International Criminal Court Statute and What the Signature Means." *Georgia Journal of International and Comparative Law* 30, no. 3 (2002): 593–615.

Broomhall, Bruce. *International Justice and the International Criminal Court: Between Sovereignty and the Rule of Law.* Oxford: Oxford University Press, 2003.

Crawford, James. "The Drafting of the Rome Statute." In *From Nuremberg to The Hague: The Future of International Criminal Justice*, edited by Philippe Sands. Cambridge: Cambridge University Press, 2003.

Dörmann, Knut. *Elements of War Crimes under the Rome Statute of the International Criminal Court: Sources and Commentary.* Cambridge: Cambridge University Press, 2002.

Gelber, Yoav. "The Lawsuit Submitted against Ariel Sharon in Belgium: Historical Background." *Justice*, no. 35 (spring 2003): 25–28.

Gross, Emanuel. "Ma'avakah shel Yisrael ba-teror bi-shnat 2002: Hebetim mishpatiim agav mivtza 'Homat Magen'" (Israel's struggle against terror during 2002: Legal aspects of the 'Defensive Shield' Campaign). *Ha-Mishpat*, no. 15 (February 2003): 84–89.

Hirsch, Michèle, and Nathali Kumps. "The Belgian Law of Universal Jurisdiction Put to the Test." *Justice*, no. 35 (spring 2003): 20–24.

"ICJ Advisory Opinion: Israel's Written Submission." *Justice*, no. 38 (spring 2004): 7–9.

Lee, Roy S. "The Rome Conference and its Contribution to International Law." In *The International Criminal Court: The Making of the Rome Statute: Issues, Negotiations, Results*, edited by Roy S. Lee. The Hague: Kluwer Law International, 1999.

Masset, Adrien. "The Supreme Court of Belgium Puts an End to the Prosecution of Sharon." *Justice*, no. 35 (spring 2003): 29–30.

Matias, Shavit, and Miri Sharon. "Beit ha-din ha-plili ha-beinle'umi." (The International Criminal Court). *Ha-Mishpat* 15 (February 2003): 14–27.

Morris, Madeline. "Complementarity and Its Discontents: States, Victims, and the International Criminal Court." In *International Crimes, Peace, and Human Rights: The Role of the International Criminal Court*, edited by Dinah Shelton. Ardsley, NY: Transnational Publishers, 2000.

Muller, A. S., Raič, D., and Thuránszky, J. M., eds. *The International Court of Justice: Its Future Role after Fifty Years*. The Hague: Martinus Niihoff Publishers, 1997.

Porat, Dina. "Ha'im Esav soneh le-Ya'akov ve-lamah? Ha-antishemiyut ha-hadashah u-me'afyeneha." (The new anti-Semitism: Trends and characteristics) *Gesher 48*, no. 145 (Summer 2002): 7–16.

———. "Durban: Mitkafah aheret al Yisrael veha-am ha-yehudi." (Durban: A different attack on Israel and the Jewish people) *Kivunim Hadashim* 7 (2002): 51–60.

Reydams, Luc. *Universal Jurisdiction: International and Municipal Legal Perspectives*. Oxford: Oxford University Press, 2003.

Robertson, Geoffrey, QC. *Crimes Against Humanity: The Struggle for Global Justice*. London: Penguin Books Ltd, 1999.

Sarfaty, Georges Elia. "Anti-Zionism: A Form of Anti-Semitism." *Justice*, no. 37 (Winter 2003): 29–31.

Schabas, William A. *An Introductory to the International Criminal Court*. Cambridge: Cambridge University Press, 2001.

Scheffer, David. "The United States and the ICC." In *International Crimes, Peace, and Human Rights: The Role of the International Criminal Court*, edited by Dinah Shelton. Ardsley, NY: Transnational Publishers, 2000.

Steinberg, Gerald M., and Simon Lassman. "The Use and Abuse of International Law by NGOs." *Justice*, no. 38 (spring 2004): 14–18.

Triffterer, Otto, ed. *Commentary on the Rome Statute of the International Criminal Court*. Baden-Baden: Nomos, 1999.

Weitz, Doron. "'Ariel be-gov ha-arayot': Mishpat Sharon veha-hok ha-belgi le-migur hafarot hamurot shel ha-mishpat ha-humanitari ha-beinle'umi." ("Ariel in the lion's den": The Sharon trial and the Belgian law to eradicate grave breaches of international humanitarian law). *Ha-Mishpat* 15 (February 2003): 90–95.

Zilbershats, Yaffa. "Universal Jurisdiction: The Walking Giant." *Justice*, no. 35 (spring 2003): 15–19.

———. "The Court Is Not Competent to Hear Political Non-Legal Submissions." *Justice*, no. 38 (spring 2004): 10–13.

Israeli Perceptions of Anti-Semitism and Anti-Zionism

Anita Shapira

After Auschwitz and 1948, the distinction between anti-Zionism and anti-Semitism can no longer be upheld.

For some reason, the world does not yet regard as natural and self-evident the right of Jews to live and exist on a footing of true equality—as of right and not on sufferance or as reward for exceptional excellence. (Jacob Talmon, "The New Antisemitism," Davar, Masa supplement, 22 June 1990)

Israelis tended to ignore anti-Semitism, as a concept that belongs to the world of yesterday and has nothing to do with the Jewish state. At the same time, they treated anti-Zionism as a separate phenomenon, rooted in Middle Eastern and world politics. Today most Israelis see both phenomena as interrelated and inseparable. In the following article, I propose to follow the changes in Israeli perceptions of both phenomena and their interrelation, since 1948. It is my contention that changes in Israeli identity affected public attitudes to both concepts. Eventually, with the growing split since the 1980s between left and right, and between religious and nonreligious sectors of Israeli society, the attitude to anti-Semitism and anti-Zionism became part of a cultural code, identifying and signifying to which camp one belongs.

*

One element of Zionist thought was the belief that the realization of the Zionist idea and the creation of an independent Jewish entity in the Land of Israel would entail the end of anti-Semitism. The Zionist endeavor in the land of Israel was to engender an essential change in the Jewish character and the relationship between Jews and non-Jews. The roots of anti-Semitism, lodged in the friction between a majority population and a visible minority, were to disappear. Conversely, Jewish traits that aroused the contempt and disgust of Gentiles—notably, Jewish alienation from manual labor, Jewish weakness and ineptness in self-defense—all these were to be rectified in the state of the Jews. The "new Jew" was to be no different from non-Jews. Hence, anti-Semitism was bound to disappear.

This conception, explicit or implicit, was formulated by numerous Zionist thinkers. Those who believed in an exodus from Europe as the response to the existential danger hovering over Jews (as did Theodor Herzl) saw the disengagement from Europe as the solution to anti-Semitism. Those who stressed the importance of the Zionist movement as a spiritual and cultural renaissance emphasized the metamorphosis in the Jewish image that would occur in the new land. Quite commonly, the generation educated in the land of Israel, who drew their picture of the world from Hebrew literature, believed anti-Semitism was passé: it had nothing to do with the new proud Jew, soldierly and independent, growing up in Palestine and Israel. Anti-Semitism applied solely to Jews who had not absorbed the Zionist creed, had not come to live in Israel. It was perceived as belonging to another time, another place. This view was widespread among the generation that came of age in the land of Israel in the 1930s and 1940s.

The approach was reinforced by the fact that after 1945, anti-Semitism fell into disrepute in the West, pertaining to the dark forces that had been defeated in World War II. Just as "Nazism" had become a dirty word, so too had "anti-Semitism," seen as its companion. In Palestine-Israel, the 1940s and 1950s were years of mass immigration, including that of Holocaust survivors. The encounter between survivors and Israeli youth at the time was marked by alienation and a lack of communication. The immigrants were different: they sounded different, looked different and were foreign to the cultural and social fabric of native Jewish youth. Soon, a conspiracy of silence enveloped the Holocaust: survivors found it hard to speak of their wartime experiences. Local youth, for their part, had no desire to hear about them. Even though the Shoah was a key issue on the public agenda, on the personal level there was a reluctance to deal with it. It was a topic everyone preferred to bury. When it did come up for discussion, there was a tendency to accuse the victims of having "gone as sheep to the slaughter." The shame felt by the country's native sons at Jewish timidity in the Shoah consciously or unconsciously reinforced the idea that anti-Semitism was a phenomenon restricted to Jews "over there"—it did not apply to Israelis.

As important as the mood of "negating exile" was in molding the approach to anti-Semitism, the greatest impact on Israel's young was the fact that they grew up in a majority society, never tasting minority life. Even though until 1948 Jews constituted a minority in the land of Israel, they nevertheless had the self-awareness of a majority; immigrants considered themselves the rightful owners of the land even when Jews comprised a relative minority.[1] Furthermore, most of the new Jewish *Yishuv* was concentrated in areas of Jewish settlement. Youth growing up in Tel Aviv lived in a milieu that was entirely Jewish, from the bus driver to the construction worker. The constant friction between an ethnic, cultural minority and the majority society was not part of the formative experiences of Israeli youth. In contrast, it may be assumed that the new immigrants, who doubled Israel's population within the space of four years, had been exposed to anti-Semitism whether they hailed from Europe or Middle Eastern states. But their experience of anti-Semitism belonged "over there"; it most likely was not transposed to their new reality.

The distinction between anti-Semitism and anti-Zionism was an important component of the Israeli self-image. Whereas anti-Semitism was considered illegitimate, based on stereotypes of the diaspora Jew, on prejudice and age-old religious hatred, anti-Zionism was considered a by-product of Zionism. Until World War II, Zionism had been a minority movement among Jews. It had aroused the opposition of the Orthodox on the one hand and of the Bundists on the other. It was attacked from the left by the adherents of world revolution, and from the right by liberal circles of assimilationists. As an issue of debate, "anti-Zionism" was primarily an internal Jewish affair.[2] The arguments more or less ended with the establishment of the State of Israel. This long public debate made anti-Zionism a legitimate concept, not to be dismissed on moral grounds, as anti-Semitism was.

Zionists did not see Arab opposition to modern Jewish settlement in Palestine in the same light as European anti-Semitism. Even though the generation that came from Europe occasionally depicted hostile Arab rioters in images reminiscent of east European pogromists, the frame of reference was different. Ze'ev Jabotinsky's sharp delineation between Zionist settlers and locals in "The Iron Wall" situated the difference in the context of relations between natives and colonizers the world over. In other words, he regarded Arab opposition to Zionism not as an expression of anti-Semitism, but as a common feature of colonizer-native relations.[3] The Palestine-Israel Jewish labor movement portrayed Arab opposition as due to a misunderstanding: the Jews after all intended to bring progress, development and other benefits of socialism to Palestine. Arab opposition no doubt was based on inadequate information or on incitement by religious leaders and large landowners (effendis), who oppressed the peasantry and feared the impact of Jewish socialism. As naïve as it may have been, this portrayal of the national conflict between the two peoples over the land of Israel does show that, as a rule, Jews did not attribute to Arabs an anti-Jewish animus. If there was mention of growing hatred of Jews among the peoples of the Middle East in the twentieth century, they tended to blame Western Christian culture and its import into the region by missionaries. Arabs, after all, like Jews are Semites and thus could hardly be accused of anti-Semitism.[4] As a result, even though growing Arab violence against Jews (1920, 1921, 1929, 1936–39) sowed rage and estrangement, the inclination to distinguish between anti-Semitism and anti-Zionism remained intact: anti-Semitism was regarded as part of the world of racist, Nazi thought, whereas anti-Zionism was regarded within the context of the Jewish-Arab struggle over the Land of Israel.[5]

Nevertheless, by the eve of Israel's establishment, there were those who already warned of a possible connection between "the anti-Semitic International" and "the enemies of Zionism." The Jewish struggle against the British, whether in the form of illegal immigration to the country or acts of terror within the country, aroused broad coverage in the British press, coverage that Jews interpreted as anti-Semitic. British newspapers depicted Zionism as responsible for rising hatred of Jews in Britain. "The anti-Semite has become anti-Zionist and apparently pro-Arab throughout the reactionary world," wrote A. Reichert, illustrating his point by citing the unholy anti-Semitic alliance between Polish General Anders and Jerusalem Grand Mufti Haj Amin al-Husseini, "Hitler's partner in exterminating the Jews of Europe and Britain's ally in thwarting the Jewish state." Referring to the Zionist assumption that anti-Semitism was to disappear upon the realization of Zionism, Reichert contended that the anti-Semitic monster, "child of Exile and its faithful companion" would continue to endanger Jewish communities throughout the world and even the state of the Jews, which would become "not only an address for those who wish us well, but also a clear target of those who wish us ill, for world fascism and its overt and covert allies."[6] His article deals with a number of motifs: first, propaganda with anti-Semitic undertones goes hand in hand with criticism of Zionist policy; second, the mention of Haj Amin al-Husseini as an example of aversion incarnate to Zionism and Jews as a whole; third, his emphasis that the foes of the Jewish people and the foes of Zion all belong to the reactionary camp of the right.

Thus, even prior to the establishment of the state of the Jews, there was visible interaction between anti-Semitism and anti-Zionism. The dynamic of using anti-Semitic argumentation in political polemics with the Zionist movement, on the one hand, and the anti-Zionist posturing of traditional anti-Semites, on the other, hints at a two-way process: from anti-Zionism to anti-Semitism and from anti-Semitism to anti-Zionism.

Most segments of the Israeli public linked the animus towards Jews and Israel to the fascist right, as Reichert did: this, when all is said and done, was the camp that had sprouted the Jews' worst enemies in the first half of the twentieth century. The left, which was associated with the world of revolution and the Soviet Union, had saved the Jews: until 1939 the Soviet Union had waged a campaign against anti-Semitism and, later, the Red Army had been the liberators from the Nazi yoke. From 1947, the USSR had supported the plan to partition Palestine between Jews and Arabs. While Western powers laid an embargo on the region, the USSR (via Czechoslovakia) supplied vital arms to Israel in the War of Independence. Above and beyond all this, Israel's left identified ideologically and psychologically with the camp of revolution. Old myths die hard: even when the brief honeymoon between the Soviets and Israel was to evaporate, Israel's left found it hard to believe that there was anti-Semitism in the USSR. Nor were these deep-set leanings changed by reports of the persecution of Jewish writers and intellectuals in the Soviet Union, which was concurrent with the "honeymoon" period; nor by reports that Zionism was a "star" defendant in the Prague Trials (1952), as the ostensible ally of American imperialism and fascism.[7]

Israel of the 1950s took little interest in anti-Semitism. The hostility of Arab states was seen as legitimate within the framework of a national conflict. In Europe at this time, anti-Semitism was on the wane. Little wonder, then, that the interest in the phenomenon in Israel was confined to historians and the generation hailing from Europe. The hatred of Jews burst into Israeli consciousness with the Eichmann Trial (1961). The long weeks of witnesses' testimony broadcast by Israel Radio caused an upheaval: Israelis began to adopt a Jewish identity and to identify with Jews. Ever since, fear of annihilation has been part and parcel of the Israeli psyche. To illustrate: even though in 1948, there were times that the fate of the fledgling state hung on a thread, there was no fear of annihilation. On the eve of the Six Day War, in contrast, during the protracted waiting period leading up to the war, the civilian population did have serious fears of annihilation.[8] *Soldiers' Talk*, a collective work by soldiers from Israel's left in the 1967 war, reveals the change in consciousness that had taken place: the young soldiers identified with Jews, Jewish fate and the dire events of Jewish history.[9] The penetration of Holocaust memory into Israel's public discourse, it appears, heightened existential anxiety and honed the sensitivity to hostility towards Israel as the state of the Jews.

Israelis, in time, came to attribute the change in attitude of the worldwide left towards them to the crushing victory they had achieved in the Six Day War: as if they had dashed the left's hopes of composing fine eulogies for them. The Six Day War in fact marked a turning point in Israel's position in the international arena. Yet the early 1960s had already seen a propaganda campaign emanating from Soviet-Arab sources and designed to delegitimize Israel, transforming its international image from a state of Nazism's refugees to a state of Nazism's adherents. In 1961, it is doubtful that Israelis paid attention to the fact that Ahmed Shukeiri defined Zionism as worse than fascism, uglier than Nazism, more loathsome than imperialism, more dangerous than colonialism; in 1964, the definition made its way into the PLO Charter.[10] Especially interesting is the definition's ideological inversion: leaders of Arab states, like Arabs in Palestine, had taken a favorable view of fascism and Nazism if only because these forces were the enemies of Western imperialist powers—"the enemy of my enemy is my friend." Now, with the acceleration of decolonization and USSR support for "progressive forces" in Asia and Africa, matters had been turned upside down.

In the past, Arabs and their British supporters had accused Zionism of Bolshevism, the dread of conservative forces in the Middle East and the Western world. Now, communism had become the accepted ideology of African and Asian peoples freeing themselves of the yoke of European powers. Now the illegitimate epithets were fascism and Nazism, symbolizing ultimate evil in league with imperialism and colonialism, everything that men of conscience had to fight against. The object of attack was not the State of Israel, since attacking it would entail indirect recognition of its existence, but Zionism, an ideology that started to be characterized in demonic terms. It is easier to attach demonic qualities to an ideology, for its relationship to reality is more nebulous; a state has more substance as an entity. "Zionism" is a catchword universally associated with Jews, but without explicitly mentioning Jews. The maneuver was initiated by the USSR, which heaped on Zionism all that it wished to heap on the Jews but could hardly do so because anti-Semitism had become illegitimate.

In 1965, two years before the Six Day War, the USSR tabled a proposal in a United Nations (UN) committee that defined Nazism, fascism and neo-Nazism as racist crimes. After consensus was reached on condemning apartheid as racism, the delegates of the United States and Brazil proposed that anti-Semitism be condemned as well. Fearing that such censure would be understood as targeting Soviet policy towards its Jews, the USSR stratagem was to demand that Zionism too be added to the list of ignominious ideologies. As a direct result of this stratagem, neither anti-Semitism nor Zionism was included in the list. It was the first signal for the "Zionism = racism" equation down the road.[11] At conferences of African heads of state, at congresses of Nonaligned States and at Arab summits at the end of 1964, there was a "clear and dangerous trend to equate the land of Israel with Angola and Mozambique and to place the State of Israel on an equal footing with Portugal and South Africa, war against them being fair game and enjoying the support of the world's enlightened people."[12] It is rather astonishing to read the following analysis in an article from 1964: "The trend is clear: to present the problem of the land of Israel not as a complex political, territorial conflict but as a plain anticolonialist, antiracist problem, to implant this view in world public opinion and thereby prepare the suitable ideological and psychological background for firm action against Israel when the time comes."[13]

Israel does not seem to have given serious consideration to the propaganda transformation taking place around it. In those days, its close ties with Asian and African states received broad coverage in the Israeli media: its general self-image was of a small, benevolent state helping the less fortunate who were winning their independence. Soviet hostility towards Jews and Israel was a sore point, but it was explained away in rational terms: it all boiled down to the USSR's courtship of Arab states, which enjoyed important strategic advantages in the Cold War face-off. The press did not highlight signs of Soviet anti-Semitism. It did not depict the discrimination against Soviet Jewry regarding national rights in the Soviet Union or emigration to Israel as singling out Jews from other national groups in the USSR. It described it as part of overall Soviet policy, which, even if distasteful, was built into the regime's guiding principles.

*

At the end of the 1960s, several processes came together: the Six Day War, the students' revolt, the USSR's invasion of Prague, the Vietnam War, the appearance of the New Left. These phenomena changed the public climate and the public discourse. The outburst of anti-Semitism in the Soviet Union and East European states such as Poland and East Germany, and the Eastern bloc's full-throated support for Arab states shocked Israelis by its venom and by the exposure of a connection between communist frustration at the failure of its arms in the Six Day War and the new legitimacy for anti-Semitism in these countries. The severance of diplomatic ties with Israel by Asian and African states in the wake of the Six Day War was a bitter disappointment. De Gaulle's description of Jews as an arrogant and domineering people astounded Israelis who, until then, had believed him to be Israel's ally. Especially baffling was the anti-Semitic tone of his words: why denigrate the Jewish People down the generations because of Israeli policy? The most disturbing developments, however, concerned the new central role played in the public discourse by young students rebelling against the Western establishment and the emerging turnabout among Western intellectuals vis-à-vis Israel.

Israel had no undue hardship dealing with criticism and virulent animosity so long as it was confined to the communist and Arab camps. The Arabs had never recognized the legitimacy of the State of Israel. The Soviet Union for the previous fifteen years had consistently wielded an anti-Israel policy; little by little, Israelis became willing to acknowledge the anti-Semitic coloring of Soviet propaganda. The real difficulty was adjusting to the new anti-Israel climate on American campuses. Less than a year after the war, an Israeli intellectual then in the United States noted the change in the position of the non-Jewish left on Israel. "Anti-Israel and anti-Jewish hysteria" was how Joseph Dan defined the leftist stance around the world.[14] Dan aptly connected the turnabout with the change in public discourse: in the division of the world between "white" and Third World countries, Israel was counted among the "white," and the Arabs among the "black." It was a value judgment, not an ethnic description: after all, Israelis originating from Arab states supposedly belonged to the same "black" camp. Nor did the definition have anything to do with economics or national wealth since the Arab states commanded vast oil reserves. It was the sense of guilt felt by the left-liberal camp over imperialism and colonialism that automatically made anyone on the "dark" side a saint, and anyone on the other side a scoundrel. Israel, being "white," was by definition disqualified. The attitude towards it, Dan argued, was not a direct result of its failings or actions, but an a priori matter of principle. Had it taken energetic steps to settle the refugees, it would have been equally faulted: "Instead of bewailing the misery of refugees in camps, liberal journalists would have described the lack of consideration and boorishness of Israel's Military Government in attempting to lodge Arabs in European-style housing and, against their will and disposition, make them conform to modern breadwinning."[15] For all his scathing criticism of liberal leftists, Dan accused them of hypocrisy, but not of anti-Semitism. He reserved his charge of anti-Semitism for the Soviets and for East European states, as well as for the Arabs. The left was disappointing, mistaken, hypocritical—but not anti-Semitic. And yet, the very fact that most Jewish liberals took a different approach towards Israel than did their non-Jewish counterparts did raise questions.

The New Left appeared on the scene in the late 1960s to early 1970s. The backdrop for its emergence was the crisis in consciousness wrought by the Vietnam War, the student unrest and the disillusionment with the Soviet Union. The New Left was anti-establishment and radical. From the start, its approach to Zionism and the State of Israel was negative: its antipathy to nationalism and specifically Jewish nationalism was a direct outcome of the cosmopolitan faith characteristic of some of its constituents. According to its worldview, there was a clear division between "white" nationalism, which is wrong, and the nationalism of the oppressed whose freedom struggle was right and just under any conditions. The New Left identified Israel as imperialistic and racist, dispensing with the need for evidence of its actions and shortcomings.[16]

Like all worldwide intellectual fads, the New Left too found a following in Israel. Their extreme censure of Israel and her policy triggered an internal crisis of consciousness. For the first time, there arose a group of Israelis who, in the name of world revolution, denied Israel's very right to exist. Numerically, the group was negligible, but not so in intellectual terms. It sparked a media brouhaha out of all proportion to its size.

The Israeli left found it difficult to swallow Israel's dubious standing in intellectual circles. The New Left was chic, with the added attraction of an anti-establishment and moral fervor, qualities that the communist bloc had long lost. The desire to identify with the progressive, enlightened, just camp, the same impetus that in previous generations had caused a blind eye to be turned to Soviet sins, now focused on the New Left: if this camp says that Zionism is essentially wrong, that the State of Israel is imperialistic and colonialist, there is probably some truth to it. Anti-Semitism had not affected the innate sense of justice at home, and basically left no traces on Israel's self-image. Anti-Zionist criticism, on the other hand, not only affected but undermined the confidence in the Zionist creed among segments of Israel's left. The process did not take place in a vacuum: the fact that since 1967 Israel had ruled over a conquered Palestinian population poured potent fuel on the flames of self-doubt. The moral erosion engendered by the occupation and its by-products evoked harsh self-criticism. The result was what poet Haim Gouri termed a transition from a society of righteous besieged to a society of guilt and remorse. The 1973 Yom Kippur War, which shattered the faith in the leadership of the Labor Party, added an additional blow to the wobbling self-confidence of Israeli society.[17]

As stated above, Israelis were hard put to accept the view that anti-Semitism related to them as well. Consequently and dialectically, they tended to blame themselves and their actions for its outbursts, which they defined as anti-Zionist but not necessarily anti-Semitic. Much of the anti-Israel hostility, for instance, they explained as deriving from the post-1967 occupation. The fact that the seeds of a pernicious anti-Zionism were already sown in the mid-1960s, prior to the occupation, attracted no attention. In the same way, a decade later, Israeli left-wing intellectuals tended to blame

Menachem Begin's government and its bellicose behavior for the unfavorable image of the State of Israel. But the fact is that the infamous UN Resolution 3379, which defined Zionism as a "form of racism and racist discrimination," was adopted in November 1975, during the first Rabin government. UN discussions leave no doubt about the grossly blatant anti-Semitic nature of the issue.[18] It was an attempt to delegitimize the existence of the State of Israel. In his analysis of the resolution, Israeli political scientist Ehud Sprinzak discerned a qualitative leap in anti-Zionism in the 1970s: "Its implication is that, from an object of delegitimization, Zionism has become an object of dehumanization."[19] In the process he described, the victim is unaware of what is happening around him because the change is not taking shape within himself but in the conceptual group invalidating him—until one clear day he realizes that not only fringe elements but also mainstreamers have ostracized him. Similarly, Zionism changed from a legitimate ideology of national liberation in 1947 into an ideology of national oppression denying legitimate aspirations. Zionism became a dirty word. Based on the paradigm of "Zionism = racism," any Israeli government is tainted to begin with, even if strictly leftist. Any Israeli war is racist and all acts of terror against Israel are kosher and admissible. The definition is particularly grave because slowly but surely it has crept into the language of Western civilization. A new stereotype made its debut: Zionism is racism and racism is Zionism. It makes no difference that Zionism never was racist—the spread of the stereotype makes the need for proof irrelevant.[20] The dehumanization of the state of the Jews went hand in hand with the dehumanization of Jews. As Leon Wieseltier said, it was a repudiation of the right of Jews to define themselves as a collective, of their historical legitimacy to be what they wish to be rather than what others expect them to be.[21]

*

The Likud Party's rise to power in 1977 signified an upsurge in Israeli society of traditionalist rightist currents. Opposite the Zionist-socialist rebellion against Jewish tradition in the form of the "old Jew," there now arose groups who stressed the continuity of Jewish history and advanced conservative views about Jews and non-Jews. As far as they were concerned, hatred of the State of Israel was an expression of the traditional hatred of Jews. They considered any criticism of the State of Israel as suspect of anti-Semitic motives and thus inadmissible. The necessary conclusion from this mode of thinking was that Israel need not concern itself with the criticism leveled at it since it was based not on her conduct but on age-old prejudice and animus.

The Likud's rise to power was concomitant with an additional change in consciousness: the Holocaust became a central component of Israeli identity. The process in Israel dovetailed with the worldwide process, which, in the West, led to a heightened consciousness of the Shoah of European Jewry. The trend paralleled the growing criticism of Israeli policy towards the Palestinians. In Israel, the European onslaught was understood as an attempt of European peoples to shed their Holocaust guilt about Israel. Begin, more so than any of his predecessors, kept bringing up the Holocaust as an indictment of the world's nations, gainsaying their moral right to preach to Israel.[22] On the Palestinian side, there was a process of appropriation and inversion of Holocaust symbolism, in a reversal of roles: in media images, Israelis were transformed from the successors of Holocaust victims into the successors of Nazis. The role reversal was first initiated by the Soviets who, back in the 1950s, had already accused Zionists of having cooperated with the Nazis in "self-genocide." These drifts were reinforced after the Six Day War when the Soviet propaganda machine invoked Nazi symbols to describe the war: the war was a *Blitzkrieg*, Israelis were a "master race," and their attitude to the Palestinians was described in such terms as "concentration camp," "SS," and "Gauleiter." Moshe Dayan and Golda Meir were likened to Hitler and his henchmen, and the military government in the West Bank, to the Third Reich.[23] The Palestinians, since 1967, have adopted the anti-Nazi frame of reference, although during the Eichmann trial (1961) they still contended that Hitler had been right, and that it was a pity that he had not completed the extermination of the Jews.[24] Now, they appropriated the terminology of Europe's anti-Nazi resistance movements, portraying the Jews as the Nazis of our times. During the siege of Beirut in the Lebanon War, Western media stations dressed the Palestinians in the image of Warsaw Ghetto fighters, poised before a formidable military machine.[25] Author John Le Carré wrote that the Israelis were on the verge of doing to the Palestinians what the Germans had done to them.[26] Preaching to the Jews was now done in the name of Holocaust memory.

Many Israelis were uncomfortable with Begin's constant reminders of the Holocaust. They regarded it as a cheapening of its memory and using it manipulatively for political purposes. But they were not aware of the use being made of the Holocaust by the other side. Israeli public opinion woke up to what was happening after the media attack on Israel during the Lebanon War. A considerable chunk of Israelis were not happy about the war and as Israel's embroilment became increasingly clearer, so too did domestic criticism. It reached a climax following the massacre of Palestinians by Christian Phalangists in the refugee camps of Sabra and Shatila. The huge demonstration held by Israel's left against government imperviousness to the war-induced human suffering sharply demarcated the moral boundaries set for the state by Israeli public opinion.

The profound differences of opinion on the war also found expression in the variant assessments of the media onslaught waged against Israel at the time. Newspapers and magazines associated with the right, such as *Ha-Tzofeh*, *Ha-Umah* and *Gesher*, dwelt on the exhibition of anti-Semitism towards Israel in the world press and media. The mantra of these groups was "the whole world is against us" and the Jews are "a people that shall dwell alone, and shall not be reckoned among the nations" (Numbers 23:9). Israel's isolation in the international arena was decreed, deriving from Esau's mythic, meta-historical hatred of Jacob.[27] Reactions in the leftist press, in contrast, were moderate. "Neither alone nor all against us," noted one writer. "Even if there were any truth to this view," he protested, "one should be careful about voicing it before the public for whom memories of Exile and the Holocaust determine much of their attitude to the nations of the world."[28] The opposition to the Israeli stance stems not from a generation-old loathing of Jews, but from rational causes related to the Cold War, the power of Arab oil, strategic and economic interests. A way must be found to explain our positions to our friends in the United States and Europe, he said, and also to talk with the Arab states just as we found a way to talk with Egypt (i.e., the peace treaty with Egypt). In a magazine connected with the Labor Party, letters to the editor lambasted the Begin government and its response to world reaction to events in Lebanon. "There is no connection between the angry reactions of the free world towards us and the traditional hatred of Jews," stated a member of Kibbutz Ayelet Hashahar, "the exaggerated use of the word "anti-Semitism," as a weapon of defense to justify deeds that bring no honor to the State of Israel, cause it to be devaluated."[29] He went on to say that, "the fact is, that in all the years of Labor movement rule, we sensed no such hostility from the peoples of the free world."[30]

The 1983 Journalists' Yearbook carried a balanced analysis by Teddy Preuss, a moderate leftist. Preuss had no illusions about the timing of the deterioration in the attitude of the world media to Israel: it had already begun during the "honeymoon" period preceding the Six Day War, before Israel had even conquered the territories. Hostility towards Israel pre-dated also Likud rule: thus, for example, the *London Times* portrayed the first Rabin government as a military high command ruling the country. But this tendency gathered momentum with the election of Begin "the terrorist" as prime minister. Preuss described the double standards employed by the world media against Israel: unseemly actions by Israel grabbed front-page headlines whereas far worse actions by others, including by Middle Eastern regimes, were reported on inside pages. The press inflated the figures of Arab casualties in Lebanon, including fictitious reports on the number of refugees fleeing from southern Lebanon. At the same time, conduct that could be viewed as favorable on Israel's part met with skepticism and meager acknowledgment in the European press—for example, the Camp David Accords and the risks Israel had taken upon itself in the peace treaty with Egypt. Preuss also cited newspapers and television networks that covered the war fairly. The day after the large demonstration on Sabra and Shatila, the world press expressed praise and esteem for Israeli moral courage, only a week after having written that Israel had lost its moral advantage and, indeed, that Israeli auxiliary forces had taken part in the massacres. Thus, Preuss believed, it was wrong of the government to present even specific criticism of Israel as a sign of anti-Semitism. However, it was necessary to expose any anti-Semitic hypocrisy and self-righteousness that took issue with Israel's right to exist, as did *Die Zeit* when it wrote that, had it not been for the Holocaust, the State of Israel would not have arisen, making Germany morally obligated towards the Arabs. Preuss suggested a criterion for the distinction between legitimate criticism and anti-Semitism—the attitude to Israel's right to exist: no state could accept criticism that cast it as a Nazi monster to be destroyed.[31]

Since the Lebanon War, public discussion of anti-Semitism and its relationship to anti-Zionism has been a permanent fixture. The Study Circle on World Jewry in the Home of the President of Israel was one of the more important colloquiums to consider the subject. In the 1984/1985 series, the topics of discussion included

"Anti-Semitism Today: Myth and Reality" and "Anti-Zionism as an Expression of Anti-Semitism in Recent Years."[32] Scholars of anti-Semitism and Israeli diplomats took part in both discussions. The main questions explored were the interaction between Israel's measures and the world's attitude to her, as well as the connection between anti-Zionism and anti-Semitism. Leftist political scientist Ze'ev Sternhell called on participants not to exaggerate either the severity of anti-Semitism or the identification of anti-Semitism—which he saw as an attempt "to destroy Western civilization and the basic components of Western culture"—with anti-Zionism, which "is primarily a political phenomenon linked ... with the war in the Middle East." He did note that his visit to Europe during the Lebanon War had been traumatic, in view of anti-Semitic manifestations, but he protested against Begin's excessive depiction of Arafat as Hitler. He did not attach much importance to the portrayal of Zionism as Nazism, ascribing the maneuver to irrational and insignificant fringe elements. On the other hand, he linked the New Left's delegitimization of the right of Jews to their own state with Israel's delegitimization of the PLO.[33] While the forum leaned towards President Herzog's diagnosis that anti-Zionism was a polite form of anti-Semitism, a distinction between the two was nevertheless maintained. Participants noted that anti-Semitic ideas and symbols had leached into anti-Zionism but they were cautious not to bracket the two together. Politically, they were on the whole either center or left. There was apparently no salient representation of Israel's right; nor of religious Zionism. It may be assumed that, had such representatives attended the discussions, the forum's positions would likely have been more polarized.

*

In 1985 a first survey polled Israeli Jews on their perceptions of anti-Semitism. Another, eight years later in 1993, checked whether attitudes to this and related topics had changed. Most of the Israelis questioned in the first sample had no personal experience of anti-Semitism. Nevertheless, a majority of those polled believed anti-Semitism to be widespread. A vestige of the period when Israelis believed anti-Semitism did not apply to them can be seen in the 1985 opinions about the causes of anti-Semitism: 41 percent attributed it to the minority status of diaspora Jewry; 22 percent cited the traits of non-Jews; and 36 percent gave precedence to Jewish traits or conduct. The relatively large last category indicates that Jews and notably Israelis had internalized some of the anti-Semitic stereotypes.

The study also found firm and positive Jewish identification among both youth and adults, although it was stronger among adults and it rose with age. Among adults, Jewish and Israeli identity overlapped. As a rule, the survey highlighted the suspicious attitude of religious and tradition-oriented Israelis to the non-Jewish world, as opposed to a more relaxed approach on the part of non-religious Jews.[34] The second, 1993, survey showed an increase in the number of respondents who said that they had never encountered anti-Semitism (from 57 percent in 1985 to 62 percent in 1993). At the same time, nearly 75 percent of respondents took an interest in the subject. The majority believed that anti-Semitism derived from social, political and economic conditions in non-Jewish society (71 percent). But prominence was also accorded to ideologies dehumanizing Jews (67 percent). Minority life appeared in third place (64 percent), the traits of non-Jews were in fifth place (58 percent) and Jewish traits and conduct were in sixth place. As in 1985, so in 1993 most respondents believed anti-Israel and anti-Zionist manifestations to be anti-Semitic (57 percent). However, whereas in 1985, about a quarter of the respondents believed that such manifestations were on no account an expression of anti-Semitism, in 1993, only 14 percent thought so. In other words, over the years, the trend of the Israeli public to identify anti-Zionism with anti-Semitism grew stronger. Nor was there any significant difference on this question between the religious and the non-religious. The same attitude also relates to the conviction of Israelis that their government's policy is the less influential factor in arousing anti-Semitism.[35] Considering that in 1993 the peace process was at its height and yet noxious anti-Israel propaganda continued, the growing association between anti-Zionism and anti-Semitism in Israeli consciousness is little cause for wonder.

Some years later, in 1995, the (socialist-leaning) Kibbutz Teachers Seminar initiated and published a study on the attitudes towards anti-Semitism and racism of two target groups: student teachers from the secular and religious sectors. This study presented a highly polarized picture of the two groups. Thus, for example, when asked what kind of Israeli behavior might help stop anti-Semitism, secular students cited "humane behavior" in first place, encompassing such elements as striving to reach a peace settlement, fostering good relations with many states; better information; liberalism and a respect for human dignity; changing our attitude to Arabs; opening the country's gates to anyone who wished to enter. In second place, they cited "active behavior," which included being a strong country, helping Jews who so desired to immigrate to Israel; demonstrating military strength. The religious respondents, in contrast, gave precedence to "active behavior" and, lagging far behind in second place, to "humane behavior." While both sectors believed anti-Semitism posed a considerable danger, the religious group attached greater importance to it. Most respondents thought it was directed primarily at diaspora Jewry, especially those easily identified as Jews. On the other hand, they also associated anti-Zionism with anti-Semitism; that is, they saw themselves too as endangered by anti-Semitism. The researchers remarked on the particularistic perspective of the young, especially the religious, on the question of racism—they identified anti-Semitism as racism, but were quick to ascribe to it specifically Jewish components, making no allowances for racism's universal aspects. The researchers recommended more intensive education towards universal love of humanity and against racist attitudes to Arabs.[36] The study sheds light on the left's concern about the erosion of humanist sensitivities in religious education as a result of an overemphasis on anti-Semitism.

In the onslaught on Israel, the role reversal between Jews and Arabs, with Jews depicted as Nazis and Palestinians as victims of Nazism, was the ingredient most infuriating to Israelis. The standard bearers of this propaganda line were the radical left. The linkage in this analogy between the history of the Middle Eastern conflict and the history of European Jewry was to no small extent responsible for the association between hatred of Jews and hatred of the state of the Jews. Any association between what was happening in the occupied territories and the Nazi regime sparked impassioned reaction. The term coined by Yeshayahu Leibovitz, "Judeo-Nazis," continued to provoke and enrage.[37] On the other hand, Moshe Zimmerman, a scholar of German history at the Hebrew University of Jerusalem, claimed that the political manipulation by Israel's government of the Holocaust guilt felt by Germany, Europe and even the United States towards Jews was responsible for the emerging image of Israel as Nazi: "Every time Israel reopened the subject, presenting itself as the victim to whom the world still owed a debt, it aroused a counterreaction and build-up of anger." "In every place that Israel used its status as eternal victim, comparisons to Nazism come up."[38] Zimmerman held that Israel could not have it both ways—both to demand for itself moralistic treatment from others in the name of Holocaust memory and to behave on the basis of *raisons d'état* whenever it suited it. Israel pretended to be guided by "Jewish ethics": Hence, it could not act according to Syrian or Russian criteria, he objected.[39]

A number of journals dealing with anti-Semitic phenomena and trends are published in Israel. The major ones are the annual *Massuah*, which is concerned with the Holocaust, and the periodicals of the World Zionist Organization, such as *Bi-Tfutzot Yisrael*, *Kivunim* and *Kivunim Hadashim*. In addition, journals identified with the right, such as *Nativ*, *Ha-Umah* and the religious daily, *Ha-Tzofeh*, frequently carried material published abroad, discerning anti-Semitism in anti-Zionist propaganda.[40] Menachem Begin used to invoke the Holocaust whenever he found himself under specific attack, whether politically or morally.[41] The growing identification of Israel's right with religious circles reinforced the trend to regard hostility towards Israel as the heritage of ages: Esau is Jacob's enemy. It is an old story. As religious imagery intensifies, the bond to the imagery of the "new Jew" slackens, fixing identity around the image of the "old Jew." The old Jew has no problem with the idea that "the whole world is against us" and the realization that the Zionist prognosis on anti-Semitism proved to be wrong.

*

But the right was not monolithic. The secular right, champions of classic secular Zionism (after Nordau or Jabotinsky), found it hard to digest the case of anti-Semitism. In two respects, the establishment of the State of Israel was supposed to have been the ultimate response to anti-Semitism: not merely as living proof that anti-Semitism was a lie, but as an end to the apologetic polemics with anti-Semites who were simply to be bypassed by Zionism. The realization that the State of Israel had not only failed to put an end to anti-Semitism but had even bred a new strain—namely, anti-Zionism—was hard to swallow for anyone raised on basic Zionist tenets. "For native Israelis, popularly known as "sabras," it was not easy to relate to the revival of anti-Semitism," declared Elyakim Rubinstein.[42] An interview given by Prime Minister Yitzhak Shamir (the erstwhile head of the pre-state Israel Freedom Fighters underground, Lehi, termed the "Stern Gang" by the British), to David Landau of the *Jerusalem Post* illustrates the complexity of the anti-Semitism/anti-Zionism approach. Shamir distinguished between the duty of the State of Israel to fight for its existence and the battle against anti-Semitism in the world arena, which he saw as the job of large Jewish organizations. World Jewry was to wage the battle against anti-Semitism whereas Israel's government was to keep the state safe and not create new enemies by opening up new fronts (the interview was held against the background of emerging anti-Semitism in Russia in the days of *Glasnost'* and the confrontation with the Catholic Church over the erection of the convent at Auschwitz). Shamir's distinction between peculiarly Israeli interests and the interests of world Jewry, in which journalist Dan Margalit detected a "thin edge of Canaanite dust" (referring to the Canaanite ideology that drew a wedge between Israelis and diaspora Jews as two separate entities), did not relate to the identification of extreme anti-Zionism (such as "Zionism = racism") with anti-Semitism. This remained intact. Nor did it relate to Israel's commitment to protect and shelter Jews, which he took for granted. But it did raise the possibility of there being anti-Semites friendly to the State of Israel. It was a reflection of Herzl's views and the unfulfilled expectations that decent anti-Semites would be happy to be rid of the Jews in their midst in an enlightened fashion.[43] To Shamir, the realization of Zionism was a lengthy process, as was the liquidation of anti-Semitism. It was his way of saying that the Zionist premise had not been wrong, but that the time was not yet ripe for its fruition. There was an essential difference between the fear of annihilation and the hysterical tone of rightist articles on the question and Shamir's approach, which took into account both the possible and the desirable from the point of view of the state, and weighed it against the ideological.

A similar complexity characterized the approach of the Zionist left. In the early 1990s, the Israeli press gave wide coverage to government reports citing anti-Semitic incidents, especially in the Soviet Union and Eastern Europe. These reports were not taken at face value: leftist political scientist Yoram Peri protested that "more than the *goyim* need anti-Semitism as a scapegoat, we Israelis need it as self-justification for our mistakes, failures, shortcomings and crimes."[44] This extremist pronouncement, in a no less extremist article, exposed the frustration of Israel's left, and not necessarily the radical left, at the stalemate on the diplomatic front during Shamir's premiership and the toughening of Israeli measures against the Palestinians in the first *Intifada*. The same Yoram Peri had published a study in 1981 pointing to the transition of Europe's Socialist International from unequivocal support of Israel to rolling out the red carpet for Yasser Arafat, without their having received his agreement to coexistence with Israel. In this article, Peri accused the socialist parties not of anti-Semitism, but of yielding to pressure, interests, and a changing policy due to changing generations.[45] Nor did he blame Israel then for deteriorating relations, even though Begin's government was already in office. A similar phenomenon can be seen in the report by Shevah Weiss (a Labor Party MK and himself a Holocaust survivor) on the Council of Europe Conference in December 1990. He spoke of Israel-bashing at Council sessions, of false horrors attributed to Israel's treatment of Palestinians, and of his objections before the Council to the lies voiced even though he was a member of Israel's

Opposition at the time. He ended the article with the remark that a year and a half earlier, when the Unity Government had proposed a peace initiative, "Israel's position in the Council of Europe had been far better."[46] But in truth, Weiss's previous report from the Council of Europe had been even worse: "In the Council of Europe, there is now intellectual terror against Israel," he had written—"Palestinians are depicted as the victims of Nazism." And: "There is no limit to the lies, no limit to the deceitful stereotypic descriptions," and so on and so forth.[47] The growing frustration of the left led to an overemphasis on the responsibility of Israel's government for rising anti-Semitism around the globe.

An extreme example of the polarized positions on the question of anti-Semitism/anti-Zionism can be found in an article by journalist Gideon Samet of *Ha'aretz*, following publication of a report by the Inter-Ministerial Forum Monitoring Anti-Semitism (25 March 1992). The report dealt mostly with the former USSR, Muslim fundamentalism, rising nationalism, anti-Semitic publications the world over, and so on. Samet wrote that "the government has now added another whining chapter to the book 'The Whole World is Against Us.'" Criticism of the Israeli government was not anti-Semitism, claimed Samet. "Dangerous demagoguery had filled our ears over the years with a muddle between anti-Israelism and anti-Judaism."[48] Most of the article is a sharp polemic against the published reports on anti-Semitism, which struck him as exaggerated in content and tendentious in timing in order to relieve pressure from the beleaguered government. The editor of *Davar*, the Labor daily, Hannah Zemer, wrote in a similar vein.[49] Government Secretary Elyakim Rubinstein, head of the Monitoring Forum, responded rather mildly that the timing hinged on the Forum's agenda, not the government's. He also pointed out that anti-Semitism in Eastern Europe was unconnected with Israeli policy in the Middle East and that the attempt to connect the two was strained and fabricated.[50] Veteran journalist David Pedhazur summed up the discussion: "This may not be self-hatred—but it is certainly typical Jewish self-righteousness." Anti-Semitism was not a disease of the Jews, he said, alluding to a statement by Holocaust scholar Yehuda Bauer: "It is a disease of the non-Jews . . .. Neither Jews nor Israel need anti-Semitism. It is needed by anti-Semites who see Jews as the prime cause of all their woes and frustrations, their troubles and disasters. It is needed by anti-Zionists who see Israel as the world's pariah Jew."[51] The article, published in *Davar*, reiterated the moderate stance of the old Zionist left, as against the radicals.

Elyakim Rubinstein and Gideon Samet may have come from opposite sides of the fence in the controversy but they shared a common denominator: estrangement from the phenomenon of anti-Semitism and a basic sense that it did not affect the existential roots of Jews in Israel. On anti-Semitism, Samet wrote, "Also for us here, who are free of one of the most contemptible social phenomena in history, this data deals a blow to the heart: in an ostensibly new world, built on the ruins of the old order, the infestation of hatred of Jews is spreading."[52] And Rubinstein explained: "I grew up in a land free of anti-Semitism, in a Jewish majority society, with a flag, [self-]governance and its own army; hatred of Jews was a faraway idea unknown first-hand to my native-born generation."[53] Acknowledging the latency of hatred of

Jews, which is built of stereotypes ingrained in Western civilization that are transferred to all parts of the globe, is hard for someone raised to believe that anti-Semitism is a phenomenon from an earlier stage of human development and that, in the present age, it has no place. Students educated in the State of Israel accepted as self-evident, as an axiom requiring no proof, the idea that the Jewish people are equal to all other nations in the world and individual Jews are equal to the rest of humanity. This was the basic essence of the Zionist idea. From this perspective, Zionism was a success story, for it changed the individual and the collective mentality and psychology. Consequently, it was especially difficult for people with an Israeli identity based on the idea of equality to accept the notion that the attitude to Jews and Israelis in the world does not live up to egalitarian expectations. This outlook was especially widespread among the non-religious Israelis, whose basic beliefs were Zionist, rather than traditionally Jewish.

Jewish tradition was ahistorical. By its lights, the basic relations between Jews and non-Jews were never meant to change until the coming of the Messiah. In these circles, hatred of Jews and the rejection of Jews as equal to other peoples were taken for granted. It fit their normative system, causing no dissonance. They were thus better equipped to accept a pessimistic view of Jewish-Gentile relations, which correlated with their inbuilt expectations.

Into this complex configuration of mindset and psychology, the component of Arab and Islamic attitudes was introduced. As will be recalled, the secular majority regarded the opposition of Palestinian Arabs to Zionism in political and social terms rather than in terms of racial hatred. Since Israelis anticipated a process of reconciliation between Jews and Arabs in the country, they tended to treat tolerantly the trickle of clearly anti-Semitic ideas and concepts into the Arab world of ideas and politics. "The fact that Muslims picked out an element hardly central to their tradition, such as anti-Semitism, and it is to be found in fundamentalist propaganda and writings from the first moment, is no doubt nourished by the Israel-Arab conflict," Islam scholar Emmanuel Sivan asserted. Further on, he pointed to "the conflicted soul of [Muslim] people, who have not yet decided whether to choose the peace process or radicalized anti-Semitism."[54] In other words, the venomous anti-Semitism of Muslim fundamentalism is a possible though not a necessary option of Islam, not anchored in historical depths. This view reflected the hopes and expectations of the Israeli left. In contrast, Israeli opponents of the peace process—whether out of a belief that the whole of the land west of the Jordan was the Jewish ancestral patrimony and that no part of it could be relinquished, or out of an inference from the system of beliefs and opinions that the nations of the world could not be trusted—described Arab and Muslim hostility towards Jews as an inbuilt quality of Islam, highlighting its explicit anti-Jewish components and those episodes in the history of Islam that were least tolerant of Jews.

*

In the final analysis, the attitude to anti-Zionism and anti-Semitism in Israeli society became a political-cultural code, highlighting the divide between left and right, and between religious and secular. Whenever an important new political issue comes up on the agenda, the political-cultural code surfaces, with one side of the fence claiming that "the whole world is against us" and the other, that "our actions will cause us to be either embraced or shunned." The attitude to the anti-Semitism/anti-Zionism issue in Israeli society does not stand alone but is part of an ideological basket, tagging one's political membership: for those on the right, anti-Semitism and hatred of the State of Israel are political navigators tabled on the agenda whenever the Israeli government takes a decision unacceptable to them. Therefore, in their eyes, the Oslo Accords are equivalent to Auschwitz and Arafat to Hitler. In the other camp, leftists will do all they can to minimize the importance of anti-Semitism and anti-Zionism, depicting them as phenomena contingent on the political context rather than immanent in relations between Israel and the non-Jewish world. This position is based on their conviction that the memory of the past should not be allowed to dictate the future. While the right portrays anti-Semitism as the root of anti-Zionism, the left chooses to put forward the contrary picture: anti-Zionism fans the flames of anti-Semitism in our generation.

The period of the 1930s and World War II still provides key elements in the West's world of images. Hence the questions as to whether the identification of our own times with the eve of World War II represents myth or reality, and whether today's anti-Semitism and anti-Zionism hint at the imminence of a new Shoah. Or maybe the two eras cannot be compared at all. These questions are topical and highly significant, and they have unmistakable political implications. On the face of it, the establishment of the State of Israel marked a quantum change in the situation of world Jewry: can the situation of the Jewish people in Europe of the 1930s even be likened to today's Israel in terms of power and freedom of action? But, on the other hand, the fact that the Holocaust did happen without prior warning places any future scenario, no matter how appalling, within the realm of the possible. The fact that millions of Muslims pray every day for the destruction of the state of the Jews is not a recipe for serenity in the Israeli psyche. The pendulum between existential anxiety and the dizziness of power are variations on a theme. The overriding majority of Israel's public is situated in the space between the two, having seemingly accepted hatred of Jews and hatred of the State of Israel as existing phenomena, attendant on their lives though not affecting daily considerations. Is this the repression of the ostrich or the wisdom of survivors?

Acknowledgments

I wish to thank Boaz Levtov, for his work as research assistant on this article.

Notes

[1] See Shapira, *Land and Power*, 55.
[2] See Avni and Shimoni, *Ha-tziyonut u-mitnagdeha.*
[3] Jabotinsky, "Al kir ha-barzel (anahnu veha-aravim)" (On the iron wall [we and the Arabs]), and "Ha-musar shel "kir ha-barzel"" (The morality of the "iron wall"], in *Ktavim,* 251–66.

[4] Harkabi, "Ha-antishemiyut ha-aravit."

[5] For more on this subject, see Shapira, *Land and Power*, 129–86.

[6] Reichert, "Medinat Yisrael veha-antishemiyut."

[7] A detailed account of this process in the Soviet Union can be found in Poliakov, *Me-anti-tziyonut le-antishemiyut*, in particular 46–87.

[8] See, for example, the story by Ida Fink, "Yulia," in idem, *Kol ha-Sipurim*, 275–76.

[9] See, for example, what Yariv Ben-Aharon had to say: "We believed we would be destroyed, if we did not win. The Holocaust bestowed or bequeathed this concept. It is a tangible concept for anyone who grew up in Israel, even if he/she did not live through the Holocaust but only heard or read about it." Shapira, ed., *Siah Lohamim*, 161; see also 167–68, 174–82.

[10] Wistrich, ed., *Ha-anti-tziyonut*, 13.

[11] Manor, "Ha-ma'avak," and *Alilat Dam*, 27–29.

[12] List, "He-hazit ha-anti-yisraelit."

[13] Ibid.

[14] Dan, "Yamin, smol, ve-hozer halilah."

[15] Ibid.

[16] "The war of the Arabs is understood by members of the New Left as a national liberation struggle, and they are not inclined to recognize Zionism as the liberation movement of the Jews." Lamm, "Ha-smol he-hadash."

[17] For more on New Left groups in Israel in the early 1970s and on other radical groups, see the series of articles by Nahum Barne'a, "Radikalizm mi-smol umi-yamin" (Radicalism on the left and right). *Dvar ha-Shavu'a*, 26 May 1972, and 2, 9 and 16 June 1972.

[18] Manor, *Alilat dam*, 36–89.

[19] Sprinzak, "Anti-tziyonut."

[20] Ibid.

[21] Wieseltier, "Antishemiyut ka-yom," 36–39.

[22] See, for example, "Begin la-eropa'im: Simu ketz le-antishmiyut" (Begin to the Europeans: Put an end to anti-Semitism), *Ma'ariv*, 26 October 1980.

[23] Wistrich, ed., *Ha-anti-tziyonut*, 17–18, 20–21.

[24] Ibid., 14.

[25] Ibid., 14–16.

[26] Cited in Preuss, "Yisrael be-itonut ha-olam."

[27] For examples of positions on the right, highlighting the connection of European attitudes to Israel and the days of Munich, 1938, see Arieh Tzimuki, "Ha-shavu'a ha-medini" (This week in politics), *Yedi'ot Aharonot*, 20 June 1980; Shmuel Shnitzer, "Patronei ha-teror" (Patrons of terror), *Ma'ariv* 17 January 1900; Shmuel Katz, "Zikhrono ha-katzar shel sar hutz leshe'avar" (The short memory of the former foreign minister), *Ma'ariv* 21 March 1980. See also Rabbi, "Sinat Yisrael le-doroteha," 156–61; Greenberg, "Utzmah yehudit," 14–19; Liebman, "Gishot klapei yehudim."

[28] Kreutner, "Lo levadad," 614–15.

[29] Hayim Hatzori, "Antishemiyut o bikoret obyektivit?" *Migvan*, no. 73 (September 1982): 69.

[30] Similar approaches can be found in Ya'akov Sharett, "Ksheha-olam kulo negdeinu" (When the whole world is against us), *Ma'ariv*, 25 March 1980; Hanoch Bartov, "Lahzor el ha-olam" (To return to the world), *Ma'ariv*, 27 June 1980.

[31] Preuss, "Yisrael be-itonut ha-olam."

[32] Bauer, *Ha-gal ha-antishemi*; Wistrich, *Ha-anti-tziyonut*.

[33] Wistrich, *Ha-anti-tzyionut*, 29–31.

[34] Herman and Farago, "Tguvot shel yehudim amerikai'im ve-yisraelim"; Farago and Levy, "Zehut yehudit."

[35] Levy, *Israeli Perceptions of Antisemitism*, 4–27.

[36] The above passage is based on Oron, Zelikovich, and Keren, *Musagim ve-amadot*, 18–60; see also Keren, Zelikovich, and Oron, *Antishemiyut ve-gizanut*, 31.

[37] Aharon Megged, "Dvarim she-ein ba-hem emet" (Words without truth]), *Ha'aretz*, 14 October 1988; A. B. Yehoshua, "Afelat ha-nefesh ha-kollektivit" (The dark side of the collective soul), *Ha'aretz*, 21 October 1988.

[38] Moshe Zimmerman, "Ha-miskenut lo mishtalemet" (Pitifulness doesn't pay), *Ha'aretz*, weekend supplement, 21 April 1989.

[39] Moshe Zimmerman, "Milkud ha-musar ha-kaful shel Yisrael" (The catch in Israel's double standards), *Ha'aretz*, 21 January 1990.

[40] For example, Ishay, "Ha-kesher ha-meshulash"; Wistrich, "Yudofobiyah islamit"; Kotek, "Motivim antishemiim"; Gerstenfeld, "Ha-demonizatziyah shel Yisrael"; Moti Zaft, "Antishemiyut be-masveh anti-tziyonut" (Anti-Semitism in the guise of anti-Zionism), *Ha-Tzofeh*, Passover Supplement, 5 April 1985; Dr. Manfred Rafael Lehman, "Mi-anti-yisraeliyut le-antishemiyut" (From anti-Israelism to anti-Semitism), *Ha-Tzofeh*, 29 June 1990.

[41] See, for example, Begin's address to the United Jewish Appeal mission, *Ma'ariv* 26 October 1980; also Tzimuki, "Ha-shavu'a ha-medini."

[42] Rubinstein, "Al ha-antishemiyut." In her work, Dina Porat has focused on studies monitoring anti-Semitism over the past decade—for example, "Ha'im Esav soneh le-Ya'akov"; Stauber, "Anti-tziyonut."

[43] David Landau's interview with Yitzhak Shamir, *Jerusalem Post*, 8 September 1989. Dan Margalit, "Antishemiyut ke-ma'avak shuli" (Anti-Semitism as a marginalized struggle), *Ha'aretz*, 11 September 1989.

[44] Yoram Peri, "Yofi, yesh antishemiyut" (Great! There's anti-Semitism), *Davar*, 11 January 1990.

[45] Peri, "Mi-ben yakir le-ven horeg."

[46] Shevah Weiss, "Yisrael al shulhan ha-nituhim" (Israel on the operating table), *Al Ha-Mishmar*, 27 December 1990.

[47] Shevah Weiss, "antiyisraeliyut antishemit" (Anti-Semitic anti-Israelism), *Ha'aretz*, 23 May 1988.

[48] Gideon Samet, "Oy, kamah she-sonim otanu" (Oy, how they hate us), *Ha'aretz*, 25 March 1992.

[49] Hannah Zemer, "Kamah tov she-yesh antishemiyut" (What a good thing there's anti-Semitism), *Davar*, 27 March 1992.

[50] Elyakim Rubinstein, "Ha-shed ha-antishemi kayam" (The anti-Semitic demon lives on), *Ha'aretz*, 5 April 1992.

[51] David Pedhazur, "Mi zakuk le-antishemiyut?" (Who needs anti-Semitism?), *Davar*, 1 May 1992.

[52] Samet, "Oy, kamah she-sonim otanu."

[53] Rubinstein, "Al ha-antishemiyut."

[54] Sivan, "Antishemiyut ve-fundamentalizm muslemi."

References

Avni, Haim, and Gideon Shimoni. *Ha-tziyonut u-mitnagdeha ba-am ha-yehudi* (Zionism and its opponents from within the Jewish People). Jerusalem: Ha-Sifriyah ha-Tziyonit, 1990.

Bauer, Yehuda. *Ha-gal ha-antishemi ba-olam shel yameinu: Mitos u-metzi'ut* (Anti-Semitism today: Myth and reality). Jerusalem: Sifriyat Shazar and the Institute for Contemporary Jewry, Hebrew University of Jerusalem, 1985.

Dan, Joseph. "Yamin, smol, ve-hozer halilah" (Right, left and back again)." *Molad*, n.s., 1, nos. 5–6 (April–May 1968): 584–89.

Farago, Uri, and Shlomit Levy. "Zehut yehudit ve-amadot klapei antishemiyut be-kerev mevugarim ve-no'ar be-Yisrael" (Jewish identity and attitudes towards anti-Semitism among adults and youth in Israel). *Iyunim be-Hinukh*, n.s., 1, no. 2 (1996): 181–200.

Fink, Ida. *Kol ha-sipurim* (All the stories). Tel Aviv: Am Oved, 2004.

Gerstenfeld, Manfred. "Ha-demonizatziyah shel Yisrael be-arav uva-ma'arav" (The demonization of Israel in Arab lands and the West). *Ha-Umah* 40, no. 150 (Winter 2002): 48–59.

Greenberg, Yitzhak. "Utzmah yehudit ke-arubah mipnei antishemiyut" (Jewish power as a guarantee against anti-Semitism). *Gesher* 29, no. 108 (1983): 14–19.

Harkabi, Yehoshafat. "Ha-antishemiyut ha-aravit" (Arab anti-Semitism). In *Ha-kayam veha-mishtaneh ba-antishemiyut be-dorenu* (The extant and the changing in contemporary anti-Semitism), edited by Shmuel Ettinger. Jerusalem: The President's Forum on Diaspora Jewry, 1968.

Herman, Simon N., and Uri Farago. "Teguvot shel yehudim amerikai'im ve-yisraelim le-antishemiyut: Skirah hashva'atit" (Reactions of American and Israeli Jews to anti-Semitism: A comparative survey). *Kivunim* 4, no. 41 (April 1993): 111–43.

Ishay, Ran. "Ha-kesher ha-meshulash: Eiropah, de-legitimatziyah shel Yisrael ve-post-tziyonut" (The triple connection: Europe, delegitimization of Israel and post-Zionism). *Nativ* 15, no. 4–5 (2002): 54–62.

Jabotinsky, Ze'ev. *Ktavim, ba-derekh li-medinah* (Writings, on the road to statehood). Jerusalem: Ari Jabotinsky, 1953.

Keren, Nili, Gila Zelikovich, and Yair Oron. *Antishemiyut ve-gizanut: Heker amadot be-kerev talmidei batei-sefer tikhoniim be-Yisrael* (Anti-Semitism and racism: An investigation of the attitudes of high school pupils in Israel). Tel Aviv: Kibbutz Teachers Seminar, 1997.

Kotek, Joel. "Motivim antishemiim ba-ta'amulah ha-anti-yisraelit be-Belgiyah" (Anti-Semitic motifs in anti-Israeli propaganda in Belgium). *Nativ* 16, no. 6 (2003): 53–57.

Kreutner, S. "Lo levadad ve-lo ha-kol negdeinu" (Neither alone nor all against us). *Tmurot* (October 1981): 614–15.

Lamm, Zvi. "Ha-smol he-hadash veha-zehut ha-yehudit" (The New Left and Jewish identity). *Molad*, n.s., 2, no. (25), 10 (June 1969): 415–23.

Levy, Shlomit. *Israeli Perceptions of Antisemitism*. Jerusalem: The Vidal Sassoon International Center for the Study of Antisemitism, 1996.

Liebman, Yeshayahu. "Gishot klapei yehudim-goyim ba-masoret ha-yehudit uve-Yisrael ha-yom" (Attitudes towards Jews-Gentiles in Jewish tradition and Israel today). *Kivunim*, no. 25 (1984): 7–18.

List, Nahman. "He-hazit ha-anti-Yisraelit veha-mahaneh ha-komunisti" (The anti-Israel front and the communist camp) *Molad* 22 (November–December 1964): 380–5.

Manor, Yohanan. "Ha-ma'avak neged hagdarat ha-tziyonut ke-gizanut" (The struggle against defining Zionism as racism). *Skirah Hodshit* 32, no. 11–12 (1985): 57–65.

———. *Alilat Dam* (Blood libel). Jerusalem: Ha-Sifriyah ha-Tziyonit, 1998.

Oron, Yair, Gila Zelikovich, and Nili Keren. *Musagim ve-amadot shel pirkhei hora'ah be-Yisrael be-yahas le-antishemiyut ve-gizanut: Duah mehkar* (Concepts and attitudes of student teachers in Israel regarding anti-Semitism and racism: Research report). Tel Aviv: Kibbutz Teachers Seminar, 1996.

Peri, Yoram. "Mi-ben yakir le-ven horeg" (From beloved son to stepson). *Migvan* 63 (September 1981): 62–67, and 64 (November 1981): 47–51.

Poliakov, Léon. *Me-antitziyonut le-antishemiyut* (From anti-Zionism to anti-Semitism). Tel Aviv: Sifriyat Po'alim, 1970.

Porat, Dina. "Ha'im Esav soneh le-Ya'akov ve-lamah? Ha-antishemiyut ha-hadashah u-me'afyeneha" (Is Esau Jacob's enemy and why? The new anti-Semitism and its characteristics). *Gesher* 48, no. 145 (Summer 2001): 7–16.

Preuss, Teddy. "Yisrael be-itonut ha-olam: Panim me'uvatim ba-marah" (Israel in the world press: A distorted face in the mirror). *Sefer ha-Shanah shel ha-Itona'im* (Journalists' Yearbook). Tel Aviv 1983.

Rabbi, Ya'akov. "Sinat Yisrael le-doroteha, ha-kavu'a veha-mishtaneh (bikoret)" (Anti-Semitism over the ages, the permanent and the changing [review]). *Gesher* 26, nos. 102–103 (1980): 156–61.

Reichert, A. "Medinat Yisrael veha-antishemiyut" (The State of Israel and anti-Semitism). *Molad* 1, no. 2–3 (May–June 1948): 108–12.

Rubinstein, Elyakim. "Al ha-antishemiyut: Mekomah ve-tafkidah shel Yisrael ba-milhamah ba-antishemiyut" (On anti-Semitism: Israel's place and role in the war on anti-Semitism). *Massuah* 31 (2003): 55–66.

Shapira, Anita. *Land and Power: The Zionist Resort to Force.* New York: Oxford University Press, 1992.

Shapira, Avraham, ed. *Siah Lohamim* (Soldier's talk). Tel Aviv: Group of Young Members of the Kibbutz Movement, 1967. Published in English as *The Seventh Day: Soldiers' Talk about the Six-Day War.* Harmondsworth: Penguin, 1971.

Sivan, Emmanuel. "Antishemiyut ve-fundamentalizm muslemi" (Anti-Semitism and Muslim fundamentalism). *Kivunim* 4, no. 41 (April 1993): 29–34.

Sprinzak, Ehud. "Anti-tziyonut: Mi-deligitimatziyah le-dehumanizatziyah." (Anti-Zionism: From delegitimization to dehumanization). *Kivunim* 25 (November 1984): 43–54.

Stauber, Roni. "Anti-tziyonut ke-bitui le-sinat ha-yehudim le'ahar ha-sho'ah" (Anti-Zionism as an expression of anti-Semitism after the Holocaust). *Massuah* 31 (2003): 37–54.

Wieseltier, Leon. "Antishemiyut kayom" (Anti-Semitism today). *Bi-Tfutzot ha-Golah* 21, no. 1 (1993): 36–9.

Wistrich, Robert. *Ha-anti-tziyonut ke-bitui le-antishemiyut ba-et ha-aharonah* (Anti-Zionism as an expression of anti-Semitism in recent years). Jerusalem: Sifriyat Shazar and the Institute for Contemporary Jewry, Hebrew University of Jerusalem, 1985.

———. "Yudofobiyah islamit: Iyum kiyumi" (Islamic Judeophobia: An existential threat). *Nativ* 15, nos. 4–5 (2002): 49–85.

The Islamic Republic of Iran and the Holocaust: Anti-Semitism and Anti-Zionism

Meir Litvak

The Ideological Basis of Anti-Judaism and Anti-Zionism

Iran espouses the most radical anti-Israeli or anti-Zionist position in the Muslim Middle East, which is epitomized in the depiction of Israel as the "Little Satan," as a "cancerous tumor" that has to be removed, and in the official slogan that "Israel must be wiped out" (*Isra'il bayad mahw shavad*). The essence of this enmity is religious as Iran does not share a common border with Israel and the two states do not have conflicting strategic or economic interests.[1] Moreover, during most of the period of Mohammad Reza Shah's reign (1941–79), the two countries were close economic and strategic allies. Anti-Zionism has become an important pillar of Iranian revolutionary ideology, which encompasses other revolutionary goals: hostility to the West, opposition to the Shah and basic enmity to the Jewish state.[2]

Anti-Zionism has been one of the few areas where the Iranian regime has remained true to its revolutionary program and has not bowed to pragmatic considerations. One could even argue that demonstrating enmity towards Zionism and Israel served in many ways as a fig leaf compensating for the many compromises that it was forced to make in other areas. It is also a unique subject on which there is almost total unanimity among all the factions within the Iranian clergy, which is divided on most other issues.[3]

The link between these anti-Jewish and anti-Zionist positions is evident in Iran's advocacy and sponsorship of Holocaust denial and its alliance with notorious Holocaust deniers in the West, who are both blatant anti-Semites and anti-Zionists. In its effort to delegitimize Zionism and present it as based on lie and deceit, Iran chooses to focus on the most salient and tragic event in modern Jewish history, which was not directly related either to Zionism or to Iranian-Israeli relations. The source and motivation of this enmity is indigenous, stemming from religious and nationalist sentiment, while the arguments are borrowed from Western sources, producing a symbiosis between European and Middle Eastern anti-Semitism and anti-Zionism, as well as between traditional and modern motifs. While the Islamic regime in Iran usually rejects Western cultural influence as anathema to authentic Islamic culture, it has not hesitated to borrow anti-Zionist and anti-Jewish themes from the same West in the service of its causes.

Iranian Holocaust denial is aimed not only at the Iranian public but also at Western constituencies, as evident in the leading role played in this effort by the two English-language newspapers in Iran, *Tehran Times* and *Kayhan International*, which address a foreign audience in Iran and the West. Iran, like Holocaust deniers in the Arab world, apparently believes that the memory of the Holocaust was the foundation of Western support for the establishment of Israel. Therefore, refuting it would severely undermine Israel's legitimacy in the West and help in its eradication.[4]

Iran's anti-Zionism emanates from two central foundations in the teachings of all Islamist movements in the Middle East, which combine both traditional Islamic elements with modern nationalist and Third Worldist concepts. The first views Zionism as the culmination of a Judeo-Western political and cultural onslaught on the Muslim world, which is the root source of the latter's deep crisis, weakness and malaise in the modern era. The second is the revival of traditional anti-Jewish attitudes in Islamic culture and history, which regard the Jews as basically hostile to Islam since its inception. These traditions regard the Jews not as a people but as a dispersed religious community destined to subordination and subjugation by the Muslims ever since they rejected the message of the Prophet Muhammad. Both elements occupy central stage in the teachings of Ayatollah Ruhallah Khomeini, the ideological founder and leader of the Islamic Republic of Iran, and have guided the Iranian government ever since the 1979 revolution.

Iran's anti-Zionism is rooted in the deep animosity towards the Jews in the teaching of traditional Shi'ism. The reason for this enmity could not have been economic as the Jews were a small and poor community that did not play any significant role in Iran's economy or society and did not compete with any social group. One possible reason for this intolerance, which was occasionally directed against heterodox Islamic sects in Iran, was the Shiʿis" sense of insecurity in the light of their own fate as a persecuted minority in the more distant past. Conversely, the majority school of Sunni Islam could afford to be more generous towards minorities, although this tolerance also subsided from the late nineteenth century with the growing sense of threat to Islam. The survival in Shiʿism of radical pre-Islamic Zoroastrian concepts of ritual purity, which distinguished the true believers from infidels, was also a contributory factor.[5]

Consequently, ever since Iran became a Shiʿi state in 1501 it had adopted the most oppressive policy towards the Jews compared with any other Sunni state (with the exception of the twelfth-century Muwahiddun dynasty in Morocco). Unlike the Sunnis, who enabled minorities to keep their religions, numerous Jewish communities in Iran were forced to convert to Islam, and some were physically eliminated during the seventeenth century, and even as late as the nineteenth century. As such they suffered far more than the Christian minority, which was economically more important.[6]

Anti-Zionism and anti-Semitism were not confined to clerical circles. Radical nationalists, who emphasized Iran's Aryan origins, also adopted anti-Jewish views during the 1920s and 1940s. To name but two of the most prominent examples, Jalal Al-e Ahmad, one of the leading writers in Iran, who had written favorably of Israel after visiting it in 1962, later adopted a strong anti-Zionist view as part of his return to religion; and Dr. ʿAli Shariʿati, the ideologue of revolutionary Shiʿi Islam, used strong anti-Jewish pejoratives in his own writings during the late 1960s. Conceivably, part of this animosity was aimed against the Shah's ties with Israel.[7]

It was Ayatollah Ruhallah Khomeini, founder and leader of the Islamic Republic, however, who made anti-Semitism a central component of Iran's Islamic ideology. Already in the first page of his major book, *Velayat-e Faqih: Hukumat-e Eslami* (The governance of the jurist: Islamic government), Khomeini charged that "from the very beginning" Islam "was afflicted by the Jews, for it was they who established anti-Islamic propaganda and engaged in various stratagems" against the Muslims. As proof of the wickedness of the Jews, Khomeini often quoted passages from the Qur'an describing the Jews as immersed in sin and as being constantly reprimanded by God for their evil doings. Following their ancestors during the Prophet's time, the Jews and Christians, according to Khomeini, conspired against Islam in the modern period as well, seeking to undermine the most important feature of Islam as a comprehensive and total system of law that governs society and state. In order to achieve their objective, the Jews joined hands with other groups that were "more satanic than they" in order to facilitate the imperialist penetration of the Muslim countries. Their main goal was the "extirpation of Islam" in addition to sowing doubt and confusion in the hearts of Muslims, since "Islam and its ordinances" were the "main obstacle in the path of their materialistic ambitions." In addition, the West, consisting of Jewish and Christian elements, resists the righteous cause of Islam to expand to the "four corners of the globe."[8] The Jews, "may God curse them," Khomeini adds, "are opposed to the very foundations of Islam and wish to establish Jewish domination throughout the world." They "meddle with the text of the Qur'an" and disseminate false translations that distort its meaning in order to slander Islam. Like other Islamic thinkers,

Khomeini sometimes describes the Jews as fifth columnists in the world of Islam and as agents of the West, and at other times as the real power that stands behind the West in its offensive against Islam.[9]

Linking Judaism and Zionism, Khomeini maintained that the most overt manifestation of the Jewish-Christian conspiracy against Islam was the establishment of Israel by Western imperialism in order to oppress the Muslims. Both Khomeini and his successor as supreme leader, Ayatollah ʿAli Khameneʾi, stated that "the occupation of Palestine [by the Jews] is part of a satanic design by the world domineering powers, perpetrated by the British in the past and being carried out today by the United States, to weaken the solidarity of the Islamic world and to sow the seeds of disunity among Muslims."[10]

Khomeini depicted the success of Zionism as a direct consequence of the crisis of Islam in the modern era, as a sort of punishment for the abandonment of religion. If the rulers of the Muslim countries truly represented the believers and enacted God's ordinances, he said, then "a handful of wretched Jews (the agents of America, Britain and other foreign powers) would never have been able to accomplish what they have."[11] In other words, Khomeini made a direct link between Zionism and the processes of secularization and cultural Westernization taking place in Iran and the Muslim world during the modern age, which threatened the foundations of Islam and subjugated it to imperialism. Since secularization is the greatest threat to Muslim societies, Zionism was directly responsible for the greatest predicament that had befallen Islam and the Muslims in the modern age.[12] Khomeini identified any harm done to Islam as serving the Jews. Israel's hostility to Islam and the Muslims was not confined to Palestine but extended to the entire Muslim world. Going further, he portrayed Israel and Zionism as the enemies not only of Islam but also of humanity in its entirety.[13]

The Shah's close ties with the United States and Israel served Khomeini's case against the Jews and made it easier for him to attack the Shah's own policies. Khomeini presented the Shah's political struggle with the clergy and his secularization policies as part of the Zionist-Western campaign against Iran. Following the June 1963 mass protests against the Shah's White Revolution, he stated that henceforth "Jews, Christians and the enemies of Islam and the Muslims are to decide on affairs concerning the honor and person of the Muslims." He attributed the government suppression of the 1963 protests to Israeli plots. "Israel does not wish the Qurʾan to exist in this country," he charged. "It wishes to seize your economy, to destroy your trade and agriculture, to appropriate your wealth."[14]

Zionism is regarded as even more detrimental to the Muslims than ordinary Western colonialism because of the widespread Islamist perception, shared by Khomeini, that the Jews were not a people at all, but a religious community that had no right to statehood. Moreover, the Jews were seen as being condemned to eternal humiliation and subordination to Muslims ever since they had rejected the message of the Prophet Mohammad. The Zionist challenge to the correct historical order, which assigns the Jews to an inferior position, is exacerbated since it has taken place in the very heart of the lands of Islam and deprives the Muslim people of Palestine, who had lived there since the time of the Biblical patriarch Jacob, of its rights to its land. It has culminated in the capture and Jewish domination of the third holiest place for Islam, Jerusalem and the al-Aqsa Mosque.[15] Therefore, the Jews' very claim to statehood is sinister and depraved by its very nature, as well as an affront to Islam and to the natural historical order, and whoever advances this claim must be corrupt and evil. Hence, Khamene'i's charge against Israel fuses anti-Zionism with animosity towards the Jews:

> What are you? A forged government and a false nation. They gathered wicked people from all over the world and made something called the Israeli nation. Is that a nation? All the malevolent and evil Jews have gathered there. ... Those [Jews] who went to Israel were malevolent, evil, greedy thieves and murderers.[16]

Enmity towards Israel was linked to an important element of Shiᶜism, which Khomeini highlighted—that is, the duty of each believer to take an active part in the struggle against injustice. Passivity in the face of grave injustice makes the believer an accessory to it. No arena is more crucial in this context than the defense of Muslim Jerusalem. The cultivation of the spirit of self-sacrifice in modern Shiᶜism added another dimension to the call for an all-out war against Israel. The struggle against Israel was portrayed as an important justification for the Iranian revolution itself. Consequently, Khomeini elevated Jerusalem to a much more important position in modern Shiᶜi discourse than it had ever had in the past. Seeking also to appeal to the Sunni and particularly Arab masses, Iran dedicates the last Friday of the holy month of Ramadan as Qods (Jerusalem) Day to express its support for the Palestinian struggle.[17]

Khomeini did not mince words about the desired fate of the Jews as enemies of Islam. Pointing to the "most noble messenger" as his model, he reminds his readers that when the Jewish tribe of Banu Qurayza, who "were a troublesome group," caused "corruption among the Muslims," the Prophet "eliminated them."[18] After assuming power in 1979, however, the Iranian leaders sought to render their anti-Jewish animosity more presentable. In addition, as jurists they may have wanted to portray Iran as a model for the conduct of Islamic states towards religious minorities. Consequently, leaders and spokesmen of the Islamic regime claimed to make a distinction between Zionists, whom they vehemently opposed, and Jews, who should be treated with tolerance, since, in Khomeini's words, "Zionism has nothing to do with religion."[19] Thus support for Israel and Zionism became a crime punishable by death, and the Islamic revolutionary courts sentenced several Jewish communal leaders to death on grounds of Zionism and connections with Israel. Concurrently, the Islamic constitution allocated one seat in parliament to a representative of the Jewish community, who also joined the anti-Zionist chorus.[20]

The most eloquent spokesman for this distinction between anti-Semitism and anti-Zionism, particularly in his statements to the foreign media, was the mildly reformist President (since 1997) Mohammad Khatami. He insisted that while "the East" had had "despotism and dictatorship," it had never had fascism or Nazism, which were purely "western phenomena," and for which the "West has paid dearly." He expressed his concern, however, that "this western anti-Semitism and anti-Jewishness might turn into a tool for the imposition of a whole range of wrong policies and practices"—that is, Zionism—on the people of the Middle East and Muslims in general. Yet, even he mentioned "greedy elements" that had reached the United States, probably alluding to the Jews.[21]

In reality, however, expressions of anti-Jewish sentiments continued to abound in the Iranian media and in pronouncements of senior government and clerical officials, and the terms "Jews" and "Zionists" were used interchangeably. Thus Ayatollah Emami Kashani, member of the powerful Council of Guardians, created a direct link between present-day Israeli policies and "Jewish atrocities" against the Muslims carried out since the first century of Islam.[22] Likewise, Grand Ayatollah Nuri-Hamadani referred to Jewish enmity towards Islam from its inception, going on to say that "at present the Jews' policies threaten us. One should explain in the clearest terms the danger the Jews pose to the [Iranian] people and to the Muslims." More importantly, he insisted that it was necessary to "fight the Jews and vanquish them so that the conditions for the advent of the Hidden Imam [i.e. the Shi' messiah] be met." In other words, he infused a messianic element into the struggle against the Jews and possible even hinged the redemption of the Muslims or even of the whole world upon their defeat. Interestingly, he referred to the Jews of Medina at the time of the Prophet as "the center of Zionists"— that is, he emphasized the historical continuity between past Jewish communities and present-day Zionists and, one is almost tempted to say, adopted the Zionist argument of the unity of Jewish history. He further explained that the execution of seven hundred of the Jews of Medina in a single day was a "step toward strengthening Islam, in order to crush the bastion of the global arrogance, and ... to eradicate this cancerous tumor," again linking the Jews then with present-day imperialism ["global arrogance" in Iranian terminology] and Israel.[23] In addition, Israel was occasionally referred to as "the Jewish entity" or as a "bunch of Jews," or the "Jewish nation,"[24] while at other times Jews in the diaspora were referred to as Zionists. To cite one example, the Iranian media used to emphasize the Jewish identity of US officials, such as Deputy Secretary of Defense Paul Wolfowitz, in order to explain their policies in the Middle East.[25]

A major manifestation of the highly blurred distinction between anti-Semitism and anti-Zionism was the serial publication of the notorious anti-Semitic tract, the *Protocols of the Elders of Zion*, in more than 150 installments by the establishment newspapers *Ettela ʿat* and *Jomhuri-ye Eslami*.[26] In 2000, the Iranian government published a special edition of the *Protocols* whose introduction was designed to show "the Zionist ... inveterate rancor against Islam and Muslims," as well as their "boundless passion for usurpation and hegemony."[27] In April 2004 the Iranian TV station al-ʿAlam aired a documentary titled *Al-sameri wa al-saher* (The golden calf and the tempter), which purported to explain how the Jews control Hollywood by the directives set out in the *Protocols*. Thus it explained that the movie *Yentl*, which Barbra Streisand starred in and also produced in 1983, "dealt with the Zionists' wish to benefit from feminism, the new women's movement."[28]

All Iranian officials and media expressed their conviction and belief that Israel is a "cancerous tumor" or "a calamity imposed by the West on the region" and "a germ which has infected the entire Middle East region with a disease that cannot be cured except by a surgical operation and by removing the germ from the region's body." Therefore, it should and would be "destroyed and shattered." According to Supreme Leader Khamene'i the only way to resolve the Middle East crisis was to destroy "the Zionist regime," the "root and cause of the crisis." Moreover, Khamene'i posited Iran's "honor, strength, unity and national interest" as depending on its standing up to the "cancerous tumor of the Zionist regime," thereby elevating the enmity towards Zionism from pure ideology to a question of national interest for Iran and an existential issue for the Islamic revolution itself. Other officials followed suit.[29]

Finally, ostensibly less hostile statements by Iranian leaders that they do not seek to "throw the Jews into the sea," but merely seek to replace Zionism with a more benign state and system of government in which Muslims, Christians and Jews could live in peace, are misleading. Such statements are a euphemism for the abolition of the State of Israel and its replacement by an Islamic system, in which Jews are deprived of their right to self-determination and are relegated at best to the status of *dhimmi*, a protected but subordinated minority under Islamic rule.[30]

Iran and the Holocaust

As part of its anti-Zionist and anti-Jewish rhetoric, Iran became a major supporter and disseminator of Holocaust denial in the Muslim world. In general it can be said that the representation of the Holocaust has become a major criterion in the examination of attitudes towards the Jews in general, and towards Israel in particular. Consequently, the greater the recognition and importance that the Holocaust acquired in Western cultural and political discourse and in Israeli collective identity, the greater was the urge among Arab and other Muslim writers to deny it.

It should be remembered that World War II is not perceived in Arab and Muslim collective memory as a war between good and absolute evil. Rather, they view it as a war in which they had no direct interest, while they had to bear the brunt of its aftermath and pay a price with the displacement of the Palestinians. The immediate context of the Holocaust for Middle Easterners has been the establishment of the State of Israel in the midst of the Arab world and its efforts to gain legitimacy. For many Arabs the Jews were the real victors of World War II. Zionism is perceived as cynically using the Holocaust, and even inventing it as a means of financial and psychological extortion, in order to create and cultivate a sense of guilt in the West. Concurrently, various Arab circles have used Nazi symbols, terminology and ideology to project them on Zionism and Israel, thus transforming victims into culprits.[31]

While Iran hosts and sponsors Western Holocaust deniers, there are some important differences between the two parties. Holocaust deniers in the West usually belong to the extreme right and represent marginal political forces. They are often racists who detest Jews as well as other foreign ethnic groups, including Muslim immigrants. In Iran, on the other hand, the senior state leaders, headed by Supreme Leader Khamene'i, have taken part in denial, and the state media were mobilized to take part in the campaign as well. Consequently, as an official government position in a non-democratic state, denial is not challenged and the Iranian public is not exposed to the more historically valid Western academic and public discourse of the Holocaust.

Deniers in the West seek to redeem the reputation of Nazism or of Hitler personally and rehabilitate the past as part of the current political battles in their countries. By contrast, Iranian Holocaust denial is not interested in Nazism per se, and its main focus is the attack on Zionism and Israel. Moreover, the deniers in Iran regard themselves explicitly as anti-Nazi; they denounce Nazism as blatant racism and as an evil regime that committed war crimes. The common enmity to Jews and to Israel enables both groups, the Western neo-Nazis and the Iranian Islamists, to gloss over the differences between them. For the Iranians it means ignoring the racist views of Western Holocaust deniers and of the radical European right. Like the European deniers, the Iranian deniers tend to relativize the Holocaust and argue for the moral equivalency between the crimes of the Nazis and those of the Allies.[32]

Themes of Denial

The "big lies" and the "Holocaust myth" are but two of the terms used by Iranian spokesmen to describe the Holocaust. The most common theme that serves the political goal behind Iranian denial is the one voiced during a solidarity conference with the Palestinian struggle held in April 2001 by Supreme Leader Khamene'i himself—that the "Zionists had exaggerated Nazi crimes against European Jewry in order to solicit international support for the establishment of the Zionist entity in 1948." There is even evidence, he added, that a "large number of non-Jewish hooligans and thugs of Eastern Europe were forced to migrate to Palestine as Jews," as part of this conspiracy.[33]

The Iranian press attributed the "Holocaust myth" to a Zionist-American alliance which exploited the common goal of struggle against the Nazis that formed during the war for the malevolent political goals of each party. The false slogan of the murder of millions of Jews in Europe by Nazi Germany was a "ridiculous pretext through which the Zionists, by fabricating and propagating it, managed to convince public opinion of the need to establish a Jewish state" in the midst of Muslim lands. The Zionists used this "myth" in order to fight anti-Zionism, which was rife throughout Europe before the war, seeking to "make the Jews look oppressed so they could achieve their murderous goals in other parts of the world." Concurrently, the United States used it as a means for expanding its influence as a superpower "searching for colonies in the world and in Europe."[34] The instrumentalist use of Holocaust denial to undermine Zionism is evident in an interview with the German-Australian Holocaust denier Fredrick Toben published by the official Iranian news agency MEHR on 29 December 2004, in which he claimed that "the state of Israel is founded on the 'Holocaust' lie" and that "exposing this lie" would help "dismantle the Zionist entity."[35]

Citing spurious statistics provided by neo-Nazi organizations and personalities, *Kayhan*, which is published by the office of the Supreme Leader, contended that the number of Jews declined from 15,600,000 prior to the war to 15,000,000 at its end, claiming thereby the fallacy of the Holocaust. Millions of Europeans "white and black and from different races and religions" died during the war, and it was natural that some Jews died among them as well, it conceded, but the claim that Hitler aimed at killing the Jews as a policy was completely "baseless" and the "Jews" most shameful propaganda lie."[36]

Like their Western mentors, the Iranian Holocaust deniers focus their attention on refuting the existence of the gas chambers in order both to shatter the symbol of the Holocaust and to grant their arguments pseudo-academic validity. The most prominent example was a seven-part series named interchangeably "the Auschwitz Lie" and the "Auschwitz conspiracy," published in the English-language daily *Tehran Times*, which relied heavily on the writings of Western Holocaust deniers such as David Irving, Robert Faurisson and Ernst Zündel, who are often described in the Iranian media as "famous historians" or serious scholars.

Tehran Times conceded that as a "concentration camp" Auschwitz was "a place of terrible human suffering" and that around 150,000 prisoners from "all nationalities" died there mostly from diseases, "insufficient nourishment and overworking." However, it highlighted the reduction of the numbers of estimated victims by credible historians from 4,000,000 to around 1,200,000 as refuting Auschwitz's role as an extermination camp for the Jews. Had it been so, it charged, "virtually no Jew would have survived, yet, the memoirs of former Auschwitz inmates "fill whole libraries." "Professional survivors," such as the "arch-liar" Elie Wiesel, who present themselves as witnesses of the "Holocaust," are a living proof that the alleged extermination of the Jews did not take place. *Tehran Times* castigated the survivors who testified in war trials as "Jewish swindlers" and "liars," who "could travel from one trial and from one press conference to the other without fear of exposure." Ironically, two of the persons it mentioned, Philip Mueller and Rudolf Verba, were not Zionists at all, pointing to the ignorance or anti-Jewish sentiment of the *Tehran Times* writers, who do not distinguish between the two groups. Concurrently, it rejected the confessions of the Auschwitz commandant Rudolf Höss that enumerated his deeds, by claiming that he was "tortured for three days by his Jewish and British interrogators before signing the statement his tormentors had prepared for him."[37]

Following the footsteps of the leading French Holocaust denier Robert Faurisson, *Tehran Times* manipulated some genuine historical facts to falsify historical reality. It cited the fate of Anne Frank's family, where the two sisters died of starvation and exhaustion in Bergen-Belsen while their father survived, to claim that there was no Nazi "extermination policy." At most, it was willing to acknowledge that Jews were "heavily persecuted and large numbers of them perished because of the bad conditions in the camps." Likewise, the story of Israeli Holocaust historian Yisrael Gutman, who "survived Auschwitz, Majdnek, Mauthausen and Gunkirchen," served *Tehran Times* to show that many Jews were transferred from one camp to another "without ever risking murder."[38]

The Iranian media was particularly annoyed at the Zionist "blackmail of the west" based on "one of the biggest frauds of the outgoing century," which resulted in payments of "huge amounts of money in reparations to the Zionist entity and the relatives of those claimed to have perished in the Nazi gas chambers."[39] Such "baseless claims," *Kayhan International* commented, "had held the German nation hostage for the past 50 years." Many Germans, it reported elsewhere, felt "highly disgusted, rather frustrated, to be forced to carry on the burden of guilt and shame for the so-called Nazi war crimes," as the "nightmare of holocaust [*sic*] is not allowed to end by the Americans." Concurrently, *Tehran Times* complained that while Germany "continues to pay billions of Marks as compensation to the Jews every year" for a crime the paper denied on other occasions, it had evaded the moral duty to compensate the Iranian victims of German-produced Iraqi chemical weapons.[40]

Presumably influenced by the Arab Holocaust discourse, Iranians often employ contradictory arguments relating to the Holocaust, particularly denial and the accusation hurled at Zionism of collaborating with the Nazis in killing Jews. Then Majlis (Parliament) Speaker Mehdi Karrubi, often regarded as a moderate reformist in Iranian domestic politics, stated at an anti-Zionist rally in October 2000 that "Hitler's massacre of innocent Jews in Germany was a conspiracy of the Zionists." "The first premier and the founder of the regime, which occupied Palestine," he added, was himself involved in these activities as he handed over 40,000 Jews to Hitler in order to carry out that plan. *Tehran Times* went into greater details, citing what it claimed to be historical evidence proving collaboration between "the Nazi regime and the Zionist lobby in purging the Jews who were considered insignificant." Some "poor non-Zionist Jews were sacrificed for the hideous goal of the Zionists, the establishment of a Jewish state," it went on, and therefore the "massacre of Jews in Germany and German occupied territories was only limited to the working class and it never affected the elite Jewish capitalists or the Zionists." On 29 December 2004, the official news agency MEHR published a review of the movie *Exodus* by Mojtaba Habibi, in which he accused the Jews of collaboration with the Nazis and of orchestrating a grand scheme of world domination together with Joseph Stalin.[41]

The TV documentary *Al-sameri wa al-saher* mentioned above claimed that "the most important film" produced in Hollywood "under Zionist guidance" in the 1960s was called *Operation Eichmann*, which "completed the false myth about the murder of six million Jews at the hands of the Nazis." Yet, it went on, the film producers failed to mention Adolf Eichmann's own testimony, in which he allegedly explained that he "was only carrying out the orders of the Zionists." "If I am guilty of the so-called killing of 6 million Jews," the fictitious Eichmann supposedly said, "then the Zionist leaders are much guiltier than I am. This is because they wanted to silence the world under the pretext that if they had stayed in Germany they would have been killed, and since they did not have a country they were forced to occupy other people's land. And that is what they did." Following similar allegations of such collaboration put forward by some Arab writers, the documentary claimed that "the Zionist authorities finished the trial quickly to avoid further commotion and hanged Eichmann in 1962 so the secrets of the collaboration between the Zionists and the Nazis would remain hidden."[42]

The instrumentalist usage of Iranian Holocaust denial as a means of delegitimizing Israel was also evident in the frequent comparisons by Iranian official spokesmen and media between Zionism and Nazism, and between the "Gestapo-like" policies of Israel and those of Hitler. While vilifying Israel, such comparisons served to belittle the scope of Nazi crimes and atrocities.[43] Thus, in his sermon on Qods (Jerusalem) day on 23 January 1998, ᶜAli Akbar Rafsanjani, the number-two man in the Iranian hierarchy, denounced Israel as "much worse than Hitler," stating that the fact that the Zionists "killed more than one million Palestinians and made millions vagrant is much worse than what Adolph Hitler did during World War II with the Jews." Priding himself as being "an expert in this field," Rafsanjani calculated that the number of Jews in Europe prior to World War II had been less than six million. He conceded that Hitler had "committed injustice against the Jews and other groups," and that he had "oppressed and persecuted Muslims, Christians, atheists [and] Marxists," but insisted that he had killed only 200,000 Jews. The figure of six million Jewish victims was therefore "only a propaganda act by the Zionists." Rafsanjani also equated Zionist ideology, which considered the Jews "to be a unique and superior race," with "Hitler's identical belief regarding the German nation' and stated that two Nazi and racist currents were pitted against each other."[44]

Likewise, the English-language *Iran Daily*, commenting on the 2001 Holocaust Memorial Day in Israel, condemned the "Zionist propaganda-mill," that "bombards the world with an unceasing and unrelenting stream of messages aimed at "perpetuating the holocaust memory in the collective consciousness of the world". The "genocidal war launched by the Jews against the Palestinian people," and the "brutality and utter callousness of Israeli repression," it went on, prompted many Palestinians and non-Palestinians to draw an analogy between "the German holocaust against Jews and the Jewish holocaust against Palestinians." Palestinian villagers "spoke spontaneously how Nablus, Ramallah, and al-Khalil [Hebron] turned into modern-day Aushwitzes, Treblinkas, and Bergen-Belsens." The growing comparison by Palestinians of "the Jewish-perpetrated holocaust against them" to "the Nazi holocaust against Jews" is likely to be dismissed as "exaggerated," maybe even a little "far-fetched" by the Zionist-influenced media in the West. However, it concluded, a close and objective examination of Israeli torment of Palestinian civilians "reveals that the Palestinian holocaust-versus-the-Jewish-holocaust analogy is anything but 'far-fetched' both at the practical and theoretical levels."[45]

The purpose of the equation was evident in the statement of Muhsin Reza'i, secretary of the powerful Iranian Expediency Council and founder of the Iranian-led International Anti-Zionist Movement. Reza'i, who counted Nazism, apartheid and Zionism as the three sinister, inhumane phenomena in the twentieth century, predicted that Zionism would finally meet a similar fate as that of Nazism and apartheid—that is, destruction.[46]

Supporting Western Holocaust Deniers

While attacking "Zionist lies" on the Holocaust, the Iranian media praised the courage and moral fortitude of Western Holocaust deniers as "experts," "scholars" and "historians" who challenged the "influence of the Zionists on Western media" and who "sought to prove the falsehood of this historical allegation on the basis of reliable evidence."[47] It highlighted the legal action taken against some of them in Europe as a manifestation of the power of Zionism but also of the arbitrary and tyrannical nature of the Western democratic and justice systems. Every one of these deniers, *Jomhuri-ye Eslami* stated, "was either eliminated or quickly isolated and restricted." *Kayhan International* shared the pain expressed by German-Australian Holocaust denier Fredrick Toben that the Germans have become "strangers in their own country," in view of the "the unjust treatment meted out to him" in Germany. "What can possibly justify the imprisonment of journalists, teachers and researchers for just questioning a historical event?" *Tehran Times* asked in righteous indignation at the Western abuse of freedom of speech so dear to the Islamic regime. "Apparently, only the Big Brother in Orwell's '1984' can decide who can think and what he can think about," was its answer.[48]

Iran went further than any Arab country in hosting and officially endorsing Western Holocaust deniers who faced difficulties in their home countries. Ahmad Rami, a Moroccan exile in Sweden who propagated Holocaust denial on his Radio Islam and was sentenced in 1990 to six months in prison and three years on parole for racial incitement, became a guest of Iran immediately after his release. Rami boasted that his case was discussed in high governing circles and the Iranian parliament (Majlis) held a special session in his honor. Upon his return to Europe he set up an internet website in ten languages, named Radio Islam, which was reportedly supported financially by Iran and which engaged in Holocaust denial and blatant anti-Semitic propaganda.[49] The Swiss neo-Nazi activist Jurgen Graff, who had been sentenced in 1998 to fifteen months in jail, fled his homeland and took up political asylum in Iran. He subsequently set out with the active assistance of his hosts to organize an international conference for the denial of the Holocaust that was to be held in Beirut during March 2001.[50] Wolfgang Fröhlich, an Austrian engineer who testified in court on behalf of Graff in 1998, also sought refuge in Iran in May 2000, claiming that his arrest by Austrian police was imminent.[51]

The Institute of Historical Review (IHR), the flagship of Holocaust deniers in the United States, took pride in the fact that "Iran's official radio" had "expressed support for Holocaust revisionism by broadcasting sympathetic interviews with leading revisionist scholars and activists." It noted in particular several interviews with IHR Director Mark Weber on the English-language service, and similar interviews with German-Canadian Holocaust denier Ernst Zündel in German and with Ahmed Rami in Arabic.[52]

The most celebrated recipient of Iran's largesse was Holocaust denier Roger Garaudy, author of *The Founding Myths of Israeli Politics*. Garaudy was tried in France in January 1998 and fined according to the Gayssot law adopted in 1990, which bans denial of the Holocaust. As a former Marxist who converted to Islam, Garaudy also represented for Iranians and other Middle Eastern Muslims an additional angle—the superiority of Islam over the West, and hence Western attacks on him were perceived as part of the West's attack on Islam.[53] The Iranian media heaped praise on Garaudy's "scholarship" and courage in exposing the Holocaust "big lie" and "myths," and associated his claims and trial with Iran's own animosity towards Jews, Zionism and the West. The conservative *Resalat* denounced the trial as a manifestation of "International Zionism's" success in penetrating Western legal systems, thereby dealing "the most severe blow to the myth of democracy in Europe and America." Unlike fascism and Nazism, which were limited and besieged, it stated, "the growth of Zionism in the West has perverted most Western political systems" and was directly correlated to the rule of capital in capitalist systems.[54] Other newspapers used the case to expose the alleged fallacy of the Western democratic and liberal systems and ideology. *Jomhuri-ye Eslami* contended that "Garaudy's trial in a country which claims to advocate freedom and democracy was a mockery of the international community's intelligence." It also "showed the falsehood of slogans of civilization and liberty in the hypocritical western society." *Kayhan International* maintained that "putting the 84-year-old French Muslim thinker" on trial in today's France was tantamount to the dawn of a dark era of witch hunts by those who claim that their country has been a cradle of the idea of "liberté." It complained that in the "twisted logic of the French legal system," Garaudy, whom it described as "one of the giants of French culture," did not have the right to challenge Zionist myths and lies, while the author Salman Rushdie had the "right to say anything and everything" about the Prophet of Islam. The trial itself, it concluded later, was "a judicial holocaust."[55]

Iran's political elite mobilized to offer its support and solidarity with Garaudy and his claims. In Tehran, 160 MPs and some 600 journalists signed petitions in his support. Students demonstrated in front of the French Embassy, while the Higher Council of the Iranian Cultural Revolution called upon the French government and judicial authorities "to end their anti-scientific, anti-cultural and worrying behavior and acquit" Garaudy. Likewise, the official Islamic Human Rights Committee protested to the French government against the "disrespect" for "the practice of freedom of speech."[56]

Prior to the trial, Rafsanjani urged Garaudy not to worry as the history of Islam and the revolution had had many victims like himself and the trial would "register him in history as a Muslim hero." In a similar vein, Ayatollah Ahmad Janati, secretary of the powerful Council of Guardians, called for Garaudy's book to be "translated into all the languages of the Islamic states" and "distributed everywhere." Referring to news that Jews were buying copies of the book to take it out of the market, Janati added that it would "be good business for businessmen. Let them continue to print it so that they [the Jews] would come to buy it. Eventually a few will reach others."[57] Even Khatami, who purported to distinguish between anti-Zionism and anti-Judaism, chose Garaudy's trial to contrast the flawed nature of Western democracies, which "do not tolerate what they consider to be opposed to their own interests," with Islamic democracy that "tolerates opposition."[58]

Following his conviction, Garaudy was invited to Iran, where he was received by Supreme Leader Khamene'i, President Khatami and then Parliamentary Speaker 'Ali Akbar Nateq-Nuri. He was also invited to address the teachers and students of

Iran's top religious seminary, the Faiziyeh Madrasa, in the holy city of Qom. Iran also helped him pay the Fr120,000 fine imposed upon him.[59]

Conclusions

Iran's anti-Zionism is a modern political articulation of both old and new anti-Semitic or anti-Jewish beliefs. It is based on the belief in Jewish enmity against Islam from its inception and in the association of the Jews and Zionism with the Western cultural challenge and threat to Islam as a religion, identity and culture. It rejects the Jews" claim to peoplehood and regards it as an affront to Islam. The other crucial component is the nationalist-based linkage, which Iran, and particularly Ayatollah Khomeini, made between the Jews, Zionism and Western imperialism. It also borrows from modern anti-Semitic ideas produced in the West.

While the basis is Islamic, Iran articulates its anti-Semitism primarily in modern terms as anti-Zionism. As such, modern Iranian anti-Semitism differs from past Shiʿi anti-Judaism and from most other Islamic movements in the Middle East which dwell more on the past "sins" of the Jews towards the Prophet Muhammad and elaborate on the evil traits of the Jews enumerated in the Qur'an. Occasionally, however, such themes that reveal the deeper anti-Jewish sentiment come to the fore in the Iranian discourse as well.

Iranian Holocaust denial, like other such manifestations in the Middle East, adopts the discourse and arguments of Western neo-Nazis and anti-Semites in order to grant it a pseudo-scientific value, particularly as these Westerners held seemingly objective views on the Arab-Israeli conflict. Conceivably, this reliance reflected subtle or unconscious esteem for, together with resentment towards, the West or Western sources.

Iranian Holocaust denial is not a consequence of ignorance of historical facts. The great effort to provide denial with a pseudo-scientific basis reflects a certain awareness of the enormity of the valid evidence on the Holocaust. In addition, the exclusive reliance on Western Holocaust deniers is a product of selective and manipulative reading and borrowing of material published in the West, and a conscious disregard for the vast scholarly, publicist and literary output dealing with the Holocaust that does not suit the Iranians" ideological convictions. It is also reflective of the broader phenomenon of the narrow and superficial cultural borrowing from the West, which is typical of Islamist movements as a whole. However, whereas in Europe Holocaust deniers represent fringe elements that are still despised by mainstream intellectual and academic circles, in Iran the most senior government officials and media play the leading role in Holocaust denial, while endorsing the Western deniers. Consequently, the Iranian public is not exposed to the other more truthful aspect of history. While Iran professes to be anti-Nazi, such denial minimizes the extent and depth of Nazi evil and brutality.

The selective reading of the Western denial literature and the contradictory arguments raised by some of the Iranian writers raise the question of their own genuine belief in their own arguments and statements. It is very likely that ordinary

Iranians, who are not exposed to the Western academic literature on the Holocaust, do believe the propaganda they are served. Concurrently, the growing skepticism among many young Iranians towards the overall ideological message of the Islamic regime may also apply to the regime's allegations on the Holocaust. While it is impossible to make any intelligent guess about the writers themselves, it should be remembered that internal contradictions abound in anti-Semitic literature in other parts of the world as well. It appears that the psychological or political need to vilify a certain party, the Jews in this case, frees the accusers from the constraints of logic and consistency.

Iran's Holocaust denial is a manifestation of anti-Semitism disguised as anti-Zionism. Using the pretext of Zionist fabrication of the Holocaust, Iran distorts and denies Jewish history and deprives the Jews of their human dignity by presenting their worst tragedy as a scam, even though this has nothing to do with Zionism per se. The very claim of Zionist invention of the Holocaust appeals to the tendency in both European and Middle Eastern anti-Semitism to charge the Jews with unscrupulous machinations in order to achieve illegitimate and immoral goals, mainly financial extortion. It aims at demolishing the legitimacy of the Jewish state, which they claim is based on the Holocaust myth. As such it is in tune with anti-Jewish and anti-Zionist sentiments in Europe, which argue that the Jews forfeited their status as victims by victimizing the Palestinians, and that Israel does not have the right to exist because the human price it requires is too high.

In a similar vein, the vilification of the Zionists as Nazis is intended to offend the most painful feelings of the Jews by equating them with their worst tormentors. Moreover, not only does this accusation deprive the Jews of their dignity and transform victims into perpetrators, it threatens them with the ultimate fate of the Nazis. Concurrently, while Iran professes to be anti-Nazi, both Holocaust denial and the equation of Zionism with Nazism minimize the extent and depth of Nazi evil and brutality, thereby serving the cause of Western neo-Nazis and other anti-Semites.

Acknowledgments

I wish to thank my colleague Esther Webman for her useful comments on this paper. Needless to say, all mistakes are mine alone.

Notes

[1] Other manifestations of this approach are the references to Israel as the "Zionist regime" or the "Zionist entity," or the insistence on using Jerusalem's Arab names, Bayt al-Muqaddas or Qods even in English texts, due to the Hebrew origins of the name "Jerusalem."

[2] See Sobhani, *The Pragmatic Entente.*

[3] An additional indication of the importance of anti-Zionism is the fact that leading figures of the Iranian regime have published books on the topic. See Rafsanjani, *Isra'il va-Qods-e ʿAziz*; former Foreign Minister ʿAli Akbar Velayati, *Iran wa-falastin*. The Institute for the Preservation of Khomeini's Heritage compiled all his articles and statements against Israel in a special book, *Al-qadiyya al-filastiniyya.*

[4] For the Arab discourse on the Holocaust, see Litvak and Webman, "The Representation of the Holocaust."

[5] Netzer, "Ha-antishemiyut be-Iran."

[6] Lewis, *The Jews of Islam*, 150–53, 181–83; Menashri, "The Jews of Iran," 353–71.

[7] Dabashi, *Theology of Discontent*, 67–68; Netzer, "Ha-antishemiyut be-Iran"; Zand, "Ha-dimui shel ha-yehudi," 109–39.

[8] Khumayni, *Al-hukuma al-islamiyya*, 7; Khomeini, *Islam and Revolution*, 27, 47, 109, 127; Dabashi, *Theology of Discontent*, 426.

[9] Khomeini was referring to rumors that copies of the Qur'an "in which all verses critical of the Jews were excised" circulated in the Palestinian Territories following the Six Day War as well as in African countries (translator's note, *Islam and Revolution*, 163). The accusation of Jewish distortions of the Qur'an are a common theme in Muslim polemics. See similar charges by Ayatollah Mahmud Taliqani in Dabashi, *Theology of Discontent*, 245.

[10] Reuters, 22 December 2000; Islamic Republic News Agency (IRNA), 24 April 2001.

[11] Khomeini, *Islam and Revolution*, 47, 196.

[12] Dabashi, *Theology of Discontent*, 426.

[13] Khomeini, *Islam and Revolution*, 195–97.

[14] Ibid., 175, 177; Khomeini, *Al-qadiyya al-filastiniyya*, 63–97.

[15] Menashri, *Post-Revolutionary Politics*, 265–66.

[16] Radio Iran, 20 July 1994 (Foreign Broadcast Information Service Daily Reports [FBIS-DR]).

[17] Menashri, *Post-Revolutionary Politics*, 266.

[18] Khomeini, *Islam and Revolution*, 89.

[19] Khomeini, *Al-qadiyya al-filastiniyya*, 47–51; Velayati, *Iran wa-Falastin*, 14.

[20] Institute of Jewish Affairs, *Antisemitism*, 122.

[21] Khatami's interview with CNN broadcast on Iran TV Network 1, 8 January 1998 (FBIS-DR).

[22] *Tehran Times*, 14 March 1998.

[23] MEMRI [The Middle East Media Research Institute] Special Dispatch Series, no. 897, 22 April 2005 (http://www.yahoodi.com/ peace/antizionism.html).

[24] *Iran*, 15 May 2003; IRNA, 17 January 1998.

[25] *Keyhan*, 13 June 2002; *Jomhuri-ye Eslami*, 20 May 2003.

[26] Menashri, "Iran," in *Anti-Semitism World Wide 1995/6*, 198.

[27] "The Protocols of the Elders of Zion, An Iranian Perspective," MEMRI Special Dispatch Series, no. 98 (7 June 2000), www.Memri.org.

[28] MEMRI Special Dispatch Series, no. 705 (30 April 2004).

[29] Radio Iran, 23 January 1998, 20 October 2000, 31 December 2001 (BBC, Survey of World Broadcasts [BBC-SWB]); *Jomhuri-ye Eslami*, 14 January 1999, 10 January 2000; *Resalat*, 11 January 2000 (*FBIS-DR*) Tehran TV, 4 October 2000 (BBC-SWB).

[30] Khatami in IRNA, 27 May, 14 December 1997; *Iran News*, 5 August 1997 cited in Menashri, *Middle East Contemporary Survey 1997*, 366; Hamshahri.net, 29 January 2002; Rafsanjani in Radio Iran, 21 November 2003 (BBC-SWB).

[31] Litvak and Webman, "The Representation of the Holocaust."

[32] For denial in the West, see Lipstadt, *Denying the Holocaust*; Shermer and Grobman, *Denying History*; Rambiszewski, *The Final Lie*. For an extensive bibliography, see Drobnicki et al., "Holocaust Denial Literature." For denial in Eastern Europe, see Shafir, *Between Denial and "Comparative Trivialization."*

[33] IRNA, 6 March 2000; 24 April 2001 (text of Khamene'i's speech). See similar assertions by *Jomhuri-ye Eslami*, 14 January 1999.

[34] *Jomhuri-ye Eslami*, 14 January 1999; *Kayhan International*, 19 January 1998; *Kayhan*, 13 June 2002.

[35] MEMRI Special Dispatch Series, no. 855 (28 January 2005).

[36] *Kayhan*, 13 June 2002.

[37] *Tehran Times*, 25 January, 29 January, 1 February, 3 February, 17 February 2001. See also the phrase "Simon Wiesenthal and his gang," referring to the Nazi hunter who resided in Vienna (*TT*, 3 February 2001).

[38] *Tehran Times*, 19 February 2001.

[39] *Tehran Times*, 8 March 2000.

[40] *Kayhan International*, 6 December 1999, 6 March 2000; *Tehran Times*, 12 April 2000.

[41] Iran TV Network 1, 5 October 2000 (http://gulf2000.columbia.edu/); *Tehran Times*, 7 May 2000; IRNA, 24 April 2001; *Kayhan*, 13 June 2002. MEMRI Special Dispatch Series, no. 855 (28 January 2005). IRNA gladly endorsed the accusation by ultra-Orthodox Jewish spokesmen that the "Zionists sacrificed religious Jews in the holocaust," whose occurrence it denied, 14 August 2000.

[42] MEMRI Special Dispatch Series, no. 705 (30 April 2004). For such allegations in the Arab world, see Litvak and Webman, "The Representation of the Holocaust" and "Perceptions of the Holocaust."

[43] *Iran*, April 2003.

[44] Radio Iran, 23 January 1998 (BBC-SWB); elsewhere he described Israel as being "imprisoned by its own Hitler-like policy in Palestine." Iran TV, 23 February 2002 (BBC-SWB).

[45] IRNA 26 October 2000, 19 April 2001. See similar comparisons in *Iran Daily*, 24 February 2001(BBC-SWB); *Tehran Times*, 9 April 2001.

[46] Radio Iran, 16 November 2000 (FBIS-DR).

[47] IRIB TV, 4 December 1999 (FBIS-DR); *Kayhan International*, 6 December 1999 (FBIS-DR).

[48] *Jomhuri-ye Eslami*, 14 January 1999; *Kayhan International*, 6 December 1999; *Tehran Times*, 12 April 2000.

[49] *Ma'ariv*, 22 November 1997; Rami to Maroc Hebdo International (no date), http://abbc.com/mh/mh-eng.htm; Webman and Rembiszewski, "The Unholy Alliance."

[50] Anti-Defamation League, "Western Deniers in the Middle East," http://www.adl.org/holocaust/Denial_ME/western_deniers.asp; http://www.radioislam.org/revisionism/confer-beiru/010303asshafir.html; http://www.us-israel.org/jsource/anti-semitism/ trend2001.html

[51] Reuters, 22 February 2001. Another Holocaust denier who enjoyed Iranian hospitality was Fredrick Toben, in December 1999; see Iran IRIB TV, 4 December 1999 (FBIS-DR).

[52] http://www.ihr.org/conference/beirutconf/background.html, 12 January 2001.

[53] For Garaudy's warm reception in the Arab world, see Webman, "The Arab World," 193–204; Webman, "Rethinking the Holocaust," 16–30.

[54] *Resalat*, 13 January 1998; *Jomhuri-ye Eslami*, 14 January; *Kayhan International*, 20 April 1998.

[55] *Jomhuri-ye Eslami*, 14 January; *Kayhan International*, 19 January, 17 February, 20 April 1998.

[56] Iran Press Service, 20 January 1998; Agence France-Presse (AFP), 12 January, 18 February 1998.

[57] IRNA, 19 January 1998; Radio Iran, 23 January, 30 January, 6 March 1998 (BBC-SWB).

[58] Iran TV Network 1, 19 January 1998 (BBC-SWB).

[59] IRNA, Iran TV, 20 April 1998 (BBC-SWB); Iran Press Service, 17 March 1998; AFP, 22 April 1998.

References

Afary, Janet. *The Iranian Constitutional Revolution, 1906–1911*. New York: Columbia University Press, 1996.

Anti-Defamation League. "Western Deniers in the Middle East." http://www.adl.org/holocaust/Denial_ME/western_deniers.asp o

Dabashi, Hamid. *Theology of Discontent: The Ideological Formation of the Islamic Revolution in Iran*. New York: New York University Press, 1993.

Drobnicki, John, et al., "Holocaust Denial Literature: A Bibliography." http://www.york.cuny.edu/~drobnick/holbib.html#general

Institute of Jewish Affairs. *Antisemitism: World Report 1993.* London, 1994.

Khomeini, Ruhollah. *Al-qadiyya al-filastiniyya fi kalam al-imam Khomeini* (The Palestinian problem in the writings and speeches of Imam Khomeini). Beirut: Dar al-wasila, 1996.

———. Islam and Revolution: Writings and Declarations of Imam Khomeini. Translated and annotated by Hamid Algar. Berkeley: Mizan Press, 1981.

Khumayni, Ayatallah Ruhallah. *Al-hukuma al-islamiyya* (Islamic government). Beirut: Dar al-Talica, 1979.

Lewis, Bernard. *The Jews of Islam.* Princeton: Princeton University Press, 1984.

Lipstadt, Deborah. *Denying the Holocaust: The Growing Assault on Truth and Memory.* New York: Free Press, 1993.

Litvak, Meir and Esther Webman. "Perceptions of the Holocaust in the Palestinian Public Discourse." *Israel Studies* 8, no. 3 (fall 2003): 123–40.

———. "The Representation of the Holocaust in the Arab World." *Journal of Israeli History* 23, no. 1 (spring 2004): 100–15.

Menashri, David. "The Jews of Iran: Between the Shah and Khomeini." In *Anti-Semitism in Times of Crisis,* edited by Sander L. Gilman and Steven T. Katz. New York: New York University Press, 1991.

———. "Iran." In *Anti-Semitism World Wide 1995/96.* Tel Aviv: Tel Aviv University, 1996.

———. "Iran." In *Middle East Contemporary Survey 1997,* edited by Bruce Maddy-Weitzman. Boulder: Westview Press, 1999.

———. *Post-Revolutionary Politics in Iran: Religion, Society and Power.* London: Frank Cass, 2001.

Netzer, Amnon. "Ha-antishemiyut be-Iran, 1925–1950" (Anti-Semitism in Iran, 1925–1950). *Pe'amim,* no. 29 (1987): 6–8.

Rafsanjani, ʿAli Akbar Hashemi. *Isra'il va-Qods-e ʿaziz* (Israel and dear Jerusalem). Qom: Azadi, n.d.

Rambiszewski, Sara. *The Final Lie: Holocaust Denial in Germany: A Second Generation Denier as a Test Case.* Tel Aviv: The Project for the Study of Anti-Semitism, 1996.

Shafir, Michael. *Between Denial and "Comparative Trivialization": Holocaust Negationism in Post-Communist East Central Europe.* Jerusalem: Vidal Sassoon International Center for the Study of Antisemitism, Analysis of Current Trends in Antisemitism no. 19, 2002.

Shermer, Michael, and Alex Grobman. *Denying History: Who Says the Holocaust Never Happened and Why Do They Say it.* Berkeley: UCLA Press, 2000.

Sobhani, Sohrab. *The Pragmatic Entente: Israeli-Iranian Relations, 1948-1988.* New York: Praeger, 1989.

Velayati, ʿAli Akbar. *Iran wa-falastin (1867–1937), judhur al-ʿalaqa wa-taqalubat al-siyasa* (Iran and Palestine: The origins of their relations and the fluctuations of policy). Beirut: Dar al-Haqq, 1997.

Webman, Esther. "The Arab World." In *Anti-Semitism Worldwide, 1996/97.* Tel Aviv: Tel Aviv University, 1997.

———. "Rethinking the Holocaust." In *Anti-Semitism Worldwide 1998/99.* Nebraska: Tel Aviv University Press, 2000.

Zand, Michael. "Ha-dimui shel ha-yehudi be-einei ha-iranim le'ahar milhemet ha-olam ha-shniyah, 1950–1979" (The image of the Jew in Iranian eyes after the Second World War, 1950–1979). *Pe'amim,* no. 29 (1987): 109–39.

INDEX

Lightning Source UK Ltd.
Milton Keynes UK
UKOW02n2354061013

218562UK00001B/12/P